ZULU WARRIORS

ZULU WARRIORS

THE BATTLE FOR THE
SOUTH AFRICAN FRONTIER

JOHN LABAND

YALE UNIVERSITY PRESS
NEW HAVEN AND LONDON

For information about this and other Yale University Press publications, please contact:
U.S. Office: sales.press@yale.edu   www.yalebooks.com
Europe Office: sales@yaleup.co.uk   www.yalebooks.co.uk

Set in Adobe Caslon Pro by IDSUK (DataConnection) Ltd
Printed in Great Britain by TJ International, Padstow, Cornwall

Library of Congress Cataloging-in-Publication Data
Laband, John, 1947-
   Zulu warriors: the battle for the South African frontier/John Laband.
      pages cm
   Includes bibliographical references and index.
   ISBN 978-0-300-18031-2 (cl : alk. paper)
   1. Zulu War, 1879.   2. Zulu (African people)—History–19th century.   3. Zululand
   (South Africa)—History, Military—19th century.   4. Sociology, Military—South
   Africa—Zululand.   I. Title.
   DT1875.L34 2014
   968.4045—dc23
                                                                                          2013041948
A catalogue record for this book is available from the British Library.

10 9 8 7 6 5 4 3 2 1

Contents

Illustrations

Maps

Abbreviations

BMS   Berlin Missionary Society
BPP   *British Parliamentary Papers*
DFH   Diamond Fields Horse
FAMP Frontier Armed Mounted Police
FLH   Frontier Light Horse
GOC   General Officer Commanding
NNC   Natal Native Contingent
NNP   Natal Native Pioneer Corps
OFS   Orange Free State (Oranje-Vrijstaat)
RA   Royal Artillery
RBL   Rifled Breech-Loader
RE   Royal Engineers
RML   Rifled Muzzle-Loader
ZAR   Zuid-Afrikaansche Republiek (South African Republic)

Note on Terminology

In conformity with contemporary South Africa orthographic practice, in words from Nguni languages the root is capitalised, but not the prefix: for example, amaZulu or amaXhosa. But in words from Sotho-Tswana languages the prefix, but not the root, is capitalised: for example, Bapedi, Basotho or Batlhaping. When the words are used adjectivally, they do not have prefixes: for example, Zulu people, Pedi people. Words which are not proper nouns are not capitalized: for example, *umuzi* or *morafe*. Note that in article and book titles and in direct quotations the original spelling of names is retained.

PROLOGUE

CHAPTER 1

The Shadow of Isandlwana

W HEN I first approached Isandlwana Mountain forty-five years ago, it was with depleted enthusiasm. We had been bumping and sliding interminably in an antique Landrover along the snaking tracks which in those days passed for roads in Zululand, and had been chugging precariously across streams swollen by the summer rains. The undulating grassy plain, punctuated by the occasional flat-topped hill with its rocky coronet, swept unimpeded to the far horizon. Only the rare sight of a ragged herd boy, desultorily driving a few scrawny cattle or goats towards a distant huddle of thatched huts, persuaded me we were not entirely alone under the enormous sky. I regretted the back-jarring journey and anticipated little of interest at our destination. At the time I knew next to nothing of the desperate battle the amaZulu and British had fought ninety years before in the dry I dongas, and among the tumbled rocks at the foot of Isandlwana, and eroded water courses, or was prepared to care rather less.

A thoroughly conventional colonial education had directed my historical concerns to the great battlefields of Europe where, we had been firmly instructed, the future of the world had been decided. Of what importance, or even interest, could some inaccessible African battlefield possibly be? Besides, like so many of my fellows, I assumed as a matter of upbringing that the technological superiority of European weaponry in the hands of professional soldiers guaranteed that they always prevailed over primitively armed warriors. The Zulu victory at Isandlwana in 1879 was consequently only some peculiar fluke, the unremarkable exception that proved the rule.

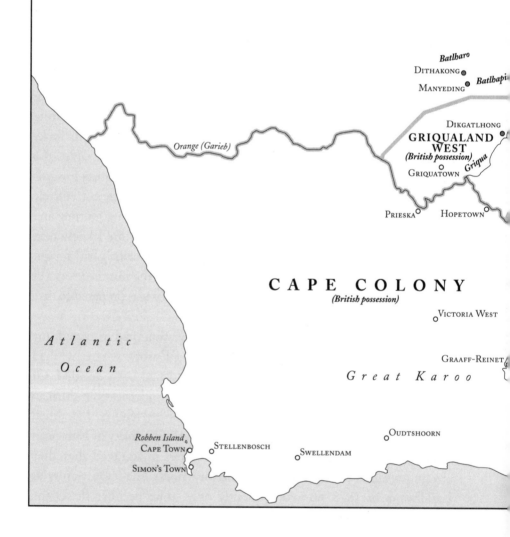

Kalahari Desert

Batlharo
DITHAKONG ●
MANYEDING ●   ***Batlhapi***

DIKGATLHONG
○
**GRIQUALAND
WEST**
(British possession)
○
GRIQUATOWN   *Griqua*

Orange (Garieb)

PRIESKA ○   HOPETOWN ○

CAPE COLONY
(British possession)

○ VICTORIA WEST

*Atlantic
Ocean*

GRAAFF-REINET

Great Karoo

○ OUDTSHOORN

Robben Island ○
CAPE TOWN ○   ○ STELLENBOSCH   ○ SWELLENDAM

SIMON'S TOWN ○

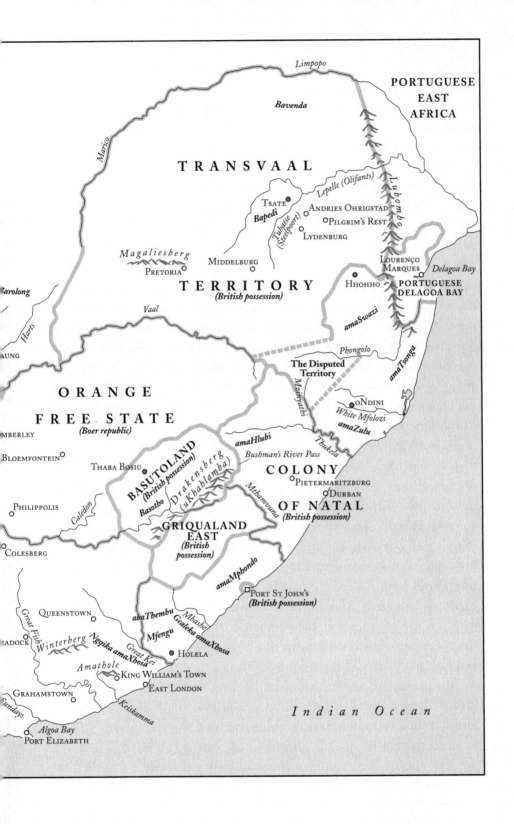

Limpopo

PORTUGUESE
EAST
AFRICA

Bavenda

Marico

T R A N S V A A L

Lepelle (Olifants)

Lubombo

TSATE
Bapedi
ANDRIES OHRIGSTAD
PILGRIM'S REST
Tabatse (Steelpoort)
LYDENBURG

Magaliesberg
PRETORIA
MIDDELBURG

LOURENÇO
MARQUES
Delagoa Bay

HHOHHO
PORTUGUESE
DELAGOA BAY

T E R R I T O R Y
(British possession)

Vaal

arolong

Harts

amaSwazi

Phongolo

The Disputed
Territory

amaTsonga

AUNG

O R A N G E

F R E E S T A T E
(Boer republic)

Mzinyathi

oNDINI
White Mfolozi
amaZulu

MBERLEY

BLOEMFONTEIN

amaHlubi
Bushman's River Pass

Thukela

THABA BOSIU

BASUTOLAND
(British possession)

*Drakensberg
(uKhahlamba)*

C O L O N Y
PIETERMARITZBURG
DURBAN

PHILIPPOLIS

Basotho

Caledon

OF N A T A L
(British possession)

GRIQUALAND
EAST
*(British
possession)*

Mthamvuna

COLESBERG

amaMphondo

PORT ST JOHN'S
(British possession)

QUEENSTOWN

abaThembu
Mbashe

Great Fish

Winterberg

Ngqika amaXhosa

Great Kei

Gcaleka amaXhosa

Mfengu

RADOCK

Amathole

HOLELA

KING WILLIAM'S TOWN
EAST LONDON

GRAHAMSTOWN

Keiskamma

Sundays

Algoa Bay
PORT ELIZABETH

I n d i a n   O c e a n

Yet, despite myself, once we had rattled to a stop under the sphinx-shaped mountain that lours over the site of the stricken British camp, and begun to clamber among the low, scattered cairns of tumbled stone that mark the graves of the British dead, quite a different mood overtook me. I succumbed completely to that atmosphere of acute melancholy and disquiet that pervades a battlefield when left undisturbed to its ghosts and the keening wind.

For when the spurious glamour of ancient wars is brushed aside, battlefields are revealed as the terrible places they really are, killing grounds where men suffered insupportable wounds and died in desperate agony. There soldiers experienced intense exhilaration or paralysing fear as they put their mettle to the test before their comrades, drawing out of their churning guts courage, fortitude and powers of leadership or, despite themselves, succumbing abjectly to terror and panic. Perhaps we all wonder in our hearts how we would carry ourselves under fire, whether we would pass the test with honour and manhood intact. And as we tramp the terrain where men once fought, trying to determine where the line of battle stood, and by what route the vanquished fled, we ponder the urgent decisions individuals made in the furious heat of battle, and how these shaped their fate and the destiny of kingdoms.

I realize now how fortunate I was to walk the desolate field of Isandlwana that afternoon, long before the bustling tourism industry insensitively transformed the site into a sanitized and over-commercialized open-air museum, all fenced and gated. Because, loitering all but alone on the battlefield and already prey to its forlorn mystique, I was unexpectedly swept up by fresh emotions. I was taken hold by a visceral intimation (for so it seemed) of the ancient, soaringly immense African landscape that embraced me, combined with a sense of marvel at the courage of those Zulu warriors—those sons of Africa—who had thrown down their lives to preserve their land and kin against would-be conquerors from across the seas.

My attempt to account for such heroism was to lie behind several books I later wrote about the Anglo-Zulu War of 1879. Yet I always felt that the explanation was escaping me, that somehow I was failing to locate the crucial thread. Then it finally dawned on me that to draw out that elusive Zulu strand was not in itself sufficient if I wished to unravel the puzzle. I had first to recognize its significance as part of a larger, interwoven pattern of African resistance to colonial conquest.

Certainly, in 1879 the Zulu kingdom under the leadership of King Cetshwayo kaMpande might have been the most powerful African state in southern Africa. But it was only one among several kingdoms clinging to their independence when faced by the accelerating British determination to unify southern Africa in a confederation of states under imperial control. To this end it was essential for the British to neuter the military capabilities of the residual independent black states of southern Africa, disarm them, and break their political power. The British accordingly embarked on a concerted, interrelated and sometimes overlapping series of campaigns which some historians now regard as the First War for South African Unification.[1] Within the concentrated span of three years the British finally crushed the Ngqika and Gcaleka amaXhosa in the Ninth Cape Frontier War of 1877–1878, subjugated the Griqua, Batlhaping, Prieska amaXhosa, Korana and Khoesan in the Northern Border War of 1878, shattered the Zulu kingdom in the Anglo-Zulu War of 1879, and extinguished Bapedi independence in the First and Second Anglo-Pedi Wars of 1878 and 1879.[2]

In a sense, what happened in southern Africa during those three bruising years of warfare was a classic case of what some historians refer to as the 'closing' of the frontier.[3] A frontier is said to 'open' when the first foreign settlers arrive and begin to interact with the indigenous people. At first—and this could be over a prolonged period—the new arrivals have neither the will nor the means to establish their dominance and there is a rough, unstable balance of power between them and the local people. Flexible alliances are made and broken that do not necessarily follow racial lines. The frontier closes when (as happened in southern Africa) the intruders finally conquer the indigenous peoples and incorporate them into their own political and economic system. This phase could be considerably drawn out, as it was in the intermittent and interminable 'Hundred Years War' on the Cape Eastern Frontier between 1779 and 1878. Or it could be startlingly abrupt, as it was in the case of Zululand in 1879.

What then struck me was that during the closing of the frontier from 1877 to 1879, when several African polities all decided to resist the

British by force of arms, they each did so in isolation, allowing the British the luxury of picking them off one by one. Why, I wondered, were these African states fatally incapable of banding together to resist the common enemy? The answer, I believe, is that their rulers, in common with most other kings right across Sub-Saharan Africa, had little or no experience in nailing together broadly based military alliances. Moreover, their festering suspicions of each other, their deeply rooted animosities, jealousies and rivalries, all precluded effective cooperation. Indeed, experience during the 'open frontier' phase in southern Africa had taught some rulers with a prescient eye to the future that while whites could be useful short-term allies against their own current African enemies, in the long term loyally collaborating with them earned their good will and, along with it, material rewards and security.

The realization that African states in southern Africa were not necessarily united in their resistance to colonial conquest is unsettling. Perhaps even more disappointing is the uncomfortable knowledge that some kingdoms were not united in themselves in facing up to the colonial aggressors. African states were by their nature loose agglomerations of subjects brought together through political convenience, self-preservation or conquest. That meant revolts by overmighty regional chiefs, vicious succession disputes within royal houses and destructive civil wars were dishearteningly common.[4] Astute Boer or British policy-makers were very much alive to these many cleavages. They were eager to exploit them to prise antagonistic factions further apart, fragment resistance and secure allies from among the disaffected in a kingdom with which they were at war.[5] Nor was it uncommon for the exiled losers in a civil war to join a colonial invasion in the hope of regaining their lost homes and power.[6]

Starkly put, a significant proportion of the African warriors who fought in the wars of 1877–1879 did so on the side of the British. That the European conquest of Africa would never have been possible without African auxiliaries has become a truism, but it is also an embarrassment for many post-colonial Africans today. Yet the fact is, these African auxiliaries provided essential logistical support for every imperial field force operating in Africa, whether British, French, Portuguese, Italian, German or Belgian. They served as wagon-drivers, herdsmen for draught-animals and captured livestock, boatmen, porters, cooks, sanitary-men and servants. As scouts, guides and interpreters they were vital for intelligence-gathering. Levies bearing arms undertook guard and reconnaissance duties, patrolled, raided, skirmished and sometimes even served in the front line of battle.

It was nothing less than essential for the British to secure African fighting men such as these for their South African campaigns of 1877–1879. The British knew they enjoyed a clear, overwhelming military advantage through the technological superiority of their machine-tooled breech-loading rifles, artillery and machine guns, as well as through their sophisticated military organization. But British regular troops in South Africa were always in perilously short supply, and had no option but to campaign in conjunction with locally raised formations. Many of these were small, exclusively white volunteer colonial units, primarily irregular horse, but the overwhelming majority in terms of numbers were African levies and auxiliaries. It is true that in southern Africa, Africans were less freely incorporated into white armed forces than elsewhere in the continent because the heavily outnumbered white settlers distrusted their loyalty. Nevertheless, sheer military necessity had always overridden these apprehensions. In the Anglo-Zulu War of 1879, 7,000 of the 17,000 British and colonial troops serving in Zululand were African, besides a further 8,000 black levies raised to guard the border of Natal.[7] Some African levies built up an extensive service record, none more so than the Mfengu (or Fingo) of the Eastern Cape who for over forty-five years loyally turned out time and again.[8] In return for their loyal service, all expected rewards in the form of plunder, and usually land on which to settle.

Because the British never once marched to war in nineteenth-century southern Africa without African allies, auxiliaries or levies, I had to concede that not one of the wars of 1877–1879 which I was investigating could be described as a simple black-on-white conflict, and that any romantic notion of racially unified African resistance had to be firmly set aside. But determined resistance there nevertheless was in this period, steadfast even in the face of inevitable defeat. The question (which first had occurred to me at Isandlwana so long ago) still remained: how to account for it?

In the 1870s, after intermittent, piecemeal colonial encroachment which had begun in the Western Cape in the mid-seventeenth century, and which tough and often skilful African resistance had frequently delayed or even staved off, African rulers were unprepared for the unrelenting determination with which the British set about slamming the South African frontier closed. In this crisis, all the indigenous armies of the subcontinent, vary as they might in everything from size to customary tactics, faced the same urgent challenge. How were they to adapt their traditional ways of war (honed effectively enough for combat against each other) to the ever-growing European military threat?

Successful resistance seemed to call for the acquisition of firearms to counter the superior colonial weapons system.[9] Yet firearms—even the most modern—were not enough in themselves. It was essential to be properly trained in handling them and to adopt new tactics and styles of military organization to exploit their effectiveness. The amaXhosa, Bapedi, and above all the Basotho, increasingly learned how to make dangerously effective use of firearms against the whites. By contrast, the amaSwazi and amaZulu did not.

Over the years I have continued to wonder why the amaZulu in particular seemed so unwilling—or possibly unable—to adapt to the rapidly changing military landscape, while other African societies were so much more flexible. It does seem that most ordinary Zulu warriors continued to rely on traditional weapons rather than on firearms not simply as a matter of supply, but also of choice. Why were they so hidebound by established military thinking that they could not accept that their old ways were no longer suitable for fighting modern colonial armies? Why did they stick to conventional warfare and the hazardous pitched battle that could decide a kingdom's fate in an afternoon? Why, unlike the amaXhosa, Basotho, Bapedi and the amaSwazi too, would they not adopt a strategy of prolonged guerrilla struggle based on impregnable fastnesses, a strategy so ideally designed to wear down the resources and resolve of the colonial forces? Could the reason have lain (I have pondered) in the pervasive world-view of the Zulu warrior that required him to prove his prowess in honourable hand-to-hand combat ill-suited to modern warfare? Or was it that traditional military systems, such as that of the amaZulu, were so integral to the very structure of African society, religion and sovereignty that to tamper with them would be to risk demolishing its entire framework?

Worrying away at these questions, I came to realize that I was back where I had started that afternoon in the shadow of Isandlwana, when I had first puzzled over the superb Zulu resolve to charge the lethal British firing-line. I saw at last that the vital connecting thread that ran through the broad weave of African resistance to colonial conquest was that of military culture. As Michael Howard put it nearly thirty years ago, wars are self-evidently 'conflicts of *societies*, and they can be fully understood only if one understands the nature of the society fighting them'.[10] And essential to that understanding is an empathetic grasp of how people made sense of the world in which they lived.[11] Thus, when thinking in terms of military culture, soldiers' choices concerning seemly behaviour, rituals, dress, weaponry and tactics may well depend upon nebulous preferences and prejudices rather than upon concrete advantages.

Admittedly, the concept of military culture can be unhelpfully opaque, but I shall endeavour to give it substance as I spool it out as the interpretative thread that holds this book together. What is certain is that military cultures can be sharply alien to each other—even when they share much the same arms technology—because they have mismatched conceptions of how warfare should ideally be conducted and value different notions of soldierly codes of honour and fair fight.[12] As the armed encounters between Africans and Europeans in south-eastern Africa in the years 1877–1879 tragically demonstrated, when each side flouted the other's conventional rules of war it served to infuriate and justify merciless ferocity and unrestrained violence which encompassed not only enemy soldiers, but non-combatants too.

My intention in this book, then, is to examine and attempt to explain the wars whites unleashed against African states in southern Africa between 1877 and 1879 primarily in terms of African military culture. I shall apply this approach to African warriors defending their lands as well as to African levies and auxiliaries in British and Boer service.

Although African military culture differed in detail from society to society, a generally accepted, continent-wide system of military values defined the warrior's place in the social order and legitimized aggressive masculinity and the violence of war. Admittedly, masculinity is a highly contested sub-field of gender studies, but for my purposes I have made my choice in the theoretical minefield. I essentially follow

R.W. Connell's concept of 'hegemonic masculinity'.[13] This term refers to the form of masculinity dominant in a society and sustained by its institutions. It defines the culturally constructed model of what it is to be a man, even if it is an unattainable ideal. Crucially, it subordinates or silences alternative visions of masculinity. In the African societies I am concerned with in this book, masculine virtue and honour (as in many other parts of the world) were closely bound up with the prowess of military heroes, and were the binding myths of the state itself, the cultural focus around which the community adhered.[14]

Face-to-face, heroic combat that sorely tried the warrior's physique, tested his skill with weapons, and proved his courage was the ultimate test of manliness.[15] Nothing better consolidated the individual warrior's reputation than to vie successfully with his comrades to be in the very forefront of the battle and ostentatiously to engage the enemy hand to hand. Since endurance was particularly highly prized as a virtue in Africa with its daily struggle for survival in a harsh natural environment, how much more so was fortitude in war! Warriors were expected to bear without complaint every form of physical hardship, as well as excruciating wounds and death. Indeed, true honour required loyalty to the death both to king and to comrades-in-arms.

These widespread notions of manly and soldierly honour motivated African warriors and help explain why they comported themselves so valiantly in war. Yet these remarkably steadfast warriors were nevertheless not specially trained soldiers with a distinctive lifestyle that set them apart from the rest of society, as was the case with contemporary British regular troops. They were not professionals but militias, part-time soldiers. Consequently, alongside their warrior-like virtues they were expected to exhibit the honourable restraint and self-control appropriate to their civilian occupations, to recognize their paramount duty to their kin and to obey their generational and political superiors. When all adult, able-bodied men of military age went to war as was expected of them, therefore, it was not simply to assert their own masculine prowess. It was also to affirm their honourable commitment to defend not only their own homesteads, women and livestock, but the entire wider community of which they were a part.[16]

Nevertheless, just because young men were home again from the wars, it did not mean that they ever forgot they were warriors, and tensions simmered. In Africa, society was under the control of the older generation of men who not only possessed all the women and cattle they wanted, but attempted to postpone the younger men's access to these desirable things.[17] As a consequence the young men, who often lived together for much of the year in warrior groups, were restlessly at loggerheads with their elders despite their obligation to respect them. Inevitably, they often formed a distinctive sub-culture, cultivating their physical beauty by ornamenting their bodies and dressing lavishly while oozing frustrated virility, insolence and aggression. And because they knew that excellence as a warrior was a passport to political office, wealth and glory, they formed the most warlike element in any state.

Hegemonic masculinity implies institutionalized male dominance over women,[18] which was certainly the case in African societies. Even so, women had their own sphere related to warfare.[19] Besides giving birth to future warriors, they played an essential part in the war ceremonies and rituals that strengthened their men against evil supernatural forces when they were preparing to march out to war. While warriors were away on campaign, their womenfolk would repeatedly perform the prescribed rituals at home to keep them safe in battle. Besides summoning supernatural protection, women contributed significantly to the war effort by supplying the warriors with food when they were gathering for mobilization, and sometimes accompanied them on campaign as carriers and cooks. While the men were away fighting, women kept the homestead and its agriculture functioning with the help of their children and the superannuated, and tended the warriors when they returned wounded or weakened by the privations of war.

Considering this cultural universe, it is hardly surprising that African rulers entirely subscribed to the pervasive warrior ethos and notions of honour. Whether under threat of attack by an African or European foe, the issue for a king was always more than a question of sovereignty or expediency: it was a matter of honour. As Cetshwayo kaMpande, the Zulu king, proudly informed the messenger whom Sir Henry Bulwer, the Lieutenant-Governor of Natal, sent in November 1876 to protest violent action the King had taken against some of his disobedient subjects: 'Go back and tell the white man this, and let them hear it well! The Governor of Natal and I are equal. He is Governor of

Natal, and I am governor here.'[20] A king was a war leader, first and foremost; his warriors were raised from birth to war and its stern demands. Rather than surrender like a coward without a fight, even in the face of hopeless odds, it was considered best by far to die honourably on the battlefield as befitted a true man and warrior.

This warrior ethos was fully shared by the African allies, levies and auxiliaries serving with the British and the Boers. Besides cannily choosing what seemed likely to be the winning side, many of them also saw how they could maintain their warrior traditions and sense of masculine honour through military service with their colonial masters. It is this perception that blunts accusations of their being mere mercenaries, despicable soldiers of fortune fighting against their black brothers for pay, rather than for any motives of loyalty or idealism.

Unfortunately for their sense of military pride, though, the British and Boers did not necessarily deploy their African 'mercenaries' in active combat roles but confined them to menial and humiliating logistical support services. When the British (and to a lesser extent the Boers) did make use of their military skills, they generally left them to fight in their traditional fashion with their own weapons, or tried only half-heartedly to give them some training in western-style warfare and military discipline under the command of white officers and NCOs.[21] In these unpropitious circumstances, what is noteworthy is not the number of occasions when the morale of African levies collapsed. Rather, it is how often these poorly regarded African soldiers proved courageous in combat and stalwart in defeat. With their fellow-Africans against whom they fought in the wars of 1877–1879, they shared a common military culture which inspired and sustained them, and which the British and Boers could not but respect and even admire.

It was my instinctive sense of this heroic ethos—even if all those years ago I was not yet intellectually equipped to give it a name—that gripped me while a young man as I stood in the shadow of Isandlwana, and which has inspired the writing of this book.

CHAPTER 2

Bushman's River Pass

A MIGHTY chain of mountains with fantastically serrated pinnacles and massive, flat-topped buttresses of precipitously sided basalt runs for six hundred miles up the eastern flank of southern Africa. This formidable barrier was known to isiZulu-speaking Africans as the uKhahlamba, or 'the row of upward-pointing spears', and to white colonists as the Drakensberg, or 'dragon mountains'. In 1873 it divided the British Colony of Natal, sprawling across the rolling hills and plains below, from Basutoland, on the high escarpment ten thousand feet above. During late spring it is typical of the climate on the uKhahlamba's eastern flanks to be incessantly wet and misty, with sudden thunderstorms, terrific lightning-strikes and thrashing hail. The foul weather should therefore have been anticipated by Major Anthony Durnford, a lean, energetic officer in the Royal Engineers sporting distinctive Dundreary whiskers—except that he had only recently been posted to Natal and the mountains were unfamiliar to him. Not that most of the eighty men he was leading up the trackless valley of the Lotheni River knew them any better. Fifty-five of them were colonial mounted volunteers of the blue-uniformed Natal and Karkloof Carbineers. They possessed scant military training and no combat experience. All carried cumbersome breech-loading Calisher-and-Terry carbines which would be almost impossible to load when mounted on their restive, poorly schooled ponies. Still, they had the advantage over the twenty-five mounted Basutos riding with them because these African auxiliaries had almost no firearms between them and would have to rely on their spears.

In the early morning hours of 3 November 1873, when his force was at about eight thousand feet, Durnford's grey pony, Chieftain, fell, rolling with him down a steep slope. Durnford's shoulder was badly dislocated and his forehead severely gashed. Despite being in considerable pain, Durnford pushed on. He enjoyed a reputation as an able officer (apparently not affected by his short temper, broken marriage and compulsive gambling), but was deeply exasperated by his failure thus far to see active service.[1] This expedition was consequently his chance to prove himself, and he was determined to see it through. His orders were to reach the top of the uKhahlamba and seize the head of the Bushman's River Pass[2] which led from the Colony of Natal (a British possession since 1843)[3] to Basutoland, an African kingdom which the British had annexed in 1868 and turned over to the administration of the Cape Colony in 1871. There, in conjunction with a force of five hundred African levies under Captain A.B. Allison who were supposed to be advancing by way of another pass some thirty miles to the north, he was to prevent the amaHlubi people under their *inkosi* (plural *amakhosi*), or chief, Langalibalele kaMthimkhulu, from crossing over the border.

The name Langalibalele means 'the sun is killing' and referred to the *inkosi*'s widespread renown as a potent rainmaker and man of power. Indeed, many Africans would come to believe that he had been exercising his occult supremacy to frustrate Durnford in his efforts to reach and seal the pass. Perceived power had its dangers, however, and in 1848 the Zulu king, Mpande kaSenzangakhona, drove him and his ally, Phutini of the amaNgwe, away from the borders of his kingdom. The Natal authorities saw that the amaHlubi and amaNgwe could serve as a buffer between the white farmers of the Natal midlands and bands of San hunter-gatherers (known as 'Bushmen' to the settlers) who were raiding the farmers' cattle from their caves in the uKhahlamba. Accordingly, in 1849 the Natal authorities settled the amaHlubi among the grassy foothills of the mountains along the upper reaches of the Bloukrans (Msuluzi) and Bushman's rivers with the amaNgwe alongside them.

Langalibalele might have enjoyed great prestige as a rainmaker, been rich in cattle and wives—they numbered forty and his children over a hundred—and exercised power over his ten thousand Hlubi adherents, but the fact was he lived in a colonial 'native location'. For thirty unbroken years, from 1845 to 1875, Theophilus Shepstone, the resolutely inscrutable, lantern-jawed son of a Wesleyan missionary in the Cape Colony, was in charge of framing and maintaining Natal's 'native policy'. In 1846 he laid its foundations by setting aside locations for important chiefdoms, like Langalibalele's, and administering them through a system of indirect rule. In other words, *amakhosi* were allowed to carry on governing their adherents according to time-hallowed African custom, but only so long as they collected the hut tax demanded by the colonial state, supplied labour when required and preserved order. Shepstone managed the system by acting as the greatest chief of all, punishing and 'eating up' delinquents and replacing them if necessary with more compliant chiefs. For many years the amaHlubi flourished on their location under the Shepstone System. The problem, though, was that they prospered all too well. They took to producing crops and stock on a commercial scale and competing successfully with increasingly indignant and envious white farmers. Even worse in the eyes of colonists, they were reluctant to enter the Natal labour market because better wages were to be had working as migrant labourers on the diamond fields.[4]

In 1867 diamonds were discovered deep in the high interior of South Africa at the confluence of the Orange and Vaal rivers, and further fabulously rich deposits were soon uncovered nearby. By 1872 twenty thousand whites and thirty thousand blacks had converged on what had become the Kimberley diamond diggings, scrambling to lay their claims in vile, overcrowded conditions where they succumbed to pneumonia, dysentery, typhoid and smallpox.[5] The initial small-fry diggers were soon being squeezed out by large-scale speculators with international finance behind them—capitalists such as Cecil Rhodes, Alfred Beit and Barney Barnato. Under them, diamonds were extracted on an increasingly industrial scale and this began to transform the economy and society of southern Africa (previously considered little more than an agricultural backwater) in what historians have dubbed the 'mineral revolution'. Ripples of capitalist enterprise and new-found prosperity lapped out across the underdeveloped subcontinent. The ports were galvanized by the huge growth in the import industry, and the trade routes that converged on Kimberley—

carrying everything from mining equipment to gin—stimulated the communities along the way. Cheap labour was required to service this burgeoning capitalist economy and its infrastructure. Africans left their homes to work on harbours, on the first railway lines and on the roads, and found good pickings driving the ox-wagons that plied them. Kimberley (second now only to Cape Town in size) attracted ever-increasing numbers of migrant male African wage labourers such as the amaHlubi. Working and living conditions there were of the harshest, and they were subjected to strict controls based on racial segregation. Nevertheless, they brought back cash with its purchasing power into their peasant communities, along with useful manufactured goods like ploughs—and firearms.[6]

White colonists felt more and more menaced by the number of firearms African migrant workers were acquiring, principally from arms-dealers at the Kimberley mines who sold them an estimated 78,000 between 1872 and 1877 alone.[7] This trade was of particular concern because most migrants were the subjects of independent African monarchs.[8] They were consequently improving the dangerous military capability of the considerable armies African rulers had at their command, a threat made worse in settler eyes by rulers themselves determinedly tapping into the often illicit, but always buoyant, international gun trade. Yet any attempts to control the trade or to prohibit the sale of ammunition to Africans faltered badly in the face of the insatiable need to attract African labour which was first effected through offering the means of acquiring firearms. When the necessary permits in British-controlled territories to deal in firearms were not granted, they were simply ignored and smuggling was rife. In any case, local officials found the duties imposed on arms and ammunition (when they could enforce them) a useful source of revenue, and tended to place immediate commercial advantage over the potential threat of allowing so many firearms into African hands.[9]

The firearms which Africans would first have acquired through trade in the 1830s—and then in the succeeding two decades increasingly from the first stirrings of migrant labour in settler territory— would have been smooth-bored, muzzle-loading, flintlock-action muskets, the quintessential firearm from the late seventeenth to the mid-nineteenth century.[10] They were commonly known as 'Tower' muskets after the mark of the Tower of London system that subcontracted manufacture to many gunsmiths. Their accuracy was poor, their effective range less than a hundred yards, and at best their rate of fire was three rounds a minute. Still, being both simple in design and hand-made, muskets were ideal for Africa since they could be easily maintained and hand-repaired. Gunpowder too was not difficult to produce and spherical musket balls could be replaced by other projectiles like stones or metal pot-legs. More and more muskets became available in South Africa during the mid-nineteenth century because European armies were adopting improved firearms, and arms-dealers were buying up the huge stocks of decommissioned muskets at rock-bottom prices to unload at a profit on the African market.

It was not long, though, before a new generation of greatly improved firearms was jostling with muskets on the African market. They are known as 'intermediate' weapons because, although not yet modern breech-loading rifles, they were a real advance on Tower muskets. Muzzle-loading they might still have been, but their barrels had three internal grooves, or rifling, which made them more accurate than smooth-bored muskets and with three times the effective range. In addition, the more reliable percussion-lock, which detonated all-weather percussion caps placed in an indentation on top of the touchhole to fire the charge in the barrel, replaced the long-established flintlock firing mechanism. Loading too was made easier by the introduction of factory-made paper cartridges conveniently holding both ball and black powder to be rammed together down the barrel.

These percussion-lock rifles rapidly became available in Africa because within slightly more than a decade after being adopted in the 1850s by European armies, they were in turn rendered obsolete by further rapid advances in arms technology. By the late 1860s they were being decommissioned to make way for the new breech-loading rifles, and arms-dealers were gleefully snapping up the 'intermediate' firearms to sell on in Africa. Africans naturally preferred to acquire these superior 'intermediate' firearms if they could, but they presented problems that would soon become acute with the introduction of truly modern firearms requiring machine tolerances. It was almost impossible to repair rifles without getting hold of the correctly manufactured spare parts, which had not been the case with the simple musket. Even more problematically, rifles could not be fired without percussion caps or the correct cartridges which, like spare parts, could only be obtained from traders.[11]

Nevertheless, such drawbacks were outweighed in the minds of Africans by the superior effectiveness of the latest weapons technology. They naturally wanted only the best, and were not content with obsolescent firearms, or even with 'intermediate' ones.[12] By the early 1870s, after another phase of transitional, experimental technology (of which the Carbineers' Calisher-and-Terry carbines were a lacklustre example), the newest and finest firearms had seven grooves in the barrel and a greatly improved range of about 1,400 yards with real effectiveness up to 700 yards. Moreover, these rifles were efficient breech-loaders that did away with the external hammer mechanism and replaced it with a spring-loaded firing pin inside the breech that detonated the inserted metal cartridges. Not only did a breech-loader require less skill to load and fire than all previous firearms, but it made for a much more rapid rate of fire with a steady six shots a minute. Critically, it also allowed riflemen to load with ease kneeling or lying prone behind cover.[13] By the 1870s all the main European armies, including the British, had adopted their own version of such rifles.[14] Of course, if Africans bought these modern rifles from unscrupulous traders, they would be as well armed as Europeans, and it was just as well from the settler perspective that at £25 each they were more than five times more expensive than 'intermediate' firearms and nearly eight times dearer than Tower muskets.[15] Even so, while very few Africans got their hands on the most sophisticated rifles, it is quite likely that by the later 1870s something like half the able-bodied African men in the subcontinent were in possession of a firearm of some sort. Many thus armed—including the likes of the amaHlubi—lived within the colonies themselves and were coming to regard guns as a symbol of status which made them the equal of whites.

White settlers generally were only too aware of this threat, and were determined to take preventative action.[16] Concern was acute in the Colony of Natal where the scant seventeen thousand whites (a third of them living either in Pietermaritzburg, the capital, or in Durban, the port) were fretfully anxious about maintaining their control over the overwhelming majority of three hundred thousand Africans. Shepstone's

System of African locations afforded them protection so long as it worked, but settlers feared all would be lost if it broke down. They were almost pathologically fearful that any disobedience or resistance in a location could herald a general uprising in which whites would be slaughtered, and the fearsome precedents of the Indian Rebellion of 1857 and the Morant Bay Rebellion of 1865 in Jamaica were constantly before their eyes. Even worse, the long history of wars along the open frontier and the dread presence immediately to their north of the militarily powerful Zulu kingdom whipped up fears that any African uprising in Natal could lead to an even more deadly 'combination' of African states intent on driving out the whites. When Anthony Trollope, the renowned novelist and perceptive travel-writer, visited Natal in 1877 he wholeheartedly imbibed the settler viewpoint in this regard. Africans, he wrote, 'must be taught to think [the white man] powerful or they will not obey him in anything', so it was essential that all the 'native races of South Africa . . . should believe Great Britain to be indomitable'. In other words, for self-preservation it was essential to maintain white 'prestige' no matter what the cost.[17]

Consequently, when more and more young Hlubi men after their six months' stint on the diamond fields returned vaunting the horses, ploughs and firearms bought with their earnings, or proffered them by labour recruiters, the settler response was nigh hysterical. By Natal's gun statute of 1859 it was necessary to apply to a resident magistrate to own a firearm, and in 1873 the colonial government decided to enforce registration rigorously. John MacFarlane, the notoriously strict and bushy-bearded Resident Magistrate of Weenen County, decided to single out Langalibalele for compliance since to bring such a prominent *inkosi* to heel would serve to cow the rest. But Langalibalele temporized, allegedly had the magistrate's African messengers beaten up, and finally refused a summons to appear in Pietermaritzburg before the recently-arrived lieutenant-governor, Sir Benjamin Pine. Yet this apparent recalcitrance was more than simple resistance to colonial authority on Langalibalele's part. It was very difficult for him to act as required as the intermediary between the colonial state and his own strident, self-confident young men who had earned their prestigious guns and horses through onerous migrant labour, and would not give them up. They were no longer amenable to the traditional control of their far more cautious elders, they possessed firearms, and to go against their wishes put Langalibalele's own prestige and authority at risk.

The colonial authorities did not see it that way, of course, and became increasingly alarmed by Langalibalele's unpardonable 'defiance', especially when they learned that he was considering leaving Natal with his adherents to take refuge in Basutoland. To add to settler panic, Langalibalele was clearly readying himself for a fight, drilling and ritually preparing his men for war. And, to top it all, he was reported to be busy exchanging messages and gifts with Cetshwayo kaMpande, the Zulu king, with an eye to securing his aid. The dreaded African 'combination' seemed to be taking shape, and sharp action appeared necessary to retrieve British prestige. Accordingly, deciding in October 1873 that Langalibalele was contemplating open rebellion and that his plans to flee to Basutoland were treasonable, the authorities mobilized all the military forces available in the colony. On 29 October Pine and Shepstone advanced on the Hlubi location at the head of two hundred men of the 1st Battalion of the 75th Regiment (1st Gordon Highlanders) drawn from the British garrison stationed at Fort Napier in Pietermaritzburg,[18] three hundred Natal Mounted Volunteers and six thousand African levies.

But Langalibalele was a step ahead. He was already leading two to three thousand male amaHlubi and seven thousand or more cattle up the dauntingly steep Bushman's River Pass into Basutoland. He had stocked the caves in the upper reaches of his location with food as places of refuge for the women, children and old people he was leaving behind, and entrusted the balance of his precious herds to the neighbouring amaNgwe, his longtime allies. It was to prevent his flight (even though the horse had already bolted) that Durnford and Allison were ordered to scale the uKhahlamba and seize the Bushman's River Pass. While they carried out their difficult joint operation, the balance of Pine's motley army would remain below the mountain's forbidding ramparts to hold the ground between them.

We left Durnford nursing his dislocated shoulder in the mist and soaking rain at the headwaters of the Lotheni River, about two thousand feet below the escarpment. His incompetent guide missed the pass up the mountain he was aiming for, so Durnford and his sodden and exhausted men had to struggle instead up the almost non-existent

Hlatimba Pass, so steep that their ponies could not be ridden but had to be led. On the way the pack mules carrying their rations and ammunition became lost, and a third of the dispirited troops simply melted away, leaving only thirty-six Carbineers and fifteen Basutos. When finally close to the top of the pass at sunset on 3 November, Durnford fainted from pain and fatigue and his companions had to pull and push him the rest of the way.[19]

He was not to be deterred by his physical collapse. The weather cleared, and after a rest Durnford mounted Chieftain and pushed his depleted force on by moonlight along the undulating top of the rocky escarpment. As day broke on 4 November they reached the rugged valley leading to the head of the Bushman's River Pass. But Allison was not there to support him with his levies as planned. It turned out that the pass shown on his faulty map did not exist, and he was still looking for a way up to the top of the uKhahlamba. Even more deflating for Durnford, it was clear that Langalibalele and most of the amaHlubi and their cattle were already through the pass and on their way into Basutoland where they hoped to settle in territory of Molapo, the son of King Moshoeshoe who had founded the Sotho kingdom.

Yet all did not seem entirely lost. A cattle guard of about five hundred men and several large herds were still coming up the pass under the command of Mabhule, Langalibalele's *induna*, or headman. Durnford resolved that he could at least prevent them from getting through into Basutoland. Leaving his troops drawn up in close formation behind him, he went forward with Elijah Khambule, Shepstone's own valued interpreter, to parley with Mabhule. Some of the Hlubi elders agreed to turn around and return to Natal, but they were at odds with the wrought-up younger warriors. Mabhule warned Durnford that he could not control them, and that it would be wise for the Major to withdraw while he still could. Durnford was not the man to comply, and when he gruffly refused to give way the young men to the rear of the elders raised a taunting clamour. One then pushed forward and threatened Durnford with his spear. An elder promptly felled him to the ground with a blow to the head with his knobbed stick, but the rest of the young warriors crowded more closely around, shouting angrily and gesticulating with their weapons. Those of the cattle guard still below the head of the pass now came running up in support. Large numbers of warriors began to take up position among the rocks on rising ground on the right flank of Durnford's men who were sitting their horses in a state of mounting apprehension.

As a precaution Durnford ordered them onto higher ground where they deployed defensively in skirmishing order. With their nerve breaking, they began pleading with him to open fire on the amaHlubi, but Pine had given Durnford strict orders not to fire the first shot, and he was determined to abide by them. It was nevertheless clear he was losing control of the situation. His jittery men were now crying out loudly that they were in a trap, and must retire. Realizing he could no longer rely upon them, Durnford reluctantly began to pull his troops slowly back over difficult, boggy ground to a higher position while a considerable number of jeering warriors shadowed their retreat. Durnford might still have withdrawn his men without a fight, but then one of the amaHlubi, Jantje kaSilele, fired a shot, and his comrades (including Malambule, one of Langalibalele's sons) joined in with a volley from behind their rocks. The inexperienced mounted troops thereupon threw up all that remained of their shaky discipline and with panicked cries simply galloped off as fast as they could in the direction of the Hlatimba Pass. Hlubi fire nevertheless cut some of them down. Katana, one of the mounted Basutos, was shot, as were the Carbineers Edwin Bond and Robert Erskine, the latter being the son of no less a figure than the Colonial Secretary of Natal. Charles Potterill's horse was shot under him, and the amaHlubi caught up with him when he tried to escape on foot. He turned at bay, and he and one of his enemies simultaneously shot each other before other amaHlubi could spear him.

Durnford and Khambule had been unprepared for the sudden rout and were left in the horsemen's wake. The amaHlubi quickly cut them off and surrounded them. Khambule's horse was speared and he was thrown. When Durnford tried to help him up behind him on Chieftain, the unfortunate interpreter was shot through the head. Two amaHlubi then grabbed Chieftain's bridle and speared Durnford in his side and in his left elbow, severing the nerves and permanently crippling his arm which he kept hidden thereafter under his tunic. Although wounded, Durnford shot both his attackers with his revolver. Freed of their grasp, Chieftain then bolted and Durnford caught up with his men. He could not persuade them to halt and make a stand and they continued riding as fast as they could over the broken terrain. The amaHlubi kept up the pursuit for almost two miles, and a few determined warriors only finally gave up the chase at the Hlatimba Pass where Durnford at last rallied his men. True to form, he tried to get them to return to the attack, but their ponies were completely blown and they had had the fright of their lives. The best Durnford could do was to keep them together and bring them down the mountain to base.

The affair at the Bushman's River Pass was a singularly discreditable military failure for Natal's forces. At the subsequent Court of Enquiry in October 1874 Durnford's leadership was severely criticized, even though his undoubted personal courage was acknowledged. He was left burning to redeem his military reputation, and in 1879 would wager all on the fatal field of Isandlwana. The three fallen Carbineers were all of prominent settler families, and this was especially shocking for a colony where no white had been killed in armed conflict with Africans since its inception. On the first anniversary of the debacle a gothic revival memorial to both the colonial and African men who had died was raised in Pietermaritzburg by public subscription. All who saw it were reminded of what might befall should existing 'native policy' fail.

That is why courts of inquiry and monuments were not enough. The colonial state had to avenge the killing of whites and send a bloody message to its African subjects that no defiance of its authority would ever be tolerated. And not only that, it must show that the occult powers of the government were greater than those of Langalibalele, the great rainmaker.[20] He was deposed as chief, and settler volunteer forces and 'loyal' African levies were dispatched on punitive expeditions to ravage the Hlubi location. They looted and burned homesteads, and the captured cattle were distributed to the levies in payment for their military services, or auctioned off to white farmers. Some two hundred Hlubi women and children were mercilessly hunted down and killed, and the survivors assigned to colonists as indentured labourers. The location itself ceased to exist and was carved up between non-Hlubi chiefs and white settlers. As for the amaNgwe who had 'disloyally' harboured Hlubi cattle, they were punished by having all their stock confiscated.

Very soon Molapo, among whose people in Basutoland Langalibalele had taken refuge, was persuaded to give him up to the colonial authorities. Captain Allison arrived from Natal on 7 December 1873 to bring him and his followers back to Pietermaritzburg where they were paraded through the streets in chains to the jeers and curses of the white onlookers. The Natal government put Langalibalele on trial in early 1874 where he was found guilty of treason and rebellion under a legally dubious combination of Native and English criminal law and banished to the Cape for life. Hundreds of his adherents were also sentenced to various terms of imprisonment. Dispatched first to the dreaded prison of Robben Island, Langalibalele was moved in 1875 to Uitvlugt farm on the dreary Cape Flats. A few of his wives were allowed to join him there, and curious visitors came to view him as if he were a caged lion. Broken, he was finally allowed back to Natal in 1887, but not to his old location.

Langalibalele may indeed have been thoroughly crushed and his people dispersed in a demonstration of colonial power, but as Trollope sagely commented, the Langalibalele Rebellion was destined to 'greatly affect the whole treatment of the Natives in South Africa'.[21] Indeed, Bushman's River Pass sent shockwaves not only through Natal but the Cape as well, raising settler fears of an African uprising to fever pitch, and leading to a redoubled clamour to formulate a common policy aimed at disarming all Africans before it was too late. And as things turned out, only a few years later the raw memories of Langalibalele's pseudo-rebellion would serve British administrators seeking the confederation of southern Africa with a popular justification for going to war against their African neighbours, especially if gun control was to be rigorously maintained thereafter.[22] As Sir Theophilus Shepstone, by then knighted and the Administrator of the Transvaal, would put the case in June 1878:

> The feeling of antagonism that has so suddenly sprung up among the coloured tribes in South Africa to the white man, and which seems to be spreading, is, I think, a direct result of this [firearms] trade; the acquisition of firearms has been to the native the acquisition of strength and confidence, hence the present state of affairs between the races.[23]

The Boer–Pedi War, 1876–1877

CHAPTER 3

Bopedi

U NEXPECTEDLY, it was neither a fresh African rebellion against colonial rule, such as Langalibalele's, nor a war against a black kingdom abutting British territory that finally precipitated the series of wars that slammed the half-open South African frontier shut. Rather, it was a spluttering conflict on the north-eastern borders of an independent, settler-ruled republic far away from the immediate sphere of British control.

When Britain formally annexed the Cape of Good Hope from the Dutch in 1814 to secure its sea route to India, some twenty-seven thousand white colonists already lived there. These Cape Dutch were derived from Dutch, Flemish, German and French Huguenot settlers and were beginning to develop a sense of their own 'Afrikaner' identity. British rule did not sit well with many of them, especially when the relatively liberal new administration interfered with their well-established and racially based notions of mastery over the African and slave majority. Some simply yearned to trek away out of the reach of the meddling, alien British so they could live their lives as they wished. But others more positively perceived the alluring economic possibilities of the expanding frontier.[1] They calculated that if they moved far enough into the interior of southern Africa they would make contact with the traders and Portuguese ports of the east coast. Once they had done so, they would no longer be dependent on the commercial network controlled by the British, and would be free to set up their own independent states.

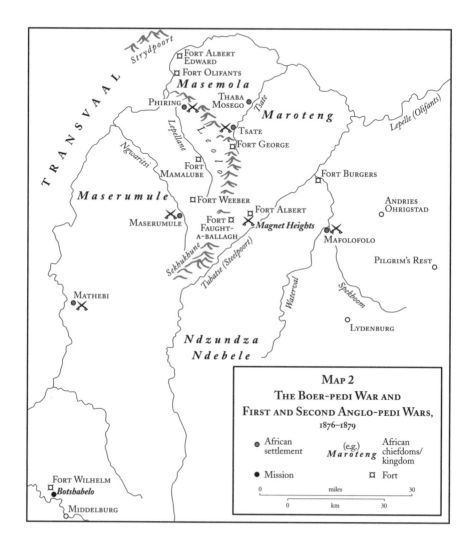

MAP 2

THE BOER-PEDI WAR AND

FIRST AND SECOND ANGLO-PEDI WARS,

1876–1879

With these objectives in mind, by 1836 an organized migration of farmers (or Boers), known as the 'Great Trek', was under way north across the Orange River. Perhaps as many as fourteen thousand Emigrant Farmers, as they called themselves, or Voortrekkers as they are now commonly known, had left the Cape by 1845 in a series of parties, taking with them not only all their livestock and goods and chattels, but also their black quasi-slaves and dependants to a number as great as their own. They violently collided with the African societies they encountered already dwelling in the boundless lands of the high-veld, and either displaced them or reduced those who remained into labourers on the immense farms they staked out for themselves.

The fractious Voortrekker parties did not find it easy to cooperate with each other. Splintering over the vast interior they founded several volatile republics which continued in a chronic state of conflict with their African neighbours and with each other. The British feared these Boer statelets were bound to create long-lasting instability in the subcontinent with likely repercussions on the Cape Colony. But it was difficult to decide how best to assert British control beyond the Cape's frontiers. Successive British cabinets throughout the nineteenth century fluctuated between pursuing formal and informal empire in southern Africa, sometimes seeking to assert political paramountcy over the whole region, only then to withdraw from direct involvement.[2]

During the 1840s the British engaged in a forward policy across the Orange River. This reached a climax in February 1848 with the setting up of the Orange River Sovereignty in the territories bounded by the Cape Colony to the south, the Vaal River to the north and west, and the Drakensberg (uKhahlamba) to the east. But this was a troublesome and unrewarding commitment and the Whig ministry in Britain very soon decided on disengagement. After all, at the time Britain was the only colonial power with a stake in South Africa,[3] so it seemed that British paramountcy could be exerted without the cost and liabilities of formal rule.[4] The first step in the imperial retreat was a settlement with the fractious Boers living north across the Vaal River who were in the habit of destabilizing the Orange River Sovereignty.

In 1849 the clutch of squabbling Boer republics north of the Vaal decided to unite under a single *volksraad*, or parliament, and entered into negotiations with the British.[5] By the Sand River Convention of

17 January 1852, the imperial power cut a deal with them. The trans-Vaal Boers agreed not to interfere with the affairs of the Orange River Sovereignty. In return, the British recognized their full independence and undertook to disclaim all alliances with 'the coloured nations' across the Vaal. Related crucially to that undertaking, the British guaranteed the Boers access to supplies of ammunition (so vital to the Boers' very survival) while agreeing to deny it to the African societies they feared. In return, the trans-Vaal Boers agreed to abolish slavery in their new republic.[6] Two years later, the British abandoned their attempt to exercise authority over the Boer communities of the Orange River Sovereignty as well, and by the Bloemfontein Convention of 23 February 1854 recognized the independence of the Republic of the Orange Free State (OFS).[7] The British retreat from the interior was completed in 1863 when British subjects north of the Orange River were freed from the jurisdiction of the Crown.[8]

The fledgling OFS retained close ties with the Cape and acted as the bridge to the north for British interests, but the 'Emigrant Boers North of the Vaal River' developed their republic in cantankerous isolation.[9] In September 1853 they officially adopted the name Zuid-Afrikaansche Republiek (or South African Republic—ZAR) for their new state, although it is often referred to as the Transvaal.[10] Agreeing on a name was one thing, but it would take the Transvalers a decade before they turned the fractured and debt-ridden ZAR into even the semblance of a viable polity. Crucially, the Transvalers found it extremely hard going to stamp their authority over the African societies they had settled among in the boundless lands north of the Vaal. Military action was hampered not merely by the logistical challenges of bringing in ammunition and essential equipment over enormous distances from the coast, but by simple lack of manpower.[11] By the late 1870s there were still only forty thousand or so whites in the ZAR to nearly a million Africans. Boer farmers in their rudimentary homesteads were sparsely sprinkled across the countryside on their six-thousand-acre farms connected by execrable tracks, and the scattering of villages usually consisted of no more than a small church, courthouse, market square and a few dozen houses.[12]

Weakness, therefore, not strength, characterized Boer relations with Africans on the porous periphery of the ZAR, and these were conducted through local agreements and compromises interspersed by occasional bursts of violence.

The Bapedi people, who went to war in 1876 with the Boers of the ZAR, know their remote, hard-faced land on South Africa's high, eastern escarpment as Bopedi. Characterized by rivers deeply incised into the rocky terrain, much of Bopedi falls under the rain shadow of the encompassing mountains. As a consequence, the summer rainfall is grudging, except during the violent thunderstorms that turn the sluggish streams into wildly raging torrents. Arable, well-watered land is scarce and highly prized, none more so than the rich valley of the Tubatse (Steelpoort) River, a tributary of the Lepelle (Olifants) River. From earliest times people have competed to settle there. The Sekhukhune Mountains run along the west bank of the Tubatse. They are almost connected to the Strydpoort Mountains in the north-west by the Leolo Mountains which traverse Bopedi diagonally with their high, conical peaks and steep gorges. In the western parts of Bopedi the featureless, treeless highveld of the country's interior gives way to the undulating bushveld. Distinctive, isolated rocky hills, or koppies, thrust out of the red soil with its dense cover of bush and low trees. On Bopedi's eastern marches the land falls away to the lowveld with its subtropical vegetation. This deceptively attractive green profusion is infested by deadly malarial mosquitoes and by tsetse flies whose vicious bites inject the fatal trypanosome parasite into humans, horses and cattle.

Yet, if the tough terrain was generally unyielding, it held one inestimable advantage: it was full of natural, rocky fastnesses which the Bapedi could fortify with stone walls and palisades and defend against their many enemies. Indeed, their rather loosely organized state was almost always on the defensive, in the final resort held together by common threats from the outside.[13]

At the time when Bopedi went to war with the ZAR in 1876, the northern Sotho Sepedi language was spoken by the majority of its people who also shared many customs. But this apparent homogeneity disguised the fact that the Bapedi actually consisted of a hotchpotch of groups with very different histories and traditions,[14] melded together in the process of forging the Pedi kingdom. Imposing the historian's clear-cut order on the shadowy events of Africa's precolonial past is an unsatisfactory, frustrating enterprise, and any account of the origins of the Pedi kingdom can—like that of any of its African neighbours—be no better than provisional.[15]

But we can be sure that the forefathers of the Bapedi, like all the other eighteenth-century Iron Age indigenous peoples of southern Africa north of the Orange River and east of the Kalahari Desert, depended on cultivated crops.[16] Furthermore, the widespread owner-ship of cattle meant wealth and power, and their exchange cemented marriage. Cattle-rich men acquired wives and manpower and emerged as the chiefs of the hundreds of small chiefdoms that clustered in localities with rivers and enough rain to support sustained agriculture.

Seemingly, the Bapedi sprang from the chiefdom ruled over by the Tswana-speaking Bahurutshe people on the fine pastures below the Magaliesberg, just north of the modern city of Pretoria. All chiefdoms, even that of the proud Bahurutshe, were susceptible to rifts because their membership always remained fluid. When drought or war suddenly destroyed a community's livelihood and wealth, a chief faced losing some of his adherents to another who could better ensure their survival. Chiefdoms might also fracture as a result of internal power struggles and succession disputes, and some groups might hive off entirely to establish new chiefdoms. In other words, no chiefdom, no matter how large and powerful, was exempt from the constant process of splitting and regrouping. And because political power was a matter of control over mobile resources like cattle, and over the labour-potential of people, chiefdoms were not bound to a particular territory. They readily migrated in search of survival and security, accumulating or shedding adherents as they went. Almost inevitably, therefore, in the 1750s various disaffected groups broke violently away from Bahurutshe rule and dispersed.

Tradition has it that when the Bapedi splintered away they eventu-ally overran the enticing Tubatse valley and set up their new chiefdom there. The Maroteng, the senior Pedi lineage, were accepted as the royal house and gave their name to the new state. Under the forceful leadership of Thulare woaMorwamotse, who reigned from about 1790 to 1820, the Bapedi began to raid assertively far and wide, taking control of the trade routes down to the Indian Ocean coast, overawing their neighbours and establishing their loose political hegemony over a wide area. Their type of state is best described as a paramountcy because it was not strongly centralized. Rather, it was a form of federation where the chiefs accepted the overall authority of the Maroteng ruler, but retained most of their local powers.

Thulare was an effective paramount, but with ill portent he breathed his last during the solar eclipse of 1820. His death unleashed an almost inevitable succession dispute. Fatally, it coincided with a much wider socio-political crisis of seismic proportions that had its epicentre far to the south-east of Bopedi, in the territory between the Phongolo and Thukela rivers. Its shock waves pulsed through much of the subcontinent and threw down the newly erected Maroteng state so completely that it had to be built up again from its very foundations.

While it is clear that during the first decades of the nineteenth century turbulent migrations of peoples violently ripped apart most of the pre-colonial societies of south-eastern Africa, their cause remains a matter of considerable academic debate. Explanations have long concentrated on ecological and demographic pressures, and more recently on growing African competition to control trade routes in ivory and cattle (and possibly slaves) with Europeans operating primarily from Delagoa Bay and north across the Orange River from the British Cape Colony. What is certain is that widespread warfare, devastation and the formation by conquest or incorporation of newly militarized and centralized states accompanied these migrations. Historians have applied the term *Mfecane* to this complex and revolutionary period. This is an isiXhosa word, derived from the root *-feca*, meaning 'to crack, bruise, or break down the maize stalks', and was employed contemporaneously to describe the general turmoil. Subsequently, historians began to use the Sesotho term *Difaqane* with reference to the wars on the highveld of the interior in the same period. It means 'those who cut their enemies in pieces', and in the early nineteenth century seems already to have gained the broader meaning of 'wars waged by wandering hordes'.[17]

By the later 1820s three centralized and highly militarized kingdoms had emerged out of the widespread chaos to dominate southern Africa north of the Cape Colony. They were the kingdoms of the amaZulu east of the Drakensberg Mountains and south of the Phongolo River, of the abakwaGaza in what is now southern Mozambique, and of the amaNdebele in the western highveld of the interior. Squeezed apprehensively between these three volatile, menacing giants were several rather smaller, defensive, less organized states that had been cobbled together out of the debris of the *Mfecane*. These included the still fragile kingdoms of the Basotho and amaSwazi (or abakwaDlamini), as well as the reconstituted Pedi paramountcy.

It is very difficult to reconcile or make certain sense of the many alternative traditions that describe what befell the Bapedi during the *Mfecane*. What does seem established is that in the first decade of the nineteenth century the two most aggressively expanding paramountcies between Delagoa Bay and the Thukela River to its south were the abakwaNdwandwe and the abakwaMthethwa. In about 1817 the abakwaNdwandwe crushed their rivals, and only the small Zulu chiefdom in the valley of the White Mfolozi River, ruled by Shaka kaSenzangakhona, a former Mthethwa tributary, remained in the field to oppose them. Despite heavy losses the amaZulu held fast over the following year, and in 1819 their military failure brought simmering tensions within the Ndwandwe ruling house to the surface. Some sections, such as the abakwaGaza under Shoshangane, broke away altogether and migrated north in the direction of Delagoa Bay. Zwide kaLanga led the senior section of the abakwaNdwandwe north across the Phongolo River out of range of Shaka's forces. This was a region already under his control, for in an earlier conflict he had driven out the hardy abakwaDlamini who were now busy consolidating the Swazi kingdom in easily defensible mountainous country to the north.[18]

Meanwhile, with the fragmentation of the Ndwandwe paramountcy, the abakwaKhumalo, one of their former tributaries, also broke away and settled under Mzilikazi kaMashobane in the highveld to the west of Zwide's relocated kingdom. There Mzilikazi incorporated refugees from the escalating violence in the interior and built up his power. By the early 1820s local Sesotho-speakers were referring to Mzilikazi's adherents as the 'Matabele', or Marauders. Mzilikazi's people proudly adopted this sobriquet and referred to themselves in its Nguni rendering as the 'amaNdebele'.[19]

The Bapedi could not escape these upheavals. It seems that in about 1821 their forces repulsed an Ndebele raid from the south. But Zwide was on the move. He was uncomfortably wedged between the amaZulu and abakwaDlamini who were both building up their military might, and was concerned about the proximity of the Portuguese at Delagoa Bay. The Portuguese had been firmly ensconced in their fort there since 1799, and while their tiny garrison was too weak to do more than defend itself, they were busy playing neighbouring chiefdoms off against each other and trading for slaves and ivory.[20] So Zwide moved further to the north-west beyond the Nkomati River to the headwaters of the Vaal River where he re-established his kingdom within much closer range of the Maroteng paramountcy. There are Pedi memories of an appalling battle in about 1822 when most of Thulare's sons perished, although it is not clear whether the victors were Zwide's forces or those of another wandering Ndwandwe fragment, the Nxaba Ngoni.[21]

Some sources suggest that, after shattering the Maroteng para-mountcy, Zwide actually settled for a period in the Pedi heartland, in the valley of the Tubatse. Certainly, by the time of his death in 1825 Zwide was the dominant power in all the lands between the Lepelle River to the north and the Phongolo to the south. But his conquests were all undone by his overconfident son, Sikhunyana, who decided the time had come to try conclusions with Shaka's amaZulu and reclaim the original Ndwandwe lands south of the Phongolo. Sikhunyana reckoned without Shaka, the rising military genius of the age. Encouraged by the defection of Somaphunga (Sikhnyana's rival for the Ndwandwe succession), Shaka resolved in late 1826 to take the offensive himself. Attached to the Zulu army that comprehensively crushed the Ndwandwe host at the izinDolowane Hills was a small mercenary force of white hunter-traders who, with Shaka's permission, had established a rudimentary settlement in 1824 at Port Natal. For the very first time, firearms had played a part in a great battle in that part of Africa. Admittedly, it was only a small one, but their mere presence on the battlefield was fraught with huge significance for the future.[22]

With that irreversible defeat at the izinDolowane Hills, the Ndwandwe kingdom crashed into sudden and absolute ruin. The survivors scattered far and wide, some transferring their allegiance to the triumphant amaZulu and others to Mzilikazi's amaNdebele. The collapse of the abakwaNdwandwe left Mzilikazi in a dominant position on the highveld. In 1827 or 1828 he led his ever-growing following further west to settle in the prime cattle country on the northern slopes of the Magaliesberg, territory that had once been ruled by the Bahurutshe and where the Bapedi had their origins. Only when in 1833 Mzilikazi finally moved further westwards yet, to Mosega on the upper reaches of the Marico River from where he could raid the prosperous Tswana communities, were the Bapedi finally out of his destructive range.[23]

Left cowering in their rocky strongholds with their prize herds lost and fields abandoned, the Bapedi found it hard to recover. Politically, the Maroteng paramountcy had fragmented with several of Thulare's surviving sons leading groups north across the Lepelle to try and regroup. The most successful of these princelings was Sekwati, a junior son of Thulare's. He wandered extensively for several years, building up his following, raiding and fighting, and in about 1828 he and his following returned to the Tubatse valley where he made his capital at the fortified hilltop of Phiring.[24]

There, just like the contemporaneous Moshoeshoe of the southern Basotho in the Caledon River valley far to the south, he built up his kingdom brick by brick by incorporating communities uprooted in the fighting of the past decade. The Maroteng state would never be as large as it had been under Thulare, but under Sekwati it re-emerged as a significant second-tier regional power.

The Bapedi in Sekwati's state lived in large villages of up to several thousand inhabitants.[25] These settlements, linked by meandering paths through the bush, were surrounded by stockades for protection against animal and human predators and were built on the less inaccessible but more defensible rocky slopes of hills and mountains and up the steep sides of valleys. Cattle, essential for providing milk, meat, hides and draught power, were also necessary for paying tribute and bride-prices, and were thus the infallible indicator of the wealth and status of their owners. Young men tended the herds in outposts on the grassy highlands some distance from the villages to avoid damaging the crops. Men also hunted, constructed the woodwork frame of the huts, prepared hides, sewed karosses of pelts, made wooden storage vessels and engaged in the specialized skills of metal workers and smiths. At peak periods in the agricultural cycle men also helped in the fields which were far below a village on the valley floor. As insurance against vagaries in the uncooperative weather, the fields were planted with a

variety of crops in the most appropriate soil for each (the Bapedi identified seven different types). It was women, though, who were the main
toilers in the village's fields, besides being potters, applying the clay to
the wooden framework of the huts (the men did the roofing), weaving
mats and baskets, grinding corn, cooking, brewing beer and collecting
firewood and water from the stream far below.

Society in Bopedi was hierarchically ordered.[26] At the apex were
the ruler and the princely members of his immediate family who
shared the same royal, Maroteng lineage. Closely associated with the
Maroteng through chiefly descent, loyalty and service were the
nobles. These chiefs found it comfortable and worthwhile to acknowledge the paramount's fairly loose overlordship which was exercised
primarily through his ritual authority, a network of marriage ties and
the ability to reward his adherents. From among his family and chiefs
the ruler selected an inner council and governed with their advice.
Subordinate to these elites were the mass of commoners who made
up the bulk of the population and were expected to render the king
and nobles tribute in the form of grain, cattle, precious items like
skins and feathers, and labour. However, they enjoyed some political
rights through the general assembly, or *pitso*, which consisted of all
the adult males of the kingdom. When the ruler and his inner council
were faced with taking a momentous decision, such as a declaration
of war, they would submit it to the *pitso* for general discussion. That
way, they were shielded from the consequences of the decision if it
turned out ill. A third, much smaller group played no part in public
affairs. These were lowly menials without livestock of their own,
despised clients and dependants, people in positions of such servitude
that it was akin to slavery.[27]

As in other post-*Mfecane* states, religious ritual in Bopedi was a
potent means of reconciling subordinate chiefs to Maroteng overlordship because the paramount was recognized as the conduit to the supernatural forces upon whose favour the wellbeing of all his subjects
depended. The Bapedi believed that while the creator god ignored the
trifling affairs of this world, the ancestors, whose shades dwelt beyond
the western horizon where the sun slips down into darkness, retained
an overzealous interest in the activities of their descendants.[28] It was
consequently essential to appease them and secure their assistance

through sacrifice, usually a libation of beer rather than the blood of a beast. Crucially, the shades retained their earthly status in the spirit world. So it stood to reason that the most powerful spirits in Bopedi were those of the ancestors of the Maroteng paramount, and that the ancestors of all other chiefs were subordinate to them. Permission to sow and harvest crops was the most powerful expression of political authority there was, and it lay with the paramount because through his ancestors he possessed a special relationship with the vegetable world and with the rain. Terrible occult forces were at work each spring and early summer as the seed lay in the ground and began to sprout, and only the paramount had the power through his ancestors to manage them and secure a successful harvest.

The paramount's ritual power extended to giving permission to subordinate chiefs to 'castrate their bulls' or hold circumcision schools; to withhold it from a recalcitrant chief prevent the creation of new age-grade regiments and disrupt the very functioning of society.[29] Since the eighteenth century the age-grade system had been evolving in many indigenous societies in south-eastern Africa to replace simple initiation into adulthood. Every few years, young people of the same sex were brought together from across a chiefdom to be formed into an age-grade regiment for the purposes of marriage, the control and utilization of labour, and for military service. In the disruptive years of the *Mfecane* enrolment in an age-grade regiment was also an effective means of incorporating new adherents into the kingdom. The more a ruler could shift control of the age-grade regiments away from regional chiefs and great nobles into his own hands, the more powerful and centralized became his own authority. Above all, the ruler needed to command the military capacity of the age-grade regiments to cow any opposition at home, enforce the payment of tribute, engage in more distant raids and see off attacks by external enemies. And for the age-grade regiments to be truly effective militarily, they had to be thoroughly imbued with an all-embracing warrior ethos.

In the chiefdoms that made up the Maroteng paramountcy, all the uncircumcised boys in their early or mid-teens and girls at the age of puberty were brought together every five years or so to be initiated. In due course they would be formed into a new male and a new female age-grade regiment, each with its own name and binding ties forged in the often harrowing experiences of initiation with its emphasis—especially for boys—on hardships and ordeals.[30]

Boys first attended a circumcision school (*bodika*). With already shaven heads they were conducted to a large lodge in a remote, wooded mountain gorge, or kloof, made of lattice work and covered in grass and branches. While secluded there they slept on one side of a fireplace down the length of the lodge and their guardians and instructors on the other. They were circumcised in order of genealogical seniority and relative rank in the political system. Once their excruciating circumcision wounds had healed, they whitened their bodies with chalk and were taught a secret language to speak only among themselves. Most of their time in the lodge was taken up by hunting, learning liturgical formulae and singing initiation songs. Boys were beaten if they forgot the words because perfect knowledge of them proved membership of the initiation group and strangers pretending to belong could be beaten or killed if they could not recite them correctly. Initiates were also subjected to earnest homilies on the desired qualities of manhood, adult responsibilities and the absolute necessity of obedience to elders and those in authority. To test their mettle boys were also made to go through repeated ordeals like picking up hot coals from the fire. They were beaten if they flinched or failed the test, and were in any case whipped daily to emphasize their subordination to their elders. Only those worthy to be men survived initiation. Finally, with their white chalk washed off along with their childhood, they emerged covered in red ochre as a sign of their new state as young adults.

A year or two later they would attend a further school, the *bogwêra*, which completed their transformation into full manhood. This time they took instruction in a lodge built in full sight of the women, and they spent their time practising their songs, hunting, collecting firewood, energetically racing each other and preening for the ogling young girls who would one day be their wives. If one objective of the *bogwêra* was to prepare young men to take part as responsible adults in the *pitso*, the other was to help them come to grips with their masculinity and to teach them how they should relate to women. The men, for so they now were, finally constituted into a new age-grade regiment under the leadership of one of their high-ranking fellows who was a member of the chiefly house.[31] Closely bonded by their common

experiences, all lived the rest of their days as if brothers and consequently could not marry one another's daughters.

In some of the highly militarized conquest states such as that of the
amaZulu, the king was able to centralize his authority through his tight
control of the age-grade regiments. This was not the case in the
Maroteng paramountcy where the ruler did not have direct command
over a large military following of his own, certainly not one powerful
enough easily to coerce subordinate chiefs into compliance.[32] This was
because the Pedi age-grade regiments did not fall under the paramount's direct command but under that of the regional chiefs who
could call on them to hunt, clear agricultural land, guard their cattle,
construct fortifications and, of course, fight. Consequently, when the
Maroteng paramount wished to mobilize the regiments for a great
hunt, to raid an external enemy, or to defend Bopedi itself when under
attack, he had to deploy all his religious and political authority to
induce the chiefs to release their fighting men into his service.

It became even more difficult to ensure their cooperation when he
required their age-grade regiments to deter dissidents and punish rebel
chiefs within the kingdom, for chiefs were often unwilling to take up
arms for the paramount against one of their own number.

From a missionary account of 1862 we know how a Pedi army was
organized as it set out on an expedition.[33] Over several days regimental
contingents dispatched by subordinate chiefs continued to arrive at the
capital to swell those from the Pedi heartland already gathering there.
Each contingent remained a separate unit in the army under its regional
commander, and fought under its own distinctive standard fashioned
primarily from ostrich feathers. When the army had fully mustered and
finally set out, the paramount himself led the centre which was made up
of the regiments from the capital and Pedi heartland. Men from the
outlying chiefdoms marched on either flank. The missionaries estimated the strength of an army at ten thousand, but it is unlikely that
the Bapedi ever mustered a force in one place even half that number. A
Pedi attacking force always tried to mislead its enemy by marching off
in a false direction before suddenly changing course in order to take its
target by surprise. The Bapedi did not take adult men prisoner, although
they regarded women and children, along with livestock, as booty and
divided them out with the lion's share going to the commanders.[34]

When it came to war, the Bapedi followed the lesson they had learned during the vicissitudes of the *Mfecane,* and if possible always stood on the defensive rather than risk a set-piece battle. The paramount and his chiefs all had their own fortified strongholds. Typically, Phiring, Sekwati's capital, was a rocky hill on which the natural defences were strengthened by stout stone walls. An attacker, baulked of a clean fight in the open field, would either have to invest the place with all the attendant problems of securing supplies over a protracted period, or have to risk an unpredictable assault on a prepared position. In the early years of Sekwati's paramountcy the Bapedi would have defended their fastnesses with hurled projectiles like spears and stones. But over the succeeding decades they began to make ever more effective use of the firearms that came into their hands in growing numbers, firearms which made them such formidable foes, not only to African adversaries, but to the Boers and British as well.

In common with other settlers in South Africa, the Boers expected Africans to fight in the heroic manner typical of the amaZulu, and to do so with their traditional weapons. Those who did not conform to the stereotype and had the effrontery to adopt novel military practices and armaments from whites were 'considered to be lacking in military virtues and competency'.[35] But for societies like that of the Bapedi who had early learned to take to their fortified strongholds against raiders, firearms made complete sense.[36] When pressure began to mount on the Bapedi from hostile neighbours, they understood they had to procure firearms to fight them off.

The problem, though, was that the Bapedi were not in a position to obtain many firearms through trade. Not only were they too far from colonial markets, but they possessed little of interest to tempt European traders since ivory was early eradicated in the Maroteng paramountcy through over-hunting. Besides, the Boers made it their business to deter any trade in firearms with the Bapedi. So the Bapedi adopted another means of acquiring firearms, and that was through migrant labour.[37]

From the 1840s Bapedi started walking along the established trade routes to seek employment as labourers as far afield as the Colony of Natal and the Eastern Cape. They worked on the harbours, roads and railways for about a year, long enough, in any case, to make enough money to buy cattle to pay a bride-price, and to acquire desirable consumer goods such as blankets, beads, sheepskin cloaks, red woollen tasselled caps, straw hats with jaunty ostrich feathers, and liquor. Above all, they earned money to lay their hands on firearms and ammunition. They bought these from Sotho gun-traders in the Eastern Cape or from the Griqua of the interior on the way home. Their chiefs welcomed the accession of firearms, and exacted welcome tribute from the migrants for permitting them to work abroad.

Soon, in what had become a rite of manhood, young Pedi men who had just been formed into their age-grade regiment were regularly making their way to the labour markets of the Cape and Natal in large, jolly groups of a hundred comrades or more under command of high-ranking officers. The Boers became increasingly alarmed by the number of firearms they were acquiring. So too did smaller, vulnerable African chiefdoms who distrusted their Pedi neighbours. They and the Boers consequently started cooperating in harassing returning Pedi migrant labourers. The migrants responded by travelling by night to avoid their patrols, and did not hesitate to fight back if any attempt was made to disarm them.

By the 1860s it seems a good third of Pedi warriors carried firearms of some sort, mainly antiquated Tower muskets.[38] Then in the early 1870s a development close by Bopedi offered an apparent opportunity to get hold of guns more easily. Small quantities of alluvial gold were discovered in 1873 at Lydenburg and Pilgrim's Rest in the eastern ZAR and set off South Africa's first gold rush, though it amounted only to 0.03 per cent of total world production.[39] By the late 1870s about five thousand 'English' settlers—or 'Outsiders'—were living in the ZAR, mainly at the gold diggings and in the small towns where—much to the chagrin and distrust of the Boers—they dominated the fledgling mining industry and related commercial activity.[40] An open arms trade developed at the gold diggings, but despite their close proximity the Bapedi were reluctant to work there for firearms. Only inferior weapons were on offer, and it soon transpired that the pay could not compare with that at the Kimberley diamond fields.[41]

The Kimberley mines were the deepest and perhaps the most dangerous in the world, subject to flooding, landslides and misfired charges. And simply to get there, migrant workers had to overcome great hazards, whether swollen rivers, lack of supplies, wild animals or bandits. Yet such challenges fitted well into the heroic warrior tradition, and were regarded as a test that proved one's manhood.[42] For the Bapedi with their long-established tradition of migrant labour, the lure of the Kimberley diggings proved irresistible, and they soon formed the largest single group at work there.[43] There they earned the cash to pay for the firearms that were not only cheaper there than elsewhere, but more modern too. No wonder that there was growing concern in the ZAR that the Maroteng paramountcy posed a direct military threat.

CHAPTER 4

Sobhuza's Dream

IF the Boers of the Zuid-Afrikaansche Republiek or South African Republic (ZAR) believed themselves to be menaced by the Maroteng paramountcy, for their part the Bapedi felt that they were being harried and raided from every point of the compass. In 1851 the amaZulu to the south of them mounted a major raid. Sekwati withdrew into his fortified capital of Phiring and defied them, eventually driving them off in considerable disarray. Even so, the amaZulu remained the dominant power in the region and Sekwati was anxious to avoid another attack. So he sent token tribute to King Mpande kaSenzangakhona in the form of ostrich feathers and other valuable items as befitted a ruler whom the amaZulu preferred to regard as one of their 'dogs'. Sekwati's successor, Sekhukhune, kept up the practice and the amaZulu thereafter maintained their distance, but their powerful potential for mischief always factored into Pedi calculations.[1]

The amaSwazi presented a much more immediate danger to the Bapedi than the amaZulu, particularly since there was always the possibility that they might ally themselves with the Boers. The members of the abakwaDlamini ruling house, securely ensconced in their fortified caves in the Mdimba Mountains in north-western Swaziland, had welded their state together in the furnace of the *Mfecane*. As a conquering aristocracy, the abakwaDlamini diffused their language and culture to the rest of their kingdom, although they maintained the distinction between themselves, the *bemdzabuko* (first people), and those subordinate to them, the *emakhandzambili* (literally, 'those with two heads'). The threat of the Zulu kingdom to the south never ceased to hang over the Swazi state, and between 1827 and 1852 Zulu armies invaded six times. On every occasion the amaSwazi, ensconced in their impregnable fastnesses, beat the amaZulu back. Their repeated successes gave the amaSwazi confidence, and from the mid-1850s they embarked on successful military campaigns to extend their domain. As a result, the amaSwazi developed into the most serious regional rival of the Bapedi. The unfortunate small groups of people squeezed between the two kept to their fortified caves in constant apprehension of being raided by one or the other.

The Bapedi had real reason to fear the amaSwazi for theirs was a far more militarized state with many of their practices borrowed from the amaZulu. Royal power in the Swazi kingdom was based on the authority of the *iNgwenyama*, or Lion, as the Swazi king was called, over the *emabutfo* (singular *libutfo*) or regiments, which were drawn from the same age-grade of young men across the entire kingdom without regard to regional loyalties and local chiefs.[2]

By the late 1840s circumcision had been abandoned. Before being formed into a *libutfo*, boys went through a tough training that prepared them for adult life as warriors. They started herding cattle when only four years old or so, and learned how to be entirely self-reliant on the open veld, hunting animals for food. Their elders taught them to wrestle and stick-fight (a dextrous skill mastered with many painful blows) and how to handle a spear. They became used to working together in military-like groups when hunting, herding, engaging in mock-battles and, as they grew up, even in love-making parties.

Every five years or so, when an age-group was considered ready, the *iNgwenyama* formed it into a new *libutfo* under the command of one of their number who had come to his attention for his leadership qualities. A *libutfo* consisted of about eight companies, each one commanded by a member of the royal Dlamini clan. A company was made up of several squads of between eight and twenty men who stood together in the dance and worked, drilled and fought as a team. Every company and regiment had its own name, war cry and dress decorations. The *iNgwenyama* was head of the army, but the actual commander-in-chief was usually a commoner, chosen for his military skills as well as his absolute loyalty.

Royal villages (or barracks) established across the kingdom served as rallying points for the *emabutfo* from which they could mount raids against neighbouring enemies. These villages also functioned as nodes of royal authority in outlying areas. Typically, a royal village was built in a great horseshoe of thatched huts encompassing the strongly palisaded cattle byre. At the top was the great hut of the member of the royal house in command, as well as the married quarters. The barracks of the *emajaha* (singular *lijaha*) or warriors were in the wings on either side. When quartered in the royal villages, *emajaha* served as agricultural labour battalions for the king and his wives, for the *iNdlovukazi*, or She-elephant, as the powerful Queen Mother was known, and for local chiefs. Work always began and ended with a *hlehla*, or war dance, in the cattle kraal, or enclosure for livestock. The young men shouted out loud boasts and individuals flung themselves into athletic solos, all intended to attract the young women who were watching with an eye to future husbands.

The *emabutfo* also played a central role at the *Ncwala*, or annual first-fruits ceremony. Like the Maroteng paramount, the Swazi king ritually ensured the fertility of the kingdom, fortified it against its enemies, and renewed the *iNgwenyama's* bonds with his people. He reviewed his *emabutfo* who had gathered from every corner of the country to pass before him in emotive massed formations, singing and dancing. They wore festival headdresses made of the streaming black feathers of the *sakabula*, or long-tailed widow bird, and white cow-tails bound around their ankles, necks and arms. Their leaders draped their loins in leopard skins.[3]

Of course, the main purpose of the *emabutfo* was to go to war, and they were constantly pressuring the king to give them permission to prove their prowess against an external foe. They raided and exacted tribute for the ruling Dlamini elite, and were themselves rewarded with cattle and goods the *iNgwenyama* redistributed to them as food and also as bridewealth when he gave the men of a *libutfo* permission to take wives from a designated female age-set several years their junior. In Zulu fashion the men then sewed on a headring symbolizing their married status.

Such largesse bound the *emajaha* closely to the king, for their future wealth and promotion to positions of power in the state depended upon his favour. Yet, concentrated in their military villages, they were not easy to control. There was blatant rivalry between the regiments to excel, exacerbated by generational differences. Young, recently formed *emabutfo* envied the authority and prestige of the older ones, some of whose members were widely celebrated warriors. They also resented the comfortable married state of the older *emajaha*, and their determination to keep the young women of their families out of the hands of the unmarried warriors. Sometimes, then, it was desirable to go to war if only to prevent the *emabutfo* from turning on each other. Naturally, the younger *emabutfo* were always more anxious to go on campaign than their elders. The veterans had homes and families to lose, while the untried warriors needed the opportunity to display their strength and courage and earn the praises of their superiors. These attitudes persisted on campaign with the veterans regularly reining in the recklessness of the untried *emabutfo*.

As in Bopedi, the decision to go to war required the *iNgwenyama* to consult senior princes and his inner council, and then to seek the approval of the *libandla*, or general assembly of adult males. If possible, the amaSwazi tried to minimize the disruptive effects of a campaign on ordinary life, and war was not normally declared until after the crops had been harvested. Care was taken to keep a sufficiently large reserve of warriors at home to protect civilians while the army was away.

Campaigns usually lasted no more than a month at most because of logistical problems. The king might send along some cattle for the road, but the *emajaha* had to carry their own provisions, staving off hunger by smoking cannabis and relentlessly foraging as they went. As the Swazi proverb has it, 'there is no case against an army'.[4] While the army was away on campaign, those left behind observed many taboos because it was believed that to fail to do so would subdue the warriors' strength and courage. Sexual infidelity by wives was considered particularly harmful, and heavy ropes were tied around their waists while their men were away.

Indeed, ritual was an integral part of warfare.[5] The success of the army depended on working destructive magic against the enemy and ritually strengthening the *emajaha*. When the army assembled preparatory to war at Hhohho, the royal capital below the Mdimba Mountains, the national war-doctors (who all belonged to the Gwebu clan and

were forbidden to use their powers for civil wars) put the warriors
through a series of rituals. These involved cutting off the foreleg of a
live, black bull and making it cavort in agony before the assembled
warriors. The doctors then skinned and roasted the foreleg, sprinkled
it with ritual medicines and tossed it to the *emajaha*. They caught it in
their teeth and ran about passing it on while ensuring that they never
touched it with their hands. That done, the warriors lined up with
shields touching. The war-doctors stalked along their ranks, jabbing
their shields with ritually potent roots and chanting incantations. The
intention was to imbue the *emajaha* with strength and courage, to
preserve them from mortal wounds and to put confusing darkness
before the eyes of their foes so that they could not effectively fight back
or escape. Warriors also ate an unborn calf ripped out of a slaughtered
cow's womb. This was supposed to make them so slippery that their
enemies would not be able to get their hands on them, and so that their
weapons would slide harmlessly off. All these powerful medicines and
ritual actions put warriors into a dangerous, supernatural state from
which they would have to be ritually cleansed after the campaign if they
were to re-enter normal society.

On campaign, warriors were armed with a variety of traditional
weapons. For disconcerting the enemy at a distance they had throwing
spears with a shaft four feet long or more and a thin, tapered blade. But
heroic, hand-to-hand fighting is what the warrior sought, and for this
he had two possible types of short-hafted stabbing spear in his arsenal,
one with a heavy, broad blade and another with a long, narrow one.
Unlike the amaZulu, but in common with the Bapedi and Basotho, for
close-in work Swazi warriors also favoured the battle axe that came
either with straight points or flanged tips. Just as effective was the
wooden knobkerrie with notches cut in its heavy head to give skull-
shattering blows greater purchase. All *emajaha* carried an oval oxhide
war shield, rounder and smaller than the Zulu version.[6] As with the
ancient Spartans, to return without it was the supreme disgrace, the
incontrovertible proof of cowardice and defeat. An awe-struck white
eye-witness in 1876 described a Swazi warrior in full war dress:

The head and face he almost conceals beneath the plumes of black
ostrich feathers. In his right hand he bears his knobkerrie and an

assegai, and on his left arm he wears his ox-hide shield, and in the hand a sheaf of spare assegais. Around his neck he wears his amulets and a hollow bone, which now and then he sounds. When marching to battle he lowers his shield before him and knocks his knees against it. The sound of these shields against the knees of thousands is like the roar of the surf upon the beach.[7]

The Swazi warrior's heroic culture embraced war as the supreme opportunity to prove his strength and courage and to gain recognition and reward. When the army marched out, scouts went ahead of it to make contact with the enemy. This particularly dangerous mission was usually assigned to members of the royal Dlamini clan as they were presumed to be particularly intrepid. Their battle formation mirrored that of the amaZulu with the young, reckless *emabutfo* forming the swiftly encircling horns, while the stolid veteran *emabutfo* anchored them at the centre.

While always applauding heroic deeds, the amaSwazi had little patience with pointless loss of life in war. Cautious commanders would normally deploy their *emabutfo* with a careful eye to the terrain, and would always keep some units in reserve as reinforcements or for pursuit. If circumstances were against risking a pitched battle, commanders saw no shame in retiring to the fortified mountain caves that had always stood the amaSwazi in such good stead.

Courageous death in battle was a special sort of death, the 'heroic-tragic culmination of manhood',[8] a glorious sacrifice made for the greater good of the kingdom. So there was no mourning for the dead warrior. *Emajaha* who had distinguished themselves were dubbed heroes, or *emaqawe*, and thereafter at festivals mimed their glorious deeds in leaping, solo dancing (*kugiya*) before their comrades. Yet, because the violent taking of life exposed the killer to an evil, occult force known as *luphalo*, returning warriors who had drawn blood on campaign, along with the weapons they had wielded, had to undergo many cleansing rituals. *Emaqawe* in addition received a *tiqu*, a necklace of wooden pegs that proclaimed their heroic status, but also magically protected them from the dire consequences of homicide.[9] Without these magical prophylactics, warriors would be exposed to the vengeful spirits of the slain who would torment them in their dreams and infect them with an uncontrollable homicidal rage they would turn against each other.[10]

On its return, a victorious army brought its plunder to lay before the king. The most sought-after spoils were cattle, and the war-doctors treated them ritually with a lighted branch to dissuade them from returning home as well as to destroy the *luphalo* they might be carrying. The king then redistributed the booty to his *emajaha*, the lion's share going to the proven heroes, the *emaqawe*.

It is notable that in their campaigns the amaSwazi made little use of firearms. That was not because they were unable to lay their hands on them from traders, as did other African societies. Nor is it persuasive to suggest that their preferred raiding tactic of surprising a sleeping village at dawn made firearms unnecessary, and that such weapons were only of marginal effectiveness in taking a stronghold by storm.[11] More likely, the cause lay in the deeply ingrained military culture they shared with the amaZulu and amaNdebele, that is, the conviction that the only true way for *emaqawe* to prove their mettle was in ferocious, hand-to-hand encounters with the enemy.

The amaSwazi, then, made for redoubtable enemies and the Bapedi were extremely wary of them. But the Swazi potential for harm multiplied greatly in 1845 when a small party of Boers, hoping to open up a commercial outlet to Delagoa Bay, settled at Andries Ohrigstad east of the Tubatse River and in easy striking distance of the Pedi heartland. What if the amaSwazi were to make common cause with them against the Bapedi? To scotch that possibility, Sekwati immediately cut a deal with Andries Hendrik Potgieter, the Boer leader.[12] Sekwati diplomatically offered to 'be his dog', or tributary,[13] and agreed to the Boers settling in what he regarded as his domain.

From Sekwati's perspective, since the land itself was inalienable, he was merely granting the Boers the use of it as he would any tributary chief. The Boers, who put great legalistic store on treaties extorted from African rulers in dubious faith, saw the matter quite differently. They insisted that the territory in question was now fully theirs. When he understood which way the wind was blowing, Sekwati refused to cede the land and resisted Boer demands for tribute in labour, ivory, cattle and children as *inboekelinge*. *Inboekelinge* (literally those 'booked in') were Africans 'indentured' to Boer masters until the age of twenty-five if male, and twenty-one if female, although there is scant evidence of their ever being emancipated. Historians now accept that slavery remained an established feature of Boer society long after its official abolition, and for decades it continued to be regularly condemned by British missionaries and officials.[14] Slavery in the ZAR would soon be forbidden under the Sand River Convention, but the republic's law created a facade behind which it persisted through sanctioning the seizure of African children who were deemed to be 'orphans'. In practice, the Boers usually captured these children in raids against African communities. Or they might demand them as tribute (as they did of the Bapedi) or trade them for hunting dogs, cattle, blankets, guns and horses with the Bapedi and amaSwazi who preyed on weaker neighbours for that purpose.

Frustrated by Sekwati's intransigence, the Boers did precisely what the Maroteng paramount had intended to prevent, and turned to the amaSwazi. Not that the amaSwazi received the Boers with open arms. Swazi oral testimony has it that King Sobhuza I (ruled *c*.1805–1839) dreamed that people of a strange species entered his country: 'They were the colour of red mealies [maize]; their hair resembled the tails of cattle; their houses were built on platforms and dragged by oxen; they spoke an unknown tongue and knew none of the courtesies of humanity. The men carried weapons of terrible destruction.'[15]

Sobhuza's dream was interpreted as a warning from the ancestors never to fight the white people. Perhaps with this in mind, King Mswati II (ruled 1840–1868) made a deal with the Ohrigstad Boers in July 1846. In return for their aid against the amaZulu threatening his kingdom, he granted them a huge swath of land between the Lepelle River in the north and the Crocodile and Elands rivers in the south. This cession included the Maroteng paramountcy and the abutting Ndzundza Ndebele, Kopa and Koni chiefdoms.[16] Obviously, these territories were not Mswati's to give away, but they provided the Boers with a legal justification (no matter how spurious) to seize them by force. In 1852 a Boer commando, supported by African auxiliaries raised from among their agricultural labourers and allied chiefs, marched on Phiring.[17] Yet, when confronted by its fortifications and the firearms in its defenders' hands, they jibbed at storming the stronghold and sat down to besiege it. Phiring's weak point was its water supply which was some distance away from the fortified hill, and the Boers sensibly tried to cut it off. They were foiled by a sortie planned and led by Sekhukhune, Sekwati's eldest son by his chief wife, Thorometsane.

Sekhukhune, born in about 1814, had grown up to be a hardened warrior in the period of endemic warfare that followed on the death in 1820 of his grandfather, Thulare. Later in life photographs show him as a thin, bearded, fierce-looking man, described by those who knew him as energetic and resourceful. He had cemented his burgeoning military reputation in 1851 when, during the Zulu invasion of that year, he played a prominent part in the counter-attack that drove the raiders away in disarray from Phiring. This time, in 1852, his successful sortie broke the Boer resolve and they raised the siege after only twenty days.

When the disgruntled Boers retired from Phiring, they drove away thousands of cattle and other livestock as booty, and seized numbers of 'orphans' as *inboekelinge*. At one level this was a severe blow to Pedi prestige and wealth, but at least the Maroteng had survived intact. Phiring, though, was shown to be too poorly sited to endure a long siege. So in 1853 Sekwati moved his capital to the Tsate valley in the mist belt on the eastern slopes of the Leolo Mountains.[18] This was an altogether better situation. The soils were rich, there were many springs and the rainfall was regular. Sekwati, his wives and some of his sons took up residence on the top of the rocky mountain fortress of Thaba Mosego. The only approach was up a steep, narrow, winding path hemmed in and overlooked by stone walls and pole fences.

Sekwati was slowly going blind, but his diplomatic skills did not desert him and in 1857 he scored a major coup. In 1849 factional splits, malaria and the tsetse fly had persuaded some of the Boers to leave Andries Ohrigstad and to found a more healthily situated community to the south at Lydenburg.[19] This fractious community had joined the ZAR, but in 1856 had seceded to set up its own independent republic. It would not rejoin the ZAR until 1860. Meanwhile, the Lydenburg Republic was vulnerable, and when its representatives sought peace with Sekwati he drove a firm bargain. In future he would not pay even the token tribute he had been committed to since 1838, and both states recognized the Tubatse River as the boundary between them.[20] This amounted to Lydenburg's acceptance that it had no claim of sovereignty over the Pedi kingdom, and in future the Maroteng would invoke the treaty of 1857 as proof of their independence.

During this same period a new, highly disruptive element entered Bopedi. For years Pedi labour migrants had been coming into contact with Christian evangelists, especially at the diamond diggings, and were carrying home hymns and texts and Christian ideas.[21] Bopedi thus seemed fertile ground for conversion, but the Boers were suspicious of missionaries because of the destabilizing effects Christian teaching might have on labour and social relations with Africans, and it was only in 1860 that the Lutheran Berlin Missionary Society, or BMS, was permitted to begin operations north of the Vaal.[22]

Dr Alexander Merensky and Albert Nachtigal immediately established their first mission station in the Maroteng paramountcy at Thaba Mosego and more soon followed. Sekwati valued the missionaries' guidance in diplomatic relations, especially with whites. Their influence was more problematic in the matter of dynastic politics, and the question of the Maroteng succession began to take on a religious aspect. Sekwati's obvious heir was Sekhukhune with his triumphant military reputation. But the young prince's very prestige made him a threat. So Sekwati turned to Sekhukhune's half-brother, Mampuru, as his preferred heir. Mampuru remained close by his father at Thaba Mosego and along with him cultivated the favour of the missionaries. Meanwhile, Sekhukhune stayed away from the capital under the protection of his powerful aunt, Lekgolane, in the south-western regions of Bopedi. There he built up a powerful personal following swelled by amaSwazi refugees fleeing vicious succession conflicts in their own kingdom. He made it clear that, in contrast to Mampuru, he had no truck with Christians whose refusal to take part in the rituals necessary for the fertility and safety of Bopedi was endangering the whole realm.

As an experienced military commander, Sekhukhune kept his eyes fixed on Mampuru's every move and was prepared to strike decisively.[23] When Sekwati breathed his last on 20 September 1861, Sekhukhune suddenly appeared at Thaba Mosego surrounded by his loyal warriors and successfully asserted his right as heir to officiate at his father's funeral rites when the old king was interred in the great cattle kraal wrapped in the skin of a black bull. Cowed and outmanoeuvred, Mampuru decided not to resist. It would have been wiser for Sekhukhune immediately to have eliminated Mampuru and his followers, who were concentrated in the northern part of Bopedi, in the Masemola chiefdom where his rival's mother came from, but he hoped to avoid a repetition of the civil strife that had followed the death of Thulare. In the event, he had considerable cause to regret his clemency. Mampuru fled Thaba Mosego in August 1862 to become a restless, dangerous exile, always on the move among hostile states bordering Bopedi searching for allies to put him on the throne occupied by Sekhukhune, and fomenting rebellions by discontented tributaries in his loathed half-brother's paramountcy.[24]

Beset by such dangers, Sekhukhune nevertheless believed the ZAR to pose the greatest threat to his state. Not only would the ZAR likely make allies of the amaSwazi and the exiled Mampuru, but the BMS missionaries in Bopedi had their eye to the long view and were prepared to work closely with the Boers. In 1863 the ZAR appointed Merensky their official representative among the Bapedi, and he set to work in the republic's interests.[25] In 1864 Merensky converted the king's young half-brother, Kgalema Dinkwanyane, to Christianity. The prince, who took the baptismal name of Johannes, was a mild-spoken man only too willing to be guided by Merensky and to be used by the missionaries as a royal stalking-horse in their conversion campaign. Enough was enough for Sekhukhune who resented the missionaries' mounting attack on many of the 'pagan' institutions on which the very fabric of Maroteng control was based. Between December 1865 and January 1866 he closed all the BMS mission stations in the Maroteng para-mountcy, and pressured Christian converts to apostatize.

Merensky responded by establishing a new mission station at Botshabelo, or the Place of Refuge, just to the south-west of the Pedi heartland.[26] It rapidly grew into a 'flourishing' settlement for over a thousand people with a church, school, stores, workshops, mill and dwelling houses.[27] On a knoll above the village Merensky built Fort Wilhelm with loopholed stone walls fifteen feet high and two flanking towers. As a consequence, Sekhukhune could not but regard Botshabelo as a direct challenge to Thaba Mosego, especially since Merensky insisted that all the tenants on the tens of thousands of acres of mission land surrounding Botshabelo should regard themselves as subjects of the ZAR. To make matters worse, Dinkwanyane (or Johannes), Sekhukhune's Christian half-brother, took refuge at Botshabelo where he acted as a magnet to Pedi converts.

Mampuru, meanwhile, after various vicissitudes including a short sojourn at Botshabelo in 1867 when he fell out with Dinkwanyane, took refuge in 1868 in the Ndzundza Ndebele chiefdom, a reluctant Maroteng tributary. There he continued to build up his support and to forge links with the amaSwazi. In September 1869, probably guided by Mampuru's adherents, the amaSwazi launched a major raid into Bopedi. It was a disaster.[28] Swazi oral tradition maintains that the Bapedi employed supernatural means to defeat the invaders. They reputedly made a wind instrument called a *luveve* out of the shin bone of a human which, when sounded, possessed the amaSwazi with evil spirits that caused them to flee.[29] Certainly, the Bapedi did always blow wind instruments when under attack which the British thought sounded just like fog horns.[30] What happened in 1869 was more mundane and even more to Pedi credit. The amaSwazi became disorientated in the broken, rugged terrain of the Leolo Mountains with its many narrow defiles, 'as ugly a place as could be wished for', a white settler later commented, 'to be cooped up and surrounded by an enemy'.[31] They fell repeatedly into ambushes where they were cut down by the Pedi gunmen firing from the cover of thick bush. The amaSwazi quickly discovered too that rocky Pedi fastnesses defended by gunfire were all but impossible to take by assault. Eventually the Bapedi trapped the demoralized Swazi army in the Tsate valley and routed it. 'Kill the locusts, the Bapedi cried during the horrible pursuit in which they gleefully cut down many Swazi chiefs and princes.[32]

The Swazi incursion had nevertheless exposed the vulnerability of Thaba Mosego. Sekhukhune immediately decided to move his capital further south down the steep-sided Tsate valley to a more defensible site. From this new base, known as Tsate to the Bapedi and as Sekhukhune's *Stat*, or Town, to the Boers, Sekhukhune began to flex his muscles. Without doubt, his stunning victory over the amaSwazi enhanced Sekhukhune's standing and marked a shift in the regional balance of power. Many of the smaller chiefdoms balancing between the Bapedi and the amaSwazi rapidly concluded it politic to acknowledge the supremacy of the Maroteng paramountcy. Late in 1869 they allied themselves with the Bapedi and ambushed and crushed a Swazi army returning from a raid to the Zoutpansberg, far to the north. This confirmation of Pedi ascendancy made it uncomfortable for Mampuru to stay on with the Ndzundza Ndebele, and in 1871 he settled in the Swazi kingdom. The amaSwazi, although twice in quick succession severely battered by the Bapedi, burned to be revenged and judged they could make use of the exiled prince to this end.[33]

CHAPTER 5

'The Boers Are Killing Me'

To the Boers of the Zuid-Afrikaansche Republiek or South African Republic (ZAR) the eclipse of the amaSwazi whom they had depended upon as a counterweight to the Bapedi was an alarming development, made worse by the concomitant local military ascendancy of the resurgent Maroteng paramountcy. Many Africans living in the open frontier zone now saw it as safe to gravitate back to the Maroteng and resist harsh and insistent Boer demands for their labour and taxes. From the Boer perspective, it was essential to cut the Maroteng back to size.[1] Quite unintentionally, the Christian Dinkwanyane brought the matter to a head.

Late in 1873 Dinkwanyane and some three hundred followers quit the Berlin Missionary Society (BMS) mission at Botshabelo and settled at Mafolofolo in the triangle of land formed by the confluence of the Waterval and Spekboom rivers.[2] The Spekboom rushes through a sheer rocky gorge, but the Waterval runs through rich, alluvial soils ideal for cultivation. Above this valley the settlement of Mafolofolo was built like a fortress around a large church. A high wall of stone incorporating natural outcrops of rock surrounded the entire village. Inside, a great rocky spur full of caves and crevasses served as the citadel. Terraced gardens spilled down the mountain slopes from the village.

Mafolofolo was a provocation, twice over. From the perspective of Albert Nachtigal (who remained in charge at Botshabelo while Merensky was on leave) Mafolofolo was draining converts away from the BMS. Merensky himself later called Mafolofolo 'obnoxious and threatening'.[3] A Christian settlement Mafolofolo might be, but the missionaries were adamant it had to go. The Boers heartily agreed. Although Mafolofolo was to the east of the Tubatse River which the treaty of 1857 defined as the boundary between Bopedi and what was now the Lydenburg District of the ZAR, Dinkwanyane refused to acknowledge Boer authority. Instead, he patched up his quarrel with the increasingly confident Sekhukhune who undertook to protect him as a tributary. Many Bapedi began to cross the Tubatse and to settle in the vicinity of Mafolofolo. This amounted to expanding the Maroteng paramountcy eastwards at the expense of the ZAR, an extension made even more galling when Dinkwanyane would not allow Boers to graze their cattle on the Mafolofolo lands, or even bear arms there.

Such assertions of Maroteng strength were intolerable for the Boers, and they turned to the amaSwazi to help them clip Sekhukhune's wings. After their recent defeats at Pedi hands the amaSwazi were reluctant to become involved, but in 1875 a Boer commando coerced the new, insecure king, Mbandzeni—who was very much under the thumb of Sisile, the Queen Regent—to sign a treaty accepting shadowy Boer suzerainty over the Swazi kingdom.[4] Technically, this committed Mbandzeni to come to the aid of the Boers in their impending show-down with the Maroteng paramountcy. And in early 1876 that moment seemed to be moving ever closer. With new-found confidence bands of Pedi warriors were roaming freely in the vicinity of Lydenburg and rustling cattle. Alarmed Boer farmers were scuttling into laagers and indignantly calling on the ZAR government to mobilize its commandos.[5]

The Boers were a militia in which no structured military training or parade-ground drill took place, and in which the popular election of officers—whose orders the rank-and-file regularly disputed—reflected their egalitarian notions.[6] Their commando system, as it was known, had first been formalized in the Cape in 1715 when the ruling Dutch East India Company developed a mobile mode of border defence against African raids. The British kept up the commando system in the Cape Colony when it came under their rule, and the Voortrekkers institutionalized it in their republics on the highveld.

In the ZAR every able-bodied free burgher (or citizen) between sixteen and sixty was required to serve without pay in time of need as part of his civil responsibility. Instead of uniform he wore his ordinary clothes which always included a wide-brimmed felt hat and comfortable corduroy trousers. A burgher was expected to provide himself with a quality firearm and ammunition. Because firearms were so essential to Boers both for hunting and for fighting, they were brought up with them in their hands and assiduously acquired the best weapons technology available. By the 1870s they were armed with the latest breechloading rifles or carbines, and carried their cartridges in leather bandoliers or in ammunition pouches sewn onto their shirts, waistcoats or jackets. A burgher was also expected to bring along a couple of horses on campaign. Horses were not indigenous to southern Africa. Boers and other white settlers generally rode the Cape Horse or *Boereperd*, a distinct breed that was a cross between horses imported to the Cape from Europe and Indonesia during the rule of the Dutch East India Company. They were accustomed to the local terrain, could survive by grazing the veld, and had largely overcome the endemic and fatal horse (or stallion) sickness caused by the bite of the tsetse fly. An even hardier variant was the tough little Basuto Pony. These were ideal for patrolling and skirmishing and were popular with Boers on commando and with other colonial mounted units and British mounted infantry.[7]

When out on commando burghers rode light, with minimum equipment and supplies, and lived mainly off the countryside. Their horses gave the mounted Boers the advantages of mobility and surprise. They also permitted swift tactical withdrawals to the convoy of ox-drawn wagons that usually accompanied them carrying supplies and which, when drawn up in an all-round defensive position, allowed Boers to maximize their fire-power and avoid being outflanked. The wagon laager, as this formation was known, made the Boers almost unbeatable in the late 1830s against traditionally armed Africans like the amaNdebele and amaZulu when they persisted in mass, frontal attacks. However, these established tactics required adjustments as enemies and technologies changed. By the late 1850s Boers in the interior were operating like mounted infantry, for to storm a determinedly defended mountain fastness (such as they would encounter in Bopedi) meant leaving horses in the rear where they were trained to stand without being held. The dismounted riflemen then worked forward towards the enemy employing coordinated infantry fire and movement tactics. Their well-aimed covering fire pinned down the defenders and made it too dangerous for them to show themselves and fire back effectively.

The great weakness of the commando system was that it was a citizen militia made up from a very small male population with few or no reserves available. Boers were consequently most unwilling to take unnecessary casualties. Hand-to-hand fighting meant sharp losses, and made no sense to marksmen. So, if an assault on an African stronghold did not progress satisfactorily, Boers saw no disgrace in living to fight another day and calling off the attack. Whatever the circumstances, the essential Boer tactics were speed in concentration and attack, and a readiness to withdraw to a more favourable position before they became too decisively engaged in a fire-fight that was going against them.

Black servants known as *agterryers* ('after-riders' or lackeys who accompanied their masters on horseback on a journey, a hunting expedition or to war) had been an inseparable part of the commando system since its inception in the Cape. *Agterryers* carried out all the support services, driving the wagons and managing the teams of oxen, grooming horses, slaughtering livestock, collecting firewood, cooking, guarding ammunition and helping with the sick and wounded, for there were no ambulance or hospital services to speak of. They took part in all the campaigns of the Boers against their African enemies, performing both their customary menial tasks and sometimes taking a direct military role as had been the practice in the Cape as well. Unfortunately, because their presence on campaign was so much taken for granted, and because the Boers tended to discount their contribution on account of their perceived racial and social inferiority, there is little specific reference to *agterryers* in the sources.[8]

Who then were these militarily essential but faceless *agterryers*? Most were the children of *inboekelinge* who grew to adulthood on Boer farms as labourers known as *oorlamse kaffers*[9] (civilized or sophisticated blacks) skilled in agricultural, pastoral, artisanal and domestic activities. They were socialized into Boer culture and taught to cultivate their sense of superiority over, and alienation from, surrounding Africans. Crucially, when their masters put them in charge of herdsmen and the livestock they were tending in the veld, they were trusted with firearms to protect them from wild animals and stock thieves. They carried them too when they accompanied their masters on hunting and trading expeditions. So it is no surprise that they bore arms on commando and fought beside their masters when required.

The Boer–Pedi War of 1876 was the product of the convoluted and mounting rivalries of the region. Yet, as is so often the case in wars that have been long a-brewing, the actual *casus belli* was trivial enough, and one can sympathize with Sekhukhune's later plaint that he did 'not know the cause of the war between the Boers and me'.[10]

On 13 March 1876 the Bapedi provocatively removed beacons set up by a settler called Jancowitz claiming land east of the Tubatse River, and seized the timber he had felled. In Pretoria, the ZAR government of President the Rev. T.F. Burgers decided it could not let the challenge to its authority go unanswered any longer, and on 16 May 1876 declared war on Sekhukhune.[11] By July 1876 the Boers had concentrated their forces at Middelburg, just to the south-east of Botshabelo. The commando was the largest ever fielded by the ZAR and was made up of about 2,000 burghers as well as some 600 African auxiliaries supported by four 4-pounder Krupp RBL mountain guns, and a supply train of nearly five hundred wagons.[12] Yet all was not well with this army. President Burgers, who assumed overall command as Commandant-General, was already held in low political esteem by many Boers. Should the campaign not prosper, he would find it difficult to hold his fractious forces together. And morale was already low, even before the Boers marched out. The Lydenburg Commando had obvious local interests to fight for. As for the rest of the burghers, the bulk of whom came from more distant regions of the ZAR, there was little reason for any personal commitment to the campaign. Many half-heartedly declared that since Sekhukhune was an independent ruler he should best be left alone.[13]

The Boers were very anxious to have Swazi support in the forthcoming operations. Yet, despite the tempting opportunity to be revenged on the Bapedi, and regardless of the very recent treaty of 1875 with the ZAR, the amaSwazi proved reluctant allies. They havered and backtracked, and would not finally commit until the Boers had agreed to protect their southern flank against a possible Zulu attack. Finally, in the first week of July 1876, 2,400 Swazi *emajaha* joined the eastern, or Lydenburg Commando of 600 burghers under the command of

Martinus Wessels Pretorius. But as such reluctant participants, the Swazi *emabutfo* could not be expected to remain committed should the campaign go wrong.

The Boer strategy was for the western division to advance up the Lepelle River from Middelburg and the eastern one to proceed up the Tubatse. Both were to reduce Pedi strongholds as they went and clear the country of Pedi forces before linking up for a joint attack on Tsate, Sekhukhune's capital. The Bapedi responded to this invasion as they had to Swazi and Zulu incursions in the past. To foil the Boers who depended largely on foraging for supplies, Pedi regiments moved rapidly across country carrying off stocks of grain ahead of the commandos and driving livestock out of their reach. The Bapedi knew that if they foolishly met the Boers in open battle they would find it very difficult to counter the enemy's mobile, mounted infantry. So they withdrew to their fortified strongholds where they could use their firearms to greatest effect, and dared the Boers to take them by assault.

The campaign opened reasonably well for the Boers. On 5 July the western commando under Commandant N. Smit successfully stormed the stronghold on the western bank of the Lepelle River held by Chief Mathebi who acknowledged Maroteng overlordship. With the fall of what newspaper correspondents called the 'kaffir Gibraltar',[14] Pedi resistance in the region collapsed. On the eastern flank, the Lydenburg Commando and their Swazi allies cleared the Magnet Heights on the eastern bank of the Tubatse on 8 July. They then turned north-east to attack Dinkwanyane's stronghold at Mafolofolo. The assault came on 13 July and Mafolofolo was overrun. When the amaSwazi broke in, they found Dinkwanyane lying sick of measles or smallpox. Their blood-lust up, they stabbed him in the right breast and groin and left him to die two days later. Nor did they spare other non-combatants, and nineteen women and thirteen children fell to their spears, besides forty-seven men who died in the fighting.[15] The survivors abandoned Mafolofolo and scattered to the winds.

The Swazi victory at Mafolofolo had not been an easy one, for they suffered thirty dead and over fifty wounded before they broke through the defences. Nor was it lost on them that while they had committed to a frontal assault at a steady trot under heavy fire, the Boers had preferred to hold prudently back, giving them covering fire from about 2,500 yards. Understandably, the amaSwazi were disgusted at being offered up as cannon fodder. So as soon as Mafolofolo had fallen, the *emajaha* rounded up the hundreds of cattle they had captured. They then marched straight home through the town of Lydenburg which they angrily plundered for food and firewood. Despite Boer pleas and promises they took no further part in the campaign. Now without the amaSwazi to take the brunt of the fighting, the Lydenburgers jibbed at attacking another stronghold and skirted all those on their path as they pressed on to their rendezvous with Smit's commando for the planned joint assault on Tsate.

Tsate was a formidable nut to crack.[16] The town of three thousand or so huts was built along the edge of the triangular valley and up the side of the rocky, steep Leolo Mountains where they tightly enclosed the lower ground from the south. Thick stone walls, one behind the other, fortified the mountain slopes. Long lines of rifle pits had been dug around the perimeter of the town, strengthened by stone walls, hedges of prickly pear and camel thorn. Entrance to the town was only through two narrow, well-defended footpaths. North of the town and in the centre of the flat-bottomed valley was the citadel, known as the 'Fighting Kopje' or Ntswaneng. This was a daunting, volcanic hill of huge granite boulders 150 feet high, 300 feet long and 200 feet broad fortified by stone-built breastworks which gave excellent cover to marksmen.[17] Ntswaneng was honeycombed with caves stocked with supplies in which civilians could shelter and further marksmen take up position. Altogether, it was strong enough to cow the most reckless assailant, let alone the cautious Boers. It was reported that before the battle, an ancient Pedi man approached the Boer laager and demanded with great prescience: 'What brings you here? Do you wish to retain all the comforts of a home and enjoy a peaceful life? If you do, return. If not, remain where you are.'[18]

While Sekhukhune and his warriors took up position to defend Tsate, his active scouts reported the precise Boer dispositions. The invaders planned a pincer movement. The Lydenburg Commando, which numbered eight hundred burghers and five hundred African auxiliaries under the command of Commandant Jan Joubert (the replacement for Pretorius who had fallen ill), was to advance over the mountains from the south. Smit's commando of nine hundred burghers and some African auxiliaries was to attack from the north.

On the dark night of 31 July Joubert's men attempted the steep ascent over the rugged mountain terrain. The Bapedi were waiting and opened a galling fire on them from their concealed positions in the rock and bush. The Lydenburgers very soon lost heart, and blundered back to their laager. Unaware that Joubert's force was now out of the picture, on the morning of 1 August Smit's men launched their own rather feeble attack on Tsate. After burning a few huts on the lower slopes of the mountain they came under the steady, accurate, increasingly heavy fire laid down by the Pedi sharpshooters (some of them mere boys) from their well-prepared positions. With too few African auxiliaries to bear the brunt of the fighting for them, and unprepared to suffer casualties themselves, the Boers flung themselves down and took cover. Indeed, they had had enough. Flatly refusing to obey explicit orders to resume the advance, they remained pinned down all day under Pedi fire until with nightfall they could fall back in considerable disorder on their laager. As an English-speaking newspaper correspondent scathingly put it, 'most of the Boers have proved themselves frightful cowards.'[19]

The next day the Boer *krygsraad*, or war council, met and resolved to renew the attack on Tsate. But the burghers were having none of it. They simply inspanned their wagons and declared that they were going home. Thereafter, among the Boers the aborted campaign was derisively known as *'die huis toe oorlog'*, or 'the go home war'.[20]

Faced with mass desertion, the Boer commanders were left with no option but to change their strategy. Clearly, it was hopeless to attempt to capture Tsate. So they decided instead to try and starve the Bapedi into submission by building two forts to command the eastern and western approaches to Tsate and the Pedi heartland. In the second week of August they erected Fort Burgers in the bushveld at the confluence of the Steelpoort and and Spekboom rivers at the foot of Morone Mountain. As no burghers were willing to garrison it, the Transvaal government had to turn to mercenaries and freebooters, promising them as inducement all the spoils they took fighting the Bapedi plus a farm of two thousand acres.[21] Despite being in contravention of the Foreign Enlistment Act of 1870,[22] enough roughs were recruited at the diamond fields of West Griqualand to make up the Lydenburg Volunteer Corps. Their commander was the dashing but dubious Captain Conrad von Schlickmann, apparently a Prussian ex-officer, but certainly one of the leaders of the aborted Diamond Fields Revolt of 1873.[23] The Boers built their second fortification, Fort Weeber, on the open plain west of the Leolo Mountains. This was manned more reputably by a hundred Middelburg Burgher Volunteers under Captain Ignatius Ferreira.

From these two strongholds the Boers sent out incessant patrols and night attacks to rustle cattle, deny the Bapedi access to their grazing lands, and prevent them from sowing or reaping their crops.[24] By numerous accounts, Schlickmann's hardened toughs committed the 'grossest outrages on humanity' by mercilessly shooting down unarmed women and children.[25] Determined to put an end to these acts, on 29 September 1876 the Bapedi attacked Fort Burgers, but the defenders successfully fought them off with rifle and artillery fire. To Pedi chagrin, their failed assault only resulted in the garrison being rein-forced by another hundred lawless, hard-bitten diggers from the diamond fields, under the command of the notorious Arthur Aylward, Irish Fenian, hater of the British, outspoken republican, journalist and another veteran of the Diamond Fields Revolt.[26]

Over the next months the Bapedi did their best to ambush the Boer patrols, and succeeded on 17 November in killing the ruthless von Schlickmann. But the situation continued to deteriorate for the Bapedi, made worse by an unrelenting drought. Suspecting they were facing disaster, a number of tributary chiefdoms shifted their allegiance away from the Maroteng to the ZAR. In an attempt to stop this rot, in November the Maroteng regiments marched out against the disloyal Masemola chiefdom where Sekhukhune's exiled brother Mampuru's stock was high, and which had rebelled once before, in 1865. The Masemola had their stronghold at Phiring, and with the assistance of a contingent of the Middelburg Volunteers from Fort Weeber they repulsed Sekhukhune's warriors when they attempted to storm it.

His defeat at Phiring forced Sekhukhune to reconsider his options. His authority was crumbling and famine was stalking the land. His people desperately needed a respite from Boer harassment and a chance to plant their crops, but it was clear he had no means of forcing the

Boers to desist. As the High Commissioner, Sir Henry Barkly, presciently reported to his superiors in London, the war had 'degenerated into a series of petty marauding expeditions, conducted with daily increasing animosity and barbarity on both sides, and tending to lead to no conclusive result'.[27] The time, then, had come for Sekhukhune to negotiate. The Boers were nothing loath since they were finding the cost of continuing military operations quite unsustainable for the already bankrupt ZAR. Merensky, back in Botshabelo from his leave in Germany, was anxious to see peace restored and offered his services as mediator.

The emissaries from the two sides met at Botshabelo and agreed to terms. The treaty itself was brought to Sekhukhune at Tsate where he ratified it on 15 February 1877. Yet nothing was as straightforward as it seemed.[28] The treaty defined the boundaries between a diminished Maroteng paramountcy and the ZAR. By its terms Sekhukhune also acknowledged himself a subject of the ZAR and promised to surrender two thousand cattle as tribute. But did Sekhukhune fully understand what he had agreed to? The circumstances under which he signed the treaty were murky with considerable evidence of deliberate Boer obfuscation concerning its provisions. And even if he did grasp all that the treaty contained, was his assent anything more than a cunning ploy to buy some breathing space from the Boers who, he lamented, 'hunted him to and fro, and shot his people down like wild game'?[29] The one thing that is certain is that he subsequently strenuously insisted that he had never, ever, agreed to become a Boer subject.

What makes Sekhukhune's motives in assenting to the treaty even more perplexing are the contents of a letter written the very next day in Sepedi and addressed to Sir Theophilus Shepstone, British Special Commissioner in the Transvaal. Shepstone had entered the ZAR in January 1877 with a small escort of twenty-five Natal Mounted Police, and carried in his valise the British colonial secretary's secret instructions to annex the republic with or without popular consent—a commission, it should be added, in blatant disregard of the Sand River Convention of 1852 by which Britain undertook not to interfere in the affairs of the ZAR.

Shepstone's unanticipated swoop into the affairs of the ZAR requires explanation. The Tories under Benjamin Disraeli, the Earl of Beaconsfield, came to power in Britain in February 1874. Beaconsfield's new colonial secretary, the Earl of Carnarvon (a great landowner and highly cultivated man whose principled indecisiveness is revealed by his unkind nickname of 'Twitters'),[30] immediately adopted a much more aggressive approach to South African union—or confederation—than had been the case under previous governments. There has been considerable scholarly debate over the reasons for this change,[31] but what is certain is that for British statesmen of the time economic issues were inextricably intertwined with increasing concerns about imperial defence. After all, this was a dangerous moment when rival great powers were showing signs of intending to acquire new territories abroad, and within a few years the notorious Scramble for Africa would be fully under way. Imperial strategists were consequently seeking to consolidate and defend the British Empire, rather than to expand it.[32] While India, rather than Africa, was absolutely central to British commercial interests and status as an imperial power, its security nevertheless depended on the Royal Navy's control of the African sea routes through the Suez Canal and around the Cape along with sufficient ports and coaling-stations for steam-driven naval vessels. Southern Africa's primary importance, then, lay in its strategic position on the way to India and it was essential for Britain to secure it firmly. The way to do this, Carnarvon argued, was through the construction of a stable, self-reliant British confederation of the white settler states of the subcontinent. What now made that possible was the gratifying transformation of the region's economy thanks to the mineral revolution. The political structure of a confederation would provide a secure environment for greater economic integration and the reliable supply of labour, as well as serve as the base for future British economic and political expansion into the African interior. Secure and economically viable, the South African confederation would then fulfil its prime purpose as an unassailable strategic link in the British route to India.

Carnarvon fully grasped that the key to any confederation was the Cape Colony. Not only was it the largest territory in southern Africa, but with 237,000 white colonists (more than twice the number of Natal and the two Boer republics put together), it was also the most populous settler state.[33] More than that, thanks to the diamond bonanza and a boom in wool and ostrich feather exports, it was also the richest. In June 1872 it had assumed greater financial control of its own administration and defence obligations when it was granted responsible government. That development had its downside, however, because if the Cape was to take up the chief burden of confederation, Carnarvon would have to persuade its prickly and parochial elected legislative assembly to go along with him.[34] The two independent Boer republics of the Orange Free State (OFS) and the ZAR posed even more of a problem because they could not be left out of his projected confederation. Not only did they stand squarely across the British path of economic expansion north into central Africa with its fabled, untapped resources—and for Natal colonists in particular access to more land and labour was a powerful motive for confederation—but by their very existence they acted as powerful lodestones for malcontent Afrikaners living under British rule elsewhere in South Africa.

Even so, Carnarvon was optimistic that he could draw the two republics into his confederation through negotiation. He possessed the requisite experience, for when he had last held office as colonial secretary he had presided in 1867 over the creation of the self-governing federal Dominion of Canada out of three separate British colonies. But, to his disappointment, South Africans proved even more difficult than Canadians to manipulate. Carnarvon found it a frustrating business getting the representatives of the various white states merely to sit around the same table, let alone to agree on some form of confederation. And to render talks even more meaningless, the ZAR was attempting concurrently to raise an international loan to build a railway line east to Portuguese Delagoa Bay.[35] Access by the landlocked ZAR to a nearby port outside British control would reduce its dependence on the imperial power's goodwill for a trading outlet to the sea and undermine the economic foundations of the projected federation.[36]

Yet the ZAR's provocative economic flirtation with the Portuguese was nothing as compared to the unresolved matter of future relations with the considerable number of still independent African kingdoms along the unclosed frontier. The endemic little wars the two Boer republics were engaged in with their African neighbours had the potential to destabilize the whole region. And they went to the heart of the one, overriding reservation many statesmen shared regarding the prospects for confederation: namely, the uncertainty of the place of Africans within this structure of British paramountcy.

Carnarvon had little doubt that the continued existence of independent, well-armed African kingdoms posed an insuperable hindrance
to confederation. In his estimation, they posed a security risk to the
settler states of South Africa—British and Boer alike—not only on
account of the likelihood of further frontier wars, but because African
rulers had the capacity to foment unrest among Africans already living
under white rule. The recent Langalibalele Rebellion seemed proof
enough of that. Consequently, Carnarvon never doubted that if he was
to clinch his ambitious plans for South African confederation, he had
first to break the military power of the indigenous peoples of South
Africa, disarm them permanently and impose some form of British
supremacy over them. Yet how was he to bring that about?

The Boer–Pedi War therefore came as a godsend. When Carnarvon
learned that the Bapedi had inflicted a decided reverse on the inept
forces of the anarchic and bankrupt ZAR, he saw that he had been
unexpectedly provided with a more or less plausible excuse to annex the
ZAR and get the bogged-down vehicle of confederation moving again.
Opportunely, the ZAR's mismanaged and unresolved war with the
Bapedi was precisely the sort of frontier conflict which the Cape
Colony so strongly insisted on seeing an end to before consenting to
join a confederation. How better could the Cape be reassured and the
wheels of confederation oiled than by marching British troops into the
annexed Transvaal to deal swiftly and conclusively with the Bapedi
where Boer commandos had singularly failed? Swept up by these bold
imaginings but requiring parliamentary sanction before taking action,
in December 1876 Carnarvon instructed the Colonial Office to draft
enabling legislation—the South Africa Act of 1877, or Permissive
Federation Bill—very similar to the British North America Act of
1867 which had provided for the federation of Canada.[37]

And Carnarvon reckoned that he had the perfect, reliable man on
the spot with extensive local knowledge whom he could entrust with
furthering his confederation schemes. That paragon was Theophilus
Shepstone. He had gone to England in 1876 to take part in a conference on confederation. The conference proved abortive, but Shepstone
and Carnarvon at once became firm political friends.[38] So when
Carnarvon saw his opportunity in the ZAR's military debacle, it was
the recently knighted Shepstone he entrusted with annexing the Boer

republic. He believed that Shepstone possessed the diplomatic skill to bring off the bold coup without bloodshed, and at first his foxy commissioner did not disappoint him. Thus, when Shepstone received Sekhukhune's letter of 16 February 1877 (the day after the paramount had signed his treaty with the ZAR), he carefully filed it away because he saw how he could make considerable use of it in his dealings with the wavering *volksraad*. Its wording unambiguously revealed that Sekhukhune placed no store at all by any agreement reached with the Boers and that he looked to the British to save him from them. 'I beg you Chief', read the letter, 'come help me, the Boers are killing me, and I don't know the reason why they should be angry with me.'[39]

The small but economically influential English-speaking community in the ZAR was eager for Shepstone to take over the government, while the *volksraad* was paralysed by factional divisions and the overwhelming burden of the national debt. Burghers were baulking at the emergency taxes the *volksraad* had levied to pay for the unfinished war against the Bapedi, and Shepstone skilfully played on their fears of a hostile Pedi–Zulu alliance from which only British troops could protect them. Consequently, when at 11 a.m. on 12 April 1877 Shepstone proclaimed that the ZAR had become the British Transvaal Territory and ran up the Union Flag in Church Square in Pretoria, Boer opposition was muted. The *volksraad* resolved to send a delegation abroad to make its objections to annexation widely known, and meanwhile appealed to citizens to refrain from violence so as not to prejudice their mission.[40] That left Shepstone, now titled the Administrator of the Transvaal, free to address the unresolved future of the Bapedi under what was now British authority.

CHAPTER 6

The 'Black Conspiracy'

W HEN on 12 April 1877 Sir Theophilus Shepstone began to
exercise his authority as Administrator of the Transvaal
Territory, he understood that the Bapedi were suffering privations as a
result of the Boer–Pedi War, and that Sekhukhune's authority and
prestige had been seriously tarnished. Nevertheless, the Bapedi had not
been defeated and their regiments were still in the field, and it was
unclear whether Sekhukhune saw himself as falling under the control
of the new British administration. Shepstone had no doubt that he
must submit. There was an irony here because, before they took over
the Transvaal, the British had found it useful politically to reject Boer
claims to sovereignty over Bopedi and to characterize the war of 1876
as 'an unjustifiable aggression against an independent ruler'.[1] Now that
the Transvaal was British, different considerations naturally applied.
On 9 May 1877 Shepstone sent a stern message to Sekhukhune giving
him the option of accepting the 'protection' of the 'Great Queen'—
along with the obligation of paying taxes—or leaving the Transvaal.
He also insisted that Sekhukhune was obliged to pay the indemnity
of two thousand cattle he had agreed to render to the ZAR by the
treaty of 15 February 1877.[2]

Shepstone adopted this uncompromising stance for two reasons: to
collect vital revenue from Africans to shore up the Transvaal's ailing
finances; and to assert British power over African states standing in the
way of the consolidation of British control of southern Africa.[3] Noting
his thirty years in charge of Natal's 'Native Policy', approving settlers

credited Shepstone with possessing a singular understanding of the workings of African society and mentality but, in fact, his perceptions were limited by an unquestioning belief in the superiority of Christian mores and western civilization. This world-view—common enough among evangelical servants of empire at the time—justified adopting a necessarily paternalistic approach to Africans if they were ever to be raised to a state of useful 'civilization'.[4] In Natal (as we have seen) Shepstone had instituted a system of indirect rule over African loca-tions from which he had extracted taxes and labour for the colony. It would obviously be highly beneficial to the Transvaal administration if the new Administrator could extend his well-tried location system to a pacified Bopedi. The additional advantage, in terms of Shepstone's world-view, was that it would benefit the uncivilized Bapedi too.

Shepstone's inscrutable demeanour did not make it easy for him to win the confidence of the suspicious Transvaal Boers in his policies. A journalist in the Transvaal described him as 'a crafty-looking and silent man, who never used an unnecessary word or gesture. He was unde-monstrative; and, rightly or wrongly, the people believed him to be utterly insincere.'[5] Critically, though, Shepstone's views as Administrator chimed perfectly with those of the new High Commissioner in South Africa, Sir Bartle Frere.

During his distinguished service in India as a high-ranking admin-istrator, Frere had proved he possessed the steely inner core, ability and vision to be the imperial statesman capable of consummating Carnarvon's design for the grand confederation of southern Africa. The Prime Minister, Lord Beaconsfield, entrusted him with the mission, and when Frere departed for the Cape in March 1877, it was not only as Governor of the Cape, but as High Commissioner for South Africa with extended diplomatic leverage over the entire subcontinent, as well as Commander-in-Chief of the British forces stationed there. Wielding his extensive powers, he was expected to complete confederation and then crown his career by staying on as the ennobled, first Governor-General of the new South African Dominion he had created, a vener-ated architect of empire.[6]

There was no doubting Frere's intellectual powers and forceful personality. An awe-struck officer in South Africa recorded his impres-sion of the High Commissioner: 'He had a wonderfully quiet, deliberate manner of speaking, never hesitating and never at a loss for the right word, giving you the idea that whatever might be the subject of the conversation he knew much more about it than any of his audience.'[7] Indeed, Frere was both highly conscientious and ruthlessly ambitious. His responsible posts in India had trained him to act on his own initiative and he never drew back from taking vigorous executive action if he considered it necessary. His concern was not to please his superiors but, rather, to ensure that his actions measured up to his own exacting standards. As a committed evangelical Christian, Frere believed it was Britain's high mission to spread the civilizing influence of Christian government and eradicate degrading, barbarous institutions through good administration and the creation of conditions for economic prosperity. To this high-minded proconsul of empire, confederation was nothing less than a Christian duty and moral objective, which would bring the myriad benefits of British civilization to all the peoples of southern Africa. But so long as independent African states existed, they would stand in the way of a prosperous, modern South Africa.[8]

In pushing forward confederation, Frere was to enjoy considerable discretion to act as he deemed fit. This was partly because of the trust the government placed in his unparalleled experience and vision, but was also a simple matter of poor communications. South Africa lay half a world away from Britain, and the subcontinent's unique problems meant that members of the government were usually ill-informed of its affairs. In cabinet they tended to defer to the colonial secretary, but he depended in turn on the knowledge of the permanent officials in the Colonial Office, and especially on the advice of the man on the spot, namely, the high commissioner. Most unsatisfactorily in this regard, communication with this official was entirely by sea until 1874 when a trans-Atlantic undersea cable was laid connecting Brazil to Europe via the island of Madeira off the north-west coast of Africa. Thereafter, messages could be rapidly telegraphed back and forth between London and the island. But there they would languish awaiting the weekly mail steamer that was to carry them on their slow sea journey to Cape Town, and would eventually bring replies back again the same way to Madeira. Consequently, even the most urgent official correspondence took about five weeks to turn about, and government decisions concerning the distant subcontinent were all too often scarcely more than belated responses to events that had already taken place. For a man of Frere's assured self-confidence, this afforded him the perfect opportunity to crack on the pace without having to concern himself overmuch with the apprehensions of the habitually cautious Colonial Office.[9]

When he arrived in Cape Town, Frere found that the Cape Parliament had already rejected in principle Carnarvon's draft Permissive Federation Bill. As we have seen, since June 1872 the white settlers at the Cape had enjoyed responsible government which gave them almost complete self-rule. Frere consequently could not impose his executive will, as he could have in a crown colony, but had to work with a prime minister and his cabinet responsible to the elected Legislative Assembly.[10] As a consequence, he had his work cut out to create conditions which would make confederation more acceptable to Cape settler opinion.[11] With this in mind, he immediately focused on closing down arenas of endemic conflict. The long-festering Eastern Cape frontier with the amaXhosa people was a major running sore he would have to address sooner rather than later. The volatile and unresolved relationship with the Bapedi was a new challenge, but Frere saw that for two intertwined reasons it was necessary to solve it urgently.

The first was obvious, because if the British could successfully bring Sekhukhune to heel after the ZAR's humiliating failure to do so, then many of the disgruntled burghers in the newly annexed Transvaal might be persuaded to acknowledge the benefits of British rule.[12] The second reason was more convoluted, but had implications far beyond the borders of the Transvaal. Shepstone dinned into Frere's ear his unwavering conviction that the ZAR's lack of military successes against the Bapedi had done enormous harm to the prestige of the white man throughout the subcontinent because Sekhukhune was acting 'as a kind of lieutenant' to the baleful King Cetshwayo of the amaZulu.[13] It is now clear to historians that Sekhukhune and Cetshwayo never formed an active alliance, and that Sekhukhune's 'old councillors' strongly advised him 'to arrange his own affairs' and to avoid becoming involved in Cetshwayo's separate disputes with the imperial power.[14]

What mattered at the time, however, was that Shepstone and Frere were absolutely convinced that Cetshwayo and Sekhukhune were hand in glove. And what made this alliance so extremely dangerous to these

British administrators was their obsessively growing belief, shared by most self-styled local white experts—settlers, missionaries, officials—that the Zulu kingdom was the political and military lynchpin of African resistance to British rule. By the end of 1878 Frere would be melodramatically yoking all the African states of the subcontinent together in what he characterized to his superiors in London as 'a common purpose and general understanding that the time was now come for the black races to shake off the domination of the white and to expel them from the country'. King Cetshwayo, needless to say, was 'the head and moving spirit' of this dangerous combination.[15] And, as Frere never tired of reporting in increasingly luridly phrased and alarmist dispatches, the 'ignorant and blood-thirsty tyrant' who ruled Zululand had in his hands a 'frightfully efficient manslaying war-machine' that was a standing menace to his neighbours.[16] Charles Brownlee, the Resident Commissioner of Native Affairs in the Cape Colony, was only stating the obvious when he declared that crushing the Zulu kingdom was the key to solving the South African 'native question'.[17] Only, it made sense to clear Cetshwayo's troublesome satellites away first.

Shepstone believed British troops should have no difficulty in subduing Sekhukhune where the inept Boer commandos had failed because, in his estimation, the Bapedi were not to be compared militarily with the warlike amaZulu.[18] Perhaps, it would not even be necessary to go to war with the Maroteng paramountcy for, at first, when faced with Shepstone's ultimatum of 9 May 1877 to accept the Queen's protection, Sekhukhune took a placatory line. Through his messengers he declared that 'he gladly accepted the conditions offered him', and that 'since he knew he was under British rule he enjoyed a sense of security he was before a stranger to'.[19] Fair words, but Sekhukhune was embarking on the delicate high-wire act of seeming to comply with the Administrator's terms while at the same time trying to maintain his independence.

The payment of the war indemnity of two thousand cattle instantly became the central issue because both sides saw its symbolic importance in signifying Pedi recognition of British supremacy. By September 1877 Shepstone had lost all patience with Sekhukhune's partial compliance and was taking a hard line. In response Sekhukhune called a *pitso*

at Tsate at which he failed to persuade the gathering to agree to a levy
of cattle from all his subjects to meet the Administrator's demands.
This popular response was an indication of the distress ordinary Bapedi
were suffering from the ongoing drought and from the dislocations of
the recent war. It was also ominous confirmation of the difficulties
Sekhukhune was having in maintaining and asserting his authority over
his wounded paramountcy.[20]

Meanwhile, Shepstone was on his way to a meeting with King
Cetshwayo's emissaries to impose his stamp on the boundary question
that had long been bedevilling relations between the ZAR and the
Zulu kingdom. Although the frontier between the Zulu kingdom and
the ZAR had been recognized in 1854 as the Ncome (Blood) River, the
frontier to the north about the headwaters of the Phongolo River was
very hazy. For decades Boers took advantage of this uncertainty to
infiltrate deep into north-western Zululand, grazing their cattle, laying
out farms, maltreating the inhabitants and erecting beacons to demar-
cate outrageously ambitious boundary lines. This region was a rich
prize with some of the best grazing in the area, highly desirable to both
Zulu and Boer pastoralists. The amaZulu and the ZAR very nearly
went to war in 1861 over what had become known as the Disputed
Territory, and there were further crises in 1864, 1869 and 1870.

During these past stands-offs, Shepstone, at that stage Secretary for
Native Affairs in Natal, had always lent the amaZulu crucial support
against the Boers because he feared the ZAR's territorial ambitions
were inimical to British interests. But now, as Administrator of the
Transvaal, he spoke for the Boers instead. So when in mid-1877 a
series of incidents in the Disputed Territory brought the issue to the
boil again, he was ready to assert the Transvaal's claims in order to
demonstrate to sceptical and intransigent Boers the advantages of being
under British rule.[21] Shepstone also calculated that if he could publicly
assert British power over Cetshwayo who was Sekhukhune's presumed
ringmaster, and from whose example the Maroteng paramount's obduracy stemmed, it would 'produce a good effect on him [Sekhukhune] as
upon all the other native tribes'.[22]

On 18 October 1877 Shepstone and a handful of Transvaal
officials, guarded by a small military escort, met a large Zulu delegation
of three hundred councillors, *amakhosi* (chiefs) and other men of rank,

accompanied by two hundred attendants. The increasingly acrimonious encounter, which lasted several hours, took place on a large, flat-topped hill (subsequently called Conference Hill) in the wide plain overlooking the west bank of the Ncome River. Shepstone was taken aback by the 'haughty' bearing of the Zulu delegates, and he indignantly reported that 'they were evidently excited, and in a very self-asserting humour, and it seemed difficult for them to treat me with the respect they had usually paid me'. As for *iNkosi* Mnyamana kaNgqengelele of the Buthelezi, Cetshwayo's chief councillor, he mortally affronted Shepstone with his obduracy and 'violent and threatening manner' in refusing on behalf of the Zulu nation to abandon any Zulu land claims whatsoever.[23]

The intransigence of the Zulu leaders on Conference Hill only confirmed Shepstone's deepest suspicions of Cetshwayo's warlike intentions. Before travelling to the meeting he had already received word that a fresh war was brewing on the Cape Eastern Frontier. He could not but see this as proof positive that a perilous African combination was forming in southern Africa which threatened to drive the white man into the sea.

THE NINTH CAPE FRONTIER WAR, 1877–1878

CHAPTER 7

EmaXhoseni

CERTAINLY, as Shepstone had been informed, in the early spring of 1877 settlers in the Eastern Province of the Cape Colony were in a fretful state. Between 1779 and 1853 eight increasingly destructive wars had been fought along the fluctuating eastern frontier that pitted white settlers, along with British troops and their African allies, against the amaXhosa people. Now, fears of renewed war against the ama-Xhosa were being buoyed up by swirling rumours about the mythical black conspiracy to drive the white man out of southern Africa. Perversely, these anxieties went hand in hand with impatience finally to clear the stormy air through another war which would close the eastern frontier once and for all. And underlying these uncertainties was settler greed, a desire to possess the potential farming lands still occupied by the amaXhosa.[1] Sir Bartle Frere sympathized with the settlers. Besides, he believed that the spiralling restlessness on the Cape Eastern Frontier was hobbling his freedom to act elsewhere in southern Africa to implement his confederation policy.[2] So it was with an eye to imposing his own solution on this troublesome region that Frere left Cape Town in September 1877 for King William's Town, the administrative hub of the frontier district.

Frere found himself in the heart of a frontier zone shaped by interminable warfare. It was an extensive, summer rainfall region, stretching between the Mbashe River to the east and the Sundays River to the west. Looming mountain chains covered by a thick mantle of forest and bush bounded it to the north, and to the south the lush coastal bush

MAP 3
THE BRITISH CONQUEST
OF THE CISKEI,
TO 1877

● African settlement   ¤ Fort

0   miles   50

0   km   50

lapped the sweeping white beaches of the Indian Ocean. Numerous rivers and streams flowed erratically down to the ocean from the mountains and hilly uplands, and it was the river valleys that possessed the best soils and pasturage where people preferred to settle.[3]

The land was so vast and the inhabitants so few that during the Iron Age cattle-keeping subsistence farmers with their iron hoes, axes and spears who reached the coastal lowlands by about 600 AD could spread steadily westwards in search of virgin fields and pastures. As they advanced, they absorbed the scattered Stone Age people they encountered. They spoke an early form of southern Nguni closely related to the northern Nguni that was the language group of the people who would later become the amaZulu and amaSwazi. The observations of European mariners combined with Xhosa oral traditions indicate that by the sixteenth century at the latest these southern Nguni-speakers were organized politically into chiefdoms with power and wealth concentrated in the grasp of royal lineages.

By then their scattered homesteads were already taking on the standard form that would persist for centuries. Each homestead accommodated the members of a family, along with their dependants, all living under the command of the married head. A homestead was typically sited facing the rising sun near the top of a ridge where it was both sheltered and well drained and close enough to the stream below. It consisted of eight to fifteen beehive-shaped huts built of a framework of branches, plastered with clay and dung and thatched with long grass. These huts faced the gate of the homestead and were arranged in a semi-circle around the cattle-byre made of mimosa thorn-branches. This enclosure was the centre of the homestead's social and religious life. Gardens of millet, sorghum, maize, beans, pumpkins, melons, sugarcane, dagga and tobacco protected by thorn fences stretched downhill between the homestead and the supply of water.[4]

The persistent westward drift of the proto-amaXhosa was eventually slowed down by the nature of the land itself. Rainfall in the lovely, open, undulating grass-covered lands west of the Great Kei River becomes increasingly erratic and periods of terrible drought more frequent, making it more difficult to sustain a way of life developed in the wetter and more fertile coastlands the people had left behind. Nor was the less hospitable land as empty as it had been up the coast, for communities of Khoekhoe pastoralists, the original inhabitants of the land before the coming of the Nguni-speakers, were already well established there. Nevertheless, by the late seventeenth century the ama-Xhosa (for so they were certainly called by then) were moving steadily over the Great Kei River into the region bounded to the west by the Great Fish River, and were assimilating the Khoekhoen into their communities along with some of their words and clicking sounds. By the early eighteenth century the amaXhosa had secured the cattle-country between the Fish and the Sundays rivers that flow into Algoa Bay. Their advance parties were probing westwards towards the valley of the Gamtoos River through the increasingly dry savannah with its dense, stunted bush of thorn trees and rich growth of aloes with their spectacular flowers. There the summer rainfall region starts to give way to a winter rainfall, Mediterranean-like climate unsuitable for the subtropical crops the amaXhosa were accustomed to cultivating.[5]

More than geography, however, was destined to throw up a barrier against the amaXhosas' westward drive. In the early eighteenth century, in the vicinity of the Gamtoos River valley, they began to make contact with another people who, like them, were migrating pastoralists, subsistence farmers and hunters. Numbering only several hundred, they appeared at first to pose no more of a challenge than had the Khoekhoen, and the amaXhosa supposed they too could be absorbed into their society. In this they were entirely mistaken.

The newcomers were *trekboere* or trekboers, migrant Dutch farmers who were pushing east from Cape Town up the wide mountain valleys that for hundreds of miles run parallel to the coast. In 1643 the Dutch East India Company had established a refreshment station at the Cape on the way to their burgeoning empire in the East Indies. The Dutch rapidly overcame the indigenous Khoesan[6] in the environs of Cape Town, reducing them to servants and labourers, and from 1685 began to import slaves from the East Indies, Madagascar and East Africa to augment the workforce in the growing settlement. Settlers in their thousands dispersed ever deeper into the interior to lay claim to vast farms and subjugate the indigenous peoples they encountered.[7] The trekboers in their extended family units were the most venturesome of these settlers. When the amaXhosa encountered them they had moved effectively out of the control of the distant government at the Cape five hundred miles behind them. They were consequently free to enter into tentative, informal relations with the amaXhosa in a situation that was characteristic of the open frontier where two communities live uneasily side by side with no single recognized authority set over them. It would be over a hundred years before this frontier finally closed.[8]

If the trekboers with their muskets, horses and wagons were objects of some initial astonishment to the amaXhosa, then many aspects of Xhosa culture were unfamiliar and unsettling to the trekboers. In stark contrast to the trekboers in their concealing European dress, Xhosa men went about essentially naked, their skin glowing with red ochre mixed with grease and herbs. Their everyday dress consisted only of a penis sheath, copper armband, ivory bangles and a necklace of animals' teeth. On formal occasions or when it was cold they negligently draped themselves in a cloak of well-worked, supple bullock-hide worn with the comfortable fur side inside and showing the skin side coloured with red ochre.

What both the trekboers and the amaXhosa had in common were their cattle, although there is no doubt that they were of far greater cultural significance to the latter. Cattle were the living wealth of amaXhosa men and owning them was indisputable proof of adult status. They conferred political power, and senior men possessed hundreds or even thousands of them, often parcelling them out in separate herds with the widely scattered members of their clan as insurance against the vicissitudes of disease or war. Cattle were transferred to the woman's family from the man on marriage, and were exchanged for goods or to cement political alliances. Above all, they were essential for ritual sacrifice to ancestors to ensure their favour. Cattle held so central a place in their world that the amaXhosa developed an extensive vocabulary to describe their every detail, and their praise poetry celebrated the surpassing shapes, colours and virtues of their precious beasts. Their doting owners recognized them individually, developed close bonds with them and lovingly decorated their bodies. No wonder that they were the most sought-after prize in warfare.

Because of the enormous value attached to cattle, looking after them was men's work and riding them their prerogative. In the gendered division of labour, women cultivated the fields, foraged, cooked and looked after the children. Above all, they were respected for their fertility. Unlike the monogamous trekboers, Xhosa men were polygamous, but only about twenty per cent were of sufficient wealth and status to keep a number of wives.[9]

Fatally for their ability to mount a unified armed response against the forces of colonialism, the amaXhosa never developed into a unified state akin to that of the amaZulu or amaSwazi, or even the Maroteng paramountcy. The senior members of their royal house headed individual, autonomous chiefdoms. A chief, as the guardian of his people, was expected to ensure that commoners all had access to the land and that they were safe from their enemies. He also resolved internal disputes, and ritually initiated the agricultural cycle with rainmaking and first-fruits ceremonies. In return, his adherents tendered him tribute, and submitted to the fines and levies he might impose. Ideally a chief stood out from his adherents, not only on account of the brass armband worn on his right wrist and his leopard-skin cloaks with the spotted fur inside revealed in the turned collar and edgings, but because of the aristocratic bravura and dignity of his deportment. Yet, despite the considerable respect accorded a chief which protected him from violence, even in warfare he exercised his authority only by consensus. His councillors, marked out by the headdress of a single crane feather worn as an indication of their rank, were always senior men of commoner lineages with followings of their own. They drastically limited a chief's freedom of action because he had always to bear in mind that dissidents could force his resignation or even desert with their adherents to another chief if he proved ineffective or unpopular.

The Xhosa paramount, instead of being a powerful, centralizing monarch, was merely the accepted figurehead of the Xhosa nation and the most senior member of the recognized royal house. His position *vis-à-vis* his chiefs was analogous to their relationship with the leading commoners in their chiefdoms. He confirmed new chiefs once they had their adherents' approval, adjudicated disputes which resisted settlement at the chiefly level and, above all, declared war on behalf of the nation. Besides that, he possessed little real authority over the chiefs and had to consult with them before taking any important decision. Lacking anything like a central bureaucracy or standing army, his status was that of *primus inter pares*, or, as the amaXhosa expressed it, of their 'oldest brother'. A Xhosa paramount chief was consequently never responsible for every action taken by other chiefs who recognized his tenuous authority, but (as shall be seen) this was a limitation never properly grasped by whites with their centralized form of government.[10]

Before the mid-eighteenth century and their first encounters with the trekboers, segmentation had been a safety-valve for the loose Xhosa polity, spurring its expansion and limiting conflict within chiefdoms. Simply put, the practice of segmentation allowed a chief's aggressive and ambitious adult sons to depart with their followers to carve out for themselves new, genealogically related chiefdoms. The most reliable of a new chief's followers would be those who had been initiated into adulthood with him and were now part of the same age-set. Indeed, in EmaXhoseni (the land of the amaXhosa), as in Bopedi, KwaZulu (Zululand) and so many other African societies, the institution of age-sets was basic to the organization of society.[11]

For Xhosa males, circumcision was integral to initiation as it was also to the closely related abaThembu people to the north of them. The initiates or *abakwetha* (singular *umkwetha*), youths between the ages of seventeen and twenty-one, left all childhood conduct behind them as they entered the initiation hut, built in a secluded spot far from any chance of ritual contamination. Diviners performed ritual ceremonies to endow the initiates with the courage and strength to resist all evil influences in this life. For three to six months following the excruciating pain of circumcision with a spear blade, *abakwetha* were put through further ordeals to probe their courage and endurance and were instructed on how to speak and act with the wisdom, dignity and restraint of a man. During this period their bodies were covered in white clay to indicate their transitional status. Periodically they would emerge from their seclusion wearing kilts and concealing headdresses of palm leaves and shoots to perform extravagant ritual dances before the young women who would become their first brides soon after their emergence as full adults. In early times *abakwetha* recently released from their circumcision lodge wore a headdress consisting of a band of hide around the forehead with bunches of blue-grey wing-feathers stitched to either side.

Even though segmentation by restless age-groups of young men was meant to limit discord, this proved to be ever less the case in the historic period. The legendary founder of the royal Xhosa lineage was Tshawe, and after him during six generations across the seventeenth and eighteenth centuries the original Xhosa chiefdom segmented into ten different chiefdoms. But then, in the later eighteenth century a major fissure occurred within the Xhosa paramountcy. Its lineaments are frustrating to discern through the swirls of oral tradition, although there is no doubt that its principal protagonists were Gcaleka and Rharhabe, the rival sons of the paramount, Phalo. Rharhabe lost in battle to Gcaleka and retreated west across the Kei with his followers to the region known later to white colonists as the Ciskei. There Rharhabe set about establishing himself as the dominant chief through interminable struggles against the other Xhosa chiefdoms, Khoekhoe pastoralists and neighbouring people such as the abaThembu. For his part, Gcaleka remained with his father Phalo in his stable polity east of the Kei, in what later became known as the Transkei, and succeeded him as paramount. When the indefatigably bellicose Rharhabe died in battle in 1778, the new paramount Khwatu (Gcaleka's heir) selected Rharhabe's grandson, Ngqika (c.1778–1829), as his successor. Unfortunately, this did little to heal the debilitating breach between what were now becoming known as the Rharhabe amaXhosa and the Gcaleka amaXhosa.[12]

Thus, when relations along the open frontier between the trekboers and amaXhosa began to deteriorate in the second half of the eighteenth century, EmaXhoseni was in a discordant state. By this period small parties of the trekboers—who numbered not more than a thousand all told including their Khoekhoe servants and a few slaves—were pushing east along the coast across the Sundays River towards the Great Fish River. This was a well-watered region, about fifty miles wide, known to the trekboers as the Zuurveld, or sour veld, on account of the nature of the grazing. The high acidity of the soil in the plains made the vegetation harmful—if not fatal—to livestock in the autumn and winter months. By contrast, the river valleys of the Zuurveld with their dense, semi-succulent thorny scrub thickets and sweetveld grasses provide good grazing all year around. When the trekboers entered the Zuurveld the amaXhosa already occupied the valleys and rotated their livestock between the winter pastures there and the summer pastures on the plains.[13]

Competition between amaXhosa and trekboers over land and grazing in the Zuurveld finally morphed into open warfare, and ushered in a century of the most protracted warfare in the entire history of the closing of the South African frontier. Nevertheless, this grim trajectory was not yet apparent from the first two Cape Frontier wars of

1779–1781 and 1789–1793 which were still similar in scale and intensity to the internecine Xhosa strife unleashed by the sons of Phalo.[14]

What was different was the composition of the armed forces the Dutch East India Company deployed against the amaXhosa. They were racially mixed, and this military amalgam of whites and Africans combating the amaXhosa would remain the hallmark of all nine of the Cape Frontier Wars. In 1739 the Dutch East India Company made part-time military service in their commandos compulsory for all frontier settlers who sometimes brought their Khoesan servants along with them as *agterryers*, or even sent them as substitutes. Because these commandos were citizen militias, they were always reluctant to spend too much time on military operations away from their farms which required their working presence; and they were uneasily conscious that their absence exposed their homes to sudden counter-raids by the enemy.[15] Precisely because the Company considered these commandos ill-trained and unreliable, in 1781 it established a full-time, regular military force of Khoesan and mixed-race servants under white officers. It became key to the Company's defence of the Cape frontier and by 1793 was known as the Corps van Pandoeren.[16]

The amaXhosa facing the racially mixed forces of the Company in the late eighteenth century were not notably warlike, and nowadays do not share the amaZulus' ferocious warrior reputation. Nevertheless, theirs was also an indubitably honour culture, the difference being that a man's high reputation or even fame could be gained through cultivating the domestic virtues of the homestead as a complement to his military heroism. Men of rank in particular prided themselves on their gentlemanlike behaviour, on their unruffled grace and courtesy, and on the sagacity of their counsel. Nevertheless, they were acutely sensitive to slights and defamation, and put a premium on their proven male virility, physical prowess and military courage. From an early age their competitive aggression was deliberately fostered in combative exercises and the hunt which prepared them for combat. Stick-fighting groups fiercely competed under the supervision of elders preparing them for circumcision. Boys could be killed in these tough bouts, but the survivors exhibited their duelling scars with pride.[17] Once initiated, young men were on constant call to serve their chief, but after marriage adult warriors were expected to restrain their aggression except when called out for war service. Then they received names of honour for their valiant deeds and composed their own praises to vaunt their prowess in public.[18]

In the early years of the eighteenth century Xhosa warfare had still retained something of the character of a tournament fought at an agreed time and place between two sides throwing spears from a distance.[19] However, by the time the amaXhosa came into serious conflict with the trekboers in the late eighteenth century, their warfare was already acquiring a sharper edge on account of the bitter conflicts between the sons of Phalo. At this stage they employed only their traditional arms. Only during the course of the nineteenth century did they add firearms and horses to their arsenal.

Their national weapon was the spear. There were eight kinds of throwing-spear for hunting or war, some barbed or serrated. Straight-bladed ones could double as an awl in leather work or as a surgical instrument for circumcision. The typically scattered formation of a Xhosa army gave a warrior the necessary freedom to throw a spear with a sharp flick that imparted a quivering motion which helped its accuracy in flight, and vibrated in the wound giving it better penetration. A good cast could transfix a body at fifty paces or more. Besides his bundle of throwing-spears which he carried with him in a quiver or held in his left hand during battle, a warrior might also heft one of the two types of broad-bladed stabbing spear and likely a stout knobkerrie as well. He used the latter as a throwing-stick when out hunting, but in battle its head the size of a man's fist cracked skulls. Most fighting was at spear-cast range, but when a battle was proving indecisive, a commander might give the order to 'get inside'. Then these weapons (or a throwing-spear with the haft broken off short) were essential for combat at close quarters.

In the eighteenth century the amaXhosa also carried a compact cowhide shield. Later, in the early decades of the nineteenth century at the time of the *Mfecane*, they adopted the larger, northern Nguni shield. But the amaXhosa soon learned that it could stop a bullet no better than a small one, and that its size was impracticable when fighting in thick bush. So shields went increasingly out of fashion, and by the 1830s warriors more often wrapped their cloak around their left arm for protection against cutting weapons.

Because the amaXhosa had no centralized military system like the amaZulu, there was no state army as such, and the Xhosa paramount had to rely on his subordinate chiefs to provide the warriors. As soon as he declared that 'the land is dead' or in a state of incipient war, he sent out heralds carrying oxtails to rally the chiefs while women spread the word by emitting their distinctive, shrill cries from hilltop to hilltop. No chief could actually compel his adherents to muster at his great place in time of war. But if they were to preserve their honour, they were unlikely to ignore the call, and knew, moreover, that they risked having to pay a cattle fine if they stayed at home. Nevertheless, they would not commit to marching off on campaign until their chief had harangued them, explained the causes of the war and persuaded them that it was a good cause to fight for. The more famous a chief as a war-leader of daring and skill, the greater the number of warriors he could expect to rally to him. Chiefs could—and certainly did—go raiding on their own account without the paramount's sanction, but technically warriors were not authorized to engage in war until the paramount himself had publicly issued his fighting orders. However, the rivalry between the sons of Phalo and their successors meant that it was increasingly seldom that the paramount could speak in time of war for the whole nation.

While they were assembling at the chief's great place, warriors would keep up war-songs as fresh contingents arrived. When all had gathered they sang the great *umhobe*, or war-anthem. War-doctors would then spray them with ritual medicines and give them others to swallow. Next, they painted a black mark on the forehead of each warrior who then washed himself in a doctored stream. The rituals concluded with the war-doctors hanging a charm around each warrior's neck. These indispensable rituals were intended to render the warriors invulnerable both to hostile occult forces and to their enemies' weapons, and also to inspire them with courage and a reckless disregard of their own lives in battle. Ritually strengthened, the warriors were ready to set off on campaign. They were organized not in age-grade regiments like those of the amaZulu and amaSwazi, but in lineage-related clans attached to the two main divisions of the army, one consisting predominantly of royal clans, and the other of commoners.

A Xhosa army moved rapidly with no commissariat to slow it down apart from a few driven slaughter cattle. Men might carry a few roasted mealies in a hide bag, but on campaign the amaXhosa relied almost entirely on foraging and raiding for supplies. Consequently, forays into enemy territory could never be long sustained, especially since the usual strategy employed by those being invaded was to fall back with their families and livestock to forests and mountain fastnesses, and to leave behind them burned pasturage and emptied grain pits. Indeed, unlike the amaZulu who were fixated on the military offensive, the amaXhosa always accepted the logic of adopting the defensive when risking a pitched battle seemed unwise.

An attacking army attempted to achieve surprise, and pairs of daring young warriors would be deployed far in advance to report back to the screen of small bodies of scouts who, in turn, sent back intelligence to the main army. That consisted of a 'chest' of younger warriors in the centre and two wings of veterans who would rush forward to encircle the enemy. Two further columns stationed at some distance on either flank had the responsibility of protecting the army from being outflanked or being taken in the rear. If the main army was repulsed, it fell back onto the reserve body. The chief, who was expected to show suitable daring without recklessly endangering himself, was usually positioned among the reserves with his bodyguard of circumcision-mates, the *amafanenkosi*, or 'those who die with the chief'.[20] It was his duty as the battle loomed to exhort his men with cryptic, heroic orders such as: 'Go! Go! As in former days (to victory) and enquire of that matter at close quarters'; or 'Go forward and die. It has ever been the fortune of men to be killed.'[21] When the warriors joined battle they uttered no single, national war-cry as did the amaZulu, but yelled formulaic cries that their comrades understood to be calls for assistance or reports that the enemy was being worsted.

In the dying years of the eighteenth century a new, aggressive power thrust itself into the fractious affairs of the Eastern Cape frontier. In 1795, in the course of its world-wide struggle against revolutionary France and its allies, Britain seized the Cape from the Batavian Republic which had been set up in the Netherlands as a client 'sister-republic' of France. It was not long before a fresh conflict, the Third Cape Frontier War, erupted in 1799. The war was still rumbling on when Britain temporarily relinquished the Cape to the Batavian Republic in 1802 in compliance with the terms of the Peace of Amiens, and left it to the returning Dutch administration to bring the conflict to a negotiated end in 1803.[22] With the resumption of the Napoleonic Wars, the British recaptured the Cape in 1806, and this time they were there to stay. By the Treaty of Vienna in 1815 the Cape was recognized as a British colony, and thereafter the tumultuous Cape Eastern Frontier was theirs to pacify.

To this end, the British commanded formidable military resources which would increasingly challenge the amaXhosa. The Cape itself furnished one colonial military unit on a permanent footing, the successor to the Corps van Pandoeren, which by 1827 was known as the Cape Mounted Riflemen (Imperial) and mustered as a battalion of mounted infantry. Its officers were British and its men Khoekhoe, armed with muskets and trained according to the standards of the British Army. These Khoekhoe troops were never other than an affront to the bigoted racial order of the frontier, and as such never ceased to be resented and distrusted by the Boers.[23] As for the Boers, they were still liable for service in the commando system inherited from the Dutch and, for want of a better alternative, the British kept it going.

The British knew that local forces such as these were not sufficient to defend their far-flung empire from internal revolt or outside attack, and that it was necessary to rotate garrisons of regular troops in and out of the colonies.[24] The Cape garrison was always several battalions strong, not only in order to guard Simon's Town, the Cape naval station of the Royal Navy which maintained Britain's nineteenth-century maritime supremacy, but also to add highly trained backbone to the local military formations. To secure the Cape Eastern Frontier from both the amaXhosa and disaffected Boer settlers, these professional troops alongside those raised in the Cape were stationed in a line of blockhouses, forts and signal posts. Some were very rudimentary—mere converted farmhouses or basic earth redoubts—but others were monuments to the skill of the Royal Engineers. Fort Frederick, which guarded the shore in Algoa Bay where troops brought by sea were landed (it took too long to move them overland), was a substantial stone redoubt; while Fort Willshire near the Keiskamma River was a complex of solidly built barracks erected in a square with bastions at the corners. Crucially, these military posts were more than a system of defence and a visual deterrent for the amaXhosa. They provided the nucleus of villages and towns for the settlers bent on expanding ever further into EmaXhoseni.[25]

CHAPTER 8

'They Must Be Humbled and Subdued'

Wᴵᵀʜ their administration established at the Cape, the British devoted almost the next seven decades to aggressively attempting to close the eastern frontier to meet white settler demands for land, labour and security, always at the expense of the amaXhosa and other Africans. When they found it difficult to defeat the Xhosa warriors in the field, the British and Cape troops increasingly adopted a brutal, total approach to frontier warfare that targeted the homes, livestock, fields and lives of civilians in order to break the spirit of the amaXhosa and bring about their submission.[1]

These wars progressively pushed the Cape frontier ever further eastwards at the expense of the amaXhosa. The Fourth Cape Frontier War of 1811–1812 drove the amaXhosa across the Fish River which the British turned into a solid barrier by establishing twenty-two military posts and blockhouses along its length.[2] This war was overlaid by civil conflict between the Rharhabe and Gcaleka amaXhosa, and the British opportunistically intervened to turn this strife into the Fifth Cape Frontier War of 1818–1819.[3] Hintsa, the Xhosa paramount, was compelled to sue for peace on behalf of all the amaXhosa.

Their victory in the Fifth Cape Frontier War allowed the British to impose a draconian settlement on the frontier. They declared all the extensive Zuurveld between the Fish and Keiskamma rivers a neutral zone, but referred to it as the Ceded Territory and treated it accordingly. Many amaXhosa were expelled and replaced with Boer settlers and five thousand British immigrants to consolidate the settler grip on the land.[4] Ominously for the amaXhosa, the white farmers, merchants, missionaries and government officials settling in the Ceded Territory were all agreed that considerably more land was required to sustain the burgeoning new economic order, and that Africans should be put to work for wages. To this end the Cape administrations set aside African locations safely distant from the new settler villages, but close enough for the segregated workers to offer their labour.[5]

The Rharhabe amaXhosa concluded they must counter-attack to halt the inexorable settler advance onto their lands. They found a leader in Maqoma (1798–1873), the eldest son of their chief, Ngqika. He had already proved a courageous war-leader in the previous two frontier wars, and had come to personify the Xhosa concept of *indumo*, or heroic fame and renown.[6] The ensuing Sixth Cape Frontier War of 1834–1835 (known to the amaXhosa as Maqoma's or Hintsa's War) was different from previous campaigns.[7] This time, under Maqoma's generalship the amaXhosa abandoned conventional tactics altogether for guerrilla warfare. They avoided attacking towns and other defensive positions, and ducked regular engagements with British regulars and the Cape Mounted Riflemen. Instead, in small, mobile parties they raided settler farms across the Ceded Territory and deep into the Zuurveld.

At length, the British forced Maqoma's warriors to retreat north to the impenetrable fastness of a range of mountains about eight miles wide, its intersecting ridges and the choked valleys muffled in thick forests and covered by snow in winter. Because of the way in which they bulked above the surrounding plain, the amaXhosa called them the 'Calves', or Amathole, for their resemblance to a herd of young cattle grazing in a grassy field. Less poetically, a British officer described the Amathole as 'broken up in the most extraordinary manner into hills and valleys, krantzes and kloofs, table-land and precipices, pasture and bush'.[8] Frustrated by their inability to come to grips with the Xhosa warriors in this impossible terrain, the British turned instead to a campaign of attrition, and systematically ravaged Xhosa territory. They also pushed on east across the Kei to lay waste the Gcaleka lands. When Hintsa entered the British headquarters to sue for peace, he was taken prisoner and treacherously shot in a supposed attempt to escape. His captors mutilated his body, hacking off his chin and ears and prying out some of his teeth as trophies.[9]

With their people on the verge of starvation, the Rharhabe ama-
Xhosa finally surrendered in September 1835. They were confined to
their locations in the Ciskei and required to surrender their firearms.
The Cape officials entered into a system of treaties with members of
the senior Ngqika lineage that now represented the Rharhabe ama-
Xhosa, the most important of whom was Sandile (1820–1878), Ngqika's
successor.[10] In an effort to secure the frontier from future attack, the
British set about constructing the Lewis Line, six new, rectangular
fortified barracks with bastions and artillery towers. To improve
communications between them, new roads and bridges were built along
with a system of stone signal towers, each with a semaphore mast on
its flat roof, known as the Fort Beaufort Line.[11]

Historians have wondered whether the amaXhosa could have
fought off the British more successfully in Hintsa's War if they had
better adapted their tactics to the firearms they possessed.[12] Certainly,
by the Sixth Cape Frontier War they knew better than to launch
suicidal frontal attacks. Rather, they were laying ambushes in their
familiar landscape of thick bush with its game trails invisible to the
stumbling British who had little idea of where the amaXhosa were
lurking. But their elusive foes always knew where they were, and alerted
each other to their whereabouts through hilltop signal fires and long
calls. The cumbersome British supply trains were particularly vulnerable to Xhosa ambush as they plodded along the winding, steep tracks
through the dense bush. The amaXhosa emerged suddenly from the
thick cover to kill the draught-oxen in order to immobilize the wagons,
and then tried to cut off the military escort as it closed up to protect
them. Another favourite tactic was to lure small parties away from the
main body of soldiers by using cattle as decoys, or by appearing at a
distance and shouting out challenges and insults to provoke the British
forces to break ranks. Nevertheless, so long as the British were still
armed with single-shot muskets it was always possible for the ama-
Xhosa to close in with these isolated groups before they could reload
and cut them down with their spears. One such cornered patrol heard
the exultant amaXhosa shout out: 'You are like a mouse in a calabash,
you have got into it, but you cannot get out'.[13]

Would muzzle-loading muskets have been more effective in this
bush warfare than spears? The amaXhosa were themselves uncertain.

In the early Cape Frontier Wars when they possessed very few firearms (and those were bought illegally or looted) they regarded them as mere ancillaries to their conventional weapons, and valued muskets more for hunting than for fighting.[14] By the early 1830s the amaXhosa were acquiring many more firearms in exchange for cattle from settler merchants and farmers, as well as from the Christian Khoekhoen and Coloureds of the Kat River Settlement below the Winterberg Mountains. The trade in firearms over the Cape border was illegal, but officials tended to turn a blind eye because it was such lucrative business. In any case, settlers complacently maintained that firearms held no danger in the hands of Xhosa savages who were incapable of using them competently. And, undoubtedly, the inferior quality of the firearms in Xhosa possession—the outmoded Tower musket or trade 'gas-pipe' gun[15]—along with a chronic shortage of powder and spares which limited the practice they had firing them, reduced their effectiveness.

Yet this Xhosa tentativeness regarding firearm technology was but one element in their uneasy adaptation of the settler civilization that was engulfing them. They were beginning to wear more and more items of European clothing and red trade blankets were supplanting their hide cloaks.[16] They were also acquiring horses from the Cape. Men of substance rode them for prestige, yet they stopped short at using them for mounted infantry along the lines of the Cape Mounted Riflemen, and confined their military employment to scouts and messengers.

During the Third to Sixth Cape Frontier Wars the British had leaned upon the military assistance of Khoekhoe auxiliaries. Thereafter, they would rely increasingly upon a new group of African allies. These were a people the colonists called the Fingo who were redubbed the Mfengu by Africanists in the 1960s.[17] There has been considerable historical debate over their origins. At the time it was assumed that the Mfengu were a destitute group of northern Nguni refugees displaced by the upheavals of the *Mfecane* who settled as inferior clients among the abaThembu, amaPondo and especially among the Gcaleka amaXhosa. In the 1820s they became the first people in the region to accept Christian missionaries. When the British attacked the Gcaleka during the Sixth Cape Frontier War, the Methodist missionary at Butterworth, John Ayliff, who had long championed the Christian

Mfengu, persuaded the British to 'rescue' them. In May 1835 soldiers and missionaries escorted nearly 17,000 Mfengu, along with 22,000 cattle confiscated from the Gcaleka amaXhosa, west across the Keiskamma River. There the British settled them on nearly half the Ceded Territory as a buffer between the Cape Colony and the Rharhabe amaXhosa. It has been argued that the majority of these Mfengu were actually impoverished amaXhosa who jumped at the chance of taking refuge with the British. Doubtless, there were Xhosa refugees among the Mfengu in 1835 who gravitated to their settlements as safe havens. Nevertheless, most were clearly Christian Mfengu with their own identity, and they would henceforth play a crucial role on the frontier in the British interest.[18]

Settled in the south of the Ceded Territory around the village of Peddie, the Mfengu did their best to be accepted into the colonial order. They made a formal vow to become Christian, acquire an education and remain loyal to the colonial government. This played well with evangelical missionaries who wished to create literate, educated and God-fearing communities in which independent peasants owned land, used ox-drawn ploughs and wagons, produced for the market, built proper, square houses and dressed decently in European clothes. The Mfengu did their best to oblige and became pioneers of Christian respectability.[19] They also expressed their loyalty to the Cape through their military service. The coming frontier wars would demonstrate their worth as light troops who could search out the enemy and operate in bush fighting which white troops found 'the most bloody and hopeless work'.[20] One should be wary, though, of dismissing the Mfengu as mere mercenaries, even if self-preservation and self-interest played a part. Living under Cape rule they enjoyed greater rights than 'foreign' Africans, and were beholden to their patrons.

The treaty system imposed after the Sixth Cape Frontier War was not long in disintegrating and the British used an incident in which a Xhosa man accused of stealing an axe was helped by his comrades to escape custody as an excuse to launch a pre-emptive strike. The ensuing Seventh Cape Frontier War of 1846–1847 (known as the War of the Axe) was the most vicious yet fought.[21]

British regulars, armed settlers, the Khoekhoe Cape Mounted Riflemen and 'Fingo Levies' confronted Sandile's Ngqika amaXhosa who adopted the irregular tactics they had followed in the previous war. This time, some of the abaThembu people living to the north of them (known to the colonists as the 'Tambookies') joined them in their attacks. At length, the British drove the Ngqika amaXhosa under the veteran leadership of Maqoma into the Amathole. As they had in the previous war, they resisted tenaciously with hit-and-run tactics and ambushes, making more extensive use of muskets than they had in the past. In this protracted bush war the Fingo Levies under their white officers began to show their worth in the arduous irregular operations as messengers, sentries, guards, scouts and spies as well as in combat. They were entrusted with muskets, even though (as a precaution) they were not allowed to enter colonial settlements bearing them.[22] And they possessed the important advantage of being less expensive than regular troops to maintain in the field because they were disbanded at the end of each campaign.

As in the previous war, the British extended the fighting to Gcaleka territory where the chief and Xhosa paramount was now Sarhili (c.1810–1893). He was a man of great nobility, a conservative who personified the traditional values of Xhosa chieftainship and was venerated by his people for his honourable humanity, dignity and decency rather than for the heroic qualities exemplified by the fiery Maqoma.[23]

With no possibility of a decisive victory in the field, both sides adopted remorseless scorched-earth tactics. Tellingly, the Governor of the Cape, Sir Henry Pottinger, ordered his commander in the field to visit on Sandile and all those supporting him 'such a measure of retribution as shall reduce them to throw themselves on our mercy, by devastating their country, destroying their kraals, crops and cattle, and letting them finally understand that, cost what it may, they must be humbled and subdued'.[24] Xhosa non-combatants were more vulnerable to this pitiless warfare than were the frontier farmers, and with their people reduced to starvation, the Xhosa leaders finally capitulated. Sarhili managed to negotiate terms that left him essentially independent, but Maqoma, the redoubtable war-leader, was sent a prisoner to Robben Island, and his people suffered an awful fate. The Cape finally annexed the Ceded Territory between the Fish and Keiskamma rivers and expelled all the amaXhosa still living there, along with their abaThembu allies.[25] The land they vacated was given to settlers and locations set aside for the Mfengu and those abaThembu who had proved loyal. Not only that, the huge region between the Keiskamma and Kei rivers was proclaimed the Crown Colony of British Kaffraria with its capital at King William's Town.

Colonial officials did not have the resources to rule British Kaffraria directly, so the Xhosa chiefdoms were squeezed into 3,050 square miles of locations which magistrates administered indirectly through the agency of the diminished chiefs. Settlers moved into the lands between the locations and established farms and villages bearing English names. A port was established at East London for their produce, and by 1850 fifteen new mission-stations had put down roots. As for the Ciskei amaXhosa, they were put to 'civilized' labour. What this meant in practice was bluntly spelled out to their chiefs by the new Governor of the Cape, Sir Harry Smith: 'You shall learn to speak English at the schools which I shall establish for you . . . You may no longer be wicked and naked barbarians, which you will ever be unless you labour and become industrious . . . You must learn that it is money that makes people rich by work.'[26]

Smith held the 'savages' in absolute contempt and his rule was hard-handed. When he deposed Sandile as the Rharhabe chief in October 1850 and declared him an outlaw, the Xhosa leaders in the Ciskei decided with heavy foreboding that they must prepare to fight again, this time for their very survival as an independent people.[27]

The Eighth Cape Frontier War of 1850–1853 was known to the amaXhosa as the War of Mlanjeni after Sandile's war-doctor. In Xhosa religion diviners communed directly with the ancestral shades and the nature spirits of the earth and water. When the world seemed out of tune and was visited by disease and disaster, people turned to them to consult the occult forces that controlled the universe and prescribe remedies.[28] Mlanjeni followed directly in the footsteps of a war prophet called Nxele who had rallied the Ciskei amaXhosa in the Fifth Cape Frontier War.[29] So, when he urged his followers to kill all dun- and yellow-coloured cattle because of their evil tinctures, it was widely understood that they represented the English.[30] Most of the Xhosa chiefs in Ciskei rose up, as did the abaThembu under Chief Maphasa, and the Khoekhoe Kat River settlers, although some leaders, like Phato of the Panther Eyes, the chief of the Xhosa Gqunukhwebe lineage, prudently sided with the British. This time, however, the Khoekhoe troops of the Cape Mounted Riflemen proved unreliable. There had been an incipient mutiny in 1838, but now they deserted rather than fight the frontier peoples. With many of the Cape Mounted Riflemen gone over to the enemy, the British had to rely more heavily than ever on their Mfengu levies.

The Mfengu fought in nearly every major engagement of the war, usually most bravely and to the admiration of the British.[31] Even so, although they carried more firearms than before and employed them better than ever, their ammunition was always rationed both as a precaution and because of their exuberant use of it. As a British officer sourly observed, 'the Levies returned firing as they always do in every direction, into the air & occasionally into us.'[32] The Mfengu were of most value to the British when fighting in the bush because—not to put too fine a point on it—they were expendable. To spare the white troops they would be sent into the rough terrain to locate the ama-Xhosa and draw them out into ambushes laid by the British troops or into the open where they were vulnerable to mounted attack. The British also preferred to entrust scorched-earth operations to the Mfengu, not only because this was a form of warfare the Mfengu revelled in, but because it had the double advantage of depriving the amaXhosa of their cattle and food supplies while turning them over to the levies as payment. Some Mfengu leaders emerged rich men from these depredations. The Mfengu were also invaluable in defensive operations. They were always deployed outside fixed positions to disrupt and absorb Xhosa attacks long enough for the amaXhosa to be caught in the open by the concentrated fire directed at them from the British fortifications. Because of their mobility and skill as marksmen (and also because of artillery support) they suffered few casualties in these exposed operations.

Sarhili, the Xhosa paramount and Gcaleka chief, did not hesitate as he had in the previous war before joining the fray. The annexation of British Kaffraria had brought the British within spitting distance of his domain, and he saw he would soon be devoured if he did not fight back. But he made the tactical error of committing his warriors to hopeless attacks on prepared British positions, and they were finally crushed in the pitched battle of Imvane in April 1851. The toughest fighting was against the Ngqika amaXhosa in the Amathole, but the British and Cape troops ultimately starved them into submission with their scorched-earth tactics. Their plight affected even hard-boiled British private soldiers, one of whom wrote home to his father that 'it would surprise you were you to see the carcases [*sic*] lying, Starvation and gunpowder has at last done for the Caffre'.[33] This time, though, the British and colonial troops suffered an unprecedented 1,400 casualties, but these were overshadowed by the 16,000 losses taken by the amaXhosa and their allies.[34] No toll would be heavier in the whole dreadful sequence of Cape Frontier Wars. The War of Mlanjeni was also by far the most brutal yet experienced, and would still be vivid in the imaginings of the British when the Ninth, and final, Cape Frontier War broke out in 1877, nearly thirty years later.

It seems that in the initial frontier wars the amaXhosa fought with their customary chivalry, sparing women and children as well as men who had done them no harm. This traditional restraint began to wilt as they were overcome by the bitterness of defeat, dispossession and the destruction of their society by a ruthless foe unwilling to differentiate between friendly and hostile amaXhosa, or between warriors and civilians. As the amaXhosa became as vicious in war as their enemies, settler opinion—and even that of the missionaries—progressively hardened, so that consensus was reached on the supposed barbaric ferocity and racial inferiority of the amaXhosa, validating their subjugation and dispossession.[35] Their irredeemable savagery was also invoked to justify systematic, unlimited warfare against them, including the refusal to take prisoners and the slaughter of women and children.[36]

Partly, it was the Xhosa adoption of guerrilla tactics that convinced the British that the laws of war no longer applied to them.[37] The case was no different in Europe where extravagant retribution was habitually visited against partisans. But the merciless British approach was also an alarmed response to the amaXhosas' increasing use of better firearms. As one officer put it, 'if we had not taught them how to fight and had not permitted the transport of and traffic of gunpowder, and arms into their country they would always have remained as innocuous as when first we came into contact with them'.[38] The British had long dreaded Xhosa expertise with their spears, but they saw how firearms increased their chances of success in the thick bush where they preferred to lay their ambushes. Night attacks, targeting the teams of oxen to bring convoys to a halt, sniping from the tops of trees and other concealed positions, picking off officers, shooting soldiers trying to help wounded comrades—all such sneaky ploys were both deeply contemptible and disturbingly effective, and justified retribution.[39]

And when the amaXhosa began mutilating and torturing their prisoners to death instead of exchanging them, this was taken as conclusive confirmation of their irredeemable savagery.[40] Yet Xhosa 'atrocities' can in large measure be explained in terms of their culture and religion. The amaXhosa always fought to kill their adversaries, as did the Mfengu, amaZulu and amaSwazi. They mutilated the bodies of their enemies to remove items believed to possess powerful magical properties which, if used as ritual war medicine, would strengthen the recipient. The liver was extracted, for example, because it was held to be the seat of bravery and courage, and the head because the skull could be used as a vessel for the preparation of war medicines. When warriors were ritually strengthened with these medicines before marching off to war, dangerous occult forces were generated within their bodies. These same potent, occult forces remained pent up in the corpse of a slain warrior and could severely injure the living. Warriors therefore feared their dead foes as much, if not more, than the living, and to dissipate the terrifying supernatural forces they ripped open the stomach. They believed that if they did not do so, these same forces would monstrously swell up their own bodies like that of a putrefying corpse, and that they would die.[41] Their enemies, especially white ones, were believed to possess occult powers. So when captives were tortured by being roasted on red-hot stones, this should be understood as a death reserved for suspected witches.[42]

Despite the general white prejudice against the Xhosa 'savages', a minority of British soldiers and settlers continued to admire the amaXhosas' determined spirit of resistance and refusal to surrender, and came to respect them as skilled, athletic, formidable enemies who 'skirmish very well and have all the advantage over the regular troops'.[43] But by the time of the War of Mlanjeni the majority of horrified whites were barely prepared to concede that the fearsome and mercilessly barbaric amaXhosa were fully human. This dehumanization of their enemies served to justify their own indiscriminate slaughter of the amaXhosa, and to excuse their own appalling collecting of trophies such as skulls and ears.[44] In any case, British officers could often distance themselves from atrocities by laying those committed by their forces squarely at the door of their wild, unreliable Mfengu levies who 'not being particular or infected with humanity slay women, children, and all they can catch'.[45]

The settlement following the War of Mlanjeni was brutal and the Xhosa chiefs were required to surrender their arms in token of their absolute submission. The Governor of the Cape, Sir George Grey, believed the enervating frontier conflict could only be brought to an end by fully exposing primitive societies to the benefits of Christian civilization and bringing about the socio-economic integration of blacks and whites. To that end, he intended to fill up British Kaffraria with white settlers to acculturate the amaXhosa.[46] The British expelled the Ngqika amaXhosa from the Amathole and confined them to a segregated reserve in British Kaffraria between the mountains and the Kei River. White settlers and Mfengu took their place in the Amathole which were proclaimed a Crown Reserve. The disloyal Khoekhoen and Coloureds of the Kat River Settlement were driven out and their land given to white settlers. The abaThembu who had fought against the British were likewise expelled from the Ciskei.

Yet, bad as things were for the deeply impoverished amaXhosa with their chiefs' households broken up, their young men put to building military roads and to labour on white-owned farms, and their children sent to mission-schools, they had not yet reached the depths.[47]

In 1853 bovine pneumonia (known as lung-sickness) arrived at the Cape on a Dutch ship. By 1855 the amaXhosa were losing five thousand head of cattle a month and their herds, so central to their entire way of life, were being wiped out. On top of this disaster, grubs, incessant rain and rot wiped out the maize harvest. What followed was the Cattle Killing between May 1856 and June 1857, an act of national, millennial atonement that was the defining event of Xhosa history.[48] In the tradition of previous Xhosa prophets such as Nxele and Mlanjeni, Nongqawuse, a fifteen-year-old prophetess, and her sister, Nonkosi, arose in Sarhili's precariously independent Gcaleka domain. She preached a synthesis of the traditional Xhosa belief in sacrifice for the good of the community with a Christian, mission-trained concept of the apocalypse, of the end of days.

Nongqawuse convinced the paramount, Sarhili, who was still strongly attached to traditional Xhosa beliefs, that the people must purify themselves of the corrupted world by destroying their remaining herds and crops in order to prepare for the coming millennium in which the ancestors would return to renew the world. People whose cattle were not dying of lung-sickness, and those who simply could not bear to sacrifice their wealth, stood aside. But about eighty-five per cent of the amaXhosa did as Nongqawuse commanded and waited for the dawn when two suns would rise and the great, cleansing wind would blow the whites into the sea.

Five times the promised day of resurrection failed to arrive. By then about 400,000 cattle had been sacrificed, besides those dead of lung-sickness. Between 35,000 and 50,000 amaXhosa died of starvation in the ghastly aftermath. Another 150,000 were displaced from their homes and many tried to find some succour in British territory. For the amaXhosa this was a disaster beyond any imagining. For the colonial government, however, it was a god-given opportunity to force the indigent amaXhosa into migrant labour throughout the Cape, to open up their depopulated territory to white settlement, to destroy the residual power of their chiefs and to impose their own, 'civilized' administration.

In British Kaffraria alone the general Xhosa population dropped between the beginning of 1857 and the end of 1858 from 105,000 to 26,000, and the sad remnant were deprived of a further 2,000 square miles of territory and squeezed into a compact location, fifty miles long and twenty-five miles across its widest point. In the same period, the number of whites living in British Kaffraria rose from 949 to 5,388.

Beyond the Kei, the shattered Gcaleka amaXhosa were broken even further by aftershocks of the War of Malenjeni.[49] In June 1857 hostilities broke out between the abaThembu, whom the British had expelled from the Ciskei, and the Gcaleka in whose Transkeian territory they were attempting to settle. The Cape authorities shamelessly took advantage of the turmoil and threw their support behind their former enemies, the abaThembu. By early 1858 Cape forces had driven the paramount and his Gcaleka warriors out of their ancient homeland and east across the Mbashe River. Then, in 1865, as part of his general settlement of the frontier, the Governor of the Cape, Sir Philip Wodehouse, permitted the Gcaleka to return to the coastal lowlands of their former chiefdom. This was an eighty-mile stretch of territory between the Mbashe and Kei rivers which was only about thirty-five miles across and constituted only a third of the former Gcaleka domain.[50] The Thembu chiefs were resettled in the northern third of the former Gcaleka chiefdom, to be known as Emigrant Thembuland. Wodehouse made over the central third to the Mfengu so as to reduce the population pressure on their crowded locations between the Fish and Keiskamma rivers. Although not officially part of the Cape, Fingoland (as this territory was named) was placed under colonial military protection because it was accepted that it constituted a particular affront to the Gcaleka whose 'dogs' the Mfengu had been before they treacherously fled to the Ceded Territory in 1835.[51]

In 1866 Wodehouse brought the drawn-out process of annexing the Ciskei to a conclusion when British Kaffraria was incorporated into the Cape Colony. Sandile's Ngqika amaXhosa remained in their location because they refused the governor's offer to resettle them in the Transkei.[52] Wodehouse was satisfied that his arrangements had finally settled the vexatious Cape Eastern Frontier. Yet, as with all previous settlements, this self-satisfied perception would prove illusionary, as Frere was to learn in 1877.

CHAPTER 9

'I Am in a Corner'

F AR from finally pacifying the Cape Eastern Frontier, Wodehouse's settlement of 1866 succeeded only in preparing the ground for the final, cataclysmic war against the Xhosa people. This was a campaign the colonials and British would wage with deliberate ruthlessness, while the amaXhosa would fight back, in Noël Mostert's haunting phrase, 'with a heroic sense of finality'.[1]

In 1869 Maqoma, the great Xhosa military hero, was released from detention on Robben Island and returned to live among his people in the Ciskei. His daunting, brooding presence so unnerved the settlers that they successfully agitated to have him sent back in November 1871 to his remote island prison where he died in 1873. His death left Sandile the unrivalled chief of all the Rharhabe amaXhosa lineages, but did not change the unpalatable fact that he ruled over only the cramped, overcrowded, barren Ngqika location. Deeply embittered but still proud, determined to maintain the traditional customs of his people and now seldom wearing European clothing, Sandile allowed the futile days to wash over him in a haze of brandy.[2] East across the Kei, the Gcaleka amaXhosa chafed in their restricted coastal lands and regularly mounted small-scale raids against their enemies in Fingoland and Emigrant Thembuland who were occupying their former territory under British protection. In 1872 Sarhili and his heir, Sigcawu, struck a particularly telling blow against the abaThembu. This military success encouraged the new generation of Gcaleka warriors to prove their mettle against their former 'dogs', the Mfengu who, to the envious

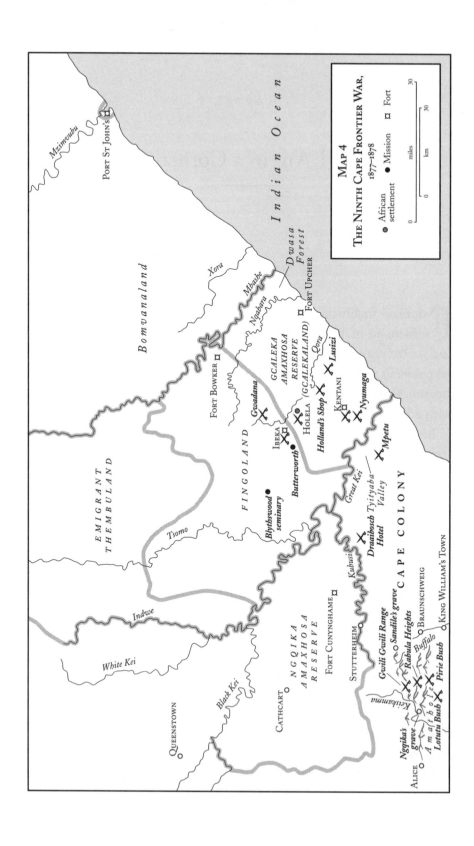

MAP 4
THE NINTH CAPE FRONTIER WAR,
1877–1878

□ African settlement   ● Mission   ¤ Fort

miles   30
km   30

Mzimvubu

PORT ST JOHN'S

Indian Ocean

Xora

Mbashe

Ngqbara

Dwasa Forest

FORT UPCHER

Bomvanaland

GCALEKA
AMAXHOSA
RESERVE

Qora

LUSIZI

KENTANI

NYUMAGA

FORT BOWKER

GWADANA

IBEKA

HOLELA (GCALEKALAND)

Holland's Shop

FINGOLAND

Butterworth

Blythswood seminary

Great Kei

MPETU

Tsomo

EMIGRANT
THEMBULAND

Indwe

Kubusi

*Draaibosch Tyityaba
Hotel Valley*

CAPE COLONY

White Kei

FORT CUNYNGHAME

STUTTERHEIM

KING WILLIAM'S TOWN

NGQIKA
AMAXHOSA
RESERVE

Gwili Gwili Range

Sandile's grave

Rabula Heights

BRAUNSCHWEIG

Buffalo

Black Kei

CATHCART

Pirie Bush

Keiskamma

Ngqika's grave

Amatbole

Lotutu Bush

QUEENSTOWN

ALICE

disgust of their former overlords, had profitably taken up sheep farming and the light American plough. Nothing would serve but to drive these despised Mfengu into the sea.[3]

In this tense atmosphere settlers in the Eastern Cape unsurprisingly became concerned about the lax regulations governing gun ownership and the number of firearms in African hands. The Colonial Defence Commission was appointed to investigate, and evidence was presented between September and October 1876. Witnesses insisted that Dutch and English merchants from Cape Town were mainly responsible for supplying firearms to Africans, and with unashamed bias some singled out amoral German and Jewish traders as primarily responsible.[4] But did Xhosa ownership of guns actually represent a threat? A few witnesses contemptuously thought them 'wretchedly bad' marksmen who could not keep a gun clean and who carried firearms largely 'for show' to 'frighten away the enemy'.[5] Most witnesses, however, contended that the amaXhosa were much more skilled with firearms than they had been in the wars of the past, and that their weapons were of better quality. In any case, they were considered 'decidedly' more 'formidable' with guns than they ever had been with their traditional weapons.[6]

The weight of evidence urged that the amaXhosa should be disarmed for the future security of the colony. But should the loyal 40,000 Mfengu living in Fingoland be disarmed too?[7] Most witnesses were against their carrying arms and being trained in their use, even if they acknowledged their loyalty in the past and could see how self-interest and fear of the amaXhosa were guarantees against disloyalty. Nor were settler fears assuaged by Mfengu evidence that the single- and double-barrelled muzzle-loaders they all carried in Fingoland were for defence against a Xhosa uprising. This rationale was no different from that of gun-toting settlers, but most whites nevertheless still saw armed Mfengu as a decided risk—even if they knew they had to rely upon them heavily in any future war.[8]

When Frere arrived in King William's Town in September 1877 he found the already twitchy frontier in a state of recently heightened 'genuine apprehension and alarm'.[9] The worst drought anyone could remember had the region in its grip, compounding the despair of the amaXhosa penned into their stifling reserves and inflaming their resentment of both settlers and their hated Mfengu neighbours. Unexpectedly, a wedding feast being held by an Mfengu called Ngcayecibi at the homestead of an Mfengu headman had set smouldering animosities violently alight. Hospitality required that the Mfengu welcome a party of Gcaleka to the beer-drinking on 3 August 1877. But the interlopers were edgy, bitter that the celebration was being held on land once theirs. Tempers cracked, and the Mfengu ended by beating up their unwelcome guests, one of whom subsequently died of a staved-in skull.[10] The Gcaleka could not accept such an intolerable affront from the Mfengu 'dogs' and launched retaliatory raids. Blood was spilt and cattle stolen. The Cape authorities rushed to offer protection to their Mfengu allies. Sarhili rightly feared the consequences for his people if the turmoil was not dampened down, but admitted that 'my people are like madmen, I cannot control them any longer'.[11]

Frere felt it incumbent on him to hold face-to-face talks with the Gcaleka leadership, but Sarhili would only treat evasively through emissaries.[12] The war-party in the Gcaleka council was in the ascendant, buoyed up by a spate of retaliatory raids against the Mfengu, and was determined to make no further concessions to the white man. As for Sarhili, that canny survivor, he too could not see how war could any longer be avoided.[13] Wearily, fatalistically, he finally told his councillors: 'I intend to fight the English. I am in a corner. The country is too small and I may as well die as be pushed into a corner.'[14]

Frere was not one to accept a rebuff from an African chief. He set up his headquarters in the barracks of imperial troops stationed in King William's Town and prepared for hostilities. He certainly did not expect to remain in these cramped, uncomfortable quarters until 26 March 1878 when, at long last, in the belief that the interminable war against the amaXhosa was effectively won, he felt justified in returning to Cape Town.[15] Never, in the pompous words of his biographer, Basil Worsfold, did he imagine that his next two years in office would be 'absorbed in the primary task of establishing the supremacy of the Europeans in South Africa by force of arms'.[16]

To prosecute the now inevitable war against the Gcaleka, Frere set up an informal war council. One of its members was Lieutenant-General Sir Arthur Cunynghame. As the General Officer Commanding (GOC) at the Cape since 1874 his command extended beyond the Colony itself to encompass all the territories of the South African High

Commission. Since the 1860s it had been British government policy to withdraw imperial garrisons from colonies of white settlement, but the Cape garrison had been exempted because of continuing African threats. In 1877 the garrison was scattered across South Africa. The 1st Battalion, 24th (Second Warwickshire) Regiment had been stationed in the Cape Colony itself since January 1875, and the 88th Regiment (Connaught Rangers) was a more recent arrival in July 1877. A Naval Brigade was usually also available at Simon's Town, the Cape naval station. The 1st Battalion, 13th (First Somersetshire) Prince Albert's Light Infantry was in the Transvaal protecting Shepstone, and the 80th Regiment (Staffordshire Volunteers) and five companies of the 2nd Battalion, 3rd Regiment (East Kent, The Buffs) were in garrison at Fort Napier in Natal.[17]

Because South Africa was not a significant or highly prized military command, those nineteenth-century generals who filled the position of GOC were seldom soldiers of much renown or experience in field command. Inevitably, they leaned heavily on the High Commissioner for support and were prepared, as was the elderly, stuffy Cunynghame, to subordinate their military authority to him.[18]

The other members of the council were two colonial cabinet ministers who happened to be at hand, John X. Merriman, the Commissioner of Crown Lands and Public Works (and in practice the Cape minister of defence), and Charles Brownlee, Resident Commissioner of Native Affairs. As a seasoned proconsul of empire Frere was accustomed to getting his own way, but he knew it would not be easy to manipulate Merriman. The latter was of like mind with the prime minister of the Cape, J.C. Molteno, who not only did not share Frere's imperial vision, but was morbidly suspicious of British interference in the newly self-governing colony's affairs. In particular, he resented the Cape having to pay for the upkeep of the British garrison which he realized was being maintained to further the confederation project beyond the Cape's borders.[19]

Unfortunately for Frere, there was no side-stepping these colonial cabinet ministers. Even although Gcalekaland was beyond the Cape frontier and the conduct of the war there consequently Frere's responsibility as High Commissioner, to wage a campaign in the Transkei required Cape logistical and military support.[20] To complicate matters,

Merriman followed Molteno in being contemptuous of General Cunynghame's military abilities and objected to his taking a leading role in operations. Besides, it was the Cape government's contention that since it was the self-governing colony's duty to protect its own territory, imperial troops were not required. Frere was decidedly sceptical of the Cape's military ability to handle a campaign on its own, but after much wrangling a compromise was hammered out.[21] Cunynghame, who took formal command on 2 October 1877 of all the troops, imperial and colonial, had his actual authority confined to military matters in the Ciskei. There, Colonel Richard Glyn, who commanded the 1/24th Regiment stationed in King William's Town, distributed his troops in military posts along the Kei to secure the Cape frontier and to hold open the lines of supply and communication.[22] The conduct of operations in the Transkei was left exclusively to colonial troops. On 26 September 1877 Frere appointed Colonel Charles Griffith, the Cape Government Agent in Maseru in Basutoland, to command them. A tough frontiersman, he had fought in the Eighth Cape Frontier War and had considerable experience commanding troops.[23]

For want of better-trained troops, African levies made up the overwhelming bulk of troops under Griffith's command. His main striking force, however, was the Frontier Armed and Mounted Police (FAMP), a paramilitary force which was the Colony's only regular military unit. Created in 1855, it accepted only whites into its ranks and increasingly took over the functions of the Khoekhoe Cape Mounted Riflemen, who were finally disbanded in 1870.[24] The FAMP numbered about a thousand men, and from 1876 they were stationed along the frontier. Initially armed with double-barrelled percussion-cap muskets, revolvers and bowie knives, in 1869 the FAMP was issued with much more effective breech-loading Snider-Enfield rifles. In 1874 an artillery unit was added to its establishment, although this did not add up to much, consisting in 1877 of one 9-pounder RML (rifled muzzle-loader) and two RML 7-pounder mountain guns. The uniform of this mobile, mounted force was appropriate for bush warfare, and consisted of a loosely cut suit of brown Bedford cord with large poacher pockets in place of pouches, overalls strapped under the boot and a slouch hat. Such attire was barely military in the eyes of British regulars who considered the FAMP had the air of sensible gamekeepers rather than of soldiers.[25] And although Molteno set great store by the FAMP, some British officers thought their training and equipment seriously neglected over the last decades of peace, and contemptuously maintained that 'hardly any of the men knew how to discharge their weapons'.[26]

Besides the FAMP, the Cape defence establishment included the commandos inherited from the period of Dutch rule. They were raised in the countryside and were made up of white and mixed-race men. The 1855 Burgher Levies Act had attempted to improve their organization and to extend their service commitments, but with little success. Instead of these problematic Burgher forces, the Cape authorities preferred to call upon exclusively white volunteer units of urban militia based on the British regimental system and formed predominantly of English-speaking settlers. The first such unit was raised in 1855, and a host of new volunteer regiments, sometimes with just a few dozen men each, were formed over the next few years. Their number and membership fluctuated drastically over the years, but improved economic conditions in the 1870s and increased colonial defence commitments under responsible government meant that after 1872 the military volunteer movement was revitalized. By 1877 there were forty-nine volunteer units in the Cape as a whole. Their military effectiveness was uncertain, however. The problem was that volunteer military units were becoming fashionable across the empire, and many raised in the Cape were little more than social clubs with few training sessions and low standards of drill and musketry.[27]

Certainly, the volunteers never lived up to British military standards, and in March 1878 a contemptuous British officer visiting one of their camps in the field described it as 'a mass of filth', and went on to comment that 'all these volunteer camps were sickening in their utter absence of sanitary arrangements; typhoid fever has been rife'.[28] Even so, the same officer could not withhold a certain ambivalent admiration for the tough, rough-and-ready colonial volunteers. He recorded in his diary:

Behind us followed volunteers, mounted on every sort of wild looking so called horse—but though a motley lot, there was something gratifying to a stranger late from England to see the sinew and bone and bold confident bearing of these sunburned colonists, as with loose but safe seats, dangling spurs, rusty bits, slouched hats, and corduroy suits of all hues they cantered along after us.[29]

The first clash between the Gcaleka and a colonial force took place on 26 September 1877 on a hill called Gwadana, or Mount Wodehouse. It started out as an operation typical of so many in previous frontier wars, with Inspector Chalmers leading a mixed force, some sixty strong, of FAMP and Mfengu, supported by a 7-pounder mountain gun, to intercept a war party of Gcaleka who had sacked an Mfengu homestead. But it was nearly a quarter of a century since the previous frontier war and the troops were inexperienced and unblooded. Leaving their horses to the rear, they extended in skirmishing order on foot on either side of the gun, which was a great mistake. The Gcaleka outnumbered them and came on with great determination in three divisions, threatening to outflank them. Chalmers's men held them off for nearly two hours, but when after firing ten rounds their 7-pounder gun (on which they placed overoptimistic store) collapsed on its improvised carriage made by local carpenters, the troops panicked and rushed for their horses.[30] As Helen Prichard, the wife of an official, drily expressed it in her reminiscences, 'the little band ... cut their way through—and—*left*.'[31] Six FAMP troopers and an officer failed to mount their bolting horses and were killed. This inglorious start to what flared out to become the Ninth Cape Frontier War shook the border country. Settlers, traders and officials resorted to makeshift strongholds. One such was the hastily barricaded Blytheswood seminary in Fingoland described by Helen Prichard. Volunteers and the FAMP turned it into an armed camp with earthwork fortifications and a wagon laager.[32]

Meanwhile, to exert pressure on the Gcaleka, Griffith established his headquarters in a small trading store at Ibeka, only five miles from Holela, Sarhili's great place. The brick-and-iron house and shop, surrounded by gum trees, was a prominent landmark at the junction of several ridges along which ran the tracks between the coast and the interior. Griffith fortified the post with a low sod wall and a ditch. To his relief, the surrounding land was not covered by the rich, dark-green

1 Photograph taken in June 1879 of the Isandlwana battlefield with wagons and other debris in the foreground and a burial party in the distance at the site of the British camp.

2 Zulu attacking in open order with spears and firearms, accurately depicted by Charles Fripp, an artist for the *Graphic*.

3 Patrol of mounted men from the Eshowe Relief Column burning *uMntwana* Dabulamanzi kaMpande's eZuluwini *umuzi* on 4 April 1879.

4 Migrant African labourers at the Kimberley diamond diggings, *c*.1873.

5 Sir Theophilus Shepstone, Secretary for Native Affairs in Natal, 1856–77, and Administrator of the Transvaal, 1877–9.

6 Sekhukhune woaSekwati, the Maroteng paramount.

7 The Earl of Carnarvon, Secretary of State for Colonies, 1874–8 and champion of South African confederation.

8 A 'young Xhosa chief' romantically portrayed by Caton Woodville, a studio artist for the
Illustrated London News.

9 Sarhili the Xhosa paramount and chief of the Gcaleka amaXhosa (d. 1892) photographed late in life in Bomvanaland where he lived in exile.

10 Sandile, the chief of all of the Rharhabe amaXhosa, sketched with his four wives in the Ngqika location.

11 Mathanzima urged his father, Sandile, in late 1877 to take up arms in support of the Gcaleka amaXhosa.

12 Three of Sandile's councillors.

13 The High Commissioner Sir Bartle Frere photographed in King William's Town with British officers and Cape officials. Seated left to right are Resident Commissioner of Native Affairs Charles Brownlee, Frere, Lieutenant-General Sir Arthur Cunynghame, Colonel Richard Glyn and Commissioner of Crown Lands and Public Works John X. Merriman.

14 Mfengu levies during the Ninth Cape Frontier War carrying both firearms and spears.

15 Cape colonial forces putting Holela, Sarhili's 'great place', to the torch on 9 October 1877.

16 Thembu levies operating in late 1877 from Fort Bowker on the west bank of the Mbashe River during the Transkei campaign against the Gcaleka amaXhosa.

17 A patrol of the Frontier Armed and Mounted Police repulsing Gcaleka forces at Holland's shop on 2 December 1877.

18 Commissariat ox-wagons of the British forces operating in the Trankei cross the Great Kei River in the early months of 1878.

19 Lieutenant-General Frederic Thesiger (who succeeded as Baron Chelmsford in October 1878) photographed in King William's Town during the Ninth Cape Frontier War. He is seated with his staff standing either side of him. From left to right they are Major John North Crealock, Captain William Molyneux, Colonel Evelyn Wood, Lieutenant-Colonel Redvers Buller and Major Mathew Gossett.

bush which flourished nearer the coast and afforded cover to the enemy, but he was also uneasily aware that the post was commanded by an eminence eight hundred yards away.[33] Griffith expected the Gcaleka to respond to his provocative presence at Ibeka, and to hold the post he rapidly concentrated a force of 180 FAMP, their artillery section of three guns and a 9-pounder rocket tube, and 2,000 Mfengu levies under Chief Veldtman Bikitsha. Indeed, as anticipated, the Gcaleka were reportedly being stung into action by the taunts of their womenfolk who declared they could no longer call themselves warriors—or even men— if they permitted the arrogant 'dogs' to hunker down at Ibeka.[34]

Duly, in the mid-afternoon of Saturday 29 September, a Gcaleka amaXhosa army of seven to eight thousand warriors armed with spears and muzzle-loaders of all descriptions appeared before Ibeka under the command of Khiva, a famous warrior and chief. Unexpectedly, Khiva's army was not deployed in the loose skirmishing order which had become customary—especially among the Ngqika—during the previous frontier wars, but in the traditional array of three densely massed columns. Apparently, this was at the insistence of Nita, a famous young woman war-doctor, who declared that the spirits of the ancestors wished the amaXhosa to attack in the manner of their forefathers. She also promised to catch the English bullets in her mouth and smeared a war mark on each warrior's forehead to protect him from bullets. The Gcaleka launched several attacks from different points but each time were thrown back in disarray, their packed ranks raked by Snider-Enfield bullets and case-shot fired by the artillery. The key to Ibeka's defences was a nearby stone kraal held by Veldtman's Mfengu who gave tellingly effective flanking fire. The young war-doctor herself fell leading the left column. (The Mfengu cut off her head and kept it in a sack of lime. When they later exhibited their trophy to Cunynghame, the general unsurprisingly found that it was 'not a pleasing object, and one look was enough'.[35]) At dusk the Gcaleka called off the attack, leaving hundreds of dead behind them. Not once had they succeeded in reaching Ibeka's prepared defences, and fire from their muzzle-loaders and array of more modern rifles had inflicted scant damage on the safely entrenched colonial forces, killing only one Mfengu.

Early the next morning, the Gcaleka valiantly tried again. They attempted under cover of thick fog to turn Griffith's position by seizing the eminence that overlooked it. But they were summarily dispersed by artillery fire. Then the Mfengu, who fought particularly well throughout the battle, sallied out in a vicious mounted counter-attack. The Gcaleka broke and fled towards Holela, Sarhili's great place, and the FAMP joined the Mfengu in pursuing them to its very gates, cutting down stragglers and burning outlying homesteads.[36]

The comprehensive Gcaleka defeat at Ibeka destroyed the credit of the previously dominant war party. Sarhili set about trying to negotiate a settlement, but Frere decided that the time had come to finish with the Gcaleka once and for all. Nothing would do but to annex Gcalekaland and include it in his South African confederation.[37] On 5 October 1877 the High Commissioner issued a proclamation demanding that Sarhili cease hostilities, relinquish his chieftainship and forfeit his territory.[38] Thirteen months later, when in December 1878 Frere framed his ultimatum to the Zulu king, he would again insist on equally impossible terms. In both cases his strategy was identical: even though the African ruler in question could not conceivably comply with his conditions, Frere had technically given him a chance to do so, and would be legally justified in smashing him militarily when he rejected them.[39]

To ram home Frere's proclamation, on 9 October the colonial forces at Ibeka marched on Holela and burned it down, withdrawing with herds of captured cattle.[40] Griffith then stood fast while he augmented his forces until they stood at 500 FAMP, 1,000 colonial volunteers (only English and Germans settlers came forward, barely any Boers[41]), and 6,000 African levies. Most of the levies were Mfengu, but some were Thembu. Their paramount, Ngangelizwe, had wavered at first, but after the resounding defeat of the Gcaleka amaXhosa at Ibeka he decided to bring his people into the war on the colonial side. Frere's Military Secretary, Captain Henry Hallam Parr, gave these auxiliaries (particularly the Mfengu) full credit for their effectiveness as 'exceedingly good light troops'. While—like every other white commentator—deprecating their reprehensibly 'unnecessary expenditure of ammunition', he appreciated how during a march they 'scoured the country to the front and on the flanks, thus saving the white troops much work', and noted how at night they bivouacked outside the camp, so reducing the danger of a night attack.[42]

On 18 October Griffith was ready to begin his advance through Gcalekaland to 'pacify' the territory. He divided his forces into three lightly equipped columns which drove along the Mbashe River and through the Dwasa forest to the coast, turning Gcalekaland as they went into a desolation of burned-out homesteads and dug-out grain-pits.[43] They encountered little opposition because Sarhili decided not to give battle. Instead, the Gcaleka warriors retreated before the advancing columns, shielding their women, children and immense herds of livestock as they made for the Mbashe River and the sanctuary of neutral Bomvanaland beyond.

Griffith's men failed to intercept them. Their advance was slowed down by the huge herds of cattle they had captured and would not relinquish and, to make matters worse, the terrible drought finally broke. The unremitting deluge turned all the tracks to deep mud and unravelled their supply-lines.[44] Besides, Griffith was proving an unenterprising commander, and his men began to accuse him of excessive caution.[45] Not that they were the least keen to prolong the campaign. Home comforts beckoned, and they had more booty than they could properly manage. Griffith understood the temper of his men. On 29 November he declared that 'the war with the Gcaleka tribe may now, I trust, be considered at an end' and called off the campaign.[46] His forces streamed home to enjoy their booty and were welcomed—for a short, heady while—as the saviours of the colony. Satisfied by the outcome of the campaign, Frere prepared to take over Gcalekaland. On 13 November notices went up offering grants of land in the conquered territory, and on 1 December Gcalekaland was duly designated a Cape magistracy.[47] The war, it seemed, was over.

CHAPTER 10

Calling in the 'amaJohnnies'

I N fact, far from being extinguished, the flames of war were about to
burst into a furious blaze. During Griffith's campaign in Gcalekaland,
some Gcaleka had sought sanctuary in the Ciskei. Frere decided these
refugees on Cape soil must be disarmed and targeted Makinana, a chief
of the Ndlambe amaXhosa.[1] When Charles Brownlee at the head of a
FAMP patrol attempted to enforce the High Commissioner's edict,
Makinana and his followers took flight to the nearby Ngqika location.
Responding to settler panic that this action might trigger an Ngqika
uprising, and without waiting to consult the prickly colonial authorities, General Cunynghame attempted to cordon off the Ngqika location with a thinly stretched line of imperial troops.[2] The Ngqika did
not resort to arms as feared, but the military presence deeply unsettled
them. Some began to urge war as a last chance to regain their lost independence, while others foresaw it would be a terminal folly. Sandile
himself was roused out of his despondent lethargy and was swept up
by the war party. As he warned Brownlee, 'a snake trodden upon
would bite'.[3]

But it was the Gcaleka who struck again, pre-empting the Ngqika.
Griffith had failed to realize that the Gcaleka warriors had every intention of returning to the fray once they had escorted their families and
herds to safety beyond the Mbashe. Having disbanded the colonial
volunteers and African levies, Griffith had only five hundred FAMP
available to patrol the long Mbashe border.[4] Unsurprisingly, a thousand or more Gcaleka, led by the redoubtable Khiva, slipped unde-

tected over the Mbashe to attack an FAMP patrol under the command of Inspector J.H.W. Bourne on 2 December 1877 at Holland's Shop. This was a burnt-out store just south of Holela, Sarhili's gutted great place on the road from Ibeka, where Griffith still had his headquarters. The Gcaleka came on in steady order during the late afternoon to within fifty yards of the FAMP's surrounded position, delivering what Bourne described as 'one of the most deadly and raking fires that has . . . ever been delivered in this war.' Under the bright moonlight they kept up an exchange of fire with the beleaguered police from behind rocks and anthills before slipping away at about 9 p.m.[5]

This inconclusive skirmish shocked the settler communities of the eastern frontier, and was very dispiriting for the overstretched FAMP who were near exhaustion.[6] Griffith urgently telegraphed King William's Town for reinforcements, but the colonial authorities had none in the field to offer him and could only suggest calling out the Mfengu and amaThembu levies. At this juncture Frere decided he had had enough of colonial dithering and incompetence. Quite simply, he did not believe that the undisciplined colonial forces possessed the military capability to contain the crisis. Ignoring colonial sensitivities, on 8 December Frere placed Cunynghame in active command of the imperial troops which he intended to send into the Transkei to deal with the Gcaleka.

On the Cape Eastern Frontier British soldiers were known as 'amaJohnnies' in both Xhosa and Mfengu slang, a derisive riposte to the soldiers' racist habit of calling every African 'Johnny'.[7] By the 1870s these amaJohnnies seemed a permanent fixture in the local landscape despite the British government's economizing desire that the Cape—along with the other colonies of white settlement—should shoulder much more of the burden of their own defence. But colonists were conflicted. As in the Cape, they insisted that their growing powers of self-government within the empire be respected, yet at the same time they persisted in believing that it was the obligation of the British garrisons stationed abroad to defend them. This meant that overseas garrisons continued to be deployed as reserve forces to be rushed to emergencies wherever they might detonate about the Empire.[8]

The army reforms carried out between 1870 and 1873 under Edward Cardwell, the Secretary of State for War, were a determined, if flawed, attempt to remedy this situation. The introduction of short service in 1870—whereby recruits spent six years in the regular army and six more in the reserve—was designed to create a large pool of trained reservists, reduce unhealthy service abroad and save money. Yet to cope with the larger turnover of men caused by short-term enlistment, the army had to lower physical standards and accept recruits from the poorest, least educated sectors of society. Moreover, because experienced soldiers now left the ranks earlier, the proportion of young recruits rose to such an extent that the efficiency of regiments on active service was undermined. All too often imperfectly trained battalions were posted to the colonies.

As for the officers who led the rough-hewn rank-and-file, although Cardwell abolished the purchase of commissions in 1871 so as to open promotion to merit and encourage the development of a professional officer corps, the social composition of the officer corps remained doggedly resistant to change. Most officers still came mainly from the gentry, the clergy and the professional middle classes, and were increasingly products of the burgeoning public schools. Yet even if too many officers continued to be promoted for their 'pluck' rather than for their military expertise, there were also growing numbers of reformist officers. They saw that for the army to perform its duties effectively in the far-flung Empire it was essential to embrace new technologies such as the submarine telegraph cable, to adopt the latest armaments and to be constantly reassessing tactics and training.[9] Yet they were constantly running up against conservative military circles that deplored reform and advanced military ideas epitomized by Cardwell's reforms, and gravitated around the reactionary Duke of Cambridge, Field Marshal Commanding-in-Chief at the Horse Guards. The charismatic Sir Garnet Wolseley, surrounded by his 'Ashanti Ring' of fellow military reformers, represented the opposite pole.[10] These antagonistic schools of military thought effectively prevented the emergence of a common military doctrine in the British Army of the time.

It was undoubtedly fortunate, then, that the late Victorian army was not called on to fight a major war, but was engaged primarily in colonial campaigns. Its enemies were irregulars in the far-flung corners of empire, from Maoris in New Zealand to Afghans on the North-West Frontier of India, who were inferior in armaments, organization and discipline, and who employed varied and unpredictable tactics and levels of military skill. Colonel C.E. Callwell famously defined such campaigns as 'small wars'.[11] These were a specialized form of combat that did not demand the same degree of technical knowledge and complex managerial expertise necessary for officers of the great continental armies such as that of Germany. Required for successfully conducting small wars was frequent experience under fire which inculcated disciplined solidarity among the men and honed tactical adaptability, initiative and flair among officers.

The organization of the Victorian army was clear-cut, on paper at any rate. The standard infantry tactical unit was the battalion. On service, the battalion was made up of a headquarters and eight companies, with a nominal complement of three officers and 110 ranks in each, or about 900 men. A cavalry regiment on overseas service normally consisted of eight troops grouped into four squadrons, and numbered about 600 men. A battery of Royal Field Artillery was made up of six guns and 174 men. Each gun had its own limber, ammunition-wagon and crew. The battery was the usual tactical unit, but was often broken up if necessary into three divisions of two guns each. Artillery was often in short supply, and had to be supplemented by Naval Brigades, landing-parties of sailors and marines trained in the use of small arms and light artillery that brought ordnance ashore from ships. Indeed, it was often more convenient to employ naval personnel than await the arrival of soldiers, for the navy was always at hand for immediate service in coastal areas. Colonial warfare had also taught the British of the need to combine the speed of cavalry with the infantry's firepower for scouting and fighting, a combination basic to the Boer commando. Mounted infantry, as they were called, were regularly raised from volunteers among the infantry battalions. A squadron of mounted infantry usually consisted of three officers and 110 men.

In the late 1870s the standard overseas field dress for British soldiers consisted of a single-breasted five-buttoned unlined serge frock. This was scarlet for infantry (except for the Rifles, who wore dark green) and Engineers. Officers wore either scarlet tunics or the dark blue patrol jacket introduced in 1866 and the preferred option in the field. The various regiments still wore their traditional facing colours on cuffs and collar (blue, black, yellow or green). Trousers were dark blue with a red welt down the seam for infantry, and were tucked into black leather boots—all too often of poor quality. Highland regiments wore tartan kilts instead of trousers. Accoutrements consisted of a black waterproofed canvas sack, or valise, supported in the small of the back by white shoulder straps. The straps were attached to a waist belt to which were fitted three ammunition pouches holding seventy rounds. The rolled greatcoat and mess-tin were secured above the valise and the wooden water bottle attached to the belt. Headgear was the light cork sun helmet, adopted for overseas service in 1877. The glinting brass shako-plate badge was usually removed on active service, and the white helmet stained light brown with coffee or mud, as were the white equipment straps and pouches.

The Royal Artillery wore dark blue tunics with scarlet facings, and blue trousers with a wide red stripe. Sailors of the Naval Brigade were dressed in an assortment of styles of blue uniform, which officers some-times varied with a white jacket and white canvas leggings or trousers. Headgear was blue (or white and blue), although a broad-brimmed plaited straw hat was often adopted. Mounted infantry wore their regi-mental frocks with dark buff corduroy trousers tucked into their boots and carried ammunition in leather bandoliers like the Boers.

Uniforms on active serve were seldom replaced, and a battalion which went through several consecutive campaigns would eventually be wearing a tattered assortment of garments, some of them civilian clothes like corduroy trousers, and everything patched and worn, including their accoutrements (which would be missing straps and other elements) and boots. Helmets would be misshapen from having been slept in throughout months of campaign and scarlet frocks faded to the colour of brick-dust. As an officer in the Pedi campaign of 1879 wrote home, 'you would laugh if you saw the state of rags our men are in'.[12] Officers in the field tended in any case to adopt an idiosyncratic assortment of non-regulation dress. Most officers and men also sported full beards on campaign, completing their wild appearance which would doubtless have dismayed the Duke of Cambridge with his insist-ence on parade ground smartness.

Campaigning in southern Africa was conducted across great distances along rudimentary tracks (or none at all), in difficult terrain ranging from dense forests to semi-deserts, from rugged mountain ranges to bare, open plains. And always, the extreme climate was

unforgiving. The essential logistical support for troops was consequently always perilously close to breaking down. Nevertheless, this
was an area where the army always tried to save money. Logistics were
in the hands of the chronically understaffed and overworked personnel
of the Commissariat and Transport Department and the Army Service
Corps. Communication between headquarters and military units and
posts was still by mounted dispatch rider or flag signal. Both were
slower but more reliable than the recently introduced field telegraph
whose line was vulnerable to being cut by the enemy, and the helio-
graph whose flashed Morse code messages were halted every time the
sun went behind a cloud. The Army Hospital Corps and Army Medical
Department provided orderlies, bearers and doctors to care as best they
could for the ill and wounded, but here too the limited personnel were
grievously overstretched.

British infantry in South Africa were armed with the breech-loading
Martini-Henry Mark II rifle, introduced in 1874. This 9-pound battle-
winner was a single-shot, centre-fire weapon with a falling block
mechanism operated by a lever. It fired a 1.1 ounce .450 calibre hardened lead bullet which flattened on impact, causing massive tissue
damage and splintering bones lengthways, stopping its victim in his
tracks.[13] It did have shortcomings, however. The Boxer pattern cartridge
with its thin rolled brass case had a tendency to jam when the chamber
was fouled and heated by the black gunpowder, and was often torn by
the ejector. Fouling also lodged easily in the rifled barrel with its seven
deep, square-cut grooves. This increased the already severe recoil, made
the barrel too hot to touch after excessive firing, and affected accuracy
since the bullet would no longer spin properly.

Marksmanship was taught and encouraged, though not practised
regularly enough, and sufficient emphasis was not given to individual
fire. Volley firing was still considered effectual in the open field and was
generally delivered by section because that way officers found it easier
to control the rate of fire and prevent wastage of ammunition. In broken
terrain, though, it was better for men to fire independently, selecting
their own target. Whatever the situation, it was important always to
avoid premature firing until the enemy was within sufficient range, and
to maintain fire discipline, as slower, deliberate, better-aimed fire was
more effective than blazing away.

The Martini-Henry was fitted with a triangular socket bayonet, twenty-two inches long, known as the 'lunger'. When combined with the four-foot-long rifle it gave a formidable reach of over six feet in hand-to-hand combat, but was of poor quality and too often bent or broke. Officers still put considerable faith in the demoralizing effect on the enemy (who were assumed to have no stomach for cold steel) of a well-timed bayonet charge. Even so, it was courting disaster to attempt a charge before the enemy had been thoroughly mauled by artillery and musketry fire and was on the verge of breaking.

Mounted infantry carried the Martini-Henry carbine and generally dismounted in action to make best use of them, as did mounted volunteers raised in South Africa whose main duties were long-range reconnaissance and vedette service, skirmishing, and patrolling the lines of communication. Regular cavalry was little employed in South Africa at this time—the final stage of the Anglo-Zulu War being the great exception—because local, irregular horse was better adapted to these duties, and because there was little call for the close-quarter shock action with the sword or lance for which cavalry was especially trained.

Both infantry and mounted troops depended on artillery to provide close fire support in combat, but the limited number of guns in South Africa at this time meant it never operated as a decisive force in its own right. The guns available were the light 7-pounder Rifled Muzzle Loader (RML) Mark IV steel mountain guns, mounted on light carriages, and the heavier 9-pounder RML. With a low muzzle-velocity and with an effective range of not much more than two thousand yards for explosive shells, shrapnel shot was usually ineffective, although the guns were much deadlier at close range firing canister shot. The Naval Brigade added their 24-pounder Hale's rockets with explosive heads to the artillery mix. Fired from a V-shaped stand, they were exceedingly inaccurate, but it was believed their hideous shrieking sound in flight and their tail of smoke and sparks had a demoralizing effect on Africans. Potentially much more effective was the Gatling gun which had come into service in 1871 and was mounted on a carriage similar to a field gun. It could fire 200 Boxer .450 rounds a minute from ten rifled barrels rotated by a manually operated crank and was fed by gravity from a revolving upright case. It could cause terrible casualties to an exposed enemy, but was unreliable on account of its tendency to jam and so was under-utilized.

'The men', opined an officer, 'are not supposed to know anything about strategy, and not much about tactics, except *Fire low, fire slow, and obey orders*'.[14] In fact, new and flexible battlefield training was filtering through to British troops in this period. The 'bush-fighting' typical of small wars constantly had to be relearned, and in the 1870s was being pushed along fast by the advent of breech-loading rifles such as the Martini-Henry. These had a revolutionary effect on the battle-field since they not only made it possible to load and fire more rapidly, but to do so while kneeling or lying down. In choosing cover and targets, individual soldiers had to learn to exercise individual judgement.

The British army in southern Africa learned to fight in loose skir-mishing order in an extended firing line, making the most of the terrain and natural cover, kneeling or even lying down. In doing so they were falling in with the instructions printed in the 1877 edition of *Field Exercise and Evolution of Infantry* which incorporated all the new tactical ideas accepted by the War Office. A section on 'Extended Order' allowed an interval of at least three paces between each file in a skirmishing line, and permitted extension to ten paces depending on circumstances.[15] When a company was extended as a fighting line, another was supposed to act in support about 150 yards to the rear. Any part of the extended line could be reinforced by throwing forward supports. If forced to retire, the extended firing line would fall back through the supporting line, and the two would continue falling back by alternate portions, each company covering the retreat of the other.[16] During the course of the Ninth Cape Frontier War the British devel-oped what seemed to be a winning tactical formation. The skirmishing lines of infantry were deployed either side of a fixed anchor of field-guns. Mounted troops or African levies were positioned on the wings to foil an enemy attempt to envelop the flanks and to act as a mobile force in counter-attack and pursuit.[17]

The problem with this extended tactical formation was that the Martini-Henry rifle depended for its effect on both range and volume, and on average it took forty or fifty rounds to kill a single enemy. The recommended rate of fire, even in a hot action, was only four shots a minute, and it remained to be seen whether a thin skirmishing line, even at point-blank range, could develop the necessary volume of fire to stop a determined charge.

Frere intended that imperial troops such as these would enter the Transkei in early December 1877 and deal with the Gcaleka since the colonial forces had been unable to end the war. Richard Glyn, the Colonel of the 1/24th Regiment, was gazetted Commander of the Army of the Transkei with the acting rank of Brigadier General, and instructed to take his battalion to Ibeka.[18] Six companies of the 88th Regiment, which was stationed in Cape Town, were ordered to be shipped to East London, along with a Naval Brigade on HMS *Active* consisting of 196 men (42 of them Marines), two rocket tubes and a Gatling gun.[19] There was scant response from colonials for volunteers, so Frere ordered Major Henry Pulleine, an officer of the 1/24th popular with the settlers, to raise a unit of four hundred volunteer infantry, or Rangers, answerable only to the imperial command. Pulleine gathered up the dregs of railway gangs, diamond diggers and the like to form a notorious gang of roughnecks known sourly as 'Pulleine's Lambs'.[20] Lieutenant Frederick Carrington, another 1/24th officer, was recalled from the Transvaal to raise a force of two hundred mounted volunteers, the Frontier Light Horse (FLH). These rough colonials had no specific uniform, but usually wore yellow or buff corduroy with black trimmings and a wideawake hat with a red puggaree. They became a tough and efficient unit under Major Redvers Buller who succeeded Carrington in command in April 1878.[21] Buller, an officer of enormous physical strength and endurance and of exemplary courage, was a protégé of Wolseley's who had served under him in the Red River expedition in Canada and in the Asante campaign in West Africa. Over the next fifteen months he would prove the most outstanding leader of irregular horse in the field.[22]

CHAPTER 11

Not the 'White Man's Dogs'

WHILE Colonel Glyn waited at Ibeka for reinforcement and concentrated his supplies, Gcaleka forces stole a march on him. They moved west to the bush-filled valleys and ravines that radiated from the lower Kei valley along the Ciskei border. From there, Khiva, the distinguished Gcaleka general, slipped through the British cordon surrounding the Ngqika location on 22 December 1877. He brought a message from Sarhili begging Sandile to bring all the lineages of the Rharhabe amaXhosa into the war. Once before, Sandile had baulked. At the time of the battle of Ibeka in September, he had refused a Gcaleka request to join them in attacking the Mfengu, protesting that 'his leg troubled him; he was getting old, and would have nothing to do with war'.[1] Sandile's response now fatefully changed the course of the struggle. He knew only too well the penalties of defeat, and many of his senior councillors urged caution. But the appeal of a great warrior like Khiva could not be ignored. While he hesitated, Sandile's son, Mathanzima, urgently joined his voice to Khiva's. Sandile took the terrible plunge.[2]

The first indication that the Ngqika had entered the war was their attack on Boxing Day on the Draaibosch Hotel, thirty miles north of East London, which they sacked and burned. The hotel was a high-profile target since travellers regularly outspanned their wagons there and traders and farmers met local Africans to deal in cattle. Within the week the Ngqika also raided and destroyed all the Mfengu homesteads in the neighbourhood and ambushed post-riders and other government officials. War parties next blockaded forts along the Colony's side of the Kei. Thrown into panic, the white farmers and their families fled to military posts in the Ciskei for protection.[3]

On 27 December, at precisely the moment the Ciskei was bursting into flame, Glyn launched the invasion of the Transkei planned by Cunynghame. The strategy he followed was nothing other than a repetition of Griffith's in October: three columns would drive to the coast, and then swing east to the Mbashe valley. As before, it proved a futile exercise. For two weeks Glyn's columns, wilting badly in the heat of midsummer, traversed most of Gcalekaland but made little contact with the enemy, killing only 120 Gcaleka and capturing a scant 2,000 cattle. Presuming, as Griffith had mistakenly done, that the Gcaleka warriors had fallen back into Bomvanaland, he had a series of earthworks constructed along the Mbashe intended to keep them safely bottled up there. But the reason his columns had found Gcalekaland practically empty of the enemy was because while they were driving east towards the Mbashe, the main body of Sarhili's forces had slipped away in the opposite direction, crossed the Kei, and joined forces with the Ngqika. The combined Xhosa army was now concentrated to Glyn's rear in the densely wooded Tyityaba valley where it kept the scattered British forces in the area fully occupied. Guarding the approaches to Bomvanaland had been rendered embarrassingly pointless, and Cunynghame ordered Glyn to pull back his columns to Ibeka. From there he was to prepare for a new offensive down the Transkei side of the Kei.[4]

It was at this moment, on 9 January 1878, that Molteno, the Cape premier, pitched up at Frere's headquarters in King William's Town. He immediately declared that he was unsatisfied with Frere's military dispositions, not least because he had no faith in British as opposed to colonial troops, considering them slow, clumsy, unnecessarily costly and unsuited to local conditions. As for Cunynghame, he and Merriman found him overcautious as a commander and an unbearable old chatterbox to boot. The main issue, however, was the question of colonial self-government, and both men intended to assert it by assuming full responsibility for the Cape's defence and prising it out of Frere's interfering hands.[5]

They would have been even more agitated if they had known that Frere, prodded by his military advisers, had written on 31 December to Carnarvon strongly requesting reinforcements, and that the Colonial

Secretary would agree to the immediate dispatch of the 90th Regiment (Perthshire Volunteers Light Infantry) to South Africa. Carnarvon believed he had to act to rescue the confederation project from the 'black conspiracy' which he imagined being stirred to violent life by the unresolved war on the Cape Eastern Frontier.[6]

Meanwhile, unaware that imperial reinforcements were to be sent out, Molteno pursued his political war against Frere. In lengthy, stormy meetings he rejected Cunynghame's sole command over all the forces on the Cape frontier, and insisted that the colonial forces would undertake their own independent military campaign in the Ciskei under Griffith's separate command.[7] Duly, on 15 January 1878 he appointed Griffith Commandant General. Frere and his military commanders were outraged. Not without reason they had no faith at all in Griffith's military capabilities, and strenuously deplored the setting up of two separate military commands in the same areas of operations which, they gloomily predicted, would imperil the entire campaign.[8]

As it happened, Glyn's campaign in the Transkei was not going badly despite the Xhosa decision in the second week of January to take the offensive and attack the camp of Glyn's Right Column which was situated in open ground near a small river called the Nyumaga, four miles to the south-west of his headquarters at Ibeka.[9] Learning that Sandile's warriors were joining up with the Gcaleka who had fought at Holland's Shop the previous month, Glyn moved out to reinforce the outpost. By the afternoon of 13 January he had his troops ready on a small plateau nearby. They consisted of two infantry companies (one each of the 1/24th and the 88th), two troops of the FAMP, fifty blue-jackets of the Naval Brigade along with Royal Marine rocket launchers and two light 7-pounder field guns. Critically, these white troops were augmented by Veldtman Bikitsha's Mfengu levies. In deploying his small forces, Glyn followed the manual to the letter: the regular troops were in an extended firing line with the artillery in the centre and a second line in support. The FAMP and Mfengu hovered on his flanks.

Facing them were about a thousand amaXhosa who breasted a ridge some way away. Apparently daunted by the British formation and reluctant to begin the fight, they fell back to the ridge behind them. Glyn then advanced his men to the ridge the amaXhosa had abandoned, and sent forward his Mfengu to draw them on. The amaXhosa took the bait and valorously streamed down to the attack. The battle became essentially a fire-fight in which the British and colonial fire-arms and artillery had a decisive advantage over the muzzle-loaders and other relatively inferior firearms in Xhosa hands. Kept at bay by steady Martini-Henry volleys delivered by the regular troops, and unable to press their attack closer than within forty yards of the British line, at sunset the amaXhosa began to withdraw. As Lieutenant Thomas Main put it, 'our Martini Henrys produced terrible havoc amongst the enemy who, having no opportunity to reload, bolted across the open plain.'[10]

The Mfengu and FAMP pursued them mercilessly, and the defeated amaXhosa dispersed into the bush of the Tyityaba valley. The British were disappointed, when they found only fifty Xhosa corpses, that their superior armament had not caused greater casualties. Follow-up operations achieved very little despite some sharp skirmishes, notably at the head of the Mnyameni valley on 30 January,[11] and the amaXhosa easily eluded the plodding British who were overcome by the summer heat. With no resolution in sight, Cunynghame decided to suspend operations until Glyn had built up more supplies and reinforcements had arrived.

Meanwhile, in the Ciskei Griffith's colonial forces opened their campaign on 14 January. They swept over the Ngqika location plundering and burning every homestead they encountered, feeding the grain they found stored in pits to their horses, driving off cattle and killing all they encountered. The Ngqika were left in no doubt that there would be no mercy shown them.[12] The colonial forces then became involved in a distracting extension to the war. On 22 January 1878 John Hemming, the Civil Commissioner for Queenstown, reported that he had initiated an expedition against Gungubele, chief of the Tshatshu abaThembu. His people had fought on the side of the Ngqika in the Eighth Cape Frontier War, but had contrived to stay in the Cape when the rest of the abaThembu had been moved over the Kei to their location in Emigrant Thembuland. Yet, resentful of the colonial authorities and embroiled in property disputes, Gungubele was wooed by the Ngqika to join them in arms. Hemming's attempt to arrest Gungubele led to stiff armed resistance on 24 January and he was compelled to call on Griffith for support. When Griffith arrived in force on 28 January, Gungubele's rebellion had spread, and with both Ngqika and Gcaleka reinforcements he now was in command of some two thousand warriors.

After three days of heavy fighting, on 4 February Griffith succeeded in dispersing Gungubele's army and the chief fled to take refuge among the Ngqika. But this explosion of violence could not be contained, and spread to Emigrant Thembuland. There Sitokwe Tyhali, the disaffected chief of the Vundle abaThembu, was at odds with his paramount, Ngangelizwe, who had decided to stick with the British. The colonial forces proved unable to subdue Sitokwe, and he remained a thorn in their flesh until the third week in March when two British columns moved in and devastated the district.[13]

At his headquarters in King William's Town, Frere was seething at Molteno's denial of his authority as High Commissioner over the Cape forces, the very forces who were botching the unnecessary 'Tambookie' campaign, as he called it. The proconsul was in no doubt that his absolute control over both the Cape garrison and the colonial troops was essential if he was to clinch confederation.[14] Matters reached a head at a stormy meeting on 31 January, and Frere decided to have done with his insubordinate ministers.[15] When Molteno and Merriman refused to resign, Frere dismissed the ministry on 6 February.[16]

The very next day, on 7 February, the Gcaleka were knocked out of the war. At the end of January Glyn had decided to establish a forward supply and operations base deep in Gcaleka territory to support further sweeps across the Transkei. Captain Russell Upcher of the 1/24th was placed in command and pitched his camp on some high ground 300 yards from the southern slope of a high hill called Kentani, 12 miles south-east of Ibeka. To defend the position Upcher laagered his wagons and built a strong earthwork surrounded by trenches and rifle-pits. The 600 white troops who held the defences consisted of 200 British regulars of two companies of the 1/24th, twenty-five blue-jackets of the Naval Brigade, ninety mounted men of the FAMP and seventy of Carrington's Frontier Light Horse. They also had two guns—a 7-pounder and a 9-pounder—and a rocket tube. Some 560 Mfengu levies under Captain Veldtman and Smith Poswa were deployed on the flanks outside the defences.[17]

While Upcher was strengthening his camp at Kentani, Sarhili and Sandile were in close consultation in the Tyityaba valley. Despite a dribble of losses already incurred in numerous skirmishes, and the much heavier casualties suffered in the mass attacks at Holland's Shop and Nyumaga, the two leaders still believed they stood a chance. With the Ngqika now fighting shoulder to shoulder with the Gcaleka the Xhosa numbers were doubled and the area of operations greatly increased, surely taxing the ability of the British to subdue them. Nevertheless, they could not stand still. The crops had failed because of the long drought and British patrols were destroying what remained. The people would starve if they could not secure supplies. Moreover, ammunition was running short for the warriors. Sandile's suggestion was to raid Fingoland for food, ammunition and firearms. But Sarhili decided all of these could be procured more effectively at the Kentani camp which, in any case, was a threat which should be countered. Sarhili was the Xhosa paramount, and his word prevailed.

Glyn had advance word that a Xhosa attack was imminent, but being unsure whether it would be on Ibeka or Kentani, with good strategic foresight he positioned a strong reserve column of infantry, horsemen and guns at the mission station at Tutura, midway between the two bases.

Very early on the soggy, misty morning of 7 February, Upcher's Mfengu scouts reported that a Xhosa army was advancing on the Kentani camp. How large it was remains uncertain, but it probably numbered about five thousand warriors. What is known is that the Gcaleka contingent led by the redoubtable Khiva and Sarhili's son, Sigcawu, was deploying to the south-west of Kentani, and that the Ngqika under Sandile himself were advancing across the eastern flanks of Kentani hill. Before battle was joined, Sarhili stirringly harangued his warriors as was customary, rousingly reminding them that: 'He was the tree his fathers had lain under, safe and sheltered, and for whom their fathers had often fought the white man. To-day they could show if they were the white man's dogs, or if they were their fathers' sons.'[18] Unfortunately for them, the Gcaleka decided to hearken to their war-doctors, as they had before the battle of Nyumaga on 12 January. Once again, they were persuaded that success depended on their fighting in the traditional, heroic fashion of their ancestors.

Consequently, the Gcaleka contingent of about two thousand warriors began their advance over the open terrain in four divisions massed in close formation, staunchly striding out in advance of the Ngqika to their right. Yet, when they came into full sight of Upcher's well-fortified position with his troops all resolutely in position to defend it, they hesitated and came to an uncertain halt. Whereupon Upcher sent forward a detachment of infantry in skirmishing order to hold a hill on their flank, and a troop of the FLH under Carrington to sting them into action with a few volleys. The dense Gcaleka columns responded as Upcher intended, and set off in determined pursuit of the FLH as they scampered back to the protection of the camp. The Mfengu deployed outside the earthworks also fell back ostentatiously, encouraging the Gcaleka to press home their advance. Accurate artillery fire opened gaps in their massed ranks, but they still pushed forward without faltering. Perhaps in the days of musket warfare the Gcaleka would have been able to close with the badly outnumbered British and overwhelm them hand to hand. But the weight of disciplined Martini-Henry fire was devastating. The infantry lining the trenches held their fire until the Gcaleka were within effective range, and then slammed their volleys into them. The concentrated fusillade was much deadlier than the Gcaleka had ever anticipated, and they at last wavered. After two half-hearted attempts to resume their advance, their nerve cracked and their columns broke up in confusion. That was the moment for Carrington to lead out the FLH to transform retreat into rout, and the Mfengu and FAMP swooped down to join the deadly chase. Within twenty minutes of the firing of the first shots of the battle the Gcaleka were dispersed in defeat. It was not yet eight o'clock in the morning.

Upcher ordered his men in the camp to stand down and eat their breakfast, but they had barely taken a bite before they spotted the Ngqika contingent beginning its advance. Unlike the shattered Gcaleka, they were not foolhardy enough to launch a frontal assault on an entrenched position. Rather, the Ngqika were wedded to the tactics of irregular warfare that had become ingrained during previous conflicts, and were relatively well equipped with their mainly outdated firearms. So when Captain Francis Grenfell led out half a company of infantry and a troop of FAMP to repeat the successful manoeuvre of earlier that morning which had drawn the Gcaleka onto the waiting guns, he fell into their trap. High grass concealed the number of warriors who were moving up, and they soon had him surrounded and cut off. Carrington, who had just trotted in from his pursuit of the Gcaleka, was sent out to extricate Grenfell. But the Ngqika rapidly outflanked him too. In a foreshadowing of the movement that would lead to British disaster a year later on the field of Isandlwana, Upcher had no choice but to detach more reinforcements from his camp to support Grenfell's and Carrington's surrounded units. As they would at Isandlwana, the infantry formed a skirmishing line with the colonial mounted men on their right. On this occasion, though, even in extended order, they developed enough fire-power to break up the Ngqika's attacks, even if the struggle was tough and sometimes hand to hand, and the warriors 'fell like grass' in the blaze of fire.[19]

When Sandile's scouts informed him that the British reserve stationed at Tutura was marching rapidly in the direction of the firing, he feared he would be caught in the rear and squeezed between the two British forces. Reluctantly, he decided he must break off the engagement. But his men were fully committed to the battle, and to disengage in such circumstances is always hazardous. Veldtman's Mfengu, the FAMP and the FLH took full advantage and grimly pursued the Ngqika to a conical hill where they rallied out of range of the artillery firing from the British camp. It was now 10.30 a.m., and Upcher called off the pursuit. The British lost only two Mfengu and four horses killed in the battle, along with nine men wounded. In stark comparison, an estimated four hundred amaXhosa perished, mainly of the Gcaleka contingent. The British located only 185 Xhosa corpses lying in the open, but they would have missed many more who died in cover, and mortal wounds would have greatly increased the death-toll.

The triumphant British celebrated Kentani as a model action and testimony to the effectiveness of breech-loading rifles. It certainly provided them with unshakeable confidence in their ability to win future set-piece engagements against African foes—a confidence that would be unimaginably shattered a year later on the field of Isandlwana.

As for the Gcaleka, their fighting spirit was utterly broken by their rout at Kentani, and they would never appear again in the field deployed as an army. Quite daunted, Sarhili fled over the Mbashe to the sanctuary of Bomvanaland. When the war-leader Khiva was killed in a skirmish on 15 March, Gcaleka resistance completely crumbled. This left the Ngqika alone in the field to carry on the war. The omens for success were not good, but the Ngqika forces were as yet relatively unscathed. At least they were free to pull back across the Kei to pursue their tried and trusted guerrilla tactics without the Gcaleka pushing them into hopeless set-piece battles.[20]

Despite his troops' victory at Kentani, General Cunynghame would not long remain in charge of the Ciskei campaign. For a few heady days he believed he was set to crown his career by subduing the Ngqika. The promised reinforcements were marching in: the 90th Light Infantry had already arrived in the Ciskei; the 2nd Battalion of the 24th was on its way, and the 200-strong Diamond Fields Horse had cantered in from Griqualand West. With a line of posts established along the railway line that now connected King William's Town to East London, Cunynghame was ready to march.[21] But politics would trip him up.

Frere had wasted little time in appointing the prominent eastern frontier politician, J. Gordon Sprigg, to replace the meddling Molteno as prime minister. The High Commissioner may have been showing evident 'traces of the severe strain he had been undergoing for several months past',[22] but at last he had a ministry he could rely upon to espouse the cause of confederation and to insist on African disarmament.[23] And final vindication would come on 18 June 1878 when the Cape parliament voted to confirm the authority of the High Commissioner 'as constitutional head of all armed forces of the Colony'.[24]

To Cunynghame's considerable satisfaction Sprigg made it clear that his first priority was to coordinate military operations once more under a single command.[25] But the sacking of the Molteno ministry had caused a great stir in the Colony, and Cunynghame had earned an embarrassing public record of 'want of cordiality' with Molteno over the direction of military policy.[26] It seemed politic, therefore, to offer him up as a placatory sacrifice to appease ruffled colonial opinion. Unbeknown to Cunynghame, on 1 February the British government had already decided on his recall.[27] On 4 March 1878 Lieutenant-General Sir Frederic Thesiger—who would succeed his father as Baron Chelmsford in October 1878—arrived at headquarters and superseded Cunynghame in command of the troops in the Cape, Natal, Transvaal and St Helena.[28] Cruelly humiliated before his own troops, Cunynghame sailed home, his career at an end. As for the upstart Thesiger who had been a good friend of Frere's since their days in India, he could boast that with the approval of Sprigg's ministry he would soon enjoy 'the entire direction of the Colonial as I have already of the Imperial troops'.[29] But how well would he exercise it in confronting the as-yet-undefeated Ngqika amaXhosa?

CHAPTER 12

'Rather Like a Rat Hunt'

——·•·——

Before Thesiger sailed for the Cape, Sir John Mitchell, who had fought in the last two Cape Frontier Wars, warned him that he should expect a protracted campaign of ambushes and skirmishes, and that he would have to adapt his military thinking to the realities of irregular warfare on the frontier.[1] Indeed, one of the real strengths of Victorian soldiers when conducting one of their many small-scale colonial campaigns was their usual readiness to adjust their military doctrine to local conditions.[2] Unfortunately, the aristocratic Thesiger had spent the greater part of his military career in India prosaically engaged with the staff and administrative duties in which he excelled, rather than on commanding forces on campaign. The Ninth Cape Frontier War was thus his first independent command in the field, and he immediately signified his preference for the conventional military doctrine he had absorbed with so much diligence as a young officer.[3]

King William's Town was teeming with refugees when Thesiger drove in on 4 March 1878 because every farm within a radius of seven miles to the north and east had been burnt out by Ngqika war bands. Even so, he was confidently informed that the war was virtually over.[4] But only five days later, on 9 March, Sandile and the bulk of his forces eluded the patrols set by Griffith to contain them. Leaving a trail of smouldering settler farms behind them, they made for their strongholds in the Amathole.[5] There, among the graves of their ancestors, they were prepared to fight and die.

Sandile, long given over to drink, now abjured it and steeled himself to take on the role of stalwart warrior. He deeply regretted deferring to Sarhili and taking part in the disastrous pitched battle at Kentani because he understood well from experience in the two previous frontier wars that only guerrilla warfare in the bush could prolong resistance. His Ngqika accordingly made for their traditional fighting-ground, known as the Pirie Bush. This was a rugged region of the south-eastern Amathole some twenty miles long, and a similar distance from King William's Town. A fractured plateau fell away to deep clefts and ravines filled with great rocks through which meandered treacherous, stony stream beds. All was overgrown by impenetrable bush through which reared the enormous forest trees strangled in wiry creepers. Captain William Molyneux, Thesiger's aide-de-camp, described the difficulty of operating in this region in awe-struck tones: 'The Bush is the primeval forest. Enormous trees overhead keep off the sunshine, while dense undergrowth with multitudes of creepers, or monkey-ropes, and wait-a-bit [acacia] thorns make movement difficult and limit the view to a few yards.'[6] Even so, what hope was there for Sandile and his brave followers? Were there enough of them to put up an effective resistance, and would not the British be able to contain the constricted area of operations and systematically snuff them out?[7]

John X. Merriman, although now thoroughly sidelined since his dismissal, could still see what Sandile's withdrawal to the Pirie Bush portended, and moaned to his mother that the Cape was now having to face 'a real old-fashioned Kaffir war'.[8] Ominously, as Hallam Parr noted, even those Ngqika who seemed to have been fully acculturated, and had worked all their lives on white farms or in government service, were readily exchanging 'their clothes for a blanket, their pen for a rifle' and going off to join the warriors in the bush.[9] Thesiger understood he must act swiftly to prevent the fighting spreading further across the eastern frontier and threw together a major offensive. He gave the command of three thousand imperial and colonial troops to the ambitious and capable Colonel Evelyn Wood, one of the special services officers who had accompanied him to South Africa in search of action and promotion.[10]

Wood's three columns converged on the Pirie Bush on 18 March and commenced a sweeping pincer movement to squeeze the Ngqika out of the bush onto the plain below where, it was intended, they would be brought to battle on the open ground and destroyed.[11] However, this entirely conventional strategy of Thesiger's did not work. The Ngqika probably numbered no more than two thousand in three main groups, but they were in their element in the Amathole wilderness, staying out of sight and always two jumps ahead of the blundering British forces. They lured one British column into an ambush and the badly demoralized troops had to ignominiously extricate themselves in the driving rain, heavy mist and freezing temperatures of the early Cape winter. Heavy shelling of the forests achieved nothing at all, and soon the offensive was in complete disarray. By 21 March many of the colonial volunteers had decided to give up and go home. Their period of employment had not quite expired, but they were disillusioned and rations were hard to get from the commissariat.[12] Thesiger abandoned the offensive on 22 March, but he was undeterred—and wiser. In preparation for the next round he ordered paths cleared through the bush to facilitate the movement of supplies, and to coordinate operations better he introduced flag-signalling between the units.[13]

On 29 March Thesiger launched a limited new offensive onto the high plateau across the Gwili Gwili Range and the Rabula Heights in the Pirie Bush.[14] The Ngqika effortlessly melted away once more. It was not surprising that recently arrived British regulars should be at a loss in this completely unfamiliar environment, but the colonial forces fared little better. The white volunteers were reluctant to risk themselves in the densely overgrown twilight of the rocky ravines, and sent the thousand Mfengu Levies (who had been recruited from within Ciskei) in first to locate the elusive Ngqika and flush them out. But the Mfengu also hung back, and were only persuaded to move in when they were promised all the livestock they could lay their hands on and £500 if they captured Sandile. Their failure to achieve tangible results disillusioned the remaining volunteers and eroded their confidence in the general. With their period of service expiring, they disintegrated as a force and went home.[15] The regulars were also dispirited with the interminable hardships of the war, and as Private George Morris of the 1/24th Regiment complained to his father: 'My clothes are worn to rags, and I have not a boot to my feet. . . . God knows I have had enough of campaigning this last few months; the weather has been very bad and wet, and many of our poor fellows have died of dysentery.'[16]

The defection of the volunteers persuaded Thesiger to bring in another thousand Mfengu Levies from Fingloland in the Transkei. They arrived on 3 April and the general was unimpressed by their lack of firearms and by their poor motivation. They were indeed unwilling recruits because they had become rich on the Gcaleka spoils of the Transkei campaign and were unwilling to risk their skins so far from home.[17] Even so, Thesiger used them on a new sweep of the bush beginning on 4 April: they were to scour the bush and identify Ngqika hideouts for follow-up action by regular troops.[18] Their performance was uninspiring, and on 5 April the acerbic Major John North Crealock on Thesiger's staff disparagingly recorded that the Mfengu fired 'wild volleys before they came to a thick bit of bush to warn the Caffres . . . At 5.30 they began to emerge, firing volleys of valuable ammunition into the air! and singing the most magnificent war songs!' In stark contrast, Crealock had nothing but admiration for the way the Ngqika were conducting themselves, writing that the 'Caffres were conspicuous in their pluck and leaving the Bush a yard or two would from behind a stone fire into us.'[19]

Despite his lack of success thus far in corralling the Ngqika, Thesiger could not afford to let up the pressure. Sandile's intrepid stand in the Amathole was inspiring other amaXhosa between the Buffalo and Keiskamma rivers in the Ciskei to throw in their lot with him. These reinforcements comprised two thousand warriors led by the veteran Rharhabe amaNdlambe chief, Siyolo, who had been released from Robben Island where he had been held after the Eighth Cape Frontier War, along with smaller forces of Gqunukhwebe amaXhosa led by Dilima, son of Phato, and by Tini Maqoma, the son of the great Ngqika war-leader. He left his refuge in the Waterkloof where he had taken up arms on threat of arrest by paranoid colonial authorities, and joined his uncle, Sandile, in his apocalyptic defiance.[20]

Caught unprepared by this new challenge, Thesiger swung his forces around to prevent these reinforcements linking up with Sandile. He launched an offensive on 6 April into the Lotutu bush where Siyolo and his Ndlambe forces were ensconced on a prominent hill called Ntaba ka Ndonda.[21] Shelling it had little effect, and the Mfengu who were supposed to clear the bush on its northern flank made no headway and fell back in disorder. The regular troops made scant impression either. After dark Siyolo withdrew his men, but Thesiger was discouraged by the day's poor work. So he returned to King William's Town, called off the offensive, and decided to rest troops for three weeks, refit and garner new reserves. The Mfengu levies were sent home for mutinous conduct and plundering. Since they had proved unreliable when they fought in return for loot, when Thesiger recruited a new contingent to replace them, this time he made sure they would be paid for their services, even if this openly turned them into mercenaries rather than allies.[22]

The amaXhosa grasped this respite to strengthen their positions in the Lotutu bush on the western flanks of the Amathole where Siyolo was concentrated, and also in the Pirie Bush to the east where Sandile remained ensconced. As for Thesiger, by the end of April he had concentrated 1,600 white and 2,400 African troops under his command and was ready for yet another new offensive.[23] His plan was first to root Siyolo out of the Lotutu bush and then to turn east to deal with Sandile. Accordingly, on 30 April four columns formed a cordon around the Lotutu plateau and advanced in a tightening noose. With much effort and sweat artillery was positioned on high ground to fire case-shot and shrapnel down the forested kloofs which were then laboriously swept by the plodding infantry who found the going extremely trying. Captain Molyneux recalled: 'What a race it was! Into holes, out again, hands and faces bleeding from thorns, knees punctured, and shirtsleeves in ribands, till after about an hour of it [we] came out on the open plateau.'[24] Yet, even though the new flag-signalling made for better coordination between the converging columns, the results were still disappointing for the British. They killed about 140 amaXhosa, but the rest had no difficulty in breaking up into small groups and slipping through the British lines. In that way Siyolo, Tini Maqoma and other leaders all succeeded in joining Sandile in the Pirie Bush.[25]

Still, even if he had not cornered and eliminated the amaXhosa in the Lotutu bush, Thesiger had at least cleared it, and was free to concentrate on Sandile's strongholds in the Pirie Bush. On 8 May 1,122 imperial troops, 920 colonial volunteers who had drifted back into the campaign, and 2,890 Mfengu levies commenced their new sweep. The intention was to drive the amaXhosa into the arms of the troops deployed along the rim of the plateau and the edges of the Pirie Bush, and to seize as many of their cattle and as much of food supplies as possible. Thesiger's forces enjoyed some minor successes, but failed in their main objective of driving the amaXhosa out of their sanctuary.[26] As Crealock observed with disgust after another day of scrappy, futile operations, 'it was becoming rather like a rat hunt'.[27]

It could no longer escape Thesiger that despite mounting five large-scale offensives he had failed to extinguish Xhosa resistance, and that colonial opinion was beginning to hold him in derision. He was a stubborn man, but even he could grasp that attempting to manoeuvre mass formations was impracticable and ineffective in the Amathole. His colonial commandants had been urging an alternative strategy on him for weeks, and at last he took their advice.[28]

Thesiger divided the Amathole theatre of operations into eleven military districts with both a mounted and an infantry force stationed in each. Manned earthworks blocked favoured Xhosa routes, while patrols scoured the country at will, never far from their supply depots. They pursued any Xhosa parties they encountered up to the border of their military district when the garrison in the next district took up the remorseless chase afresh. Much depended on the effectiveness of tough, colonial district commandants who knew the terrain, and on their determination never to ease up the pressure on the amaXhosa. This meant sending their men out on dangerous missions such as night attacks to surprise the enemy, or into caves to search out amaXhosa hiding there. It also entailed capturing what pitiable supplies of food the amaXhosa still had left, and destroying their wretched shelters. This was harsh, merciless warfare in which no prisoners were taken and the Xhosa bands were systematically located and eliminated.

The new campaign opened with a drive that ground on for three remorseless weeks without a pause.[29] Winter was beginning to bite and the defenders were cold, wet and quite famished. By mid-May many amaXhosa could take no more punishment and began trying to wriggle through the iron British grid. Siyolo made his escape to the Fish River valley, and Tini Maqoma crept back to the Waterkloof. Starved and desperate, the shattered Xhosa bands would not give themselves up as a matter of honour, but would fight when they could neither hide nor escape. The British became increasingly embarrassed by destitute

Xhosa women and children from the devastated Ngqika location and from the Amathole who flocked into the military camps for succour and had to be fed from military supplies.[30] The winter brought much hardship and sickness to the British garrisons in the Amathole highlands as well, but their sufferings were as nothing compared to those of the Xhosa fighters still pathetically lurking in the sunless ravines.

During late April and early May, concurrently with the launching of Thesiger's new strategy in the Amathole, the British opened a new offensive beyond the Transkei to finish off any residual Gcaleka resistance. Several companies of imperial infantry, along with some troops of the FAMP and three thousand Mfengu levies, crossed over the Mbashe into Bomvanaland from Gcalekaland and pursued Sarhili and the remnants of his forces as far as the Qora River. They took little booty (the Gcaleka had little livestock or other possessions left to relinquish), but the operation brought the fighting in that sector to an end.[31]

The campaign in the Ciskei was also drawing to its cruel end. On 31 May 1878 Sandile and his Ngqika bodyguard attempted to break out from the Buffalo River valley where they had been hemmed in. Near isiDenge Hill in the north-eastern plateau country of the Pirie Bush they ran into a small patrol of Rupert Lonsdale's Mfengu levies which he had raised in the Keiskammahoek district where he was the special magistrate. Three of Commandant Friedrich Schermbrucker's FAMP in their drab uniforms joined the fire-fight. Sixteen Ngqika were shot dead. A Snider bullet smashed through Sandile's side above his right loin, fracturing two ribs. His surviving companions carried their mortally wounded chief away with them, but after days of agony he died on 5 June. During this terrible war only mission-trained Ngqika ever paused to bury their dead. So it was not exceptional for his companions to slip Sandile's body into the bush under a great rock to rot before resuming their flight. Word of Sandile's death was brought to the British, and on 7 June a patrol was guided to the naked corpse. Wild animals had been feeding on it. The right arm was eaten almost to the bone and the left eye and cheek were badly gnawed. Even so, the body was clearly recognizable as Sandile's on account of his withered leg and items such as his walking stick, covered in blood.

The British slung Sandile's body over a horse and brought it back to the isiDenge camp. They washed it and laid it on a sheet of canvas in a shed with its arm crossed over the chest and the head averted to hide the eaten face. The curious viewed the body and cut off the hairs of Sandile's almost white beard and the still black hair on his head as souvenirs. Mfengu warriors were allowed to dance past the corpse, jeering, laughing, chanting and shaking their weapons in victory over their reviled enemy, the 'Tiger of the Forest'. On 9 June the British finally gave Sandile a decent, but not military funeral. He still lies buried in that forlorn spot, and a portrait bust has been placed above his grave. Recent excavations—overseen by the local Xhosa community—have confirmed the body's identity and dispelled centuries-old rumours that Sandile was posthumously decapitated.[32]

After Sandile's death desultory mopping up continued for several weeks more.[33] Mfengu patrols killed other Xhosa notables including Siyolo who was shot in the Fish River Bush in early June. Many Xhosa warriors, rightly fearful they would be killed out of hand, continued to lurk in the Pirie Bush. Colonial forces including the volunteers were sent in to flush them out, and they performed their task with vengeful callousness, tracking the amaXhosa down and shooting them as if they were little more than vermin. Embarrassing reports began to trickle out of the abuse and summary execution of prisoners. At last, on 2 July the Cape government proclaimed an amnesty for any fighters still in the field, and the killing ended. The poor remnant of Xhosa warriors knew they had comported themselves as true men, and little honour would be conceded in surrendering when all was lost. In July, Sandile's sons, Edmund and Mathanzima, who had fled to Emigrant Thembuland, gave themselves up, and were sentenced to prison for life. Gungubele of the Tshatshu abaThembu was also taken. Tini Maqoma, who also surrendered, was sentenced to death for treason, but the sentence was commuted to life imprisonment.[34] In early August Glyn finally brought his forces back from Gcalekaland, thereby signifying the territory was pacified and the war officially over. Sarhili, nevertheless, was still at large. With a reward of £1,000 and 500 cattle on his head, the Xhosa paramount remained in hiding like 'a baboon in a hole' in an inaccessible refuge deep in Bomvana territory. He declined to emerge even when offered a free pardon in 1881, but eventually acquiesced and accepted British rule, dying in 1892 at eighty-three.[35]

An estimated 3,680 amaXhosa warriors died in the Ninth and last Cape Frontier War, something like an appalling fifty per cent casualty rate. This number does not include other fighting men who died off the battlefield of their wounds or privations, or Xhosa non-combatants who perished of starvation. Only 171 men were taken prisoner, testifying to the ruthlessness of the campaign. More than 45,000 cattle and some 579 horses were lost too. Most painful of all, perhaps, was the fate of the 4,000 Xhosa women who had taken refuge with the British. They were taken off by steamer from East London to earn a bare living labouring in the environs of Cape Town.[36] In startling contrast, British and colonial casualties numbered no more than 60 white and 133 African soldiers killed.

The settlement the Cape government imposed on the defeated amaXhosa was unrelenting. Commandant Friedrich Schermbrucker set the tone when on 6 June he addressed the men of the Amatola Division who were drawn up in a hollow square around the grave where Sandile had been interred:

> This is the last Chief of the Gaikas [sic]; let his life and death be a warning to you. The man who lifts arms against his Queen will sooner or later meet a fate like this. Sandilli [sic] has been laid low, his tribe dispersed, scattered, and stripped of all they once possessed; instead of being lords and masters in the country they once owned, they will now be servants.[37]

The decision was taken to expel all the Ngqika across the Kei, even pro-government chiefs and those of Sandile's adherents who had not taken up arms. In early September 1878 Charles Brownlee informed them that their lands were forfeit and would be sold to white settlers, and that they would be relocated to a location set aside for them in the western half of the former Gcalekaland. The reluctant, pitiful exodus of nearly eight thousand people commenced on 6 September 1878. About half the Ngqika succeeded in avoiding expulsion by seeking work as wage-earning labourers on white-owned farms in the Ciskei, or by agreeing to be transported to the distant Cape Peninsula as indentured labourers. As for Sarhili's adherents, most of the Gcaleka were settled in a location next to the resettled Ngqika, in the eastern remnant of the former Gcalekaland. With their lands otherwise occupied by Europeans, this was the dénouement of the protracted Xhosa tragedy.[38]

The Mfengu were left the dominant ethnic group in Ciskei, but if they anticipated they would be accorded privileged treatment for the loyal and vital role they had played in the recent war, they were rapidly disabused. Sprigg, the new Cape premier and Frere's willing cat's paw, was determined that the frontier would never again experience a war between the races, and that the peace—unlike those that had imperfectly concluded previous frontier wars—must be no patch-up affair. Africans therefore had to be left in no doubt that they were conquered, and that the whites were now the unassailable masters of the land.[39] This meant ensuring that colonial forces defending the Cape would be exclusively white, and that there would be no place in future for African levies, not even for loyal allies like the Mfengu. The FAMP were augmented and renamed the Cape Mounted Rifles, the volunteer units were strengthened, and all other able-bodied white males were brought into either a yeoman force of reservists or the burgher commando structure. For, as Sprigg was reported to have forcefully stated in a public speech:

> The defence of the colony ought to depend on European inhabitants alone, for otherwise there was a great danger of giving rise to a feeling on the part of the natives that the white men could not do without them . . . it would be a good day for them when they felt that there was no chance for them against the European race (hear, hear).[40]

And to absolutely make certain of this, it was essential to disarm all Africans without exception, including even those who had time and again proved their loyalty in war. The Gun Commission of 1876 had recommended gun control; now Frere and Sprigg made disarmament the cornerstone of their native policy. Not unexpectedly since they were a conquered people, the Gcaleka and Ngqika were required by proclamation to surrender all their weapons.[41] But, in addition, Sprigg pushed the Peace Preservation Act of 2 August 1878 through the Cape parliament. The Gun Act, as it became known, not only disarmed all amaXhosa in the Cape, but the amaThembu and Mfengu as well.[42]

Cape officials wasted no time in implementing the Gun Act and whipped up a storm. The defeated amaXhosa were resigned to being disarmed, but the amaThembu were wildly resentful. As a Thembuland magistrate reported: 'From time immemorial, arms have been regarded as the insignia of manhood; and to part with, or be deprived of them, is, in the eyes of a native, an indelible disgrace.'[43] No wonder that the abaThembu believed disarmament was but the first step in a process that would lead to their land being taken away from them and culminate in their wives and children being sent to the Western Cape as slaves.

As for the Mfengu who had made up by far the majority of the colonial forces in the recent war, and whose military contribution had been even greater in 1877 and 1878 than in previous campaigns, they too were to be disarmed. With the warlike and resilient amaXhosa conclusively subdued at last, the Mfengu had lost their significance as military allies. Henceforth they were to become yet another subject African people, their previously close association with the colonial power set at naught. The Mfengu were deeply distressed at being disarmed, but they accepted that it was in their own interests to comply as cheerfully as they could. Their prosperity depended on producing goods for the colonial market, and they understood that any attempt to hang on to their arms would be construed as a sure sign of their disloyalty.[44]

Complete disarmament remained a chimera, and inevitably some arms were concealed and so remained in African hands. Even so, between August 1878 and March 1880 Cape officials collected 10,860 firearms and 15,764 spears. The crucial point was made that henceforth no African under Cape rule could legally own a firearm and would play no future military role in its affairs other than as a rebel.

The Ninth Cape Frontier War had dragged on for nearly a year, but as a consequence the Cape Eastern Frontier had finally been pacified after a century of warfare. A significant block on the way to confederation had thereby been removed, encouraging Frere to continue down that road, even though his patron, Lord Carnarvon, had resigned as Colonial Secretary on 23 January 1878.[45] His successor, Sir Michael Hicks Beach, strikingly handsome, aloof, and known as 'Black Michael' for his biting tongue,[46] was mindful of Britain's overstretched global reach and the continuing Russian threat, now focusing on Afghanistan and hence on India, Britain's paramount imperial possession. Hicks Beach was therefore not at all in favour of Frere following an aggressive forward policy that might result in unnecessary and distracting South African military complications. Unfortunately, because the recent frontier war had proved a relatively inexpensive victory in terms of both casualties and treasure, Frere remained in thrall to the mirage of cheap and swift military interventions aimed at clinching the confederation deal.[47]

Breaking the power of the Zulu kingdom remained Frere's ultimate target. As a military commentator expressed it in the midst of the Ninth Cape Frontier War, 'no rational being believes in the struggle with that military nation being postponed much longer'. And when it came, the amaZulu would have to be 'struck down with an iron hand'.[48] Certainly, they promised to be the toughest African enemy Frere would face. The defeated amaXhosa thought so too. Captain Hallam Parr, Frere's Military Secretary, took good note of the words of an old Gcaleka warrior: ' "You have beaten us well, but there," says he, pointing eastward—"there are the AmaZulu warriors! Can you beat them? They say not! Go and try. Don't trouble any more about us, but beat *them*, and we shall be quiet enough."[49]

Nevertheless, before trying conclusions with Cetshwayo, Frere had to clear his decks. It made sense to finish first with Sekhukhune and the Bapedi in order to secure the Transvaal. He knew that Africans were reported to be knowingly asking of each other: 'If the bull-calf [Sekhukhune] has to be let alone, what will happen when the elephant [Cetshwayo] attacks the white man?'[50] Yet, besides the Bapedi, one additional matter remained to be dealt with militarily before the High Commissioner could focus all his attention on Zululand. This was the revolt in Griqualand West, 400 miles north-north-west from the Cape Eastern Frontier, which had broken out in April 1878. Fighting was still going on there, deep in the dusty interior of southern Africa with its incongruous diamond riches, when it had already ceased in the wasted lands of the amaXhosa.

The Northern Border War, 1878

CHAPTER 13

A 'Hideous and Disgusting Place'

O N the far edges of the arid Great Karoo, the remote, dusty little frontier settlement of Hopetown in the Cape Colony straggled along the breathlessly hot south bank of the Orange River. The Khoesan called the wide stream with its little islands the Garieb, or Great River, and along its verges green bush stood out against the drab, surrounding thirstlands. Hopetown owed its existence to a drift that crossed the great river there, some sixty miles upstream of its confluence with its main tributary, the Vaal River, which allowed passage to the territory of the independent Boer republic of the Orange Free State (OFS) on the north bank.

It was close by in 1867 that a 'Klonkie' and Erasmus Jacobs turned up what proved to be a diamond, exultingly dubbed the 'Eureka'.[1] Eager fortune-hunters flocked to the region. Scattered diamonds were discovered at dry diggings across the Orange River, and even more at river diggings further to the north, at the confluence of the Vaal and the Harts rivers. The indigenous inhabitants, Khoekhoen, Batlhaping, Korana and Griqua, entered the frenetic search for more deposits. They were already exchanging ivory, skins and ostrich feathers with colonial traders for the firearms and ammunition they needed for hunting, and now added the dull but inexplicably desirable little pebbles to their goods on offer. Then, in 1870 a great deposit of diamonds was found in the core of an extinct volcano at Bultfontein. The following year an even richer pipe of diamondiferous gravel was located on the farm of

TRANSVAAL
TERRITORY

✕ BOTHIKONG

Kuruman

Mashowing

GAMOPEDI ●✕   ✕ DITHAKONG

Korannaberg

BATLAROS ●   *Moffatt Institute* ●

Kuruman Mission ●   ● MANYEDING

Langeberg

KONING ●   ✕ *Kho*

Gbaap Plateau

Harts

● TAUNG

● PHOKWANI

Gobatse Heights   ● BORIGELONG

✕ *Paarde Kloof*   *Cornforth* ✕

Vaal

Witsand

DANIEL'S KUIL ○   ✕ DIKGATLHONG

G R I Q U A L A N D   W E S T   ● BARKLY WEST

CAMPBELL ○✕   O R A N G E

GRIQUATOWN ○✕   ○ KIMBERLEY

Modder

Jackal's Vlei   BLOEMFONTEIN ○

KOEGAS
⊠ ✕   F R E E   S T A T E

Riet

*'Eureka'
diamond, 1867*

PRIESKA ○   HOPETOWN ○

C A P E   C O L O N Y

Orange (Gariep)   ○ PHILIPPOLIS

Caledon

MAP 5

THE NORTHERN BORDER WAR,
1878

● African   ⊠ Fort
settlement
● Mission

0   miles   100

0   km   100

the De Beer family not far from the east bank of the Vaal River, about 85 miles north-east of Hopetown.

The diamond rush was on, and by the end of 1871 many thousands of miners were in the area, living in impermanent mining 'camps', trying to lay claim to their fraction of what their frenetic digging would soon turn into the Big Hole. By 1878 the enormous mine was already 399 feet deep, and by the time the deposits ran out would have delved 2,600 feet into the earth. The settlement (known initially as New Rush) that sprung up around the mine was all a boom town should be, squalid, rough and ready. In 1872 a digger described the typical scene to his father: 'Restaurants, a circus, photographic saloons, inns, and surgeries are mixed up with the little square tents where diamond buyers sit with their scales.'[2] The unruly Diggers' Mutual Protection Association ran New Rush, not only to ward off monopolists and to establish some order to claims, but to defy attempts by local African and Boer political authorities to take it over. The British hastened to intervene. By 1873 the mine and its surrounding territory were being sketchily administered by a lieutenant-governor as the Crown Colony of Griqualand West, and New Rush was re-named Kimberley after the British colonial secretary of the time. The problem was that British annexation came at the indignant expense of African and Boer claimants to the diamond fields, and involved the subjugation of previously independent chiefdoms and the alienation of much of their land to white settlers. Bitter resentments consequently ran deep, and it was these which exploded into a full-blown rebellion in 1878 that coincided most uncomfortably for the British with the Ninth Cape Frontier War.

Kimberley pants in a sun-drenched plain of parched, sparse grasses and acacia thorn trees, broken by rocky outcrops. West across the Vaal, over 125 miles away, the range of the Langeberg, its modest, rounded peaks no higher than 6,000 feet, rises abruptly above the Ghaap Plateau. The summer rainy season in this arid savannah country is short and unreliable, tumultuous thunderstorms delivering most of the mere sixteen inches of rain a year. Winters are bone dry and achingly cold. The people who had long dwelt in this harsh land could never depend entirely on their cultivated crops like pumpkins, melons, beans and sorghum for survival. Instead, they turned to hunting the wild game that still roamed over the plains that stretched to the far horizon, and placed most reliance of all on their cattle, sheep and goats for milk, meat and leather. Finding sufficient grazing in this desiccated land with its seasonal streams that dried out in the winter was a challenge, and livestock had to be parcelled out to distant posts under the care of boys and teenagers. Living for months in crude shelters away from their villages, they learned how to be tough and self-reliant and to develop hunting skills that would translate into martial ones.[3]

Before the coming of the diamond diggers, Batswana and Griqua chiefdoms ruled the land. The Setswana-speaking Batswana could trace their ancestors back to people who had moved slowly westwards from the highveld, intermarrying with the Khoesan hunter-gatherers of the increasingly parched terrain until they came to a halt on the uninhabitable margins of the Kalahari Desert. The scarcity of water meant they could not live in scattered communities like the amaZulu and amaXhosa in their well-watered lands to the east. Instead, they packed into compact, dense settlements of round wattle-and-daub and thatched huts in those rare places where there was sufficient water for their crops and herds. They worked iron acquired through trading the ivory and skins garnered in great game drives when they stampeded wild animals into pitfall traps to be killed.[4]

In Setswana, the word *morafe* (*merafe* in the plural) means a geographical area as well as the people who recognized the authority of a *kgosi* (*dikgosi* in the plural), or chief. A *kgosi* exercised all executive and judicial authority, allocated the land and directed all economic activities, exacting tribute in return. Nevertheless, in common with indigenous rulers elsewhere in southern Africa, he was no tyrant. He would regularly consult his subjects in a *pitso*, or general gathering, and was bound by the norms and conventions of society. However, shortages of agricultural land and pasturage, along with competition for trade and regular succession disputes, kept *merafe* in a state of endemic warfare, while the vast stretches of unoccupied land made it easy to secede and move away. The Batswana consequently seldom succeeded in forming large, enduring states. The Barolong lineage developed one in the seventeenth century with its capital at Taung on the Harts River, but by the late eighteenth century it had splintered into four *merafe*. One of these was the *morafe* of the Batlhaping (the 'people of the place of the fish') which in the late eighteenth century Phuduhutŝwe established west of the Vaal River on the Ghaap plateau. Most of his people lived in the capital, the large central town of Dithakong, which at its height in the early nineteenth century had ten thousand inhabitants. Its name meant 'place of stones' from the ancient animal enclosures (kraals) nearby, and the site long retained its special spiritual meaning for the Batlhaping.[5]

The Batlhaping intermarried with another group, known as the Korana.[6] They were settled along a line of springs in the valley of the lower Orange beyond its confluence with the Vaal, and regularly intermarried also with the small, wandering bands of hunter-gatherer San, the original people of the land. These Korana were the descendants of Khoesan who had been progressively pushed out from the fertile southwestern Cape by Boer pastoralists trekking north in search of new hunting grounds and lands to settle. In the process, they adopted elements of the culture of their enemies, peppering their speech with Dutch words, adopting Dutch names and wearing items of Dutch clothing. Most significantly of all, they took to riding horses and carrying muskets, and exploited them to become highly efficient and mobile raiders, preying on neighbouring settled communities. They were made doubly formidable on account of their stronghold on a slew of small islands stretching for some fifty miles in the middle of the Orange River above the Aughrabies falls. These were covered in dense bush which concealed the narrow channels between the islands and provided ideal cover for snipers defending them.

Towards the end of the eighteenth century another group of colonial outcasts settled in the same region as the Korana.[7] They were people of mixed-race origins, the offspring of white male colonists and Khoesan women or female slaves imported from the East Indies, Madagascar or East Africa, and the progeny of intermarriage with the Batswana. They spoke a dialect that was the simplified form of Dutch that would become the Afrikaans language, and wore only European-style clothing. They were equipped like the Boers with muskets, horses and wagons, and were known as the Oorlams, a word derived from Malay that refers to riding and shooting skills. Although they had lived at first among stock-farming Boers on the far, northern margins of the Cape, these dark-skinned versions of the colonists found themselves increasingly rejected on racial grounds. Squeezed out, they made their

home among the Korana and began to seek their fortunes north of the
Orange River, in what was known as Transorangia. By the early nineteenth century the Cape authorities began to recognize them as distinct
from the Cape's 'brown people' and by the 1860s were categorizing
them ethnically as 'Coloureds', differentiated from the 'Natives' of the
interior like the Batswana. Recently, Paul Landau has suggested that
the term 'métis' is an appropriately vague one for all these culturally and
biologically intermixed people of the Cape and highveld borderlands.[8]

There they lived in semi-nomadic hunting communities, sometimes called *drosters*, or gangs, on account of their widespread cattle-
raiding and slave-taking from other communities. When raiding,
they operated just like Boer commandos, or mounted infantry. By the
early nineteenth century they were established as the most mobile and
feared fighters on the highveld. Several main bands emerged, the
Oorlams proper, the Bergenaars, the Hartenaars and the Basters
(self-proclaimed racial Bastards) led by Adam Kok and Barend
Barends. The latter would play a significant part in the history of
Griqualand West.

The Basters were already nominally Christian, and Barends saw
how the evangelical missionaries of the London Missionary Society
(LMS) could help bring his people around to 'civilized' occupations
instead of living by raiding. The LMS was invited in 1804 to establish
a mission station at Klaarwater, and the roving Basters began to settle
around it. In 1813 the Revd John Campbell persuaded the Basters to
change their rather too explicit name to Griqua, and Klaarwater was
renamed Griquatown,[9] which developed as an important trading
centre.

As part of their drive to convert the Griqua to more civilized behaviour, the missionaries persuaded them to adopt a written constitution
for a fledgling, independent statelet governed by a *Kaptyn* (Captain)
and advised by a council. Adam Kok II and Barend Barends were the
first *Kaptyns*, but political stability was not easy to impose. The Kok
and Barends families were soon at odds with another grouping led by
Andries Waterboer. Waterboer was of Khoekhoe descent and gained
respectability by closely allying himself with the missionaries. By the
early 1820s he had established his political predominance in Griquatown.
The British found they could deal with Waterboer's stable little state,

and in 1834 concluded a treaty recognizing his sovereignty and right to the land his people occupied. Adam Kok II, Waterboer's main rival, conveniently left the picture. In 1826 he moved east across the Vaal with his followers to settle at Philippolis, and in 1861 his successor, Adam Kok III, trekked off again, founding his new chiefdom of Griqualand East over the Maloti Mountains in the 'No Man's Land' between the Basotho and amaMphondo.[10]

Meanwhile, the LMS was bringing its mission to the Batlhaping. In 1812 Mothibi succeeded as *kgosi* of the Batlhaping *merafe*, and allowed the missionaries to settle at Dithakong. In 1823 the Revd Robert Moffatt, Scottish Congregationalist and future father-in-law of the famous missionary and explorer David Livingstone, had been at Dithakong only three years when Mothibi's capital was threatened from the east by masses of refugees displaced by the turmoil of the *Difaqane*, as the wars on the highveld contemporaneous with the *Mfecane* were known.[11]

The Batlhaping way of war was still largely traditional. Boys and girls from across an entire *morafe* went through *bogwera* (initiation schools) to be inducted into the culture, religion and mores of their people. For boys, the process culminated in circumcision and entry into full manhood. Thereafter they were formed into age-grade regiments under the command of fellow-initiates drawn from the *kgosi*'s royal kin. As warriors responsible for the security of the *morafe*, they were the *kgosi*'s essential instrument of political power. Each warrior was armed with a bundle of long-shafted throwing-spears, and often carried a battle-axe with a crescent blade set into a stout, knobbed stick. For protection he had a small, light, cowhide shield cut distinctively into a pattern resembling an H turned on its side, the four wings designed to deflect cast spears rather than for tough, close combat. Mothibi understood that this time-hallowed way of warfare was no match for the Griqua with their muskets, and was already beginning to acquire fire-arms for war and hunting when the *Difaqane* burst upon him.[12]

Many polities neighbouring the Batlhaping were dislocated, and thousands of their adherents scattered to the winds. The Batlhaping were fortunate that Robert Moffatt persuaded Andries Waterboer and the Griqua—lured on, it is true, by the prospect of booty and captives—to come to their aid. At the battle of Dithakong on 23 June 1823 two hundred Griqua horsemen, armed with muskets, handily repulsed the

Phuting, Hlakwana and (possibly) Fokeng raiders while the Batlhaping regiments stood by in reserve. The raiders, who were armed with their traditional weapons which closely resembled those of the Batlhaping, to whom they were closely related culturally, simply could not stand up to the Griqua volleys.[13]

The battle of Dithakong did more than save the Batlhaping from being overrun. It confirmed that firearms were essential for warfare, and that they must obtain them along with horses and ox-wagons. Mothibi rewarded Moffatt for securing victory by granting the LMS a fertile site in 1824 for their mission on the Kuruman River south of Dithakong. Kuruman duly became the missionaries' base from where they progressively eroded the traditional practices of the Batlhaping in the interests of Christianity and civilized behaviour. They discouraged the heathen *bogwera* initiation schools, and under their influence the Batlhaping abandoned their former dress of skins along with the red-clay ochre they smeared over their bodies as protection against sun and parasites. Instead they took to wearing broad-brimmed hats, jackets and trousers in the Boer style, and became indistinguishable in dress from the Griqua.[14]

The Batlhaping *morafe* also fragmented in these years. Drought in 1828 compelled them to move away from the Kuruman mission where they had concentrated since the upheavals of the *Difaqane*. Mahura, Mothibi's younger brother, led half the *morafe* of five thousand people back to Dithakong. Mothibi moved south towards the confluence of the Vaal and Harts rivers with the rest of the *morafe*. In 1839 Gasebonwe, Mothibi's son by his first wife, moved further north up the Harts to Borigelong and Phokwani with his adherents. Jantjie, Mothibe's son by his second wife, who (unlike Gasebonwe) was under strong missionary influence, took charge as *kgosi* of the Christian section. In 1841 he established his capital at Dikgatlhong, just west of the Harts at its confluence with the Vaal. In this Christian community the buildings were rectangular and brick-built in the European style, literacy and useful technical skill were encouraged, and men driving ox-drawn ploughs began to take over agriculture from women.[15]

But for the Batlhaping at Dikgatlhong modernization went beyond acquiring farm implements. By the 1840s Jantjie and the other prominent men in his *morafe* were engaged in trade with Cape merchants, exchanging firearms, wagons and horses against the ivory and skin karosses they obtained on extended hunting expeditions to the north. Firearms were naturally the most desirable commodity of all for hunting and for war. From their youth, the Batlhaping were trained in handling them proficiently and gained an enviable reputation as crack shots. Many missionaries were opposed to the arms trade (along with that in liquor), but some took the approach that it could be justified in terms of good relations and conversions. And it must be said that some of the pitifully underpaid missionaries traded firearms to keep the wolf from the door. In any event, by the 1860s Kuruman Mission was becoming the central market where firearms were exchanged for ivory, and boasted two trading stores and a secure magazine for arms and ammunition.[16]

For the Batlhaping, firearms were becoming ever more essential for protecting themselves against the Boer republics to the north-east of them. The ZAR interpreted the Sand River Convention of 1852 to claim sovereignty over all territory north of the Vaal which, to the Transvaalers' way of thinking, gave them the latitude to fix their western boundary wheresoever they willed. They lacked the military heft to enforce their pretensions, but from the 1850s they began steadily to encroach on Batswana territory.[17] This border-creep did not yet directly affect the Batlhaping for whom the ambitions of the OFS were far more threatening.

A crucial armed encounter took place at Kousop on the Vaal in July 1858. *Kgosi* Gasebonwe and his son, Botlasitse, at the head of a force of mounted men armed with muzzle-loaders, confronted Free State Boers raiding across the river for children to seize as *inboekelinge*. The Batlhaping, who always dismounted to fire when out hunting, found themselves at a real disadvantage against the Boers who were used to loading and firing from the saddle, and were worsted in the affray. The Boers did not let the matter rest there, and the following month dispatched a commando against Gasebonwe's town of Taung further up the Harts River from Borigelong. The Boers ruthlessly sacked Taung, killed Gasebonwe in the fighting and, to the horror of the Batlhaping, beheaded him. In the wake of this defeat, Mahura of Dithakong was forced as the senior Batlhaping *kgosi* to sign a treaty with the OFS agreeing to pay 'war expenses' and to surrender wagons, cattle, and children as *inboekelinge*. The last demand was intolerable, and in the end Mahura never paid the agreed-upon 'war expenses'. The OFS then declared that if he did not, his country would be forfeit to them. And so matters rested, unresolved. For the Batlhaping the lesson was clear. They needed many more firearms for protection, and they must learn to fire them from the saddle, just like the Boers.[18]

The discovery of the diamonds changed everything, and Jantjie's Dikgatlhong *morafe* found itself at the storm-centre of the dispute over the ownership of the diamond fields. In his capacity as High Commissioner, the new Governor of the Cape, Sir Henry Barkly, was vested with the power to represent British interests outside the colony. Wasting no time, in January 1871 he travelled straight to the diamond diggings to ensure the British got their hands on them.[19] But while Britain had no obvious legal claim to the diamond riches, five other parties did. They were the ZAR, the Barolong, the Batlhaping, the Griqua led by Nikolaas, the eldest son of Andries Waterboer, and the OFS. In a fine show of impartiality as an honest broker, Barkly appointed the Bloemhof Committee to take the complex and contradictory evidence presented by the various claimants, and to refer it to Lieutenant-Governor J.R. Keate of Natal for arbitration.

Barkly grasped how Britain could gain control through the Griqua claim, for Nikolaas Waterboer was prepared, if the dispute was decided in his favour, to seek British 'protection' and surrender his sovereignty to the British. His case was based on his spurious claim to be overlord of the Dikgatlhong and Borigelong *merafe*. The OFS, which had a watertight case based on its natural river boundaries, simplified things for Keate by refusing to accept arbitration. The Keate Award duly found for Waterboer. According to plan, he then offered his territory—which was taken to include the diamond diggings as well as the Dikgatlhong and Borigelong *merafe*—to Britain. Barkly immediately proclaimed it the British Crown Colony of Griqualand West on 27 October 1871.

Jantjie soon discovered that the new colony encompassed most of his Dikgatlhong *morafe*, but did not include Manyeding on the Ghaap plateau beyond its northern boundary. Deeply disgruntled, Jantjie moved to Manyeding but continued to regard his adherents still living in Griqualand West as his subjects. Botlasitse's *morafe* was also split, with Borigelong left in Griqualand West but with his main town of Phokwani on the other side of the border. And to add salt to the two *dikgosis*' wounds, the British decided to recognize Mankuruwane of Dithakong, Mahura's successor, as paramount of all the Batlhaping left outside the boundaries of the new crown colony.

The Keate Award created enormous resentment in the Boer republics. The OFS continued to protest and in 1876 the Cape Supreme Court, under instruction by the British government to end the issue, found that Waterboer had in fact no claim to the disputed territory. The Crown paid the OFS £90,000 in 'compensation'—a bargain if ever there was one. Jantjie and Botlasitse received nothing for the loss of their territory, even though Waterboer's claim to it was entirely discredited.

Barkly was anxious to slot Griqualand West securely into the envisioned South African confederation, and hoped that the Cape would make this easy by incorporating the new colony. But Molteno's ministry, which drew much of its support from the 'Old Colonists' (those descended from the original Dutch settlers), saw the annexation of Griqualand West as a betrayal of Boer—and especially OFS—interests, and would not cooperate. So there was nothing for it but to ensure that the fledgling crown colony was put on a sufficiently stable footing for it to take its own place in the confederation. The daunting commission was assigned to Major Owen Lanyon, another of Wolseley's 'Ring' who had served under him during the Asante campaign, and he took his post as Administrator of Griqualand West on 26 September 1875.[20]

Lanyon was melancholic and unapproachable.[21] He developed little empathy for Griqualand West, which he dismissed as 'the most hideous and disgusting place it has ever been my misfortune to enter'.[22] Nevertheless, he was highly ambitious and efficient, and being a professional soldier he ran his administration on military lines. As Carnarvon's approved man on the spot, and fully committed to the confederation idea, he did his best to groom Griqualand West to play its part. Yet by March 1877 he was certain it could only do so under Cape administration, just as Barkly had originally intended. He persuaded his superiors accordingly, but the solution was messy. The Griqualand West Annexation Act of 27 July 1877 placed Griqualand

West under Cape rule, but the approval of the Cape parliament was still necessary before this act could actually come into effect. Such approval was not forthcoming until 18 October 1880, and by then confederation was already close to being a dead letter.[23]

Meanwhile, Lanyon pushed on with reordering Griqualand West. He decided that entitlement to land must be determined by valid, individual title deed only, and in 1877 gave Major Charles Warren of the Royal Engineers the task of framing a land settlement based on this principle. Warren's settlement allowed only some sixteen per cent of Griqua title claims. It thereby dispossessed the Griqua of most of their traditionally held land and turned them into squatters on the farms held by land speculators and new white settlers. This was hardly what the Griqua had envisaged when they embraced British rule in 1871, and they were deeply disaffected.[24] As for the Batlhaping, Lanyon instructed Warren to set aside locations of arable land where they were already settled in concentrated numbers, and to exclude the large tracts of grazing land that had been so essential to the indigenous economy. This freed-up pasturage was earmarked for freehold settler farms, and surveying commenced in November 1876. And lest there be any doubt where power now lay, in August 1876 Lanyon made it clear that former African rulers no longer possessed any political authority in the crown colony.

Unsurprisingly, the Batlhaping were deeply angered by what they regarded as the seizure of their land, and rejected the boundary which divided those Batlhaping living inside Griqualand West from those who found themselves outside the crown colony. The Batlhaping inside the colony started removing the offensive surveyors' flags demarcating settler farms, and Botlasitse's people regularly knocked down the stone boundary beacons that divided their *morafe* in two. In 1877 Botlasitse, settled now in Phokwani north of the border, began demanding tribute from white farmers who had settled on his old lands in Griqualand West. Provocatively, he started collecting 'compensation' from them by way of cattle raids. By October 1877 (just when Griffith was ravaging Gcalekaland) Lanyon had come to the conclusion that something decisive had to be done to teach the bumptious Batlhaping who was master in Griqualand West.[25]

What gave him pause was the number of firearms he knew to be in Batlhaping and Griqua hands. As he subsequently put it to Frere, the 'moral effect of giving a native a gun is to make him think he is on a par with the European', whereas 'he should be treated as a child, and as such, dangerous weapons should be kept out of his reach'.[26] The problem was that Kimberley merchants were proving only too pleased to profit by the arms trade. When he saw trouble brewing in the colony in 1877, Lanyon tried to put a hold on the trade. He had a strong supporter in the Colonial Secretary, Sir Michael Hicks Beach, who agreed that 'the possession of arms by natives is a source of great danger to the South African Colonies'. However, as Hicks Beach was well aware, 'the effectual repression of the evil' required that all the states of South Africa adopt a common policy of arms control, and by the time he wrote stating so in April 1878, fighting had already broken out in Griqualand West.[27]

CHAPTER 14

Resisting with 'Fixity of Purpose'

B Y late 1877 the British authorities in Griqualand West were aware that many Batlhaping were declaring openly that the British had unjustly encroached on their lands and that 'they would resist by fighting even if they lost'.[1] It was Andries Mothibi, *Kgosi* Botlasitse's intemperate half-brother, who turned words into action. In October 1877, with armed men at his back, Andries ordered white settlers off the land around Borigelong, just within the borders of Griqualand West and formerly part of Botlasitse's *morafe*. The magistrate stationed at Barkly West scurried north and arrested him, but a threatening crowd of some two hundred Batlhaping men, many of them armed, rescued Andries who slipped back across the border. Even though Lanyon smartly led fifty of his constabulary north from Kimberley and arrested seventeen of the Borigelong 'rioters', he found that the Batlhaping were undaunted and continued to threaten and raid farmers, driving their rustled cattle back over the border to Phokwani.[2]

Lanyon, ever one for swift, decisive action, resolved that he must punish Botlasitse to put an end to these incursions. Yet to mount a successful punitive raid required sufficient military force, and there were no imperial troops stationed in Griqualand West. The only full-time force available was the armed constabulary. From the outset the administration in Kimberley had encouraged the formation of volunteer settler units along the pattern in the Cape on order to help maintain law and order, and the Kimberley Light Horse and Du Toits Pan Hussars had been formed in 1876. They had amalgamated in 1877 as the Diamond Fields Horse (DFH),[3] and the young bloods who filled its ranks were keen and active. But in January 1878 Lanyon had to respond to urgent calls from the theatre of the Ninth Cape Frontier War for mounted infantry, and rushed the 110 volunteers of the DFH to King William's Town under the command of Major Charles Warren, RE. That left Lanyon as the sole professional officer in Griqualand West. Not that this fazed him. He relished the opportunity to excel in his own little war, and set about raising further volunteer corps from among the hardy diggers and farmers. In the coming months they would serve cheerfully under his strict but proficient command, and Lanyon would be proud that they did their job so well that he never once had to request the aid of imperial troops in putting down the 'disturbances' in Griqualand West.[4]

On 21 January 1878 Lanyon rode out of Kimberley for the northern border to deal with what he termed the 'Battapins'. He had under his command about two hundred white volunteers eager for adventure and avid for booty (because that was the only form of payment they could expect), along with about a hundred African mercenaries recruited at the diggings and paid in cash to exercise their warrior skills.[5] Botlasitse hurriedly decamped before Lanyon could arrive, leaving the women, children and the elderly behind in Phokwani. Lanyon restrained his hard-bitten volunteers from looting and raping, but had them scour every house for firearms, and they collected a fine haul of muskets as well as a few modern rifles. When he withdrew, Lanyon drove off 445 cattle as a 'fine' and auctioned them off in Kimberley. Lanyon was promoted lieutenant-colonel for his successful strike but, as the missionaries at Kuruman feared it would, the raid simply roused the Batlhaping in a universal call for vengeance.

To complicate matters for Lanyon, trouble was brewing at the very opposite end of Griqualand West, along the Orange River. At the time of the *Mfecane* a small group of amaXhosa had settled along the Orange River below its confluence with the Vaal in a vicinity known as Prieschap, or 'the place of the she-goat' in Khoesan. Now the remote Karoo village of Prieska, it was directly south of Griquatown. From the 1850s these Prieska amaXhosa—or 'Pramberg Kaffirs', as they were known to the colonial authorities; also called 'Kaal [Naked] Kaffirs' to distinguish them from the Griqua and others who wore European dress—were steadily shouldered out of their grazing lands south of the Orange by advancing colonial settlement. They consequently began to graze their herds on Griqua land between Prieska and the Langeberg, the remote, desolate mountain range on the margins of the southern Kalahari Desert straddling the Griqualand West border. When he made his land settlement in 1877, Warren refused to recognize any of the Prieska amaXhosa land claims north of the Orange River, leaving them deeply resentful.[6]

In late 1877 when news began to filter through from the Eastern Cape of early Xhosa successes in the Ninth Cape Frontier War, the disaffected Prieska amaXhosa were greatly encouraged. They too were warriors of the same stock, and burned to prove it. By March 1878 rumours were circulating in Griqualand West that they were urging the other indigenous peoples that the moment had arrived to throw off the white oppressors. The Batlhaping outside the province still held back, but many Griqua, dispossessed in their land and betrayed by the British, were eager to act. Their grandfathers had raided far and wide, and they too could prove themselves men of mettle. Others remained cautious. One prominent Griqua, Gert Bezuidenhout, later admitted that he had 'heard whispers of this foolish undertaking for six months past' but that he had warned people that 'any resistance to the English government would be useless'.[7] Nikolaas Waterboer himself also prudently held back, but the authorities were nevertheless certain he was surreptitiously implicated, and Lanyon exiled him to Hopetown.[8] Certainly, few Griqua would have been unsympathetic towards those who actively rebelled. Many Korana were also disposed to answer the call to rise up in revolt because they too had suffered in Warren's land settlement, and possessed a tradition as fearless, resourceful fighters. They took to their impenetrable island stronghold in the middle of the Orange River and recommenced their old raiding ways.[9]

Rebellion finally broke out along the Orange River in April 1878. The widely recognized leader was Donker Malgas, and his three hundred or so followers-in-arms were a combination of Prieska ama-Xhosa, Griqua and Korana.[10] The 'rebels' (which is what the British invariably called them) raided trading stores and farms south-west of Griquatown, killing a few herdsmen and colonists and then driving off the large herds of rustled cattle, sheep and goats over the colonial border to the southern Langeberg. These mountains already had an unsavoury reputation as a haunt of gunrunners and bandits who traded stolen livestock. Gravely alarmed, white farmers in the area on both sides of the Orange River began to trek away or to go into laager.[11]

Lanyon had to act at once to suppress the 'rebels' with what forces he had available—and, in truth, he welcomed the opportunity to demonstrate his military skills at the head of his tough settler volunteers, eager as ever for excitement and loot. On 2 May Lanyon reached Koegas on the Orange River (two hundred miles from Kimberley) with a force of about 150 volunteers, constabulary and a motley taggle of burghers and loyal Griqua.

The campaign began as it would continue over six gruelling, exasperating months of ambushes, skirmishes and indecisive fire-fights, all waged over the harshest, most unforgiving terrain of stony, arid, limitless plains, and in deep kloofs surrounded by krantzes, rocky, overhanging cliff-faces. Most of the fighting took place during the bitter winter months with nights of hard frost and intense cold that made camping in the open intensely miserable for all combatants and cruelly probed inadequate clothing.

On 3 May a British patrol was lured into an ambush and the unsalted troops fled in such a panic that Lanyon, who came up with reinforcements, could not rally them. He let them go, and with his fresh troops settled down to a fire-fight of two hours, at the end of which the insurgents retired to a strong position made up of a succession of steep ridges. Lanyon dared not attack them without artillery support, and pulled back to his entrenched camp at Koegas to await developments.[12]

This stand-off set the pattern for the coming months. The 'rebel' forces were determined, mobile, entirely familiar with the lie of the land and knew how to make effective use of the terrain for cover. As hunters they were skilled, practised marksmen. The inventory of firearms confiscated from Nikolaas Waterboer's house in mid-June 1878 gives some indication of the variety in the hands of the 'rebels', and of the high proportion of good, modern weapons: seven flintlock muskets, two muzzle-loading rifles, two breech-loading carbines and four excellent rifles of the latest design.[13] As Warren ruefully reported after an encounter in late June:

the enemy engaged with a greater fixity of purpose, far greater
knowledge of military tactics, and more determined resistance than
the Kafirs [amaXhosa] have as a general rule shown in the Colonial
frontier war, and possessed a far greater proportion of good shots
and superior weapons, there being many rifles of long range among
them.[14]

Indeed, as the British would discover in 1880/81, fighting these
Africans was little different from engaging Boer forces in the Transvaal.
Lanyon soon learned that in this scrambling, skirmishing style of
warfare mounted men were of limited value, and that 'all our work will
be best performed by infantry'.[15] Casualties were kept low as the two
sides typically sniped at each at a distance from behind rocks or breastworks for hours at a stretch. In the end what regularly gave the British
an edge was artillery fire from their 7-pounder RML steel mountain
guns with their maximum range of 3,200 yards.[16] Explosive shells and
shrapnel bursts disrupted insurgent manoeuvres over more open ground,
and flushed them out from behind their defences, giving the British the
opportunity to advance and capture their positions.

Lanyon was no sooner back in Koegas in May 1878 than the magistrate in Griquatown was appealing for aid against fresh 'rebel' forces
raiding determinedly between the town and the Orange River. Lanyon
rode to the rescue with thirty-four horsemen and on 22 May engaged
the insurgents three miles south of Griquatown at Jackal's Vlei.
Throughout the skirmish he was exposed to enemy fire on his 'old white
horse' but was only struck by a few rock splinters. Once more the
fighting was indecisive, and the insurgents fell back on Langeberg where
they were too strongly ensconced to be attacked.[17]

Distances were too great over the vast, empty spaces of Griqualand
West and the British forces too small to keep a close watch on 'rebel'
activity which began hotting up again close to the Orange. Fortunately
for the British, the various insurgent groups lacked coordination, so
even if it was a stretch, it was possible to contain them in detail. Thus,
on 29 May while Lanyon was still in Griquatown, about six hundred
insurgents, both mounted and on foot, attacked the entrenched camp
at Koegas held by Inspector R.E. Nesbitt and a reduced garrison. For
an hour and a half the 'rebels' kept up their fire from the surrounding

hills and the cover of a nearby donga before slipping away.[18] Fortunately for the Koegas garrison, Warren (now a lieutenant-colonel) was at last on the march back from the Eastern Cape with the DFH in response to Lanyon's urgent request, and reinforced Nesbitt on 31 May. Strong enough now to take the offensive, he led out a mounted patrol on 3 June, surprised the insurgents and captured 1,700 sheep.

On 9 June Warren sallied out again from Koegas and engaged the 'rebels' at Whitehuis Kloof where they had concentrated with their herds and families. He adopted successful tactics that were to become the British hallmark in the coming months. Aware of Warren's advance, the insurgents held the mouth of the kloof in force to deny entry to the British, and had their livestock penned behind them. Warren sent part of his force up the steep hills to surprise the 'rebels' in their rear, and a tough fire-fight then ensued among the krantzes and kloofs. Warren was engaging the insurgents for the first time, and found that their adept use of cover made them 'difficult folk to shoot off the rocks'. He also discovered, as he would again in the future, that while they were prepared to resist 'with tenacity at close quarters', their firing, which was accurate at a distance (as it would be for hunting), fell off markedly during the stress of looming hand-to-hand fighting. The discomforted 'rebels' slipped away, leaving behind their livestock, sheep, cattle and some horses, which were their material wealth and main means of subsistence. Warren claimed to have killed about thirty 'rebels', a number matching Nesbitt's tally six days earlier. However, these body-counts were always impressionistic and routinely exaggerated. By contrast, livestock were more accurately tallied because they possessed a monetary value and were subsequently publicly auctioned.[19]

It seemed to Warren and Lanyon that the 'rebels' were now on the run and holed up in the southern Langeberg, and that a knock-out blow against their stronghold at Paarde Kloof (where scouts reported them to be assembled) must end the campaign. After toiling through heavy sands, Warren's column halted for the night on 17 June six miles from Paarde Kloof. He had under his command 140 white troops: the DFH, the volunteer units called the One Star Brigade and Diamond Light Infantry, and burghers. Crucially, they had dragged a mule-drawn 7-pounder field gun along with them. Twenty-six Zulu auxiliaries completed the force.[20] The insurgents spied their campfires that night, and prepared for the attack they knew would come the following morning. Paarde Kloof is a deep valley cutting into the Langeberg with krantzes and hills rising eight hundred feet on either side. The ledges of living rock form natural breastworks behind which the approximately 350 defenders ensconced themselves, banking on holding off the British with superior marksmanship.

Warren moved to the attack at 7 a.m. on the morning of 18 June, and tried to form his men up in a skirmishing line at the entrance to the kloof across which the insurgents had erected and manned stone breastworks. The British found themselves caught in a galling cross-fire from the hillsides about 600 to 800 yards away, as well as facing fire from the breastworks straight ahead. Warren admitted the 'rebels' made 'excellent shooting', and that Samuel Fortuin, a famous Griqua crack shot, was among them. Warren realized the flanking krantzes were too strongly held to be taken, so he ordered the 7-pounder to shell the breastworks straight ahead. It did so with accuracy and subdued the fire coming from them. Warren, with himself in the lead, charged the breastworks in a sudden rush, broke through, and then started rolling up the insurgent flanks. The entire British line then advanced and slowly drove back the insurgents who tenaciously disputed every position. It was now the turn of the British to catch them in an enfilading fire, and the 7-pounder shelled them whenever they tried to make a stand at the next line of rocks.

At that moment, with the battle already won, Lanyon arrived in a cloud of dust and bugle calls at the head of seventy-five mounted men after a dramatic night march from Griquatown. But he stood back and allowed Warren to complete the operations he had begun. The kloof was crammed with livestock—two thousand oxen, two thousand sheep and two thousand horses—and the insurgents tried to drive them over the mountains as they retreated. But the British prevented them with artillery fire and continued skirmishing until sunset, flushing the insurgents out of every crevice and from behind every rock. At the end of the day, besides abandoning all their precious livestock, the retreating fighting men left behind a hundred women along with their wagons. The British lost one man killed and the 'rebels' about thirty-five, including a number of leaders, among whom the victors optimistically numbered Donker Malgas who, in fact, lived to fight another day.

Lanyon and Warren kept up the pressure. After a few days of preliminary skirmishing, on 25 June they attacked the insurgents who had fallen back further to the heights above Witsand.[21] This was extremely rough and rugged terrain, a jumble of high hills and deep kloofs, strewn with large boulders. Lanyon divided his forces of 230 men into two columns with the intention of catching the 'rebels' in a pincer movement. Lanyon advanced his men across a wide valley, keeping them under the cover of a ridge of rocks. From this cover he pinned the 'rebels' down in a fire-fight and waited for Warren to appear in their rear. When he did, the insurgents retired, as ever doggedly disputing every position. Some made a final stand in a cave in a deep kloof, and kept up a constant fire on Warren's men who worked forward close enough to the cave to parley. The defenders shouted they would die there, but were eventually persuaded first to send out the women and children, then the old men, and after them the boys. In the end the die-hards surrendered too. About eighty fighters fell prisoner to the British as well as five hundred women and an even greater number of children who were sheltering freezing and famished in nearby caves. The British were satisfied that three of their principal leaders had perished in the fighting, namely Samuel Fortuin, the crack shot, Gamka (alias Jean Pienaar) and Stoffel van Wyk.

Highly satisfied with the results, on 26 June Lanyon departed for Kimberley leaving Warren as Officer Commanding Griqualand West Field Forces to mop up what was left of 'rebel' resistance. While on his way Lanyon reached the little settlement of Campbell where he learned that an insurgent attack was being planned. He vigorously set about preparing the place's defences, and on 28 June was in command to face an attack mounted from all sides by a mixed force of Griqua, Prieska amaXhosa and Batlhaping. Lanyon's men finally drove off the attackers after several hours of heavy firing by making a dashing sortie that caught them in the flank.

Meanwhile, Warren had been sending out patrols to find where the defeated 'rebels' had gone, and ascertained that except for small parties of marauders they had moved north, out of Griqualand West. Satisfied that the Langeberg was now clear of insurgents, Warren moved north up the far, or western, side of the Langeberg with a column of 216 white troops and 20 amaZulu to cut off the 'rebels' who had attacked

Campbell. He reached Daniel's Kuil after a very difficult, thirsty march in intense cold under louring snow clouds, and there received word that the Batlhaping territory beyond the northern border was now aflame.

On 25 May 1878, at the very moment when Lanyon was being hard-pressed to contain the spreading revolt in the southern parts of Griqualand West, twenty armed men surrounded a small trading store in the north close to Daniel's Kuil. The raiders were a mixed group of Griqua, Batlhaping and Batlharo, another Batswana people from the dry regions to the west of Kuruman. They all held grievances against the store's owner, James Burness, who was a local field-cornet and was actively involved in enforcing adherence to the surveyor's beacons in the region.[22] They gunned Burness down on his verandah as he attempted to reason with them, shot his brother when he went for his shotgun, and then killed his distraught wife as she bent over his body. Their nasty work done, the raiders fled over the border to the territory of *Kgosi* Morwe of the Batlharo whose chief town was Batlaros, downstream of Kuruman, and holed up in his secondary town of Koning, twenty miles to the south of the mission.

It seems Morwe was eager to begin a general uprising, but Jantjie and the Batlhaping were still unwilling to be sucked in, and Jantjie did his best to convince the missionaries and traders at Kuruman that they had nothing to fear. But they knew that the more than five hundred guns and ammunition arms dealers had stashed at the mission would make an irresistible target. The Revd John Mackenzie advised all whites in the vicinity to take refuge in the recently completed and solidly built training seminary, the Moffatt Institute, across the river from the mission. It was none too soon, for on 26 May Morwe and a party of armed men camped outside Kuruman and then rode provocatively through its streets. For his part, Jantjie found it increasingly difficult to dissuade his zealous young warriors from taking up arms to assert their manhood, and fled to the improvised fort at the Moffatt Institute to take sanctuary with Mackenzie.

In Kimberley, Lanyon had left Judge J.D. Barry in charge while he was away on campaign. Barry responded to the Burness 'outrage' by ordering John H. Ford, the government surveyor (and surely a provocative choice in itself considering the widespread resentment over the land settlement), to muster a force of mounted volunteers and proceed north to arrest the killers. Lanyon approved, for he intended to give 'these people . . . so severe a lesson as will prevent their again going against us'.[23] Nevertheless, he urged some caution. Not only did he place little faith in the untested Ford's military competence, but he did not wish to antagonize *Kgosi* Mankuruwane at Taung (whom the British regarded as the Batlhaping paramount) by crossing his territory uninvited to attack Morwe's town of Koning.[24] So on 16 July he ordered Ford to make no more than a 'demonstration' of force on the British side of the border, and only to ride to the rescue of Kuruman if it was directly threatened.[25]

Ford was soon on his way with eighty mounted settler volunteers, ten white infantry and a force of thirty-two Mfengu and other African auxiliaries recruited from the diggings. He was spoiling for a fight. He secured Mankuruwane's permission to enter his territory, and on 30 June crossed the border in disregard of Lanyon's orders.[26] Luka, Jantjie's son, was at Manyeding when he learned that Ford's commando was advancing in his direction. On 2 July he led eleven mounted men forward to reconnoitre. At Kho they encountered five scouts riding out ahead of Ford's column who called on them to halt. When they would not, Captain D'Arcy of the Barkly Rangers opened fire and injudiciously pursued Luka's men who fell back firing expertly from the saddle until they reached a little rise. Six more of Luka's men were stationed there on foot, and the horsemen dismounted to join them in making a stand. The eighteen Batlhaping—all of them experienced hunters and splendid shots—pinned down D'Arcy's scouts. Ford sent up another thirty men in support, but although outnumbered two to one, Luka's men still had the best of the fire-fight which went on all afternoon from about 3 p.m. until sunset. When Ford's chastened men finally withdrew, they carried back five dead comrades and Ford's son, who was mortally wounded. Ford himself was wounded in the lower leg. By a strange coincidence, Luka was also wounded below the knee, but only one of his men was killed.

Kho was only a minor skirmish, but ever since the Batlhaping have kept its memory alive as a great victory over the invading English.[27] More prosaically, the encounter meant the Batlhaping could no longer avoid being drawn into hostilities with the British. Jantjie himself left Kuruman and withdrew with most of his family to Dithakong, thirty miles away. Ford and his mauled column holed up in the Moffatt Institute on 9 July. Except for a patrol by the Barkly Rangers that attacked Koning and drove off the surviving defenders to the northern Langeberg, Ford remained inactive in Kuruman waiting to be rescued.

When Lanyon arrived back in Kimberley on 4 July and learned of Ford's humiliating debacle, he ordered Warren's column at Daniel's Kuil to hurry north to relieve Ford and restore British prestige. Warren reached Kuruman on 14 July and started putting some backbone into Ford's demoralized troops. Lanyon himself rode wearily into Kuruman on 16 July and wasted no time before going onto the offensive. An eighteen-mile night march up the dry Kuruman valley with half his available forces (about 250 men) and a 7-pounder field gun[28] brought them at dawn on 18 July to the Batlharo village of Gamopedi where Lanyon believed some of the Burness killers had taken refuge.[29]

Lanyon's field gun lobbed six rounds into the slumbering village before the rudely aroused men in Gamopedi could rally on a ridge to the south-west of the village where they hastily threw up stone breastworks. For an hour they kept the British back with accurate fire, killing two of the Zulu auxiliaries. Finally, outflanked by Warren at the head of the DFH, Diamond Contingent and Barkly Rangers, they fell back to the surrounding hills. Lanyon's men then overran and plundered the village. At least fifty of the defenders, and numbers of women and children too, were killed by the artillery fire and in the fighting, and the British rounded up their cattle, sheep and goats for subsequent auction in Kimberley.

Meanwhile, at the town of Dithakong where Jantjie, Luka and many of their adherents had taken refuge, *Kgosi* Merwe of the Dithakong agreed to join the common cause in defending the Batlhaping *morafe* against the British invaders. News of the carnage at Gamopedi only determined them to make a stand at the historic Batlhaping capital. Generations of Batlhaping had regarded it as their inviolable stronghold, and it was the site of the famous battle of 23 June 1823 when they had thrown back the raiders unleashed by the *Difaqane*. Now, Dithakong must withstand the British. Over the following days further armed men trickled in until about five hundred were gathered at Dithakong.

Preparations for the defence of Dithakong against Lanyon's inevitable attack were assigned to Luka, the victor of Kho.[30] The town lay on the southern side of the dry river bed of the Mashowing, defenceless as Gamopedi had been against artillery. But on the far side of the river bed steep slopes rose up to a long ridge north-east of the town. Luka and his lieutenants decided to hold the ridge rather than the town, and concluded that the British would storm it across the open plain from the north rather than from the south across the river bed. In the days before the British attacked, the Batlhaping frantically improvised defences along the ridge. The ridge was studded with 508 circular live-stock enclosures, each about sixteen feet across, which had been built centuries before of rough, dry-stone walling. The defenders connected these kraals with more stone walling to create a stone network with interconnecting passages they hoped would foil any attacker. They also strengthened the stone walls along the northern foot of the ridge.

By 23 July Lanyon was at Bothikong, thirteen miles north-west of Dithakong, with about four hundred men. In preparation for the coming battle, *Kgosi* Merwe sent all the civilians away from Dithakong, and Luka, because he was still suffering badly from the wound to his leg, left too in a wagon with his father, Jantjie. They journeyed north for over two hundred miles until they had crossed the Molopo River to find sanctuary among the Bangwaketse people in what is now Botswana.

The armed Batlhaping at Dithakong took up their posts on the evening of 23 July in the stone enclosures along the ridge. All of them carried firearms, and all wore coats, trousers and hats although they kept warm during the icily clear, starry winter night under traditional skin karosses. As Luka had correctly anticipated, on the morning of 24 July Lanyon's force approached from the north-west, halting out of rifle range before the ridge. At about 10 a.m. Lanyon's three field guns began their bombardment of the ridge. For the next three hours the defenders took what cover they could from the explosive shells, suffering most of the casualties inflicted on them that day.

At 1 p.m. Lanyon decided the Batlhaping defences were sufficiently softened up to order the assault. The artillery ceased firing as the section of troops on Lanyon's right—a troop of DFH, Barkly Rangers and Zulu auxiliaries—advanced to the western flank of the ridge while the main body—Warren and rest of the DFH, the Diamond Light Infantry and the Diamond Contingent—attacked it directly along its length. The ridge was certainly a formidable position to take by assault.

The well-armed Batlhaping had plenty of ammunition and their firing was disconcertingly well directed. But the attackers were not Ford's amateurs. They were troops well seasoned in the campaign against the Griqua and their allies, and they advanced steadily, taking cover behind the rocks strewing the slopes. After hotly exchanging fire for over an hour with the attackers, the Batlhaping decided the enemy had come too close and pulled back down the southern slopes of the ridge to their rear. Like the Griqua and Korana, theirs was the Boer style of sniping warfare at a distance, and they had little stomach for actual hand-to-hand fighting in the complex of kraals and stone walls.

The defenders left thirty-nine dead behind them. Despite having stormed a fortified position, Lanyon lost only two white troopers and two Zulu auxiliaries. He was cock-a-hoop at his victory which, because of the historic significance of Dithakong, he later declared to have been 'by far the most decisive during the war'.[31] Over the next few days after the battle the victors scoured Dithakong and the villages and cattle-posts in its vicinity for booty with which to pay the volunteers. The haul this time was prodigious, and left the Batlhaping seriously impoverished for years to come. The loot was put up for sale in Kimberley on Tuesday 13 August and continuing every day for the rest of the week. Among the items advertised for sale were 3,600 head of cattle, six thousand sheep and goats, 63 wagons with their spans of oxen, as well as ostrich feathers, ivory, karosses and rifles.[32]

Before Lanyon could return to Kimberley, however, he had unfinished business to complete in Taung. On 18 July, the same day as the fight at Gamopedi, about two hundred raiders under a number of Botlasitse's brothers had attacked Francis Thompson's farm at Cornforth Hill. They killed Thompson, although his son and badly injured nephew managed to escape. The raiders then fled north beyond Taung to Modimong in Mankuruwane's *morafe*. This placed Mankuruwane in an extremely uncomfortable position. To placate Lanyon who was steadily approaching with all his forces, the paramount himself attacked Modimong to prove his loyalty, informing Lanyon that he was 'still the friend of the Queen as before'.[33] Awkwardly for him, though, Botlasitse and the rest of his family were far too conveniently allowed to escape. Thoroughly unimpressed, Lanyon imposed a fine of a thousand cattle on his unreliable and now very disillusioned ally.[34]

Lanyon and the volunteers returned to Kimberley on 19 August to a rousing welcome as conquering heroes, but he knew very well that Griqualand West was still not entirely pacified. On 22 September, in a final push to snuff out all lingering resistance, he dispatched two forces from Kimberley. The stronger column under Warren went north to Batlhaping territory to finish off Botlasitse, and the smaller force south to the Griqua country where, undeterred and stubborn, insurgents had returned to the Langeberg and recommenced their raiding.

While Warren was still on the road to Dikgatlhong, a die-hard force of Prieska amaXhosa, Griqua and Khoesan sallied out from their stronghold in the Langeberg and attacked the southern column, driving it into Griquatown. Warren immediately wheeled about to assist. Alarmed that this redeployment left his northern frontier exposed, Lanyon secured fifty Mounted Infantry from the Transvaal to secure Kuruman. As for the Langeberg raiders, once they realized Warren was marching in their direction they hurriedly fell back to the mountains.[35]

Exasperated that he had not eliminated the Langeberg 'rebels' in his earlier June campaign, Warren was determined that this time they should not get away. Dividing his column of five hundred men into three detachments because of the severe lack of water for horses and oxen, he hurried in pursuit across the arid wastes. In the second week of October Warren caught up with the insurgents in a rocky kloof of the Langeberg, about four miles in length, through which the insignificant Gamayana stream trickles from the heights above to dissipate westwards into the sands of the Kalahari.[36]

At this season, before the coming of the scant summer rains, the river was completely dry, and over 1,300 fighting men and their families were crowded into the basin, along with their horses, cattle and sheep. The Prieska amaXhosa were under Donker Malgas, the Griqua under Gamka (alias Jean Pienaar) and the Khoesan under Sampu. Nonetheless, it seemed a good place to make a stand because the only feasible approach was along the valley from the west. The insurgents constructed a breastwork of rocks and boulders across the entrance and believed their flanks and rear to be protected by the high rocky krantzes either side.

Indeed, when Warren advanced on 11 October up the valley as anticipated, his men spent a very uncomfortable day pinned down before the barricade by the insurgents' accurate fire. Warren therefore had to try a different approach. He decided to attack the 'rebels' from behind the position they were defending and over terrain they believed inaccessible, and fixed on the Gobatse Heights, overlooking the valley a thousand feet below from the north-east. This was hardly an easy approach, and it took Warren's men seven hours on the morning of 14 October to scramble to the top of Gobatse, lugging along a 7-pounder mountain gun with its limber and ammunition. They got the gun into position by mid-morning before the defenders at the barricade became aware that the British had completely outflanked them and now commanded their position. When they did catch sight of the British above and behind them, the defenders experienced considerable initial alarm and confusion. Then, with commendable military acumen, they rapidly did a complete about-face and took excellent cover on some ridges of boulder-strewn krantzes that faced the British a mile away across the low-lying hills of the valley basin. Rather taken aback by the effective Griqua response, Warren extended his line along the heights on his side of the valley, and ordered the advance.

While two dismounted troops of the DFH went down a ridge on Warren's extreme right to outflank the 'rebels' behind the nearest krantz, the gun shelled the floor of the basin ahead of them to deter the insurgents who were trying in turn to outflank them. The rest of the British forces then came straight down the steep hillside, Mounted Infantry on the right, the Diamond Light Infantry to their left and a detachment of African levies from the mines of Kimberley beyond them. The well-armed insurgents again proved themselves more than competent shots, and to move forward the discomforted troops had to make crouching rushes from boulder to boulder, finding it disconcertingly 'like fighting experienced and desperate white troops'.[37] Consequently, as on the initial day's fighting at the breastwork, and as in so many previous engagements in this campaign, the British advance turned into a stalemate with both sides exchanging fire from behind cover.

Then after five hours, the defenders lost heart and probably began to run low on ammunition as well. As soon as they began to fall back and their fire weakened, Warren ordered the charge with fixed bayonets. Once again, the insurgents baulked at close fighting to which they were entirely unaccustomed. They abandoned their positions along the lines of krantzes and withdrew westwards over the slopes behind them. At about 4 p.m. those still manning the breastwork across the valley entrance also fled, joining what had swiftly turned into a rout. The defeated 'rebels' rapidly fading into the desert beyond the Langeberg left behind them nine hundred cattle, twenty-two wagons, all their old people, women and children and those too lame or ill to escape. The fighting in the Langeberg was over.

A fortnight later, on 2 November, a patrol of burghers from Victoria West in the Northern Cape tracked down the last resisters along the Orange River in the thick bush near Koegas. The hunted band of Prieska amaXhosa and Khoesan were at their last gasp. They had only three firearms between them, and had to rely mainly on their bows and arrows to defend themselves against the well-armed burghers. Unsurprisingly, the encounter turned into a massacre, and the patrol killed forty-six men along with ten women and children caught in their fire.[38]

This atrocity caused some fleeting concern in Cape official circles, and was not the first in the campaign to do so. Six weeks before, Lanyon had indignantly refuted charges by the Aborigines' Protection Society that his Griqualand West volunteers—whom (he declared) it had been his 'pride and pleasure to lead'—had committed atrocities.[39] But Warren rather gave the game away when he drew attention to the 'treacherous nature' of his adversaries and their many wiles such as feigned surrender which, he obliquely admitted, made it dangerous to take them alive.[40] Quite clearly, armed 'rebels' were regularly shot rather than allowed to surrender, and there could be no denying that this had been a cruel, dirty campaign, only too typical of counter-insurgency operations.

Following his victory at the Gobatse Heights in the Langeberg, Warren returned to Batlhaping territory. He spent the next three months on an intimidating military tour between the Griqualand West border and the Molopo River to the north, ensuring the submission of the Batswana *dikgosi* who (for fear of being attacked or fined) routinely requested British protection.[41] On 13 November Lanyon signed an amnesty for all insurgents 'save those principally engaged',[42] and Warren's commission was to round up the main offenders still at large. The submissive northern *dikgosi* scrambled to demonstrate their new-found loyalty, and Luka, Botlasitse and others whom the British wanted were all handed over and imprisoned in Kimberley. Only the aged Jantjie was allowed to retire to Manyeding to live out his days.[43] Most of the prisoners were released in January 1879 and indentured as labourers to white farmers. Others were put on trial in

June 1879 for murder, but all except five were acquitted for lack of evidence. Those found guilty were jailed on the lesser charge of 'public violence or riot and assault'. Luka, Botlasitse, Merwe and other prominent men remained in Kimberley as 'state prisoners'. Finally, as part of the arrangement to merge Griqualand West into the Cape Colony, and because he believed peace was fully restored, Frere decided in 31 May 1880 to let them go free to their locations.[44]

The suppression of what a relieved Lord Chelmsford[45] characterized as 'a very troublesome rebellion' in Griqualand West[46]—a campaign officially called the Northern Border War—meant the removal of a distracting obstacle from the high road to confederation. More parochially, it spelled the final closing of the Northern Cape frontier and the subjugation of the Griqua, Batlhaping, Prieska amaXhosa, Korana and Khoesan. Their subject status was reinforced in the aftermath of Isandlwana in January 1879 when Warren ordered the general disarmament of all 'natives' in Griqualand West and they surrendered hundreds of firearms.[47] White landowners were content because their land claims were now secure and their African labourers back at work. The members of the One Star Contingent (one of the volunteer units Lanyon had led during the rebellion) expressed the settler position perfectly in an address of thanks in which they stated their admiration for the manner in which their old commander had 'unflinchingly shared the hardships and dangers in the late struggle between advancing civilization and barbarism in this Province and neighbouring territories'.[48]

Lanyon's superiors were equally pleased with his services, all the more so since they agreed with him in viewing the suppressed rebellion as yet another manifestation of the widespread black conspiracy threatening to sweep away white supremacy everywhere in southern Africa.[49] As Lanyon put it to Frere in November 1878 when insisting upon the absolute need ruthlessly to check 'armed disaffection' everywhere in South Africa:

> There is much evidence of concert between distant and apparently unconnected outbreaks here [Griqualand West] and elsewhere, and if there is anything like a combination among the evil-disposed in different Kafir tribes, there is no surer means of encouraging its spread than by delaying the complete reassertion of the authority of the Government.[50]

The First Anglo-Pedi War, 1878

CHAPTER 15

'The Ground Was His'

U NNERVED and smarting from his humiliation on Conference Hill in October 1877 at the hands of the representatives of the Zulu nation, Shepstone, the Administrator of the Transvaal, wrote to Carnarvon that 'the sooner the root of all evil, which I consider to be Zulu power and military organization is dealt with the easier our task will be.'[1] Meanwhile, because Shepstone firmly believed that Sekhukhune, the Maroteng paramount, was Cetshwayo's obedient ally,[2] he was determined to bring him to heel and force him to acknowledge that he was a subject of the Transvaal.

In fact, Sekhukhune was unwilling to become embroiled in Cetshwayo's disputes with the British. His overriding concern was not to surrender his status as an independent ruler. To that end he had to restore his authority over the Maroteng paramountcy which had been severely shaken by the Boer–Pedi War of 1876 to 1877 (see chapter 5).[3] Many subordinate chiefdoms—particularly those west of the Leolo Mountains, such as Masemola with its long history of revolt—had taken the opportunity to slip the Maroteng leash and sidle up to the authorities in Pretoria, first the Boers and then the British. Sekhukhune tried to bring his straying tributaries back through negotiation and when that failed he decided in early 1878 to use force. In taking that warlike path, he clearly believed that circumstances had shifted in his favour since the grim, drought-stricken months of late 1877. The new harvest promised to be a good one, and when he looked about him, he realized that Shepstone had no armed forces available in the vicinity of Bopedi with which to interfere with his plans.

Indeed, in June 1877 the cash-strapped Administrator had disbanded both the Middelburg and Lydenburg volunteers and had abandoned their bases at Forts Weeber and Burgers.[4] The only British troops in reach were three companies of the 1/13th Regiment forming the Pretoria garrison, but Shepstone dared not allow them to leave town. The delegation of disaffected Transvaal Boers contesting the legality of British annexation in April 1877 had recently returned bootless and angry from London. On 28 January 1878 a large, excited gathering at Naauwpoort had appointed a *Volkskomitee*, or People's Committee, to collect signatures protesting annexation. Shepstone was concerned this popular movement would lead to outright sedition and required the troops close by to keep a lid on discontent.[5]

Believing therefore that he had a reasonably free hand to act, Sekhukhune decided to tackle the Maserumule chiefdom west of the Leolo Mountains. Maserumule had been the most powerful of the Maroteng tributaries. In 1877 it split between supporters of Lekoglane, Sekhukhune's widowed sister, whom he had appointed regent for her young son, and Phokwane, the deceased chief's younger brother. Raid followed counter-raid between the two adversaries. On 8 February 1878 Sekhukhune at last threw his weight onto the scales and sent a regiment to assist his sister. But Phokwane had been making friendly overtures to the British, and they could not leave their useful ally in the lurch, especially since they preferred to suspect that in attacking him Sekhukhune was 'acting under the influence' of Cetshwayo.[6]

With no British troops to spare, in February 1878 Shepstone instructed Captain M. Clarke of the Royal Artillery, the Commissioner he had appointed to administer the Lydenburg District, to 'avail himself' of 'all the friendly Native tribes' in raising a force capable of protecting the people threatened by Sekhukhune.[7] Clarke responded in his own preferred way by putting together a force of twenty-five white volunteers, the Provisional Armed and Mounted Police, or PAMP, and sent them under Native Commissioner C. Schultz to re-occupy Fort Weeber which was close by Lekoglane's stronghold. Clarke reinforced them with a further 107 men of the Native Police Force under the command of L. Lloyd. Known popularly as the Zulu Police, these were Africans Shepstone was recruiting from Natal where he had so much residual influence with the black population. The Boers did not appreciate their armed presence, and suspected Shepstone of using his old African allies to overawe them. Be that as it may, Clarke believed he had gathered sufficient force to impose his will on Lekoglane. He peremptorily informed her that he was deposing her for allying herself with Sekhukhune, and that she must first pay a cattle fine and then go into exile.[8]

Sekhukhune was now in an impossible situation. He could not stand by and allow his sister to be displaced by Phokwane because this would be the signal for other chiefs west of the Leolo Mountains finally to shake loose from their allegiance to the Maroteng. Yet to take military action would bring on a clash with Clarke who was supporting the usurper and threaten to re-ignite the war against the Transvaal administration. Sekhukhune nevertheless attempted to thread the needle. On 2 March his emissaries informed Clarke that he was not 'a child', but was 'a man', and was going to 'punish these people who were once my children', but that 'the white people must remain quiet' and that he did 'not want to fight them'.[9] Clarke was unimpressed and sternly ordered Sekhukhune to take no action. But the paramount resolved that as the independent ruler he still firmly saw himself to be, he could brook no more interference, come what may. He responded uncompromisingly that Clarke 'and the English Government had gone the wrong way to work with him; that he would return to the Boers; that [the British] were afraid to fight . . . that the country was his . . . that he was quite ready for war . . . that he would not trouble the people at Fort Weeber, but that the ground was his'. On receiving this unequivocal message, Clarke gloomily concluded that although not at all well prepared for a campaign, a 'collision cannot now be avoided'.[10]

Sekhukhune immediately struck out both east and west. On 6 March a Pedi regiment appeared at Fort Burgers where George Eckersley (a former lieutenant in the Lydenburg Volunteers) was stationed as Clarke's eyes and ears. Eckersley wasted no time in decamping. Pedi warriors then began to roam the Lydenburg District, burning farmhouses and taking cattle. Panicking whites went into laager. To the west, Clarke pulled his forces out of Fort Weeber and the Bapedi burned it to the ground. Having demonstrated his willingness to defend his interests by military action, Sekhukhune then stood on the defensive.[11]

In Pretoria, Shepstone was thoroughly spooked by these developments. Harping on his favourite string, they were to him proof positive that Sekhukhune was being manipulated by Cetshwayo for his own fell purposes. To make matter worse, Shepstone and Clarke also believed that Sekhukhune was being egged on by seditious Boers in the Lydenburg District. Their suspicions fell primarily on Abel Erasmus, a prominent farmer who felt hard-done by the new British administration. Erasmus certainly had close contacts with Sekhukhune, keeping him informed of political developments and providing him with guns from Delagoa Bay in return for Pedi labour on his farms. It also seemed too much of a coincidence that when the Pedi regiments raided the Lydenburg District they left Boer farms alone and targeted only English-owned ones.[12] Perhaps not too much should be made of Sekhukhune's special pleading when held in captivity in December 1879 that 'it is the Boers who misled me and counselled me to resist.'[13] While there were certainly many Boers eager to find allies in their resistance to the British administration, Sekhukhune was doubtless as prepared to use them to achieve his own goals as they were to manipulate him.

Whatever the truth of the matter, at the time Shepstone and his officials (and the Berlin Missionary Society missionaries too, for good measure) all believed that a sinister Bapedi–amaZulu–Boer conspiracy was brewing. Already on 23 February 1878 Shepstone had written histrionically to Carnarvon that he needed more troops in the Transvaal because if Sekhukhune's power was not broken, there was a real risk of 'a general rising among the numerous native tribes'.[14] Armed with the latest news from Bopedi, Shepstone was absolutely convinced that the 'black conspiracy' to drive the whites out of the subcontinent was real and activated. To his mind, the only consolation was that because Africans were 'incapable of precise combination', whites would be 'alright' if they could 'roll one stone out of the way at a time'. And Shepstone had no doubt that 'Sikukuni is my first stone, confound him!'[15]

How to dislodge him, however, was the problem. In early March the only British forces in the Lydenburg District were the inadequate Zulu Police, the PAMP and whatever African levies could be raised from allied chiefs. But the imperial troops Shepstone had requested earlier were beginning to arrive. On 12 March three companies of the 90th Regiment marched from Pietermaritzburg for Utrecht to relieve three companies of the 1/13th Regiment stationed there. These in turn set off for Pretoria in order to free the garrison in the capital for operations in the eastern Transvaal. Meanwhile, the irregular forces there were beefed up. A second troop of mounted men for the PAMP were raised under Arthur Aylward to strengthen the defences of the town of Lydenburg, and a body of fifty special constables was organized from men of the gold fields to protect Pilgrim's Rest.[16] In addition, a force of fifty mounted white volunteers under Captain Gerrit van Deventer set off from Pretoria for Bopedi. As a result, Clarke over-optimistically believed that he could concentrate enough men without the assistance of regular troops to strike a blow at the stubborn Lekoglane and, through her, her brother Sekhukhune.

By the end of March 1878 Clarke had succeeded in assembling a respectable force at Fort Weeber, which he had reoccupied and rebuilt. It consisted of the Zulu Police, van Deventer's Pretoria volunteers and two Krupp 7-pounder guns, an African levy of a hundred and sixty men from the Waterberg District close to Pretoria, two hundred men furnished by Phokwane, and some four hundred more from other local chiefs who had decided to break loose from Sekhukhune's overlordship. On 5 April this motley force assaulted Lekoglane's fastness which was known by the same name as the chiefdom, Maserumule. Typically, it was built around a rocky conical hill with its sides densely covered with thorn bush. Clusters of huts had been constructed around the hill on platforms artificially levelled. Each cluster was defended by a wooden stockade and a hedge of prickly pear. The hillside was in places scarped, and the approaches leading from one platform to another were artfully fortified and flanked by rifle pits, creating a perilous labyrinth. Lekoglane's men were determined to defend the fastness, and Clarke found it far too tough an objective to carry by assault. Daunted, his African allies hung back under cover at the base of the hill and never went forward at all. The Zulu Police and volunteers got some way up the northern side of the hill before prudently withdrawing with several hundred captured cattle.[17]

This embarrassing setback forced Clarke and Shepstone to accept that with such forces they had no hope of capturing a stronghold such as Maserumule.[18] Instead, they fell back on the strategy the ZAR had adopted after its failure to take Tsate (see chapter 5). They built Fort Mamalube close to Fort Weeber in the west, and Fort Faught-a-ballagh ('Clear the way' in Gaelic) near Magnet Heights in the east to control the passes to the Tubatse valley. From these two small sod and stone forts surrounded by ditches, the mounted volunteers rode out to raid and disrupt Pedi agriculture and starve them into submission. This new approach worked well west of the Leolo Mountains. By June 1878, local people were telling Clarke that 'you know we are hungry and will be more so'.[19] Increasingly isolated and harried, towards the end of April Lekoglane gave up the struggle. She took refuge with Sekhukhune and her followers were broken up and redistributed among chiefs loyal to the British.[20]

Sekhukhune realized that with this debacle he had finally lost control of the subordinate chiefdoms west of the Pedi heartland. Ominously, he would have been informed that in mid-April three companies of the 1/13th Regiment (which had been relieved by the three companies from Utrecht) were marching in his direction. They were to garrison Middelburg and Lydenburg and defend them from any Pedi attack. In addition, in early June 103 volunteer officers and men of the DFH arrived in Lydenburg from Kimberley, bringing all the mounted volunteers in the district to about five hundred. The Zulu Police were also still in the field along with nebulous numbers of allied African contingents.

East of the Leolo Mountains Sekhukhune gamely kept his own forces mobilized. His regiments raided farms and engaged in minor skirmishes with British patrols in which the Bapedi had the best of the fighting. They enjoyed a major success on 7 April when at the Dwars River they ambushed eighty-three men of the DFH who had been patrolling the Tubatse valley. The Bapedi quietly surrounded the mounted volunteers during the night, and following a well-prepared plan fell on the grazing oxen early in the morning. In the course of a scattered fire-fight they drove forty-eight away with them. The horses grazing nearer the volunteers' camp took fright and galloped off, and the Bapedi captured fifty-two of them. Without horses the DFH were all but useless. Already driven close to mutiny through lack of provisions, they and many other volunteers who were finding military discipline irksome began to go home. At the same time, the Zulu Police had to be disarmed for mutiny. In all, it had become embarrassingly evident that mounted volunteers and African levies could not finish the Pedi business off, and that it had become necessary to call on the regular troops.[21]

Lt-Gen. Thesiger, hot from successfully concluding the Ninth Cape Frontier War, established his headquarters in Pietermaritzburg on 9 August 1878 to begin preparing for the inevitable Zulu campaign. It was obvious that he should finish off the nagging Pedi business beforehand. He knew that by the end of October horse sickness would bring the campaigning season to an end, but he hoped for a rapid, decisive blow before then. To land it, he had first to reinforce the troops in the Transvaal. In order to free up the detachments of the 1/13th Regiment which were scattered in garrisons for the coming campaign, he ordered the 80th Regiment which had been stationed in Natal to relieve them. The arrival in Durban of the 2/24th Regiment from the Cape, where they were no longer needed, in turn kept up the strength of the Natal garrison. Having set all the pieces in motion, on 13 August Thesiger placed all the forces in the Transvaal, whether imperial or colonial, under the command of Colonel Hugh Rowlands, VC.

Rowlands also had at his disposal some two hundred seasoned, hard-bitten veterans of the FLH under Major Redvers Buller. The conclusion of the war in the Eastern Cape had threatened them with disbandment, and they eagerly embraced this new adventure. Rowlands further managed to extract five hundred Swazi *emajaha* (warriors) from the reluctant King Mbandzeni who decided to do the minimum to keep the British sweet. His *emajaha* were not earmarked for action, but were kept to garrison and general duties at the various fortified posts.[22]

In all, Rowlands had 1,216 infantry and 611 mounted men at his command for the campaign to conquer Sekhukhune's stronghold of Tsate. But because he suspected Sekhukhune would attempt to break out if the fighting went against him, he detached much of this force to garrison the posts he established around the perimeters of the Pedi heartland to prevent him from doing so. On 6 September Rowlands and his headquarters column from Pretoria met Captain Clarke in the valley of the Lepelle River. The plan was to move past Fort Weeber to set up an advance base for operations against Tsate at the abandoned Fort Burgers. Lydenburg would serve as the main base for the campaign.

Leaving an entrenched camp held by a company of the 1/13th at the Lepelle, Rowlands crossed the river on 8 September. The Bapedi resorted to their habitual tactics of harassment and ambush which had proved so effective against other invaders in the past. They occupied the high hills on either side of the track the British followed through the rugged terrain, but Rowlands brushed aside their skirmishers with little trouble. On 19 September the British encamped at the Spekboom River near Fort Burgers and concentrated their resources for the advance on Tsate itself.

At last, on 3 October, Rowlands marched with 130 men of 1/13th Regiment, 338 men of the FLH and Mounted Infantry, and the two 7-pounder Krupp guns of the mule battery. Tsate was twenty-five miles to the west, and the object was not to assault it immediately, but to occupy a position nearby. The idea was to undertake damaging raids from this fortified camp and, as had been the case when Lekoglane had been pressured into abandoning Maserumule, to induce Sekhukhune to surrender.

Undaunted, the Bapedi determinedly skirmished with the British as they scrambled through the very rugged country, firing on both flanks of the column from spurs and bluffs projecting out of the thorn trees and bush that obscured the track. The British nevertheless pushed on. By the afternoon of 4 October, the second day of their march, they had crossed the watershed dividing the Tubatse and Lepelle rivers and bivouacked in a square formation near what should have been a flowing stream. But the season was exceptionally hot and dry. The watercourses had ceased to flow and the country was totally denuded of any pasture for the column's horses and slaughter-oxen. The soldiers dug in the sandy bed of the dry gulley and found enough water which they filtered to slake their desperate thirst, but left nothing for the suffering livestock. The Bapedi were watching. Just as the British were settling in for the night, the Bapedi launched an attack at about 8 p.m. against three sides of the bivouac, pouring in an unexpected volley followed by independent firing. The panicked livestock stampeded while the British scrambled to return fire. After about half an hour the Bapedi retired, scooping up all the straying slaughter-oxen. Fortunately for the British, their horses had been hobbled and it was possible to recover most of them.

Rowlands resumed the march the next day and reached an amphi-theatre in the hills where there was sufficient water in two pools for men and remaining livestock. A koppie commanded the place and several Bapedi were stationed on top. The FLH drove them off in a slight skirmish. The British then dragged themselves to a new camping ground to the north. There it was again necessary to dig holes in the sand for an inadequate supply of water of which there was enough for the men, but only for about a third of the suffering horses and draught-oxen. Rowlands realized this simply could not continue. Without water and forage, it was clearly impossible to maintain an armed camp as planned to menace Tsate. Besides, the Bapedi were proving tenacious skirmishers and Rowlands's column was manifestly too small to deal with them effectively. As so often in colonial warfare, Rowlands had underestimated his enemy and the harshness of the inhospitable terrain. Disconcertingly, his horses were already beginning to die of the dreaded, wasting horse sickness. It was not understood at all that it was caused by the bite of the tsetse fly and the following year, when in his turn General Wolseley was campaigning in Bopedi, he noted in his journal that 'if anything is really known about the "horse sickness", it is that eating the wet grass in the early morning brings it on'.[23] But however misdiagnosed its cause, Rowlands knew that once horse sick-ness broke out in full force it would be impossible to continue opera-tions. All things considered, there was no option but to retreat, and all his officers concurred.

At dawn on 6 October Rowlands pulled his weary, dispirited troops back by the way they had come. It was an awful march with tempera-tures reaching 110°F in the shade. The Bapedi held the hills commanding what little water there was. Rowlands did not attempt to dislodge them, but pushed his men on as fast as they could stumble. Exhausted and dehydrated, they and their surviving horses reached their base at Fort Burgers late in the afternoon of 7 October. The unfortunate draught-oxen had been eleven hours under the yoke and thirty hours without water. Human casualties were negligible with only one man wounded, but the blow to British prestige was considerable.

Before suspending further operations, though, Rowlands needed at least one success to recover dented British pride. On 27 October he targeted a Pedi stronghold only about five miles away from his camp at

Fort Burgers, so logistical problems would not again upset his plans. Typically, it was a strong position with rocks and caves giving cover to the defenders. But with three 7-pounder guns, 140 mounted men, 340 British infantry and 250 African levies Rowlands possessed over-whelming force. His men stormed and burned the place killing sixteen Bapedi to eleven British wounded. And with that last flourish the campaign—which the British later dubbed the '1st Sekukuni War'— came to an end. With horse sickness gaining hold and with supplies still an intractable problem, Rowlands abandoned Fort Burgers and all other advanced posts. Following Thesiger's orders, he withdrew the troops to various garrisons in the Transvaal, concentrating them along the Swazi and Zulu borders for the anticipated, inevitable campaign against the Zulu kingdom. Even if these troops were not diverted within the next few months to the Zululand theatre, Rowlands did not see the next campaigning season in Bopedi opening until late April 1879.[24]

Sekhukhune had survived thanks as much to the drought as to the determination and skill of his regiments. Yet he could have entertained few illusions about how dangerous the next British onslaught would prove. Shepstone was naturally taken aback by the humiliating outcome of the campaign, not least because military expenditure in the bankrupt Transvaal jumped from £51,064 in 1877 to £299,572 in 1878,[25] and all for nothing. He admitted to Rowlands that with hindsight he had miscalculated, and that 'Sikukuni's powers to resist or to defend himself were underrated from the beginning'. But then Shepstone was a man of the oddest illusions, and went on to add bizarrely 'that to subdue Sikukuni was a more difficult task than to subdue Cetywayo'.[26] He could not have been further off the mark.

The Anglo-Zulu War, 1879

CHAPTER 16

Preparing to 'Draw the Monster's Teeth and Claws'

O N a bright, chilly winter's day in July 1878 an eagle was plying the thermals above the Mahlabathini plain in the very heart of the Zulu kingdom. Scattered across the open, rolling plain were thirteen enormous, elliptical arrangements of beehive huts of thatch. These were royal military homesteads, or *amakhanda* (singular *ikhanda*), where the king's age-grade regiments, or *amabutho* (singular *ibutho*), periodically mustered to serve their ruler. The greatest *ikhanda* of them all was oNdini, Cetshwayo's chief residence, with a circumference of 2,375 yards. At the head was the *isigodlo*, or private royal enclosure, where the king lived with his wives and over four hundred maids-of-honour. Two great wings of a thousand or more huts, arranged in three rows, curved out from either side of the *isigodlo* to enclose a great parade ground. There the warriors quartered in the encircling huts danced, exercised and praised the king. An outer palisade of stout timbers eight feet high enclosed the whole vast complex.[1] At the top of the parade ground, directly below the *isigodlo*, was the royal cattle enclosure. The king sacrificed there and consulted with his inner council of state, or *ibandla*, drawn from the ranks of royal princes, or *abantwana* (singular *umntwana*), hereditary chiefs, or *amakhosi* (singular *inkosi*), and *izinduna* (singular *induna*), the trusted officers of state he had appointed.

The *ibandla* was in conclave when its members, wrapped in their distinctive grey blankets, noticed the eagle soaring majestically far above them. Suddenly, to their consternation, four hawks swooped down upon it and drove the great bird away. Filled with foreboding, King Cetshwayo consulted his *izangoma*, diviners inspired by the ancestral spirits. Glumly, they declared that the *ibandla* had witnessed a portent that the states bordering the Zulu kingdom would soon combine to destroy it.[2] Yet, unwelcome as this divination was to the king and his *ibandla*, it merely confirmed their growing conviction that war with the British was imminent.

On 9 August 1878 General Thesiger, basking in the formal thanks of the Cape parliament for winning the Ninth Cape Frontier War and made a Knight Companion of the Bath on the recommendation of a grateful British government,[3] set up his headquarters in Pietermaritzburg, the capital of the Colony of Natal. He was there to prepare for the invasion of the Zulu kingdom. Sir Bartle Frere, misled by the relative ease of the general's recent success against the amaXhosa, fondly imagined that the amaZulu could similarly be subdued at the price of a minor campaign.

The High Commissioner was still adamant in his conviction that Zululand must be removed as the lynchpin of resistance to white rule in southern Africa.[4] Shepstone had drummed into his ear that to convince the Transvaal Boers of the advantages of British rule it was essential not only to finish off the Sekhukhune business, but also to resolve Boer–Zulu friction over the Disputed Territory in the Transvaal's favour (see chapter 6). Frere was thrown off balance, however, by the unexpected intervention of Sir Henry Bulwer, the fussy and self-important Lieutenant-Governor of Natal. Bulwer feared that, if Frere supported the Transvaal in the border dispute, war with the amaZulu would follow, and he wanted to keep Natal out of the fray. So he offered to mediate. Frere was then mired in the Ninth Cape Frontier War and gave him his head. Cetshwayo agreed to mediation with considerable relief, and the Boundary Commission began sitting at Rorke's Drift on 17 March 1878. Three months later, on 15 July, Frere received its scrupulous report. To his dismayed frustration its findings in large measure vindicated Zulu territorial claims and threatened to cause a political explosion in the increasingly truculent Transvaal. Frere believed the report would be read there as proof positive that the British could not guarantee its security against hostile African neighbours, and he feared this would finally spark off a Boer rebellion in the

Transvaal. His fevered nightmare was that such an uprising would draw in the Boer Republic of the Orange Free State as well as anti-British Boers in the Cape and Natal, and that hostile Africans would be encouraged to fall upon the whites while they fought each other. And naturally, to his way of thinking, the amaZulu would be the leaders in the general uprising.

It was essential, therefore, not to make the findings of the Boundary Commission public until he had found a way to neutralize them. Events played into Frere's hands. A series of minor incidents along the jittery borders of Zululand between July and October 1878 alarmed settler opinion and provided opportune justification for military action. By September Frere's commanders were preparing on a contingency basis for war, and during November and December they moved troops in a steady trickle to the border. Yet Frere still could not get a clear run at the war he was fomenting. In London, the government was becoming increasingly uneasy with his bellicosity. The Second Anglo-Afghan War broke out in late 1878, relations with Russia were dangerously strained, and at the Colonial Office Hicks Beach made it clear he wanted no war in Zululand complicating the already alarming scenario. When Frere requested the reinforcements his military advisers considered necessary for the impending war, the government proved reluctant and urged that the troops already along the Zulu border should be used solely for defence against a Zulu invasion.

But Frere was not prepared to 'decline the contest'.[5] The time had come to solve the so-called native question once and for all, and that meant settling with Cetshwayo. As he wrote to Shepstone, he had to 'draw the Monster's teeth and claws',[6] and he could not achieve that while the dreaded Zulu military system remained intact. To destroy it would take brute force, not fair words. So Frere pushed ahead with the military plans he knew the cabinet would not sanction while coolly exploiting the conveniently slow communications with London to keep the ministers in the dark.[7] He knew he risked his distinguished career, but he had been assured by his military men that a Zulu campaign would be swift, cheap and decisive. Any censure for disobeying instructions would be wiped away by his triumphant clinching of confederation. By late 1878 he had also worked out how a disarmed Zululand would be slotted into the new British order and the South African frontier finally closed. Drawing on his extensive administrative experience in India, he did not envisage Zululand being annexed. Rather, he saw it taking its assigned place in the confederation like an Indian 'subject ally', or princely state, ruled indirectly through a compliant chief under a British resident.[8]

Supremely confident in his objectives, Frere took the final steps to war. With the advice of Shepstone, Bulwer and other colonial administrators, he drafted an ultimatum to the Zulu king. It was delivered to Cetshwayo's emissaries on the Natal side of the Thukela River on 11 December 1878. The Zulu delegation was first appraised of the Boundary Award, but their jubilation was swiftly snuffed out when they absorbed the terms of the ultimatum that followed it. Among other stipulations, it demanded that the Zulu military system be abolished and the king submit himself to a British resident. Cetshwayo's representatives understood as well as the colonial officials delivering these terms that they could never be accepted by their king. War must surely follow when the ultimatum expired on 11 January 1879.

In planning and executing the Zululand campaign, General Thesiger, now Lord Chelmsford, faced many handicaps, not all of his own making.[9] His main striking-force would be his battalions of British infantry, but the unintended consequence of the recent Cardwell reforms meant that those serving abroad were often imperfectly trained and consisted of physically immature, untried soldiers and inexperienced NCOs. Although some of his battalions, particularly those which had served in the Ninth Cape Frontier War, were campaign-hardened, Chelmsford would have to make do with green troops whose performance often left much to be desired. As he was to complain, 'drafts will not be of much use, as they are certain to be composed of boys'.[10]

British infantry serving in South Africa might not have all been up to standard, but they were still too valuable and scarce to dissipate on garrison and convoy duties which were better undertaken by African auxiliaries. Moreover, as Chelmsford had found with his Mfengu levies in the Cape, in the absence of sufficient mounted troops they were also useful in reconnaissance, skirmishing and pursuit. So Chelmsford set about raising African levies in Natal. Colonial officials warned that they would make only poor soldiers, and most settlers feared the security risk of arming them. But Frere supported his general and Chelmsford got what he wanted. With a few recent exceptions, historians have tended to ignore these black soldiers in favour of their Zulu adversaries, even though when Chelmsford invaded Zululand in January 1879 they made up fifty-two per cent of his army.

To raise the Natal Native Contingent (NNC),[11] Chelmsford had to turn to Bulwer who, in his capacity as Supreme Chief over the African population in Natal, had the right to exact *isibhalo*, or compulsory labour and military service. Magistrates accordingly raised levies from the chiefs of the Natal Native Reserves, encouraging recruitment with promises of captured cattle and pay. Thousands came forward through loyalty to their superiors, for the reward, because they were political exiles from Zululand and because they welcomed the opportunity to show the amaZulu that they too were warriors and men. The levies were then transferred to the general's command as imperial, rather than colonial, troops. In the Transvaal Colonel Evelyn Wood raised six hundred Wood's Irregulars and Vos's Natives, for the most part labour tenants on white farms pressed into service by the landdrosts (or magistrates).[12] They too were maintained as imperial troops, as were 250 levies drawn from the Swazi kingdom and known as Fairlie's Swazis.[13]

Chelmsford planned for the NNC to comprise 7,000 infantry, 250 mounted infantry and 300 men of the Natal Native Pioneer Corps (NNP) to repair roads and construct earthwork fortifications during the campaign. All were placed under white colonial officers and NCOs and commanded by seconded or former British officers. Following British military style the NNC was organized in companies, battalions and regiments—initially three regiments of seven battalions—and drilled to instil discipline and tactical utility. The men received no uniforms but wore a red cloth tied around the head to distinguish them from the Zulu who were similarly dressed only in loin-covers. They were also issued with blankets of a different colour for each battalion. Chelmsford did not intend them to take a major role in a pitched battle, and issued the infantry with only one obsolete muzzle-loading percussion-lock Enfield rifle for every ten men. This, he believed, was sufficient to give them confidence against the amaZulu when serving as light troops in support of the British regulars. The NNP were uniformed in red tunics and white trousers, and some of them were issued modern rifles. The mounted African troops were the elite. They were volunteers from the Natal Native Reserves and the Christian community at Edendale outside Pietermaritzburg, and formed the Natal Native Horse and several other troops under the command of white colonial officers. They supplied their own horses, but the War Office maintained them in the field, issued them with smart uniforms and slouch felt hats, and armed them with standard British carbines. The war correspondent, Charles Fripp, noted that what marked them out from similar accoutred white mounted irregulars were 'their assegais in a sheath bound to the saddle' and their preference for riding without boots 'with the big toe only in the stirrup'.[14] Chelmsford also recruited several essentially mercenary units of African horsemen such as the Mounted Basutos, the Sesotho-speaking Tlokwa adherents of *iNkosi* Hlubi kaMota Molife.[15]

To Chelmsford's disappointment, it was soon apparent that the NNC infantry were of doubtful morale and effectiveness. They did not grasp the point of British parade drill and were much more familiar with their traditional spears than with their ineffective muzzle-loaders. To make matters worse, their white NCOs were usually unmotivated and unversed in military matters. Many of their officers did not know isiZulu (although some who had served in the Eastern Cape could speak the related isiXhosa) and their commands were more often than not incomprehensible to the NNC.

Doubt therefore hung over the utility of the NNC infantry in the coming campaign, but more essential to its success were the mounted African troops. They had proved pivotal in the latter stages of the Ninth Cape Frontier War, and would be crucial in Zululand not only for reconnaissance and raiding, but for the pursuit of a broken enemy. Yet as Chelmsford was uncomfortably aware, he had not nearly enough of them for his purposes. Regular cavalry would not be made available until the closing stages of the campaign so, besides the Natal Native Horse, he had to rely on a motley collection of mounted units. Some were well trained, such as the scant two squadrons of British Mounted Infantry and the white settler Natal Mounted Police in their smart black uniforms who approached the discipline and profession- alism of regular troops. Then there were the Natal Volunteer Corps, contributed by Bulwer in his capacity as Commander-in-Chief of Natal. First raised in 1855 and drawn predominantly from English-speaking colonists, the Volunteers elected their own officers, and provided their own equipment, arms and horses. In October 1878 the 430 officers and men of the eleven mounted corps volunteered for active service in Zululand.[16] And, finally, among several units of irregular horse raised from whites living in the Transvaal and Cape there was the veteran FLH, hardened in the Ninth Cape Frontier War and the First Anglo-Pedi War, as well as the Dutch Burghers, a commando from the eastern borders of the Transvaal. A young British officer attached to the irregular horse later wrote of them:

> they appeared to be rough, undisciplined and disrespectful to their officers, fearfully slovenly and the veriest drunkards and winebibbers that ever took carbine in hand. On the other hand they looked, what they eventually were, just the rough and hardy men to wage a partisan warfare against an active enemy.[17]

Indeed, while professional British soldiers inevitably held poorly trained and inadequately armed African auxiliaries in low esteem, there was considerably less reason for them to look down their noses at these white colonial volunteers who knew the terrain and were skilled in arms. Still, there was no avoiding the clash of military cultures between the regular soldiers with their inflated self-esteem and the rough-and-ready colonial militia, even if the latter would play a role in the Zululand campaign out of proportion to their small numbers.

The shortfall in horsemen for intelligence-gathering was of particular concern to Chelmsford because the lack of accurate maps of Zululand meant he was dependent on mounted reconnaissance to relay him information about the terrain to be traversed, and to locate the enemy.[18] Unfortunately, Chelmsford's gentlemanly-amateurish disregard of the need for the professional accumulation and analysis of intelligence compounded the problem. His small staff had been selected for compatibility rather than for talent, and he was in any case reluctant to delegate, spending time and energy on routine duties more appropriately performed by his subordinates.[19]

Nevertheless, Chelmsford did acknowledge the need to understand beforehand the military system of his prospective foe. To that end he had booklets prepared for his officers describing in detail the Zulu military system and way of war, and providing instructions on how British troops should be managed in the field.[20] Unfortunately, neither Chelmsford nor his officers seem to have believed what they read about the fighting qualities of the amaZulu. In fact, it is clear that they wholly underrated them. Naturally, their well-ingrained sense of racial, cultural and technological superiority to 'savages' would have played its usual part, but their recent experiences in the Ninth Cape Frontier War contributed greatly to their over-confidence. The amaZulu could be expected to be tougher adversaries than the amaXhosa, but they were assumed nevertheless to be essentially in the same league. As the staff officer Major Cornelius Clery later put it, 'the easy promenade' in the Cape made 'all go into this business with light hearts'.[21] The consequence, he explained, was that:

> the general and his staff not only did not anticipate that the enemy would venture to attack him, but if they should do so that the only thing to be apprehended was that the fire of our people would frighten them so much that they would never come near enough to suffer any serious loss. So that to take any precautions against an attack, such as entrenching, etc., such a thing was never dreamt of.[22]

Consequently, when Chelmsford set about framing his strategy for the coming Zulu campaign, he based it on a dangerous underestimate of the fighting qualities of the amaZulu. His planning would also lack flair for—as the recent operations against the amaXhosa had demonstrated—the general was reluctant to adapt orthodox military thinking to colonial conditions unless absolutely pressed. In mitigation, though, he had not been dealt a free hand.

For one thing, he had to make arrangements to secure Natal from Zulu counter-raids when he invaded the kingdom. To this end, he persuaded the Natal government to raise a field force of African levies to hold the countryside between the border posts which were to be garrisoned by imperial troops and colonial volunteers. This Natal Border Guard was placed under the command of white officers and stood at about 2,800 men. They rotated at intervals with the members of a larger reserve, thus allowing them time to attend to their crops and herds. Inevitably, this did little for their military preparedness. They were not drilled in the British style like the NNC, but were expected to fight in the traditional way with spears and shields. Technically, they were under colonial command, but Bulwer initially conceded that Chelmsford had the right to dispose of the colonial troops stationed along the border as he saw fit.[23]

Despite these arrangements, Chelmsford knew that the borders remained vulnerable and this affected the timing of his invasion. The rivers between Natal and Zululand were generally unfordable between January and March on account of the summer rains, and so formed a natural line of defence. Chelmsford confidently expected that if he invaded early enough in the year the campaign would be won before the rivers subsided. He also needed to begin his advance while the summer grazing was plentiful for his draught-animals, and so he worked with Frere on the political front to ensure that he could launch the campaign in January, the height of summer.[24]

Effective logistics were the key to a rapid, decisive campaign, and here Chelmsford faced insuperable difficulties. Since supplies could not be obtained from the theatre of war, they had to be carried. For months before the invasion Chelmsford was engrossed in collecting and organizing supplies and transport with little help from the alienated Natal authorities who were not in favour of war. By the end of the campaign Chelmsford would have hired or bought from colonial civilians the 27,125 oxen, 4,653 mules and 748 horses necessary to draw the 1,770 wagons and 796 carts he required. Eager to profit from the unexpected windfall, they charged him exorbitant rates.[25] He was also let down by his own understaffed Commissariat and Transport Department whose inexperience in purchasing and in looking after its draught-animals in South African conditions helped drive up costs.[26]

Chelmsford's dependence on slow-moving and vulnerable supply-trains which averaged no more than ten miles a day over the broken and rain-sodden terrain meant that his manoeuvrability would be compromised. The larger the convoy, the slower it moved, so Chelmsford decided he must send in a number of smaller columns, unfortunately echoing his initial, unsuccessful deployment in the Ninth

Cape Frontier War. Nevertheless, he was sure that the strategy of converging columns was appropriate for Zululand because (he convinced himself) they would discourage Zulu counter-thrusts against Natal and the Transvaal. He accordingly selected invasion routes in sectors he believed vulnerable to Zulu attack: No. 1 Column of 4,750 men (including the 2nd Regiment NNC) under Colonel C.K. Pearson would protect the Natal coastal plain; No. 3 Column of 4,709 men (including the 3rd Regiment NNC) under Colonel Richard Glyn—reinforced by the 3,871 African troops of the 1st Regiment NNC and Natal Native Horse with No. 2 Column under Brevet Colonel Durnford—would shield central Natal; No. 4 Column of 2,278 men under Brevet Colonel Evelyn Wood would cover the Utrecht District of the Transvaal; and No. 5 Column of 1,565 men under Colonel Hugh Rowlands would take care of the volatile eastern Transvaal that abutted the Pedi, Swazi and Zulu kingdoms. These invading columns were supposed to converge on oNdini, King Cetshwayo's capital, despite all their logistical and intelligence deficiencies, let alone Zulu resistance.[27]

Shepstone had convinced Frere that under the stress of war opposition to Cetshwayo within his kingdom would grow, and that political disarray, compounded by military defeat, would bring the kingdom to its knees. Chelmsford hoped to exploit these divisions by encouraging disaffected chiefs to defect, and instructed his commanders to accommodate surrendered Zulu notables and their followers behind their lines.[28] But any unravelling of the Zulu kingdom required British military ascendancy, and Chelmsford was determined to avoid the desultory, protracted warfare he had experienced in the Eastern Cape. Instead, he intended to conclude the campaign expeditiously with a decisive pitched battle, and was confident that the amaZulu, true to their heroic warrior tradition, would oblige him. So Chelmsford's operational gambit of dividing his army into several columns was also bait intended to entice the amaZulu into attacking these small and deceptively vulnerable forces. Then, as the amaXhosa had previously discovered to their sorrow, the Zulu warriors' mass attack would be shattered by the disciplined, superior firepower of the British soldiers.[29]

CHAPTER 17

The Meat of Heroes

WHILE growing numbers of British troops menaced the kingdom's borders and Frere wound the political crisis to breaking-point, King Cetshwayo and his *ibandla* discussed the threatening situation with mounting concern.[1] In September and again in October 1878 they partially mobilized the *amabutho* in response to border alarms. Cornelius Vijn, a white trader who found himself detained in Zululand during the war, noted that bitter resentment of those 'very bad people', the British, began to sweep the country. Widespread rumour had it 'that the Whites had come to capture all the males, to be sent to England and there kept to work, while the girls would all be married off to (white) soldiers, and their cattle would, of course, all belong to the English government'. Warriors responded by declaring that 'when it came to fighting, they fought not for the King only, but for themselves, since they would rather die than live under the Whites.'[2]

In its debates the *ibandla* had been divided. *uMntwana* Hamu kaNzibe, the king's deeply ambitious brother, had undoubted designs on the throne and always opposed Cetshwayo, while his chief *induna*, *iNkosi* Mnyamana kaNgqengelele of the Buthelezi, and his powerful cousin, *iNkosi* Zibhebhu kaMaphitha of the Mandlakazi, wished to maintain good relations with Britain and realistically feared the consequences of going to war with them. Yet so draconian was the British ultimatum, so fatal was it to Zulu independence, that even they could see no alternative but to fight. In early January 1879 the *amabutho* mustered at oNdini where they were 'doctored' for war and readied themselves to affirm their masculinity and prowess through the death of the invaders.

In 1904 Ngidi kaMcikaziswa proudly verified a central Zulu cultural predilection when he informed James Stuart, a white magistrate recording Zulu oral history, that the amaZulu 'are always talking of war and battles, even at this day'.[3] Indeed, violence defined the Zulu kingdom which rose and fell within the span of a long-lived person's lifetime. It was born of King Shaka kaSenzangakhona's conquest in the 1820s of neighbouring African chiefdoms, but during the reign of King Dingane (1828–1840), Shaka's half-brother and assassin, nearly succumbed in 1838 to the armed migration of the Voortrekkers from the Cape Colony. The kingdom was next close to being shattered by vicious civil wars of succession. In 1840 *uMntwana* Mpande overthrew his half-brother Dingane at the battle of Maqongqo; and in 1856 Mpande's rival sons, Mbuyazi and Cetshwayo, fought to secure the right to the succession. Cetshwayo won and duly succeeded Mpande on his natural death in 1872.[4] But the forces of colonialism were pressing ever harder on Zululand, and it was for British forces, waiting impatiently along its borders, finally to bring the kingdom crashing down in January 1879.

Frere and his colonial advisers were not wrong in seeing Zulu military style and organization as central to Zulu society, although they misconstrued and exaggerated the threat. Like the amaXhosa, the amaZulu were essentially pastoralists and reckoned their wealth in cattle, although they also kept goats and scant-haired sheep.[5] Over twenty thousand scattered, circular, palisaded homesteads (*imizi*, singular *umuzi*), looking like so many tiny villages, dotted the rolling countryside. An *umuzi* consisted of a crescent of four or more hemispherical, beehive-shaped thatched huts (*izindlu*, singular *indlu*) sheltering on average four people each, so the Zulu population stood at somewhere around three hundred thousand people.[6] The *izindlu* of an *umuzi* surrounded the central cattle-byre in which grain was stored during the winter in deep pits, their funnel-shaped mouths carefully disguised. Each *umuzi* was supported by its own grazing and agricultural land and was home to a married man, his several wives, children and dependants. The male head of the *umuzi* tended his allegiance to his regional *inkosi* who, in turn, gave his allegiance to the king on behalf of all his adherents. In male-dominated Zulu society agriculture was primarily women's work, while to men exclusively fell the more prestigious activities of caring for livestock, building and repairing the *umuzi*, discussing politics, and going out to hunt or fight.

Oral traditions tell of constant raiding from earliest times in what would later be the Zulu kingdom to acquire herds by force from neighbours. The warriors who raided each other would have had their fighting skills honed by participation in organized hunting parties. European sailors in the late seventeenth century saw them using long throwing-spears and finishing off their victims with short stabbing-spears. These would remain the basic Zulu weapons for the next two centuries. By the mid-eighteenth century at the latest hunting parties were developing into large-scale military formations, or 'regiments', known to the amaZulu as *amabutho*. These *amabutho* were based on age-grade units which had developed out of the now defunct circumcision schools marking the transition from youth to manhood. It is impossible to say which particular grouping in what later became the Zulu kingdom invented the *amabutho*, but it is certain that by the eighteenth century they were increasingly being deployed as the chiefs' instruments of coercion, and that to keep them fed and rewarded necessitated raids against neighbouring chiefdoms.

The most successful of these warring chiefs was Shaka who in about 1816 seized the throne of the little Zulu chieftainship in the valley of the White Mfolozi River from his half-brother. More than any other man, he exemplified the warrior hero as conceived by the amaZulu. Magema Fuze (who in 1922 penned the first history in isiZulu of his people) quoted with awe from Shaka's praise-poem which was intoned to invoke the spirit of the great king and which hailed Shaka's aura of naked power and insatiable ferocity:

The blade that vanquishes other blades with its sharpness.
He who roars like thunder as he sits . . .
Shaka, a fearful name I dare not utter.
The long-armed robber who robs with violence,
Who destroys always in a furious rage,
With his ever-ready shield on his knees.[7]

It was Shaka's full development of the military potential of the *amabutho* which enabled him to extend and consolidate his rule over the entire region between the Phongolo River to the north and the Thukela River to the south.[8] For him and all his successors the *amabutho* remained the central instrument of royal power holding together the political structure of the Zulu kingdom. All the men as well as the women of the kingdom were grouped into *amabutho* under the king's direct ritual authority rather than remaining under that of their regional *amakhosi*—as would have been the case in the Pedi and Xhosa paramountcies. Girls stayed at home until it was time to marry. But boys between the ages of fourteen and eighteen would gather at the nearest of the various *amakhanda*, the great military homesteads sited at strategic points around the kingdom where they functioned both as regional centres for royal influence and as mobilization points for the *amabutho*. There youths would serve for two to three years as cadets. Once enough boys of the same age-group had trained at the various *amakhanda* across the kingdom, the king would form them into an *ibutho* with orders to build themselves a new *ikhanda*. Members of a male *ibutho* could not marry until the king gave them permission to wed women of the female *ibutho* he designated. The king usually withheld permission until men were about the age of thirty-five because, until then, they technically remained youths under the supervision of their elders and thus more thoroughly under his control. Once a man was allowed to marry, he assumed the *isicoco* (the distinctive married man's polished headring of fibres and wax twisted into the hair) and at last established his own *umuzi* as a fully fledged adult.

A new *ibutho* would serve continuously at its *ikhanda* for seven to eight months immediately after formation, and thereafter for only a few months a year. For the rest of the year its members lived at home playing their part in the subsistence economy of their *imizi*. After marriage, the men's wives might accompany them during their annual service at their *ikhanda*. While serving, an *ibutho* would make repairs to its *ikhanda*, tend the king's cattle and fields and take part in the great national ceremonies. The most notable of these was the annual *umKhosi*, or first-fruits festival, when the army was ritually strengthened and the power of the king reaffirmed. During such ceremonies the *amabutho* would don their elaborate ceremonial attire that distinguished them from one another and comprised many fragile and rare skins and feathers. By the 1870s, when hunting had seriously depleted supplies, attire was simpler than it had been in the past. Even if headdresses in particular were becoming less lavish, cow-tails tied above the elbows and below the knees remained standard, as did the loin-cover of a bunch of tails in the front and an oblong of cowhide behind.

Besides commanding their labour, the king also fully controlled the military might of his male *amabutho*. They collected tribute, partici-pated in great hunts, enforced internal control (which included attacking recalcitrant regional *amakhosi*), and served as his army against external enemies. When going on campaign they wore a much abbreviated version of their precious and constricting festival attire—a choice which differentiated them from the amaSwazi who went to war in full befeathered and beskinned panoply—although officers might sport some feathers and others conspicuous items as a sign of their rank. All carried a selection of the basic traditional weapon, the spear. The dead-liest variety was the short-handled, long-bladed stabbing-spear (or *iklwa*, plural *amaklwa*) intended for close fighting. A warrior would also carry several throwing-spears with long shafts. Used primarily for hunting, the *isijula* (plural *izijula*) could find its target up to thirty yards away. Many fighting men might also heft a brutal wooden knobbed stick or *iwisa* (plural *amawisa*) to beat out an enemy's brains. Like the amaSwazi, the *amabutho* also carried a great war-shield of cattle-hide, the *isihlangu* (plural *izihlangu*). By the 1860s it had generally shrunk to two-thirds of the man-height stipulated by Shaka. Nor did the uniformity of shield colours and patterns any longer differentiate the *amabutho* as they had once done. Only two *izihlangu* could be cut from a single beast, and there were no longer sufficient cattle available with the required markings. Nevertheless, younger *amabutho* carried predominantly black or reddish *izihlangu* and married *amabutho* mainly white ones.

The British first became aware of the military power of the Zulu kingdom when in the late 1820s King Shaka's *amabutho* raided as far south as the borders of the Cape. The hard-fought war of 1838 between the invading Voortrekkers and the amaZulu cemented the reputation of the *amabutho* as warriors greatly to be feared. Thereafter, Zulu campaigns against the amaSwazi and Bapedi until the early 1850s

and subsequent spear-rattling kept apprehension among their neighbours alive, as did the periodic alarms over the Disputed Territory. Yet
was the fearsome Zulu military reputation entirely deserved? The
amabutho were a militia, after all, and not the standing British army
with its professional soldiers.[9]

When the campaign experience of the *amabutho* mustering in the
Mahlabathini plain in January 1879 is examined, what strikes one is the
lack of it. The last mobilization that had resulted in an actual campaign
against whites had been in December 1838 during the Voortrekker-Zulu
War, forty-one years before. The record against neighbouring African
states was little different, and the last time the amaZulu raided the
amaSwazi had been in 1852. Ironically, the most recent campaign the
amaZulu had waged had been the civil war of 1856 when *uMntwana*
Cetshwayo and his half-brother Mbuyazi fought for the right to the
succession. Cetshwayo had triumphed at Ndondakusuka which saw the
heaviest casualties in any battle ever fought by the amaZulu. But that was
twenty-three years before, a considerable hiatus in active service, one
might say, for such an apparently ferocious warrior nation. Compare this
record with that of the men of the 24th Regiment who were battle-
hardened veterans of the Ninth Cape Frontier War only the previous year.

Naturally, this does not mean that many individuals who had fought
in earlier campaigns did not do so again in 1879, and most of the senior
commanders in 1879 had taken part in the Swazi wars or the battle of
Ndondakusuka—but they had done so in a more junior capacity. Four
of the *amabutho* that fought in the Anglo-Zulu War were aged between
forty-one and forty-seven, namely the iSangqu, uThulwana, iNdlondlo
and uDloko, and they had all been present at Ndondakusuka. Other
veterans of Ndondakusuka like the iNdabakawombe and uDlambedlu
(who were aged fifty-eight and fifty-six respectively) were considered
too old for active campaigning and were mainly kept in reserve in 1879
to protect the king. Otherwise, not one of the other twelve *amabutho*
who fought in the Anglo-Zulu War had seen the field of battle: this was
to be their very first campaign. Even the most prominent *amabutho* in
the war—the uMbonambi, uKhandempemvu (or uMcijo), uMxhapho,
iNgobamakhosi and uNokhenke—were previously unblooded warriors
between their mid-twenties and mid-thirties, while the recently formed
uVe were younger still.

20 Ngqika amaXhosa recovering their wounded during a skirmish in 1878 with Cape and British forces. Note their combination of European and traditional dress and the muzzle-loaders they are firing.

21 The sweep into the Lotutu bush on 6 April 1878 by British regulars, African levies and colonial mounted volunteers to dislodge the Rharhabe amaNdlambe from Ntaba ka Ndonda, the prominent, flat-topped mountain in the distance.

22 Feeding destitute Xhosa women and children who had fled from the devastated Ngqika location in May 1878.

23 Mfengu levies celebrating over Sandile's corpse at the isiDenge camp on 8 June 1878.

24 Watched by both black and white inhabitants of King William's Town, the Diamond Fields Horse from Griqualand West, who volunteered in January 1878 for service in the Ninth Cape Frontier War, parade under Major Charles Warren.

25 Botlasitse Gasebonwe, the Batlhaping *kgosi* (seated left) and Nikolaas Waterboer (seated right) photographed with their councillors in 1874.

26 Major Owen Lanyon, Administrator of Griqualand West, *c.*1877.

27 British troops during the First Anglo-Pedi War on the march to Fort Weeber in September 1877.

28 *uMntwana* Dabulamanzi kaMpande, the Zulu commander at Rorke's Drift, photographed in 1873 in conversation with the hunter-trader John Dunn who supplied firearms to the Zulu kingdom.

29 A company of the Natal Native Pioneer Corps drilling in camp outside Pietermaritzburg. The men wear old British greatcoats and blue pillbox forage caps encircled by a yellow band.

30 The Border Guard stationed at White Rock Drift on the Natal side of the Thukela River, c.May 1879.

31 The final repulse of the amaZulu at the battle of Gingindlovu on 2 April 1879, based on an eye-witness sketch by Lieutenant-Colonel J. North Crealock.

32 Charles Fripp's sketch of Wood's Flying Column on the march through Zululand in mid-June 1879.

33 Melton Prior, artist for the *Illustrated London News*, setting fire to a Zulu *umuzi* during the final advance on oNdini. He is being watched approvingly by members of the Natal Native Contingent who are looting it.

34 With the oNdini *ikhanda* in flames in the background, members of the Natal Native Contingent bear away British soldiers wounded in the battle of Ulundi on 4 July 1879.

35 King Cetshwayo kaMpande on board the *Natal* in early September 1879 on his way to exile in the Cape after his defeat in the Anglo-Zulu War.

36 The ambitious Sir Garnet Wolseley posing proudly soon after being made Knight Grand Cross of the Order of St Michael and St George in 1874.

37 Swazi *emajaha* and colonial mounted volunteers at the entrance to the cave where Sekhukhune took refuge on 30 November 1879 after the Pedi defeat at the battle of Tsate.

38 The captured Sekhukhune being brought under escort into the British camp on 2 December 1879.

None of this is to suggest that the *amabutho* were not desperately eager to face the British in battle and were not confident of their ability to beat them. But that is precisely the problem. Who among them had any experience in facing disciplined soldiers armed with modern rifles? It is true that the four *amabutho* who had fought at Ndondakusuka had all faced the firepower of the iziNqobo, the hundred-odd African hunters and Natal Frontier Police who had fought as *uMntwana* Mbuyazi's allies.[10] Yet their firearms had been flintlock or percussion-lock muzzle-loaders, not nearly as effective as the modern rifles and artillery the *amabutho* would be facing in 1879. In 1856, despite heavy casualties, they had overwhelmed the iziNqobo in traditional hand-to-hand combat with their *amaklwa*. Yet could courage and tenacity make up for the inadequacy of such tactics when pitted against Chelmsford's forces bristling with modern rifles and artillery?

Compared to the Bapedi, amaXhosa and the various communities in Griqualand West, the amaZulu permitted firearms to play only a very tentative part in their military culture. In 1910 Singcofela kaMtshungu explained to James Stuart that *iqungo* (a form of super-natural insanity which afflicts a person who has killed another) 'affects those who kill with an assegai [*iklwa*], but not those who kill with a gun, for with a gun it is just as if the man had shot a buck, and no ill result will follow'.[11] Unlike a firearm which is used at a distance, the *iklwa* was wielded only at close quarters, when an underarm stab—normally aimed at the abdomen—was followed without withdrawing by a rip. This was the weapon of the hero; of a man who cultivated military honour or *udumo* (thunder) and who proved his personal prowess in single combat.

John Iliffe reminds us how the Zulu heroic ethos pervaded male life, stressing physical strength and beauty and expressing itself in the complex, elaborate parade costumes and towering headdresses of skins and feathers worn by the *amabutho*.[12] These preening Zulu males lived in public among their peers every day of their lives from the moment they first mustered as teenagers at the *ikhanda* nearest them. From the outset individuals were in strenuous competition with each other, and would select forceful, courageous youths from among their own ranks as the junior officers of the future. Mtshapi kaNoradu, a member of the uKhandempemvu *ibutho*, told James Stuart in 1918 that even a cadet who had not yet been inducted into a new *ibutho* would begin to *giya*, or to perform a war dance accompanied by the praises his mates had conferred on him. In Mtshapi's words: 'One who did not *giya* was called a coward. For praises would cause a person to become roused. He would remember his praises when the battle was on, feeling that he would be worthless if he did not fight fiercely.'[13] So even if *amabutho* spent the bulk of each year at home, their culture was a highly militarized one that was crucial to notions of masculinity and the creation of Zulu identity as a warrior nation.

The warrior ethos was played out most fully in battle. There the tactical intention was to outflank and enclose the enemy in a flexible manoeuvre, evidently developed from the hunt, which could be readily adapted to a pitched battle in the open field or to a surprise attack. The amaZulu did not attack in a solid body, shoulder to shoulder, but advanced in opening skirmishing order. They only concentrated when upon the enemy, casting a shower of *izijula* to distract the foe as they rushed in to engage in hand-to-hand fighting with their *amaklwa* or *amawisa*. After a few vicious minutes of frenzied stabbing or clubbing they would fall back and regroup before re-engaging as many times as was necessary before the enemy broke. No quarter was given to the defeated foe who was pursued to his complete destruction.[14]

In this sort of fighting a man's prowess was under the constant scrutiny of his comrades. After the battle the king would discuss with his officers which *ibutho* had the distinction of being the first to engage the enemy at close quarters. Men who were members of that *ibutho* and who had killed in battle were designated *abaqawe* (heroes or warriors of distinction) and the king ordered them to wear a distinctive necklace made from small blocks of willow wood (known as *iziqu*) which was looped around the neck or slung across the body bandolier-style. If a man distinguished himself in battle again, he would increase the length of his *iziqu*. On the other hand, if a man who wore the *iziqu* subsequently disgraced himself in war, the king might order his *iziqu* to be cut as a public humiliation.[15] Indeed, those who failed to live up to the required ideals of heroic masculinity, and whose courage deserted them in combat, were publicly degraded. Mtshapi informed Stuart in 1918 that cowards' meat:

would be roasted and roasted and then soaked in cold water. It was then taken out of the water and given to the cowards, while the king urged them on to fight. Upon this they would begin to steel themselves, saying, 'When will there be war, so that I can leave off this meat?' If the coward was then reported to have acquitted himself fiercely in battle, the king would then praise him and say, 'Do not again give him the meat of the cowards; let him eat the meat of the heroes.'[16]

Muskets first entered Zululand in 1824 with traders and hunters from the Cape Colony who settled in Port Natal. Shaka was not above employing these white men as mercenaries in his wars, a precedent followed by his assassin and successor, King Dingane. Yet the full potential of firearms only became apparent during the Voortrekker invasion of 1838. The amaZulu discovered at the battle of Ncome (or Blood River) on 16 December 1838 that, because of the heavy musket fire, they could not get close enough to the Voortrekkers' laagers to make any use of their amaklwa or of their amawisa in the toe-to-toe fighting to which they were accustomed.[17] As Ngidi ka Mcikaziswa ruefully admitted to Stuart, 'We Zulus die facing the enemy—all of us—but at the Ncome we turned our backs. This was caused by the Boers and their guns.'[18]

The thorough defeats at Voortrekker hands only confirmed the chilling efficacy of firearms and the need to possess the new weapons. Yet at the battle of Ndondakusuka in 1856 involving 35,000 combatants, the firepower of the handful of iziNqobo did not affect the outcome, and the iklwa and cow-hide war-shield again won the day, reinforcing the traditionalist Zulu military ethos and wiping away memories of the disastrous war against the Voortrekkers.

Nevertheless, the new weapons technology could not be ignored. As we have seen in the case of the Bapedi, from the late 1860s firearms began to spread rapidly throughout South Africa thanks in large part to the demand for African labour at the diamond fields which allowed the migrant workers to buy firearms.[19] The amaZulu perceived that they should not fall behind in the new arms race, but because no Zulu man was permitted to leave the kingdom because he had to serve the king in his ibutho, Cetshwayo had to import firearms thorough traders. The enterprising hunter-trader John Dunn, who gained Cetshwayo's ear as his adviser, cornered the lucrative Zulu arms market, buying from merchants in the Cape and Natal and bringing in the firearms (mainly antiquated muskets) through Portuguese Delagoa Bay to avoid Natal laws against gun trafficking.[20] The Zulu paid mostly in cattle which Dunn then sold off in Natal.[21]

It is not possible to gauge how many firearms entered Zululand during Cetshwayo's reign (1872–1879) because the statistics given by different contemporary sources differ widely. Still, the report of the British vice-consul in Mozambique gives a reasonable indication. He estimated that between 1875 and 1877, twenty thousand percussion-lock muzzle-loaders along with percussion caps passed through the port, along with five hundred breech-loaders with cartridges, as well as ten thousand barrels of gunpowder. Three-quarters of these goods reportedly found their way to Zululand.[22]

If, conservatively, twenty thousand guns entered Zululand during Cetshwayo's reign, it seems they were not necessarily in the hands of the *amabutho* who would be using them in battle. Mpatshana kaSodondo of the uVe *ibutho* told Stuart in 1912 that when the Zulu army was concentrating at oNdini preparatory to marching off to fight the British invaders in January 1879, 'Cetshwayo came out by the inner gate at 9 a.m. He said, "Is this the whole *impi* [army, plural *izimpi*], then? Lift up your guns." We did so. "So there are no guns?" Each man with a beast from his place must bring it up next day and buy guns of Dunn.'[23]

What this evidence makes clear is that as instruments of power and as a valuable form of largesse Cetshwayo wished to keep the control of firearms in his own hands. They were not necessarily widely dispersed into the hands of ordinary warriors, and many had little (if any) practical training in their use. This being the case, we cannot wonder at the oft-repeated British assertions made during the Anglo-Zulu War about the very poor quality of Zulu marksmanship. Naturally, part of the reason for this doubtless lay with the known ineffectiveness of the many obsolete and inferior firearms in Zulu possession, with the unskilled way in which they were maintained, with the often poor quality of their gunpowder and shot and with shortages of percussion caps and cartridges. But these mechanical shortcomings were exacerbated by lack of musketry instruction. For example, the amaZulu were accustomed to the curving trajectories of thrown spears, and aimed firearms high with the not unnatural expectation that bullets would behave similarly.[24] Put simply, most amaZulu did not shoot well because they had scant practice in it. Little wonder then that in terms of effectiveness they regarded guns in the same light as throwing-spears, and regularly cast both aside before getting down to the real business of fighting hand to hand.

It was the Zulu elite then, rather than ordinary warriors, who monopolized most of the many firearms in the kingdom and valued them for the mystique of power they conferred upon the possessor. It is in those terms that we must view Cetshwayo's bodyguard of armed young women, drawn from those serving him in his *isigodlo*, because these 'amazons' were purely for show. Mpatshana 'never heard of their fighting', and with defeat in the Anglo-Zulu War the king took care to disband them so that they could take refuge out of harm's way.[25]

If these 'amazons'—along with men of status—had the ammunition to improve their marksmanship, so too did a select handful of men recruited and trained in the use of firearms by white hunters such as John Dunn. Hunting had become one of the most important economic activities in southern Africa because of the international value placed on tusks, hides and feathers, and amaZulu proficient in firearms were necessary to help procure them.[26] Otherwise, as we have seen, the bulk of *amabutho* were unfamiliar with firearms and continued to treat them like throwing spears, to be discarded before the real hand-to-hand fighting began.

With a gun culture failing to take deep root in their military culture, and with no experience in facing modern weaponry, is it any wonder—in the shamed words of Ndungungunga kaNgengene—that the amaZulu would ultimately find themselves 'completely beaten off by the artillery and bullets'?[27] Rather, we should regard with awe an honour society with such deeply ingrained expectations of what was appropriate conduct for a fighting man that it would prosecute a hopeless war for six terrible months before surrendering. Yet, in truth, there was no alternative, for what gave a man authenticity as a warrior was the lauded deed of valour which his descendants would celebrate down the generations when they declaimed his praises.

CHAPTER 18

'We Shall Go and Eat Up the White Men'

FROM the spies he deployed in Natal, the Transvaal and Delagoa Bay, Cetshwayo learned the precise strength and intentions of the British columns poised to cross his borders.[1] Zulu kings habitually employed spies to keep then apprised of what was occurring throughout their kingdom, and in time of war the king expected his subjects to report on the enemy's movements and gather intelligence in hostile territory. The British were aware even before they crossed the border that they were under constant Zulu surveillance, but it took them some time before they realized that the deserters and refugees they succoured or even employed as camp servants were actually spies.[2]

Knowledge of the extent of the threat and the limits of his own resources caused Cetshwayo to cast around for allies. If he really had been the prime mover of the 'black conspiracy' it should have been no challenge to summon up aid from across southern Africa, but Cetshwayo could not play the role Frere and his lieutenants had assigned him. Even though African rulers maintained diplomatic relations with each other as a matter of course, sectional advantage continued to be placed before wider, common interests, and it is the hard truth that during the closing of the frontier from 1877 to 1879 no large-scale alliance was ever formed.[3]

Despite Cetshwayo making some friendly overtures in late 1878, there was never any prospect of aid from Swaziland.[4] To the contrary, the amaSwazi had for too long been the victims of Zulu raids and threatened attacks, and King Mbandzeni looked eagerly forward to the elimination of Zulu military might. Nor was there any likelihood of cooperation with the Mabhudu-Tsonga, the dominant chiefdom across Zululand's trade routes north to Delagoa Bay. Although they had long paid tribute to the amaZulu, relations had been poor since the 1860s when they clashed with their overlord over control of the lucrative trade routes and smaller chiefdoms of the region. Muhena, the regent of the Mabhudu-Tsonga, consequently welcomed the prospect of the breaking of Zulu power. Further afield, Cetshwayo had even less chance of raising black polities under British suzerainty against their white over-lords. Despite some activity by his emissaries in late 1878, he had absolutely no success with the Basotho who had been under Cape administration since 1871, nor with the amaMphondo on the southern borders of Natal.[5] It should perhaps have been different with the Bapedi. After all, the British were convinced that Sekhukhune was being directed and manipulated by Cetshwayo, his puppet-master.[6] There is in fact evidence that the two rulers were considering a common anti-British front but, in the end, no active alliance was formed. Sekhukhune seems to have decided that it was too dangerous to allow his unresolved conflict with the Transvaal to be sucked into Cetshwayo's explosive dispute with the British. In any case, he was aware that Colonel Rowlands's No. 5 Column was strategically positioned between his territory and the Zulu kingdom. Doubtless, holding back in early 1879 was a miscalculation he came to regret, because once the British had dispatched the amaZulu they turned on him in late 1879, and he had no ally left to come to his aid.

Aware that no other African state would rally to their cause and unsure of being able to wage a successful aggressive campaign over their borders, in January 1879 Cetshwayo and his advisers opted for a defensive strategy. This approach made sense both militarily and politically. Cetshwayo learned from his white advisers—in particular from John Dunn, the white hunter-trader who supplied him with guns and whom he had rewarded in return with a large chiefdom in south-eastern Zululand—that the British had limitless resources and were capable of remaining in the field far longer than could the amaZulu. The problem was that Zulu logistics were rudimentary.

When a Zulu *impi* marched off to war, boys older than fourteen (*izindibi*) accompanied it as carriers of sleeping mats and other equipment, and also as drovers of cattle which would be slaughtered for consumption. Daughters and sisters of the warriors bearing supplies kept up with the *impi* for a few days until their stocks were exhausted. The warriors themselves carried iron rations in a skin sack. But these varied sources of food soon began to give out. The hungry *amabutho* tried to spare their own civilian population along the line of march as far as possible, and camped when they could at *amakhanda* where stores of food had been amassed. In earlier wars, when an *impi* campaigned in enemy territory, it foraged ruthlessly as it advanced, raiding the grain-pits in the abandoned *imizi*, stripping the vegetable gardens, driving off the livestock and demolishing *izindlu* for firewood. Yet when forced to operate entirely on their own soil, as they were in 1879, the hungry *amabutho* could not afford to be squeamish about pillaging their own people. For their part, Zulu civilians took the same precautions against them as against an enemy, removing their grain which was vital as seed for the next season's planting, driving off their cattle and taking refuge themselves out of the *impi*'s path.[7]

So, from the Zulu perspective, the campaign had to be short for logistical reasons. Politically, it also had to be decisive if Cetshwayo was to have any chance of negotiating a cease-fire which he believed he could manage best from a position of military strength. Yet here was the paradox. The British were unlikely to enter into any negotiations with him if his *izimpi* followed up a victory on their own soil by invading British territory. For his political strategy to succeed, Cetshwayo had to convince them that he had absolutely no hostile intentions against neighbouring British colonies. Therefore, it was essential to fight only within the borders of Zululand so that he could present himself as the victim of an unwarranted attack, legitimately defending his own. As he would declare to Cornelius Vijn soon after the battle of Isandlwana: 'It is the Whites who have come to fight with me in my own country, and not I that will go to fight with them. My intention, therefore, is only to defend myself in my own country.'[8] Cetshwayo would stalwartly maintain this stance while held prisoner after the war, and eventually public opinion in Britain would veer around and come to perceive him as the hapless victim of aggression.[9]

Having decided on this broad strategy, the next issue was how best to deploy Zulu forces for the coming war. The problem was that the kingdom faced attack from every quarter and there were not enough fighting men to go around. The numerical strength of the *amabutho* is difficult to estimate with any certainty, and alarmist settler tallies went as high as 60,000. Chelmsford and his staff made their plans with the figure of 41,900 warriors in mind. In fact, the Zulu army probably did have a nominal strength of about 40,000 men, but some of the senior *amabutho* were past active service, and actual effectives—those who were in an age-band between their early twenties and late forties—were unlikely to have numbered more than 29,000.[10] In addition, Cetshwayo could count upon an approximate 5,000 irregulars joining the *amabutho* on campaign. These included the people of the Tsonga chiefdoms to the south of the Mabhudu-Tsonga who were in a strong cultural and tributary relationship with the neighbouring Zulu kingdom, and people such as the Kubheka living in the disputed north-western region of the kingdom who owed Cetshwayo a shadowy allegiance.

In making his dispositions, Cetshwayo correctly decided to discount the possibility of a sea-borne invasion.[11] By January 1879 it was clear the British were not intending to land troops at Portuguese Delagoa Bay or at St Lucia Bay to its south, nor would they be advancing from the north-east picking up Mabhudu-Tsonga auxiliaries as they went. Nor were they going to attempt an amphibious landing further down the Indian Ocean coast despite a serious effort in August 1878 to iden-tify a suitable landing-place along a shoreline frustratingly deficient in natural harbours.[12] The king was far less confident in leaving his borders with Swaziland undefended. Nevertheless, he gambled rightly that Mbandzeni would not risk entering the conflict allied to the British until he was absolutely certain they would win. Despite repeated overtures by Norman MacLeod, the Swazi Border Commissioner, Mbandzeni prevaricated and would do no more than keep his warriors embodied, but uncommitted.[13]

The upshot was that Cetshwayo could safely ignore his northern border and coastline to concentrate on the British forces to the south and west. His spies correctly informed him that the British No. 3 (or Centre) Column operating out of Rorke's Drift was the strongest, and that Chelmsford himself was accompanying it. This intelligence persuaded Cetshwayo that the Centre Column was the main British force and that the maximum effect would be gained by defeating it. He

consequently resolved to direct his main army against it, while a subsid-
iary army would break away to confront the No. 1 (or Right) Column
preparing to advance up the coast across the lower Thukela River.
Local irregulars in the Nkandla forest in southern Zululand would
oppose the No. 2 Column if it crossed the middle Thukela (in the event
it moved west and joined the Centre Column). He also sent some reinforcements to support the irregulars in the north-west who were
confronting both the No. 4 (Left) and No. 5 Columns.[14]

In early January Cetshwayo sent out orders for his *amabutho* to
assemble at oNdini to prepare for war. Kumbeka Gwabe recalled: 'The
regiments gathered there had so many men in them that they seemed
to stretch right from there to the sea. The first thing our king did was
to give us cattle and beer to drink.'[15] During the days following the
expiry of the British ultimatum the *amabutho* mustered in the *amakhanda*
in the Mahlabathini plain were 'doctored' for war.[16] The amaZulu
believed in an overlap that existed between this world and the world of
the spirits. This was expressed by a mystical force, *umnyama*, which was
darkness or evil influence, and was represented by the colour black. As
Mpatshana explained, it could overtake an *impi* in the form of 'paralysis
of action caused by fear . . . futility or stupidity of plan when engaging
their assailants, being overtaken by a mist when it is clear for their foes,
etc.'[17] It could also be contagious in its most virulent forms. Because
such pollution was a mystical rather than organic illness, it could be
cured only by symbolic medicines. Death by violence, expressed as
umkhoka, was an especially powerful form of *umnyama*, as the killer
himself was polluted. Thus *amabutho* on campaign were in special spiritual danger, and needed to be ritually purified of evil influences and
strengthened against them.

Before marching out to war, members of an *ibutho* caught and killed
bare-handed a black bull from the royal herds upon which all the evil
influences in the land had been ritually cast. *Izangoma* (singular *isangoma*)—diviners possessed by the spirits of the ancestors (*amadlozi*),
which made them a link between this and the spirit world—cut strips
of meat from the bull, and treated them with black medicines to
strengthen the warriors and bind them together in loyalty to their king.
The strips of meat were then roasted on a fire of wood collected by the
warriors the previous day. The *izangoma* threw the strips up into the air

and the warriors, who were drawn up in a great circle, caught and sucked them. Meanwhile the *izangoma* burned more medicines and the warriors breathed in the smoke and were sprinkled with the cinders.

Weapons too were incorporated into the ceremonies of ritual purification and strengthening, and with firearms mystical forces were expected to compensate for lack of practical skill in hitting a target, just as they would protect a man from wounds and death. Mpatshana described in detail how before the Isandlwana campaign an isangoma 'made all those with guns hold their barrels downwards on to, but not actually touching, a sherd containing some smoking substance, i.e. burning drugs, fire being underneath the sherd, in order that smoke might go up the barrel. This was done so that bullets would go straight, and, on hitting any European, kill him.' The isangoma also 'made marks on our faces . . . and declared that the Europeans' bullets would be weakened . . . and not enter'.[18]

Finally, in order finally to expel all evil influences, each warrior drank a pot of medicine, and a few at a time took turns to vomit into a great pit. The ritual vomiting was also intended to bind the warriors in their loyalty to their king. Some of the vomit was added to the great *inkatha* of the Zulu nation, the sacred grass coil which was the symbol of the nation's unity and strength. The following day the warriors went down to any running stream to wash, but not to rub off the medicines with which they had been sprinkled. With the completion of these rituals the warriors (who had undergone a symbolic death) could no longer sleep at home nor have anything to do with girls or women since they themselves had now taken on a dangerous state of *umnyama*.

While the warriors were thus setting themselves apart from ordinary life and dedicating themselves to war, Cetshwayo called up pair after pair of the *amabutho* into the royal cattle enclosure to boast of their courage and to issue ritual challenges to outdo one another in the coming campaign. Mpatshana described the ritual encounter between the uKhandempemvu and iNgobamakhosi which lasted until sunset: 'A man from the iNgobamakhosi got up and shouted, "I shall surpass you, son of So-and-so. If you stab a white man before mine has fallen, you may take the kraal of our people at such-and-such a place; you may take my sister, So-and-so." ' Having made his challenge he then commenced to *giya*, or to perform a leaping war dance with his dancing shield and stick, while his companions loudly called out his praises. The member of the uKhandempemvu thus addressed answered in like kind while Cetshwayo held out his arm towards him, approvingly shaking two extended fingers at him.[19]

For the amaZulu, good fortune in a military enterprise depended on the approval of the *amadlozi* who lived under the ground and were interested in every aspect of their descendants' lives. Because the spirits maintained the status they had enjoyed while alive, it was particularly necessary before proceeding on campaign to secure the favour of the *amadlozi* of the king's royal forebears since they were necessarily concerned with the welfare of the entire Zulu nation. The way the living propitiated the *amadlozi* was through cattle sacrifice when the spirits partook of the burnt offerings and 'licked' the meat set aside for them. So, before the *impi* marched away to war, Cetshwayo ensured that the royal *amadlozi* were satisfied with a generous sacrifice from the royal herd. Now the *amadlozi* would accompany the warriors and deploy their powers against the enemy.

Before he dispatched his ritually prepared armies to the frontiers, Cetshwayo issued his generals with careful tactical instructions.[20] The king well understood the dangers involved in trying to storm prepared positions similar to the Boer wagon laagers in 1838. He therefore categorically forbade his commanders from attacking any form of entrenchment where they would be pitilessly exposed to concentrated fire-power. Rather, he cautioned them to bypass defensive works and to threaten the British lines of supply and the territory to their rear. That would force the enemy out to protect them. Then, Cetshwayo instructed, 'if you see him out in the open you can attack him because you will be able to eat him up'.[21] After all, it was in a pitched battle in the open field that the heroic virtues of the *amabutho* were most likely to prevail. On the other hand, if the British could not be brought swiftly to battle, the Zulu armies would founder for lack of logistical support. But if they won a great victory, then the king might be able to bring off his peace offensive and strike a deal with the British that would save his kingdom from destruction.

Nzuzi of the uVe *ibutho* recalled that before the *impi* finally marched out to war, the king addressed it as it stood around him in a great circle:

I have not gone over the seas to look for the white men, yet they have come into my country and I would not be surprised if they took away our wives and cattle and crops and land. What shall I do?' . . . 'Give the matter to us,' we replied. 'We shall go and eat up the white men and finish them off. They are not going to take you while we are here. They must take us first.[22]

CHAPTER 19

'How Can We Give You Mercy?'

———•◦•———

With the expiry of the ultimatum on 11 January 1879, the British Centre Column already concentrated at Rorke's Drift on the Mzinyathi River began its laborious advance into Zululand.[1] The amaZulu did not seem appropriately awed by the spectacle of military might, and taunted the British, calling out ' "What were we doing riding along there?" "We had better try and come up;" "Were we looking for a place to build our kraals?" etc., etc.'.[2]

Chelmsford inevitably overshadowed Colonel Glyn, the veteran of the Ninth Cape Frontier War and the column's nominal commander, and assumed active control of its direction. His forces scored an easy success in a skirmish at kwaSogekle (the stronghold of Sihayo kaXongo, the Qungebe *inkosi*) on 12 January. The amaZulu failed to make a determined stand which seemed to confirm British expectations that they would not prove to be any more formidable than had the amaXhosa.[3] When during the skirmish Major Clery wished to send in some mounted men 'rather widely to flank', Major Crealock, Chelmsford's military secretary, checked him:

'Do not do that as it will cause what actually happened in the last war—the enemy to take flight and bolt before we can get at them.' Again, the general issued an order that the artillery was never to open fire until the enemy were within 600 yards of them for fear of frightening them, and so deterring them from coming on, or making them bolt.[4]

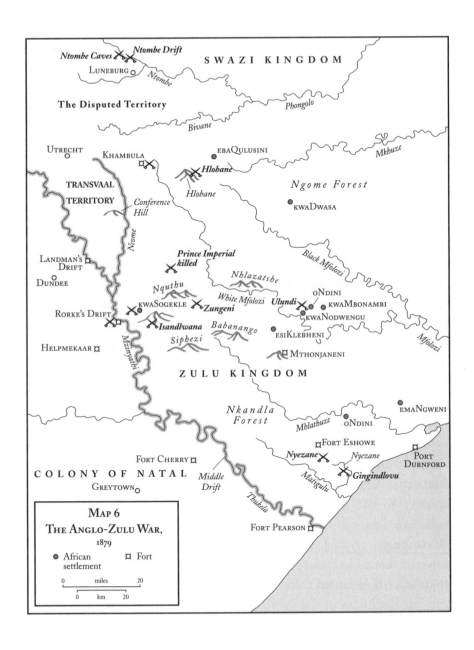

Ntombe Caves ✗ ✗ **Ntombe Drift**

LUNEBURG ○ *Ntombe*

SWAZI KINGDOM

The Disputed Territory

Phongolo

Bivane

UTRECHT ○ KHAMBULA ○✗ ebaQULUSINI ●

Mkhuze

✗ **Hlobane**

TRANSVAAL
TERRITORY

Conference Hill

Hlobane

Ngome Forest

kwaDWASA ●

Ncome

LANDMAN'S ✗
DRIFT
DUNDEE ○

Prince Imperial
✗ **killed**

Nhlazatshe

Nquthu

White Mfolozi **Ulundi** oNDINI ●

Black Mfolozi

RORKE'S DRIFT ✗ ○ kwaSOGEKLE ✗ **Zungeni**

✗ **Isandlwana** *Babanango*

kwaNODWENGU ● kwaMBONAMBI

HELPMEKAAR ✗

Siphezi

esiKLEBHENI ●

Mfolozi

Mzinyathi

✗ **Mthonjaneni**

ZULU KINGDOM

Nkandla Forest

emaNgweni ●

Mblathuze oNDINI ●

FORT CHERRY ✗

COLONY OF NATAL

GREYTOWN ○

Middle Drift

✗ FORT ESHOWE

Nyezane ✗ *Nyezane*

✗
PORT
DURNFORD

Matigulu **Gingindlovu**

Thukela

FORT PEARSON ✗

MAP 6
THE ANGLO-ZULU WAR,
1879

● African
settlement

✗ Fort

0   miles   20

0   km   20

To his annoyance, Chelmsford found that the rain-sodden, muddy ground rendered a rapid advance impossible. On 20 January he halted and set up camp at the eastern base of the sphinx-shaped Isandlwana Mountain while he prepared to reconnoitre the way forward. The position was potentially difficult to defend because it was overlooked by a spur of the Nyoni Hills to the north, and the layout of the camp was overly extended. But since Chelmsford regarded the camp as temporary, and considered a Zulu attack most unlikely, no attempt was made to entrench it. Nor were the wagons laagered because they were required to bring up supplies from Rorke's Drift. Colonists, harking back to their experience in the Boer–Zulu War of 1838, urged the general to form a laager, but it had not been the practice to laager temporary camps when on the march against the amaXhosa. In any case, until he learned better, Chelmsford regarded a laager more as protection for oxen than as a redoubt for soldiers.[5]

The Zulu response to the British invasion was rapid. After parading past the graves of King Cetshwayo's ancestors to secure the blessings of the *amadlozi*, the main Zulu *impi* of 24,000 men under the joint command of *iNkosi* Ntshingwayo kaMahole Khoza and *iNkosi* Mavumengwana kaNdlela Ntuli began its march on 17 January. Morale was high, for the *amabutho* believed in their cause and were exuberantly confident that they would scatter the *amasoja ebomvu*, or red soldiers.[6] On 20 January the *impi* bivouacked by Siphezi Hill, only just over twelve miles east of Isandlwana, and its scouts made contact with the British. Chelmsford, however, had no inkling of the enemy's close proximity. Instead, he was concerned that the local Sithole *inkosi*, Matshana kaMondisa, might be gathering a force in the broken country to the south-east of Isandlwana in order to interrupt his column's line of supply once it advanced further into Zululand. Accordingly, on 21 January Chelmsford sent out a reconnaissance-in-force to scout the area south-east of Isandlwana. It consisted of more than half his mounted men under Major John Dartnell and the bulk of the 3rd Regiment of the NNC under Commandant Rupert Lonsdale who had commanded Mfengu levies in the Ninth Cape Frontier War. Confronted by several thousand of Matshana's men on the hills to their front, the two commanders bivouacked nervously for the night on the Hlazakazi Heights.[7]

Meanwhile, the joint Zulu commanders, who had indeed been considering a flank march to Chelmsford's east to join with Matshana and cut the British column off from Natal, decided instead to take advantage of the general's division of his forces. They detached men to reinforce Matshana, but on the same evening of 21 January and during the next they transferred the main army across the British front to the deep shelter of the Ngwebeni valley. This was a truly masterful manoeuvre. The *amabutho* moved rapidly in small units, mainly concealed from the Isandlwana camp nine miles away by the Nyoni Heights. The British mounted patrols that sighted some of the apparently isolated Zulu units had no inkling an entire army was on the move.

During the moonless night of 21/22 January there was a false alarm and needless panic among the NNC encamped in a hollow square on Hlazakazi,[8] but Dartnell nevertheless urgently requested support. Chelmsford was convinced that Zulu movements in the area indicated that the main Zulu army was pushing down the Mangeni valley to the east, and decided he must move out to intercept. Colonel Glyn, accompanied by Chelmsford, accordingly advanced at 4.30 a.m. with about half the force still at Isandlwana, leaving the camp with a garrison of two 7-pounder guns, five companies of the 1/24th Regiment and one of the 2/24th, some mounted troops, and four companies of the 1/3rd NNC.

Before he left, Chelmsford ordered up Brevet Colonel Anthony Durnford from Rorke's Drift with the available men of No. 2 Column to reinforce the camp. Still smarting from his debacle at the Bushman's River Pass in 1873, Durnford was keen to retrieve his military reputation. Until he arrived—when the troops in camp would amount to 67 officers and 1,707 men (approximately half of whom were Africans)—Brevet Lieutenant-Colonel Henry Pulleine (another veteran of the Ninth Cape Frontier War) would be the senior officer. As Clery later commented, 'nobody from the general downwards had the least suspicion that there was a chance of the camp being attacked'.[9] Indeed, as Captain Henry Harford (a regular officer seconded to the NNC) later noted in his journal, some officers 'were terribly disappointed at the thought of being left behind in Camp and lose [*sic*] the chance of a fight, and begged hard to be allowed to find substitutes'.[10] Even when later that morning a thousand or more Zulu appeared fleetingly on the hills to the east of the camp, no officer was disconcerted. For, as Lieutenant Henry Curling of the Royal Artillery (one of the few officers to survive the battle) later wrote to his mother: 'We none of us had the least idea that the Zulu contemplated attacking the camp and, having in the last war [the Ninth Cape Frontier War] often seen equally large bodies of the enemy, never dreamed they would come on.'[11]

Chelmsford's relief force reached Hlazakazi at about 6 a.m. on Sunday 22 January 1879, bringing the troops operating in the area to about 2,500. They skirmished until early afternoon with the Zulu forces that were pulling away north-east towards Siphezi. Meanwhile, Chelmsford scouted about, and at 9.30 a.m. while breakfasting with his staff he received a message Pulleine had sent at 8.05 a.m. cryptically reporting that that enemy were advancing on the camp. No one suspected this could be the main Zulu army, and there seemed no sense of urgency in the message. Chelmsford himself, when Clery asked him what action he should take, nonchalantly replied: 'There is nothing to be done on that.'[12] With nothing apparently amiss, therefore, somewhere between 10 a.m. and 11 a.m. Chelmsford sent orders to Pulleine to strike camp and move up. Meanwhile, he continued scouting with a small mounted escort, and the unpredictability of his movements meant that for hours urgent messages concerning the unfolding battle at Isandlwana failed to find him.

Having finally decided on a suitable campsite on the Mangeni River above its spectacular horseshoe falls, seven miles to the south-east of Isandlwana, Chelmsford ordered the relief column under Glyn to concentrate there. As its units straggled in during the early afternoon, sounds of artillery fire were heard from the direction of Isandlwana, and messages from the camp's garrison at last reached Chelmsford. Clery afterwards wrote that he heard Crealock superciliously exclaim: 'How very amusing! Actually attacking our camp! Most amusing!'[13] Shortly after 1.15 p.m. Chelmsford examined the Isandlwana camp through field glasses from a hill just north of the Mangeni campsite. All seemed quiet, and the tents had not been struck as were the regulations during an engagement. Chelmsford therefore concluded that if there had been a Zulu attack, it had been successfully repulsed.

Finally, though, at 2.45 p.m. he decided to return to Isandlwana with a small escort to investigate. About five miles from the camp he was encountered by a shattered Commandant Lonsdale who had nonchalantly ridden back to Isandlwana to arrange for supplies to be brought up, and had barely escaped the amaZulu who were in possession of the camp. Chelmsford was appalled, reportedly exclaiming in disbelief: 'But I left over 1,000 men to guard the camp.' He nevertheless immediately decided he must retake the fallen camp, and by 6.30 p.m. had concentrated all his scattered, exhausted troops within three miles of Isandlwana. Clery later described 'the look of gloom and pain' on Chelmsford's 'expressive' countenance which clearly mirrored his inner turmoil.[14] Indeed, a soldier wrote home that he was 'very near crying'.[15] But Chelmsford never 'flunked' his duty and, anticipating Zulu resistance, addressed his dismayed troops with determination:

Men, the enemy has taken our camp. Many of our friends must have lost their lives defending it. There is nothing left for us now but to fight our way through—and mind, we must fight hard, for we will have to fight for our lives. I know you, and I know I can depend on you.[16]

The men cheered lustily in response. Chelmsford then advanced in darkness with his force in battle array. But the victorious amaZulu had already withdrawn except for a few stragglers, and Chelmsford reoccupied the camp at about 8.30 p.m. without resistance. What then followed was an horrific night spent bivouacked, as he laconically informed Frere, 'among the bodies from dead soldiers and of the enemy'.[17]

For the loss of about a thousand men, the amaZulu had killed 52 of the British officers left to defend the camp, including Pulleine and Durnford, along with 739 white troops (almost all of those in the camp), 67 white NCOs of the NNC and 471 recorded black troops. This was a 75 per cent casualty rate, an utter rout which was the rarest of rare occurrences in a colonial campaign, all the more shocking for that. How had the amaZulu achieved their stunning victory?

Late on the dull, cloudy morning of the battle the Zulu *impi* was still bivouacked in the valley of the Ngwebeni stream while small parties were out foraging and scouting. Its commanders were in conclave, discussing their next move. It was not their intention to fight that fateful Sunday because, as Mpatshana explained: 'That day the moon had waned. It was not customary to fight at such a time . . . a young woman does not dance that day . . . a garden is not reaped, a hunting party is not sent out.'[18] But, as a 'Zulu Deserter' of the uNokhenke *ibutho* related, while the *impi* was 'sitting resting', a party of mounted British scouts in pursuit of Zulu foragers driving along a small herd of cattle suddenly came over the Mabaso Heights overlooking the valley, just above the mettlesome uKhandempemvu *ibutho*. The uKhandempemvu 'at once jumped up and charged', and their fierce if ill-disciplined example was taken up by the other younger *amabutho*.[19] There was considerable disarray in this impromptu advance, and the Zulu commanders were hard-pressed to restore some order. They did succeed in keeping back four of the more experienced *amabutho* in reserve and putting them through the final ritual preparations for battle which their younger comrades had forgone—although (according to Mpatshana) many had taken the precaution of 'carrying drugs in their medicine-bags' with which to 'doctor' themselves.[20]

As it drove on towards the British camp, the *impi* deployed into its time-hallowed chest and horns formation with the intention of enveloping the British position. Pulleine made his initial dispositions without any true idea of the size of the Zulu forces bearing down on him and unaware that they were intent on outflanking him. So in copy-book fashion he pushed forward an extended firing line in an arc on either side of his two 7-pounder guns. Their position was nearly half a mile north-east of the camp in order to support outlying units falling back, and to command the dead ground to their front. Colonel Durnford—who earlier that morning had rashly ridden off for several miles to the east with his mounted men to support Chelmsford (so he believed) from a Zulu rear attack—conducted a fighting retreat to a deep donga on Pulleine's right flank.

When the Zulu centre spilled over the Nyoni Heights where the Zulu commanders halted to take up their stations, they were pinned down by the British rifle fire. Even though the troops were in skirmishing order, it was quite heavy enough to stall the daunted *amabutho* who had never, ever experienced the like. The Zulu commanders sent officers running down the hill to rally the *amabutho*, pointedly reminding them of their ritual challenges before the campaign. Sikizane kaNomageji shouted to the iNgobamakhosi: 'Why are you lying down? What was it you said to the uKhandempemvu?'[21] Another exhorted them: 'Never did his Majesty the King give you this command, to wit, "Lie down upon the ground!" His words were: "Go! And toss them into Maritzburg!"'[22] Then, as a 'Warrior of the uMbonambi' recalled, 'they all shouted "uSuthu!" [the national battle-cry] and waving their shields charged upon the soldiers with great fury'.[23]

The Zulu chest's determined charge coincided with an attempt by the British to fall back from their exposed forward positions and concentrate on their camp because they realized they were being outflanked by the rapidly deploying Zulu horns. With scarcely a month's training behind them, the two companies of the 1/3th NNC in the centre of the British line were not up to a disciplined withdrawal. They broke and ran, and the exultant *amabutho* of the Zulu chest poured through the gap. The Court of Inquiry Chelmsford later set up to investigate the 'loss of the camp' blamed the collapse of the British line on the NNC's poor performance, and Chelmsford gratefully seized on this convenient African scapegoat for the bad judgement of the British commanders on the spot.[24]

The amaZulu allowed the withdrawing British no opportunity to rally. Mehlokazulu kaSihayo remembered that: 'When the soldiers retired on the camp, they did so running, and the Zulus were then intermixed with them, and entered the camp at the same time. . . . Things were then getting very mixed and confused . . . what with the smoke, dust, and intermingling of men, footmen, Zulus and natives [NNC].'[25] The *amabutho* finally had what they so ardently desired, a brutal hand-to-hand struggle as they drove the British through the camp. The Zulu horns almost succeeded in encircling the camp and entered it from the rear. Some of the British mounted men, pursued and harried the entire way by the amaZulu, succeeded in getting away down the treacherous 'Fugitives' Path' to the Mzinyathi River which was lethally swollen by the summer rains. Small units of British infantry attempted to rally and fight their way out, or at the very least to make a gallant last stand. Nzuzi grimly recalled that as the amaZulu fell upon the white men: 'many . . . said to us in our own tongue: "Spare our lives. What wrong have we done to Cetshwayo?" "How can we give you mercy", we replied, "when you have come to us and want to take our country and eat us up? ... uSuthu!" ' And with their eyes 'dark' in battle fury the warriors 'stabbed everything we came across'.[26]

During battle a ritual many Zulu warriors followed was to *hlomula*, or to stab an enemy who had already died fighting courageously. This practice was connected with the hunt, and was observed only when a fierce and dangerous animal like a lion had been overcome. But killing in battle or participating in the *hlomula* ritual severely contaminated the warrior with an especially virulent form of *umnyama*. A notable warrior might be praised for being 'wet with yesterday's blood',[27] but when he pushed his *iklwa* into the victim's yielding flesh, or battered out his brains with an *iwisa*, the victim's blood which spurted over him and his clothing formed a fearsome bridge between the living and the world of the dead. All sorts of special ritual precautions then became necessary to gain ascendancy over the vengeful sprits of the slain.[28] One essential ritual was to slit open the belly of a slain foe, to *qaqa*, so that *umnyama* would not affect the killer and make him swell up like the dead. The killer would also put on items of the dead man's apparel in place of his own—which would have been contaminated by the harmful influences of the victim's blood—in order that he might *zila*, or observe the customary abstentions after a death until ritually cleansed.[29] The British, when they later found the disembowelled bodies of their comrades, naturally saw their mutilation in a very different light. To them it was a horror and an abomination which changed the whole nature of the war and justified merciless retaliation.

Once the fighting had died down somewhere after 2 p.m., the exultant *amabutho* set about comprehensively looting the camp in the sickly light of a partial solar eclipse.[30] Firearms and ammunition were the most highly prized booty, especially the modern Martini-Henry rifles. About eight hundred fell into Zulu hands, and in later encounters Zulu marksmen familiar through hunting with modern firearms were able to make effective use of them. Pillaging continued until, towards evening, the *amabutho* saw the dilatory Chelmsford at last approaching. Sated, they pulled back with their booty to their bivouac at the Ngwebeni. They did not bury the fallen, but as Mpatshana recalled, the bodies 'were here and there covered over with their shields—it is put over by a relative or friend'.[31]

While their comrades were relentlessly pursuing the fugitives down towards the Mzinyathi or exuberantly pillaging the camp, between three and four thousand of the Zulu reserve who had not taken part in the battle advanced in orderly fashion on their right flank. Under the command of the headstrong *uMntwana* Dabulamanzi kaMpande they went on to cross the Mzinyathi onto Natal soil in direct disobedience of Cetshwayo's instructions to his commanders not to do so.[32] Having missed the battle at the camp, it seems their intention was to salve their honour and reputation by ravaging the plain between the river and the heights of Helpmekaar. But then, in the recollection of Munyu of the uThulwana, 'they said, "O! Let us go and have a fight at Jim's!" '[33] This was the small British supply depot at Rorke's Drift, formerly a mission station. Its small garrison of eight officers and 131 men had enough time to improvise rudimentary fortifications from wagons and sacks and boxes of supplies with which they linked up the scattered buildings.

The defenders 'were in a corner',[34] as the amaZulu meaningfully put it later, fighting for their lives with nowhere to escape, but the *amabutho* made poor work of the business. They commenced their attack at 4.30 p.m., assailing different sectors of the perimeter in separate waves rather than in a concerted assault. The British were forced to evacuate the hospital and draw in their defensive position, but they held. After ten hours and prolonged periods of desperate hand-to-hand fighting, the amaZulu disconsolately withdrew in the early hours of 23 January. Rather than confirming their manhood, this botched affair disgraced them in the eyes of the local Zulu population who thought them 'shocking cowards' and jeeringly told them: ' "You! You're no men! You're just women, seeing you ran away for no reason at all, like the wind!" '[35]

For the amaZulu, Rorke's Drift was a painful reverse. Not only were 350 or more killed in the failed assault to seventeen of the British, but when Chelmsford brought his surviving troops back across the Mzinyathi after their frightful night among the disembowelled dead, some vented their anguished fury on the hundreds of wounded or exhausted amaZulu they found in the vicinity of the post or hiding in the fields and undergrowth. Commandant Hamilton-Browne of the NNC later wrote without an ounce of shame that: 'My two companies of Zulus [NNC] with some of my non-coms. and a few of the 24th quickly drew these fields, and killed them with bayonet, butt and assegai. . . . War is war and savage war is the worst of the lot. Moreover our men were worked up to a pitch of fury by . . . the mutilated bodies of the poor fellows lying in front of the burned hospital.'[36] Rorke's Drift was, moreover, a double defeat for the amaZulu. For the British, their successful defence of the post against overwhelming odds supplied them with a thoroughly welcome propaganda coup to offset the Isandlwana disaster. No less than eleven Victoria Crosses were awarded to its defenders for their outstanding gallantry, and the spurious but useful word was spread that Rorke's Drift had saved Natal from a major Zulu invasion.

Yet nothing could really disguise what a disaster Isandlwana had been for the British, one made even worse, somehow, by having to leave their dead unburied for four months in an overwhelming stench of decay until the tide of war had turned. It was only on 21 May 1879 that Chelmsford felt able to return to commence the grisly interment of the pathetic and by now desiccated remains. Still, in a sense Major Clery was surely right to reflect that Chelmsford had been singularly 'unlucky'. If the main Zulu army had gone against either of the two other columns invading Zululand instead of his, doubtless 'the same thing would have happened to them'[37] since they fully shared the general's misplaced confidence. But, as it happened, their initial encounters only reaffirmed it.

The day after the Zulu *impi* marched out on 17 January, a force of about four thousand men detached itself from the main body and marched off south-east to confront Colonel Pearson's Right Column, picking up several thousand local reinforcements as it went. Its commander, *iNkosi* Godide kaNdlela Ntuli, Mavumengwana's elder brother, was nearly seventy years old and most likely had fought the Voortrekkers in 1838. What he had learned then was probably in his mind when he attempted to ambush the British in the hills to the north of the Nyezane stream early on the morning of 22 January—the very same day as Isandlwana—while they were strung out on the march. The amaZulu called this encounter Wombane after the hill which was the key to their position, and what they attempted was certainly a sensible and appropriate military ploy.[38] It failed largely because Godide was in command of second-rate troops since most of the crack *amabutho* were with the army fighting at Isandlwana. Godide's forces neither had the stomach to press home the attack, nor were they sufficiently disciplined to coordinate their movements effectively. The men of the 1/2nd NNC in Pearson's column did not acquit themselves well either, with one company scouting in advance running away when they encountered the Zulu vanguard. Pearson was nevertheless able to close up his convoy, form a steady skirmishing line and bring superior, concentrated fire to bear from rifles, 7-pounders, rockets and the new wonder-weapon, the Gatling gun. In this fire-fight Zulu firearms were completely outclassed and the warriors never got close enough to fight hand to hand as their comrades would later that day at Isandlwana. To Sihlahla of the uMxhapho *ibutho* the effects of the British fire were devastating: 'The whites shot us down in numbers, in some places our dead and wounded covered the ground, we lost heavily, especially from the small guns. . . . The "itumlu" [Rocket] killed people but the small guns are the worst.'[39] Godide called off the Zulu attack and Pearson pushed on to the abandoned mission station at Eshowe which he immediately began to fortify.

While the Zulu *izimpi* were engaging Chelmsford's and Pearson's columns, in the north-west local forces did their best to harass Wood's and Rowlands's columns. The latter did not venture further south than its base at the little mission station at Luneburg where it skirmished with the Kubheka of *iNkosi* Manyonyoba kaMaqondo who had his stronghold in the caves of the Ntombe valley just to the north of the settlement. Wood's Column advanced east across the Ncome (Blood) River, raiding far and wide and skirmishing with the irregulars of Mbilini waMswati—an exiled Swazi prince who had lost a succession dispute in 1866 and given his allegiance to the Zulu kings—and the abaQulusi under their *induna*, Msebe kaMadaka. The abaQulusi formed a distinct *ibutho* drawn exclusively from the men living in the vicinity of the ebaQulusini *ikhanda* which King Shaka had established to dominate the region. They were thus different from the men of other *amabutho* who were drawn from the same age-group across the whole kingdom, and regarded themselves as the Zulu king's own special followers.[40] Wood nevertheless forced them to take refuge on Hlobane, the enormous flat-topped mountain which was their traditional stronghold, and seemed thoroughly in the ascendant when the shattering news of Isandlwana reached him. In the circumstances he considered it prudent to retire north-west to Khambula Hill where on 31 January he formed a strong entrenched camp. For his part, when Pearson learned of Isandlwana he decided to hold fast in Fort Eshowe and remain a thorn in the Zulu side, diverting them from attempting to invade Natal.

Certainly, it was immediately clear that his defeat at Isandlwana had comprehensively shattered Chelmsford's invasion plans. The heavy loss of life, weapons, ammunition and transport meant that he could make no further advance before his forces had regrouped and been reinforced, and before fresh transport assembled. Until then, he would have to stand on the defensive and do his best to rally the defences of Natal where panicking colonists were in daily expectation of a Zulu invasion. True, the stout defence of Rorke's Drift had certainly somewhat neutralized the shattering effects of Isandlwana, but it was now clear that if the British were to maintain their prestige in southern Africa they had to prosecute the war until the Zulu were utterly destroyed in the field. Paradoxically, Cetshwayo's great tactical victory had ensured the defeat of his political strategy. Henceforth, the British would entertain no negotiations with the king that stopped short of complete Zulu compliance with the terms of their ultimatum.

In tactical terms, Isandlwana had been a condign field defeat for the British. It administered the stern lesson that a massed Zulu charge could break through an extended infantry line no matter how superior its armaments, and that the rapidly manoeuvring Zulu horns would always turn its flanks and envelop it. Pearson's success in brushing off a poorly coordinated Zulu ambush notwithstanding, it was now painfully clear that the most effective way to concentrate fire and stem the enemy's rush was to place troops in prepared all-round defensive positions such as fieldworks, wagon laagers or infantry squares. And duly, after Isandlwana's awful lesson, it became Chelmsford's overriding tactical concern to entice the Zulu into destroying themselves against such fixed positions.

And here we encounter the concominant problem in Zulu tactical thinking. Isandlwana had been a victory because of faulty

British dispositions which, in the dispersal of units and the presentation of vulnerable flanks, were similar to an escorted convoy or column on the march. The repulse at Wombane was surely not reason enough to abandon what remained a potentially effective ploy against the British when strung out on the road. This was a situation where the amaZulu could apply their proven ability to bring up large forces undetected by the British, make the best use of their speed in attack, and consummate their fervid desire for hand-to-hand combat. By the same token, after the failure at Rorke's Drift to capture even improvised defences with all the advantages of overwhelming numerical odds and relative surprise, how could they imagine that they would succeed in the field by throwing themselves against laagers or entrenchments? Were the bulk of Zulu commanders and the rank-and-file of the amabutho simply too embedded in their established military culture to envisage alternative tactics? The next round of hostilities would tell if there was such a paralysis in Zulu tactical thinking.

Meanwhile, the amaZulu had to come to terms with the heavy cost of the first round of battles. Four days after the battle of Isandlwana, Muziwento, whose umuzi was close by, went with other boys to inspect the battlefield. What he found was horrific: 'We saw the soil that it was red. . . . We saw countless things dead . . . everything was dead. . . . Mdeni took some biscuit, but I and my brother declined. We said . . . "Sit there if you please, with your little bits of bread smelling of people's blood!" '[41] More than two thousand amaZulu probably died in those opening days of the war, including many amakhosi and prominent men at Isandlwana. Untold numbers of the wounded, their bullet-shattered bodies beyond Zulu medical skill to heal, died as they tried to drag themselves home. The few survivors from gun-shot wounds were left scarred and crippled for life. Cornelius Vijn described mourners who 'kept on wailing in front of the kraals, rolling themselves on the ground and never quieting down; nay, in the night they wailed so as to cut through the heart of anyone. And this wailing went on, day and night, for a fortnight.'[42]

CHAPTER 20

'No Quarter, Boys!'

————•◦•————

THE deadliness of British firearms left many Zulu warriors—even those who had been victorious—severely shaken, and they immediately dispersed to their homes instead of returning to oNdini to report, as was expected of them. Those who did follow the custom were in a highly contagious state of ritual contamination and had to be purified before they could see the king. For four days they were separated from their companions in special *imizi* and fed on cattle captured in battle. Daily, they washed ritually in a river and returned to *ncinda*, or to suck medicine from their finger-tips and spit it in the direction of their enemies. In this way they gained occult ascendancy over the vengeful spirits of their victims, the blood from whose fatal wounds formed a dangerous bridge between the living and the spirit world. On the final day the *izangoma* completed the warriors' ritual purification by sprinkling them with medicines before they presented themselves in the royal cattle enclosure before the king. There they exchanged accounts of the fighting and repeated the ritual challenges made before setting out to war. The king duly praised some individuals for bravery, humiliated others for cowardice and honoured and rewarded the uMbonambi *ibutho* which had most distinguished itself by being the first into the British camp at Isandlwana.[1]

For his part, the Isandlwana disaster severely affected Chelmsford's health and morale and for a time he seemed on the verge of a breakdown.[2] His incompetent conduct of the war was excoriated in harsh parliamentary debates and was subjected to angry public criticism in both Natal and Britain. The general's staff attempted to mend his tattered reputation by throwing the blame for Isandlwana on Durnford, Glyn, the NNC or anyone else they could conceivably finger.[3] The government, under fire for starting the unfortunate war in the first place, nevertheless reluctantly decided for the time being to stand by Chelmsford. Its members did not yet possess an authoritative picture of what had actually happened at Isandlwana and charitably believed that it would be premature summarily to fire their commander in Zululand. In any case, and no matter what the cost, they were now obliged to pursue the war there to a victorious conclusion, both to avenge Isandlwana and to reassert British military paramountcy in southern Africa in the most unambiguous fashion. Consequently, on 16 February 1879 the government agreed to Chelmsford's urgent request for reinforcements and dispatched six battalions, two cavalry regiments, two artillery batteries and a company of engineers to Natal.[4]

The poor performance of the NNC seemed to have vindicated scepticism in Natal about the wisdom of raising them in the first place, but Chelmsford still needed their manpower and set about improving their structure and training. He disbanded the 3rd Regiment which had suffered so badly at Isandlwana and only reassembled it in April as the Weenen Contingent. He broke up the 2nd Regiment (which Pearson had sent back from Eshowe) and the 1st Regiment into five independent battalions. The new battalions received abler commanders than previously and at least one officer in every company was required to speak isiZulu. The existing, highly unsatisfactory white NCOs were transferred to newly raised mounted units and African headmen took their places. Several hundred breech-loading Sniders and Martini-Henry rifles were issued to each battalion in addition to their old Enfields, and the men were given uniforms and drilled until they became proficient. They would be altogether better units when Chelmsford marched them into Zululand again.[5]

But that would not happen until Chelmsford had completed the reorganization of his forces and absorbed the reinforcements being sent him. Meanwhile, low-intensity fighting continued on the coast and in the north-west. In Eshowe, Pearson's lack of initiative and dearth of mounted troops meant that he lurked defensively behind the walls of his fort waiting to be relieved. He refused to be drawn out by the several thousand Zulu forces living in the vicinity who, under *uMntwana* Dabulamanzi's command, were cutting his lines of communication back to Natal and harassing his patrols and foraging parties. For their part, the amaZulu dared not assault the fort which the garrison improved daily, so two months of enervating stalemate ensued.[6]

The north-western front was rather different. In early February Chelmsford confided to Colonel Evelyn Wood, the energetic commander of No. 4 Column, that he was 'fairly puzzled' when he contemplated future operations, and wished he saw his way 'with honour out of this beastly country'. In the same letter he added that he was depending on Wood and his dashing commander of mounted troops, Lieutenant-Colonel Redvers Buller, to pull him 'out of the mire'.[7] They did their best to oblige, repeatedly sallying out in mounted raids during February and early March to burn the ebaQulusini *ikhanda*, raid Hlobane Mountain, and attack Manyonyoba in the Ntombe caves. They captured great herds of cattle and the amaZulu within their reach began to withdraw or to submit.[8]

In the second week of March *uMntwana* Hamu, Cetshwayo's discontented rival, decided to defect to Wood's camp with many of his Ngenetsheni adherents. This act of treason sent shock-waves through the Zulu kingdom for it was the first clear indication that some Zulu notables had decided that the game was up, and that it would be best to come to terms with the British. In the aftermath of Isandlwana Cetshwayo had been adhering to his political agenda by making peace overtures to the British, but they had all been brusquely dismissed.[9] This failure, coming on top of Hamu's deplorable defection, persuaded him and his advisers to seize the initiative and go over onto the offensive before the British were ready to invade again. Wood's camp at Khambula would be the objective since his activities were currently presenting the gravest threat to the kingdom. So, in the second half of March the *amabutho* began to reassemble at oNdini for the new campaign. The king and his council knew that the very existence of the kingdom would hinge on its success. In earnest of the seriousness of its mission, the *impi* was placed under the supreme command of Mnyamana, Cetshwayo's chief councillor and the second man in the kingdom. Ntshingwayo, the tough victor of Isandlwana, would lead it into battle.[10]

The attack on Wood's camp was clearly intended to be a reprise of the victorious assault on Chelmsford's at Isandlwana, and would inevitably take the form of a pitched battle—ideally in the open field—where there was little doubt that the amaZulu would repeat their customary tactics. There was a certain irony in this likelihood. During the course of the fluid war of raid and counter-raid in the north-west, the abaQulusi, Mbilini's irregulars and Manyonyoba's Kubheka were repeatedly demonstrating the effectiveness of flexible skirmishing tactics and the advantages of fighting like the amaSwazi or Bapedi from behind the rocks and breastworks of their strongholds. These fighters were at least as valiant as the *amabutho*, and in the long run more successful too, for Wood would never manage to subdue them entirely and at the end of the war they would be the very last Zulu units still fighting in the field.

In March these irregulars scored two successes which came second only to Isandlwana in the number of casualties they inflicted on the British. On 12 March Mbilini caught a convoy of supplies escorted by a company of the 80th Regiment (which formed part of the 5th Column that had been attached to Wood's command on 26 February) asleep at dawn. Their ill-formed laager at a drift across the Ntombe River not far from Luneburg was not defensible, and in the complete rout the British lost sixty-one of their officers and men besides eighteen wagon drivers.[11]

The British debacle on Hlobane on 28 March was even more disastrous and occurred at the unanticipated intersection of several military movements.[12] At the end of March Chelmsford was at last ready to march to the relief of Eshowe and instructed Wood to create as much of a diversion as he could in his sector. Accordingly, he raided the Ntombe valley again on 25 March, and decided to attack Hlobane next. It was a significant target because the abaQulusi and Mbilini's warriors were again using the great mountain with its coronet of sheer, rocky cliffs as their base and as a refuge for their livestock. On 27 March Wood led out a mixed force of 1,300 mounted men and African auxiliaries (Wood's Irregulars and Hamu's Ngnetsheni) from Khambula. The following, rainy morning one wing under Buller stormed the eastern summit while another waited in support below the enormous mountain's western flank. Buller pushed westwards across the mountain with his captured cattle, but he had fallen into a trap. As the story went in Zululand after the battle: 'When the Whitemen got to the top, seeing the mountain a nice level plain . . . but not the Qulusi, who were hiding, they said "Hlobane is a fine place! It's like a man's head-ring." But the Qulusi heard all that, and sprang up on all sides and stabbed them.'[13] Certainly, Buller found himself surrounded, with the abaQulusi across his route back down the eastern side of the mountain. Even worse, the British had failed to heed intelligence that the main Zulu army was on the move towards Khambula. Buller's men were aghast when the *impi* appeared in battle array below Hlobane to the south, scudding across the spreading plain like the shadow of an appalling cloud. Several *amabutho* were detached to support the abaQulusi, and the British were nearly cut off as they scrambled despairingly down the precipitous 'Devil's Pass' on the western side of Hlobane to make their escape back to Khambula. In the ignominious rout (during which Buller and four others earned the Victoria Cross for gallantly aiding the fugitives) the British lost ninety-four officers and men and over a hundred African auxiliaries, along with most of their captured cattle.

The amaZulu were naturally exultant at this unanticipated victory, but they had forfeited any advantage of surprise. While the *impi* bivouacked for the night near the Black Mfolozi River, at Khambula Wood used the respite to ready the 2,086 men under his command (only 132 of whom were African) in his defensive complex of fort, wagon laager and stone kraals. Cetshwayo had repeatedly warned his *amabutho* to avoid precisely this sort of fixed position and 'not to put their faces into the lair of the wild beasts, or else they would get clawed'.[14] Rather, with the lesson of Rorke's Drift before him, he exhorted his commanders to attempt to manoeuvre so as to draw Wood out and fight him in the open. But, as Mehlokazulu recounted, 'the regiments were anxious to attack, but we went there cross, our hearts were full, and we intended to do the same as at Isandhlwana'.[15] Indeed, the *impi*, especially the pairs of fanatically competitive rival *amabutho*, was too buoyed up by victory at Hlobane to heed caution. Consequently, when on 29 March the advancing *impi* halted at midday four miles south of Khambula, the firebrands had their way. As Cetshwayo later complained, 'an insubordinate regiment—the iNgobamakhosi—said they would attack, and actually advanced to do so, contrary to orders. Mnyamana seeing this, then decided to attack with the whole army.'[16] Deploying into a fearsome crescent extending over ten miles, at about 1 p.m. between seventeen and twenty thousand warriors began their menacing, deliberate advance on Khambula from the south-east. Full of bravado, they began to sing out as soon as they came within earshot of the apprehensive defenders: 'We are the boys from Isandhlwana!'[17]

But this time, the outcome would be very different for the *amabutho*, even though the impending battle would be by far the most prolonged and fiercest they would ever fight.[18] At about 1.30 p.m. Buller's mounted men ranging outside the camp stung the overeager right horn into a premature attack which stalled under heavy fire from the British rifles and six 7-pounder guns. Zulu strategy was unhinged, and thereafter, for four grinding, murderous hours the *amabutho* launched a series of uncoordinated attacks from three directions which (as had been the case at Rorke's Drift, but on a much smaller scale) allowed the British to meet each one in detail. Even so, the amaZulu stormed the cattle kraal, chasing out its defenders, and came up to the very perimeter of the laager. For a moment the *amabutho* scented victory. Wood had urgently to reposition his artillery, and daring British sorties were required to drive the *amabutho* back at bayonet point. Zulu sharpshooters armed with captured rifles caught the British in enfilading fire and had to be silenced by the artillery. But the strong Zulu tide began to ebb once it became clear that it would never sweep over the British defences. As Mehlokazulu of the iNgobamakhosi *ibutho* (which bore the brunt of the fighting on the Zulu right) remembered with horror, 'we . . . were lying prostrate—we were beaten, we could do no good. So many were killed that the few who were not killed were lying between the dead bodies, so thick were the dead.'[19]

By about 5 p.m. all the *amabutho* were exhausted and dispirited and the *impi* commenced an orderly withdrawal under fire. That was the moment for Wood to launch his counter-attack. Buller charged out with three columns of mounted troops aching to exact revenge for the loss of so many comrades on Hlobane the day before. Captain Cecil D'Arcy of the FLH crowed that his men had been 'butchering the brutes all over the place' and that he had told them: 'No quarter boys, and remember yesterday.'[20] A Zulu *impi* had last experienced a mounted sortie at the battle of Ncome forty years before, and once again its commanders could not rally their demoralized *amabutho*. Retirement broke down into utter rout. The remorseless British pursuit in which no prisoners were taken continued as far as Zungwini Mountain ten miles away, and was only called off with the fall of darkness.

The British counted 785 Zulu corpses within a mile radius of their camp, and noted how many of the men were in the prime of life and horribly disfigured by their wounds. Many hundreds more lay dead along the line of flight or rotted undetected for months in the long grass. Probably, nearly two thousand amaZulu perished, and the amaZulu calculated that more men of high rank were killed at Khambula than in any other battle of the war. The British lost only three officers and twenty-five men. Wood was luckier than Chelmsford, for his decisive victory at Khambula over the best army the amaZulu could muster effectively blotted out his undeniable disaster the day before at Hlobane. Without it, he too would have been pilloried.

Mnyamana did his best to keep the shattered Zulu army together to return in some order to the king, but for the most part the men were too shocked by defeat to obey. It seemed even the valorous *amabutho* could be daunted, and as Sihlahla of the uMxhapho later expressed it: 'Not one in our force doubted our being beaten, and openly said they had had enough and would go home.'[21] Despite their previous experiences at Isandlwana, they had found the intensity of the British fire and the ferocity of the mounted pursuit unimaginable. While being held prisoner, Sihlahla described how:

> Everyone in the iNgobamakhosi lay down as the safest, for the bullets of the white men were like hail falling about us. It was fearful, no one could face them without being struck. . . . I found myself near a large white stone placed there by the white people [a range marker]; behind this I got and remained there until the force gave way and fled. We were then pursued by the horsemen from the camp, who rode after our retreating army and turned them about like cattle.[22]

In an undated letter he scrawled to Wood in mid-April, the usually punctiliously courteous Chelmsford could not bring himself to squeeze out generous praise for his far-too-successful subordinate, and wrote only: 'One line to congratulate you upon your successful repulse of the attack made upon Kambula laager—I am up to my ears in work & cannot say as much as I could wish.'[23] The reason for Chelmsford's ill-disguised jealousy was that only four days after Khambula, on 2 April 1879, he had scored his own victory which Wood's threatened to eclipse.[24]

When he had marched to the relief of Eshowe, Chelmsford was determined to avoid his previous mistakes. This time he organized effective forward reconnaissance, and while on the march scrupulously laagered at every halt. On the early morning of 2 April, a day's march from Eshowe, the 5,670 men of the Eshowe Relief Column under his 'personal command' (his official dispatch hums with a deep sense of personal vindication) routed the Zulu force of ten thousand men mustered to intercept his advance under the command of Somopho kaZikhala, the *induna* of the emaNgweni *ikhanda* further up the coast. Thanks to Chelmsford's painstaking precautions, the Eshowe Relief Column was securely positioned within its entrenched laager near the burned-out kwaGingindlovu *ikhanda*. The Zulu attack developed at about 6 a.m. The warriors came on at the double in two divisions deployed in open order and taking advantage of the coastal bush for cover. They all but surrounded the laager, but their determined assaults all broke down at about twenty yards from its perimeter. There they came under the concentrated fire not only of the rifles, but of two 9-pounder guns, rockets and Gatling guns positioned at the laager's four corners. By 7 p.m. the Zulu attackers were pinned down everywhere, and Chelmsford ordered out his mounted men (150 white and 130 African) to charge them. The amaZulu had suffered enough and broke, hotly pursued. The two thousand men of the 4th and 5th Battalions of the NNC who had been kept in reserve during the Zulu attack were now unleashed to mop up behind the mounted men and kill all the Zulu wounded—a task they performed with gusto. A British soldier wrote home that 'we sent our blacks out amongst them . . . and some of [the wounded amaZulu] asked our blacks for a drop of water: yes and they gave them water too—they put their assegais through them and stuck them to the ground.'[25] The NNC were particularly active along the banks of the Nyezane stream where fleeing amaZulu had abandoned their wounded to their grisly fate.[26] In all, the amaZulu lost somewhere close to fifteen hundred dead to nine British soldiers and seventeen African troops. Chelmsford relieved the Eshowe garrison the day after the battle and then evacuated it to the Natal border to regroup.

If Chelmsford was now victorious and readying himself for a second major thrust into Zululand to finish the war, the situation was very different for the amaZulu. Their crushing, almost simultaneous defeats at opposite ends of the kingdom spelled nothing but ruin for their cause. Not without reason 'the King was very angry with us when we went back', later admitted a warrior of the uThulwana. 'He said we were born warriors, and yet allowed ourselves to be defeated in every battle.'[27] The problem was that their tactics were time and again proving ineffective in pitched battles against fortified positions. Cornelius Vijn recalled that the amaZulu were intensely indignant at the British way of fighting which revealed the yawning gap between British military culture and their own. 'Why', they complained:

> could not the whites fight with us in the open? But, if they are too much afraid to do this, we have never fought with men who were so much afraid of death as these. They are continually making holes in the ground and mounds left open with little holes to shoot through. The English burrow in the ground like wild pigs.[28]

Meanwhile an absurd 'war' of a different sort had broken out on another front.[29] When the British went on to the defensive after Isandlwana, Chelmsford greatly reinforced the Border Guard with levies from the interior of Natal (such as the Ixopo Native Contingent), and by the end of May its strength was probably about 7,700 men. Chelmsford insisted that these border levies make diversionary raids across the border into Zululand as part of what he termed the 'active defence'.[30] Bulwer baulked since the lieutenant-governor correctly anticipated that a damaging cycle of raid and counter-raid would be initiated. As he saw it, the border levies had been raised solely to protect Natal from Zulu attack and were under his command, not Chelmsford's. Frere agreed with Bulwer that the raw levies would be better reserved for the 'passive defence' within Natal's borders.[31] But with his credit and prestige fatally damaged by the Isandlwana disaster, the High Commissioner drew back from intervening aggressively as he had done in the Cape in 1878 to resolve the issue of divided command. His sights were in any case set on the Transvaal Territory where the irreconcilable Boers were agitating against British annexation, and he left Natal on 15 March to negotiate directly with them.[32] With Frere a broken reed, both Bulwer and Chelmsford bombarded their respective superiors in London with inordinately long and intemperate dispatches.

This shrill dispute was a final straw for a British government that already perceived Chelmsford to be demoralized, uncertain of his strategy, and unable to bring the increasingly expensive war to a speedy conclusion.[33] So, while on 19 May Hicks Beach indicated that he supported Chelmsford's claim to the 'full command of any forces, whether European or Native',[34] this decision was rapidly followed by another, altogether crushing one. Lord Beaconsfield's exasperated cabinet decided this was the moment to rein in its entire pack of squabbling, unsatisfactory senior officers and officials in southern Africa by creating a single, unified command for the troubled parts of the region. On 28 May the chief civil and military authority in south-eastern Africa was placed in the hands of the reformist and incorrigibly thrusting General Sir Garnet Wolseley. As full general he would outrank Lieutenant-General Chelmsford, as Governor of Natal he would subordinate Lieutenant-Governor Bulwer, and as Governor of the Transvaal and High Commissioner for South East Africa he would sideline Frere to the Cape Colony.[35]

When Chelmsford finally launched his long-delayed second invasion of Zululand he was unaware that he had been superseded. Only on 16 June would he learn informally of Wolseley's appointment.[36] Then, the sure knowledge that Wolseley was on his way spurred him on to defeat the amaZulu in a final, decisive battle before his rival could rob him of the credit.[37]

CHAPTER 21

'The Army Is Now Thoroughly Beaten'

IN Zululand, as Sibhalo kaHibana revealed under interrogation, rapidly spreading word of the devastating defeats at Khambula and Gingindlovu 'where so large a number was killed, shook the country'.[1] With his *amabutho* scattered in disarray to their homes and his strategy for prosecuting the war in ruins, Cetshwayo was left perplexed by what to do next. Ironically, so too was Chelmsford.[2] He knew he had entirely regained the initiative, but he was taxed in deciding how best to employ the embarrassing number of reinforcements rushed out to him by the anxious government. Besides, the growing concentration of troops in Natal was putting intolerable strain on his Commissariat and Transport Department which had already been revealed as unequal to the demands placed upon it. Of one thing Chelmsford was certain: this time he would exercise extreme caution to avoid a repetition of Isandlwana. Cavalry would carefully reconnoitre the route ahead, the troops would laager every night, and he would regularly halt to establish fortified supply depots along the lines of communication.[3] Appropriately, Chelmsford's own uninspiring motto of 'slow and steady wins the race' would characterize the second invasion of Zululand.[4]

Chelmsford's senior officers (and he now had four newly arrived, self-important major-generals to accommodate)[5] advocated sending in a single column to place less strain on the Commissariat and Transport Department. Nevertheless, Chelmsford eventually decided to deploy two widely spaced columns to screen the Transvaal and Natal from a possible Zulu counter-blow. The 1st Division of 7,500 men under

Major-General Henry Crealock (Chelmsford's military secretary's equally insufferable brother) was to advance on oNdini up the coast. The 2nd Division of 5,000 men under Major-General Edward Newdigate (accompanied by Chelmsford) was to march on oNdini from the north-west instead of following the route of the ill-fated No. 3 Column. It would take longer and the unfamiliar route required considerable reconnaissance, but for reasons of morale it was considered wise to avoid the stricken field of Isandlwana. On the way it was to rendezvous with Wood's 3,200 men, now renamed the Flying Column.[6]

Despite the number of British regulars under his command, Chelmsford still found the five battalions of NNC infantry, six mounted African troops, and three companies of NNP indispensable. The mounted Africans, in conjunction with similar small colonial units, were far more versatile and observant in scouting than were the two regiments of ponderous regular British cavalry now serving with the 2nd Division; while the African infantry were essential for protecting the increasingly attenuated lines of supply and releasing British troops for combat operations. And when it came to battle, they would again be invaluable in pursuit of the broken enemy.[7]

Zulu resistance to the new British two-pronged advance which began to gain momentum during May 1879 was distinctly muted. The amabutho were still dispersed, and only small, irregular units occasionally skirmished with the invaders. Thirty years later conservative amaZulu were still inclined to deride fighters who 'waylaid' their enemies 'in forests and fastnesses' because real warriors 'would have taken up a position in the open and come face to face with the foe'.[8] Even so, in 1879 there were some innovative commanders willing to break the conventional mould. On 1 June a scouting party of thirty or more ambushed a small mounted British patrol, opening the attack with a fusillade from thick cover before charging. In hand-to-hand fighting they killed the young Prince Imperial of France, the pretender to the Bonapartist throne, who was accompanying Chelmsford's headquarters as an observer. The Prince's death occasioned as much consternation in Britain as the battle of Isandlwana, and further damned Chelmsford in the public eye.[9] Four days later, on 5 June at a cluster of four imizi on the slopes of Zungeni Mountain known as eZulaneni and belonging to *iNkosi* Sihayo, three hundred amaZulu, most of them carrying firearms, successively repulsed three hundred British irregular horse and then the five hundred regular cavalry which charged up to support them. Effective Zulu skirmishing tactics and the correct exploitation of the terrain and cover had again proved their potential.[10] This encounter, which disconcerted the British, was an example of what the amaZulu were capable of achieving—although too seldom attempting—when they followed the style of fighting adopted by irregulars in north-western Zululand.

Embarrassing as they were, skirmishes such as these were as mere pin-pricks to Chelmsford in the wider context of the campaign. His ultimate objective was to break the neck of the Zulu power in one final, cataclysmic pitched battle from which it would never recover. In order to drive Cetshwayo and his *amabutho* to this extremity, he pursued a strategy requiring both a carrot and a stick.

Even before the first invasion, Chelmsford had known the Zulu kingdom to be riven by tensions between the king and his ambitious royal relations and great *amakhosi*. He hoped to exploit these divisions to the British advantage by encouraging disaffected chiefs and their adherents to follow *uMntwana* Hamu's example, and defect. As the carrot, Chelmsford offered easy terms of surrender to Zulu notables while remaining steadfast in requiring that Cetshwayo submit entirely to the tough terms of the British ultimatum. The stick involved harsh measures against the civilian population. It is true that Chelmsford forbade unauthorized excesses against the civilian population on pain of 'flogging',[11] but he hoped that by rendering the Zulu population hungry and depriving it of shelter he would provoke Cetshwayo's desperate subjects into deposing him and surrendering. In this he was no different from other commanders in Queen Victoria's 'small wars' who accepted civilian suffering as an unfortunate ancillary to victory. Accordingly, as Crealock, his Military Secretary, wrote of Chelmsford in late June, the general did 'not wish to prolong the war or in any way inflict any unnecessary hardship on the Zulus; but war can't be made with kid gloves'.[12] In any case, ever since Isandlwana and the disembowelling of the slain, the British attitude to ordinary amaZulu had hardened considerably. As the war correspondent Charles Norris-Newman reported:

The fallacy of fighting with an uncivilised race with the same feelings of humanity that dictate our wars with civilised races was thoroughly proved; and it thus was shown that in Zululand neither men, kraals, cattle, nor crops should be spared on any pretence whatever, except on the complete submission and disarmament of the whole nation.[13]

So besides systematically destroying the two dozen *amakhanda* in Zululand—which as rallying-points for the *amabutho* and depots for Zulu supplies could be considered legitimate military targets—the British also remorselessly attacked the Zulu people's basic means of survival.[14] Tactically, widespread pillaging in the area of operations denied the opposing Zulu forces bases, shelter and supplies, and thus created an extensive zone free of Zulu forces around the British columns when vulnerably extended while on the march. But following a scorched-earth policy also helped demoralize ordinary amaZulu and sap their desire to resist. Repeated and ruthless mounted patrols were sent out to burn *imizi* or to demolish their *izindlu* for use as fuel, to destroy standing crops and grain stores, and drive off cattle, goats and sheep. As one colonial newspaper correspondent ruthlessly put it:

By deprivations of all kinds the Zulu . . . must 'feel' the miseries of war, and nothing will bring home to them the horrors of war better than being deprived of the shelter of huts in these cold nights. Fire, sword and rifle must never rest, day or night, to make every Zulu man, woman or child at last cry for peace.[15]

Other correspondents, however, could not help recommending a 'little sympathy' for the enemy, even if 'in campaigns of this kind one is apt to look lightly on the sufferings of the enemy who, happening to be of a darker hue, is often supposed to be utterly devoid of the gentler feelings possessed by the superior white man'.[16] Those with eyes to see noticed the human plight of victims of a mounted raid and reported: 'As usual, some Zulu women and children were brought in. It was strange to see a Kaffir woman in tears. Most likely, she had had her home burnt, and all that she cared for was scattered.'[17] Indeed, the devastation the British visited upon ordinary amaZulu should not be minimized. Even allowing for the fact that great stretches of Zululand were never visited by British patrols, they nevertheless destroyed many hundreds of *imizi* and captured tens of thousands of cattle and other livestock.

Yet what is noteworthy about the Zululand campaign is that the worst that befell civilians who fled the mounted patrols for the security of the nearest mountain or wooded valley was the loss of their homes and possessions. Those who were rounded up were in little or no danger of being killed by their captors. The very limited number of atrocities perpetrated against Zulu civilians—as opposed to wounded Zulu warriors who were routinely slaughtered—can plausibly be attributed to their usual reluctance to wage guerrilla-style warfare. Consequently, the British were not stung (as is typical in counter-insurgency operations) into wild reprisals against civilians who might be harbouring fighters. It is no coincidence that the worst incident in the whole course of the war occurred in north-western Zululand where from the outset the inhabitants had been fighting a guerrilla-style campaign. Even then, when on 8 September the British blew up some caves in the Ntombe valley killing about thirty die-hard Kubheka defenders and the civilians sheltering with them, it could be argued (admittedly by a considerable stretch) that the action was legitimate since the Kubheka refused to surrender and were still fighting back.[18]

As the two British divisions crept methodically but remorselessly towards oNdini—the 1st Division was derisively known as 'Crealock's Crawlers'—ordinary amaZulu fleeing British raids could see that the tide of war had turned irreversibly against them. Unsurprisingly, the previous trickle of Zulu defections and submissions became a flood. This was particularly the case along the coastal plain where the whole-sale surrender of the demoralized civilian population—even before the final battle of Ulundi had been fought on 4 July—was not simply a consequence of the disheartening record of absolute lack of Zulu military success in that theatre. What made it feasible were the easy terms Chelmsford instructed his commanders to offer *amakhosi* increasingly willing to lay down their arms.

For weeks Cetshwayo and his advisers seemed to have been paralysed by the inexorable British advance before finally reacting. In the king's own recorded words:

During June and July Cetshwayo had decided on no definite plan of operations. He received information that Lord Chelmsford's division and General Crealock's would meet on the Mthonjaneni [Heights overlooking the Mahlabathini plain from the south] and move together on oNdini. On the arrival of Lord Chelmsford's force there [29 June], he saw it was impossible for General Crealock to come up in time, so he decided to give his whole attention to Lord Chelmsford. He called up men from all the districts, leaving only a few in the coast country to protect the cattle.[19]

While waiting for the *amabutho* to muster, which they did with grim foreboding and greater reluctance than in the past, Cetshwayo made increasingly desperate efforts to negotiate with Chelmsford. But Chelmsford knew that Wolseley was making every effort to reach the front in order to take up his command,[20] and he was determined that Zulu resistance should continue until he had achieved the crushing victory in the field he believed essential for polishing his tarnished reputation.[21] So, while he continued to advance, Chelmsford deliberately spun out negotiations by insisting on terms he made increasingly crushing and impossible for Cetshwayo to accept.

On 30 June Chelmsford moved down to an entrenched camp just across the White Mfolozi from oNdini. In a last-ditch effort, Cetshwayo tried to send a herd of his prized royal white cattle to the British as a peace offering. To his frustration, as he later informed the Governor of the Cape, the uKhandempemvu *ibutho* 'drove them back and said they would fight. . . . I then asked [them] why they would not allow the cattle to be taken to the English. And they said, "We will all rather die." '[22] So, to the very last, the *amabutho* were determined to assert their heroic honour, no matter how terrible the likely cost. But, as Cetshwayo grimly warned them: 'If you prod the ground with your stick, the earth will be hard.'[23]

And so it proved. Chelmsford was determined not to confront the Zulu army from an entrenched position as he had at Gingindlovu, but in a great, hollow infantry square. By finally defeating the amaZulu in the open field which favoured their style of warfare, he hoped to impress on them the invincibility of British arms. Since he intended to fight the climactic battle in the Mahlabathini plain in the midst of the

great *amakhanda* clustered there, on 3 July he sent in a mounted reconnaissance of about five hundred men under Buller's command to find
the best location for it. One last time a Zulu commander of considerable dash showed what the amaZulu might have done under more
innovative leadership. Zibhebhu kaMaphitha was the *inkosi* of the
Mandlakazi in north-eastern Zululand, a cousin of the king's and
senior *induna* of the uDloko *ibutho*. Nevertheless, although his personal
courage and skills as a commander were widely acknowledged, he had
been kept out of high command on account of his relatively youthful
age of thirty-five. When on 3 July Buller led his sortie across the White
Mfolozi, Zulu horsemen with Zibhebhu at their head skilfully drew the
British into an ambush where several *amabutho* lay hidden in the long
grass. Fortunately for the British, the opening Zulu volley at only fifty
yards was fired high and they managed to extricate themselves in a
scrambling fighting retreat. The Zulu pursued them all the way to the
river's edge in excellent skirmishing order, but their victory was less
complete than they had planned.[24]

At about 1.30 a.m. that night the British were awakened by the
amabutho at the kwaNodwengu *ikhanda* 'singing a war song, thousands
of voices and a grand chant, it came echoing up the river magnificently
. . . as more and more voices swelled it'.[25] Although the awed listeners
could not know it, never again would the gathered manhood of the
Zulu kingdom join in raising their stirring *amahubo* (*ihubo* singular),
the sacred ballads honouring the mighty deeds of the ancestors and
great warriors of the past, for the coming day would see them scattered
in final defeat.

At very first light on 4 July, Chelmsford advanced his square to a
position one-and-a-half miles west of oNdini itself.[26] His force totalled
5,170 men, of whom a thousand were African. The infantry were
drawn up four ranks deep supported by six 9-pounder and six 7-pounder
guns, as well as two Gatling guns. The irregular horse, cavalry and
African infantry waited inside the square. Between 15,000 and 20,000
amaZulu under the command of *uMntwana* Ziwedu kaMpande,
Cetshwayo's brother, were concentrated in the plain. At about 8 a.m.
they advanced on the square in loose undulating lines with large masses
in support, preceded by waves of skirmishers, and within half an hour
they had completed their encirclement.

The British irregular horse then sallied out to draw the advancing amaZulu into effective firing range. However, experience in previous battles had given the *amabutho* a chastened sense of the effectiveness of close-range, concentrated fire. So they came on warily in crouching positions behind their shields, taking advantage of the natural cover and the dense smoke from the British weapons and burning *amakhanda* nearby. Zulu veterans admitted that after their recent, severe defeats 'we did not fight with the same spirit, because we were then frightened'.[27] From within the British square Wood was of the same opinion, writing in his reminiscences that 'the Regiments came on in a hurried, disorderly manner, which contrasted strangely with the methodical, steady order in which they had advanced at Kambula. . . . [I] could not believe they would make so half-hearted an attack.'[28] Many of the Zulu reserves never joined the battle. Among the *amabutho* who attacked the British square there were those who hung back out of effective range, but others pushed forward with great courage and determination. Yet even they were almost all pinned down a hundred yards from the square, unable to penetrate the zone of point-blank fire. Only the iNgobamakhosi and uVe came close to breaking through the cordon of fire at the right rear corner of the square where they made good use of the shelter provided by the burning kwaNodwengu *ikhanda*. When a dense column of reserves moved out in support from oNdini they were summarily dispersed by artillery fire.

Increasingly daunted and disordered, at about 9.20 a.m. the discouraged *amabutho* began a demoralized, ragged withdrawal. That was the moment for the 17th (Duke of Cambridge's Own) Lancers and all the other mounted troops to sally out of the square in a devastating counter-attack. Supported by artillery fire they drove the amaZulu from the field in complete disarray and did not rein in until they reached the hills two miles away. The 2nd Battalion NNC and Wood's Irregulars then gleefully burst out of the square to assist the irregular horse in dispatching the Zulu wounded and in putting all the *amakhanda* in the plain to the torch. Thirteen died on the British side compared to some 1,500 amaZulu.

With the gathered military might of the Zulu nation crushed and scattered in the very heart of their kingdom, a grimly satisfied Chelmsford could be assured that British arms had been vindicated throughout southern Africa, and that Isandlwana had been avenged. As for the defeated amaZulu, they were disconsolately aware that their nerve and heroic resolve had at last splintered at what many called oCwecweni, the battle of the corrugated-iron sheets. The flashing of the British bayonets, swords and gun barrels doubtless gave rise to this impression, but perhaps the apparent 'unfairness' of the British defences helped salve their loss of honour. What was certain in all Zulu minds, though, was the decisiveness of their defeat. Ndungungunga kaNgengene declared immediately after the battle: 'The army is now thoroughly beaten, and as we were beaten in the open, it will not reassemble or fight again.'[29]

Nor did it. After Ulundi the Zulu army speedily dispersed all over the country and no organized forces remained in the field.[30] King Cetshwayo himself did not witness the battle because he had left oNdini the day before for the kwaMbonambi *ikhanda*. Once runners informed him that his army had been routed, he immediately retired northwards with the idea of making a further stand. But his *amabutho* would not respond to his order to reassemble, and Cetshwayo accepted that the game was up. So he sent further word for them to disperse for, as Magema Fuze reported, 'he did not wish his people to come to an end, for they had now fought a good deal and had suffered greatly'.[31] While Cetshwayo sought refuge in remote *imizi* far to the north, the great men of the kingdom, 'deadened like stones', saw that 'the Zulu house must go to the ground'[32] and made ready to treat with the conqueror.

It would not be with Chelmsford, however. Having won his great victory before Wolseley could arrive to supersede him and rob him of the credit, Chelmsford promptly resigned his command on 5 July 1879. He believed he had salvaged his reputation, but his many, vociferous critics in England disabused him. He would never be trusted with another field command, and lived out the rest of his life as a purely ornamental soldier and courtier.[33]

Wolseley took dynamic charge the moment Chelmsford left Zululand and hastened the process of Zulu submissions.[34] He understood that the predominant Zulu attitude was that they had seen enough of fighting, and that they wished for peace and the opportunity to go home to resume the normal course of their lives. On 19 July he took the formal surrender of the coastal *amakhosi* who had already submitted to General Crealock, but further efforts were needed to persuade the other great chiefs to give in. Accordingly, on 26 July he let them know that all who surrendered with their arms and royal cattle[35] would be permitted to retain their own herds, land and chiefly status in the new Zululand where both the monarchy and the military system were to be abolished. Wolseley thus placed the *amakhosi* in a position where they could preserve or even augment their local positions by coming to terms with the British, while the livelihood of their adherents would not be disrupted.

With symbolic intent, on 10 August Wolseley moved his headquarters to the kwaSishwili Camp amid the burned-out *amakhanda* in the Mahlabathini plain. Captain Alan Hart was disconcerted by the great number of Zulu skeletons lying in the grass which seemed to possess a ghoulish 'life of their own'. Some, he uneasily decided, 'look angry, some threatening, some foolish, some astonished, and those that are on their faces seem to be asleep'.[36] There, in this landscape of carnage and devastation, Wolseley received the submission of most of the important *amakhosi* of central and northern Zululand between 14 and 26 August. Simultaneously the *amakhosi* in the south-west surrendered at Rorke's Drift. Nevertheless, it remained imperative for Wolseley to kill or capture Cetshwayo to prevent him from providing a rallying-point for renewed resistance. He candidly wrote to his wife that he 'should be quite happy if some kind friend should but run an Assegai through him'.[37] But, since no one would oblige, he had to track down the fugitive king.

Wolseley had already sent the greater part of the British forces in Zululand marching home, but he retained two reduced columns to enforce final pacification and corner Cetshwayo. To scotch possible resistance in the difficult terrain of southern Zululand which had seen no British forces, Brevet Colonel Charles Clarke's column was sent back to Natal by way of Middle Drift. It met with no overt resistance and exerted grudging submissions as it went. Lieutenant-Colonel Baker Russell's Flying Column made for the north-west where Wolseley feared the abaQulusi and Kubheka might mount a last-ditch resistance. Colonel Villiers approached the same region from the north with a motley force of mounted irregulars, Hamu's Ngenetsheni and Swazi allies. At this very late stage King Mbandzeni had decided it was safe to come out on the British side against his people's traditional foe and—incidentally—take a share of the spoils.[38] The amaSwazi cheerfully joined the rest of Villiers's ill-conducted troops in comprehensively devastating the country between the Phongolo and Bivane rivers. Luckily for them, they met no resistance, not even from the abaQulusi. Under their principal *induna*, Mahubulwana kaDumisela, the abaQulusi remained unswervingly loyal to Cetshwayo, but they disbanded and submitted on 1 September on receiving a secret order from the king to lay down their arms because he had at last been taken prisoner.

The Zulu *amakhosi* were conscious that they would not secure a final peace with the British so long as Cetshwayo remained at large. So Mnyamana, the king's former chief councillor and always the political pragmatist, elliptically gave the information necessary for a patrol to capture Cetshwayo. He was run to earth on 28 August at the remote kwaDwasa *umuzi* deep in the Ngome forest.[39] The fallen king passed through Wolseley's camp under escort on 31 August, impressing all with his dignified royal bearing despite his unbearable humiliation and physical exhaustion. Even so, when he learned that he had been deposed and would not be allowed to remain in Zululand, his resolution finally slipped, and the tears ran down his cheeks. On 4 September he was taken off through the surf at Port Durnford and put on board the steamer *Natal* bound for exile.[40] When he was driven through Cape Town on 15 September to the Castle where he would be detained in the Flagstaff Bastion, he was overwhelmed by the extent of South Africa's largest city and cringed at his presumption in pitting his people against such evident power. 'I am now a very old man', he was heard to moan to himself.[41]

With Cetshwayo bound for exile, the *amakhosi* could with a relatively clear conscience publicly accept Wolseley's terms for a settlement. While it had been Frere's unswerving intention to break the military potential of the Zulu kingdom and destroy the unifying power of the monarch, it had not been part of his plan to burden Britain with the future administration of the territory. It was sufficient to ensure that the amaZulu would never again either pose a military threat to their colonial neighbours, act as a rallying-point for other African states, or generally hinder the confederation process. Wolseley had all these objectives in mind when at an assembly at kwaSishwili on 1 September he imposed his settlement on the *amakhosi*. The Zulu monarchy was suppressed, and its main prop, the military system, abolished. In line with Frere's preference for indirect rule in the style of the Indian Empire, Wolseley did not annex Zululand, but divided it up into thirteen independent territories under the nominal supervision of a British resident. Following considerable consultation with colonial advisers, Wolseley appointed a rag-bag of likely chiefs to rule over the thirteen fragments of the former kingdom. He cynically calculated that out of self-interest most of them could be relied upon to uphold his settlement and to ensure that there would be no resurgence of the centralized Zulu monarchy.[42]

Disregarding prescient rumblings that his railroaded settlement had consigned the Zulu people to civil war and ruin, Wolseley and his staff departed Zululand for the Transvaal. The last British troops marched out on 21 September, and in Natal the African auxiliaries and colonial troops were disbanded by early October.[43] The war was over.

John W. Colenso, the Anglican Bishop of Natal, had antagonized settler opinion in March 1879 by preaching that in Zululand too the people were suffering 'the terrible scourge of war' and required mercy. With the end of hostilities he feared that the amaZulu were now threatened by starvation because their last harvest had been destroyed by British patrols.[44] Yet Colenso's apprehensions were exaggerated. Vast areas of north-eastern and south-central Zululand had never seen so much as a single British soldier, and the people's livelihood had never been directly threatened. Even in areas that had borne the brunt of the destructive British columns, by August civilians were back planting in their fields for the new season and rebuilding their *imizi*. In late July a newspaper correspondent wrote of the coastal plain which had been subjected to heavy mounted raids from May to July:

Not long since the neighbouring fertile lands were the scene of battle, desolation, and other evils attending war. . . . Now everything presents a peaceful aspect. . . . Visits are repeatedly paid to camp by these Zulus . . . as if the war had never disturbed them. . . . [Yet] there is scarcely a family which has not lost one of its members, while numbers of them have lost some of their cattle, which is the

Zulus' treasure; and many have even felt the pangs of hunger, which has probably hastened their surrender,—which none regret.[45]

Still, even if the normal patterns of everyday life were resuming in Zululand, none could ignore the aching gap left by the men who had died in battle defending their kingdom. There were at least six thousand of them—quite probably thousands more—all in the productive prime of their manhood. What added considerably to the death-toll was the scant number of those who survived the massive tissue damage and splintered bones inflicted by bullets which flattened on impact. So many died in this way that the amaZulu came to believe the British bullets were poisoned. Yet from another perspective, the high 20 per cent Zulu casualty rate was not much higher than the 17 per cent of British soldiers lost—killed in action, from disease or incapacitation from wounds: a total of 2,334 men.[46] Expressed in another way, that amounted to one British casualty to every three Zulu, a quite astonishing ratio in a colonial 'small war'. Whichever way one takes these figures, they testify to the relative success of the completely outgunned Zulu war effort. And what made British casualty figures even worse in the eyes of the military hierarchy was that in colonial campaigns combat losses were never expected to exceed deaths from disease, and in Zululand they were a staggering three times higher.[47]

Almost as telling a blow to the familiar fabric of Zulu society as the death of so many men in battle was the spectacular destruction of the *amakhanda*, those centres of royal authority, and the barracks of the *amabutho* who had sustained the monarchy. Thanks to Wolseley's settlement, political power was devolved once more to the great *amakhosi* and British appointees, and the young men of Zululand, rather than serving the king in their *amabutho* as they had since the days of King Shaka, fell once more under their chiefs' localized authority. As for the kingdom itself, forged first in war in King Shaka's day, a scant sixty years later it had been undone by war in the reign of his nephew, King Cetshwayo, and was no more.

The Second Anglo-Pedi War, 1879

CHAPTER 22

'Short, Sharp and Decisive'

———•·•———

O N 26 February 1879 Colonel Rowlands's No. 5 Column in
garrison on the Phongolo River was attached to Colonel Wood's
command in north-western Zululand for the remainder of the Anglo-
Zulu War. This meant there were no British troops left deployed in the
vicinity of Bopedi to exert pressure on Sekhukhune. Buoyed up by his
success in the First Anglo-Pedi War of 1878, his regiments went on
the offensive, capturing cattle to make up recent losses and striking at
chiefdoms that had repudiated their ties with the Maroteng paramountcy. Yet, as was soon to be made apparent, this military flourish
was Sekhukhune's last.[1]

By the autumn of 1879 there could be no doubt that the Zulu
kingdom was going down in defeat and that the Transvaal had little
more to fear from that quarter. The Territory was by then under new
management. Colonel Owen Lanyon, basking in the approval of his
superiors for the efficient part he had played in the Northern Border
War of 1878, had been translated from Griqualand West on 4 March
1879 to replace Sir Theophilus Shepstone as Administrator.

In contrast to his successor, Shepstone had proved a grave disappointment to his superiors in the Colonial Office. He had failed to
reconcile the Boers to British rule, or to replenish the exhausted
Transvaal exchequer, or extinguish Pedi independence.[2] Lanyon
believed he could do much better. Always vigorous in action, he
concluded that it was necessary to put a quick end to Sekhukhune's
'open rebellion' and prove that the British administration could 'enforce

its authority'.[3] So he immediately reoccupied the abandoned forts hemming in the Pedi heartland and patrols rode out once more to harry the inhabitants. But Lanyon had reckoned without his immediate superior, Sir Garnet Wolseley, who was sailing out to South Africa as Governor of the Transvaal and High Commissioner for South East Africa. Wolseley decided Lanyon's half-cock military activities could only dangerously provoke the Bapedi at a time when there were few troops available to repel them. Consequently—and much to Lanyon's frustration—he ordered an end to all offensive operations in the Transvaal until he was in a position to take charge of them personally.[4]

With Cetshwayo at last a prisoner and his controversial settlement of Zululand in place, Wolseley arrived in Pretoria on 27 September 1879 at the head of imperial reinforcements. The pushy and self-confident general lost no time in consigning a fretful Lanyon to the background, and for three months ruled the Transvaal in his place.[5] Hot from forcing the thirteen appointed chiefs in Zululand to accede to his terms on 2 September, Wolseley assumed that Sekhukhune could also be compelled to accept whatever conditions he laid down.[6] Nevertheless, as he tersely informed Hicks Beach, if the Maroteng paramount should be so foolish as to reject his terms, then it would 'be necessary to destroy Sekukuni's power by force'.[7]

Sekhukhune's ten emissaries made their way to Fort Weeber on 10 October 1879 where Captain M. Clarke, the Commissioner of the Lydenburg District, bluntly informed them that he must pay a fine of 2,500 cattle for not accepting British rule. In a matter of such crucial importance the paramount could not take a decision without bringing the matter before a *pitso*, or general assembly of all adult males. His own, realistic inclination was to submit and pay the cattle fine for he could not see how he could successfully continue the war. But popular feeling, reflecting the deeply ingrained warrior culture of the men, was indignantly on the side of continued resistance. A straight-speaking petty chief, Putlakle, had the temerity to say to Sekhukhune: 'You are a coward, let the white people fight for the cattle if they want them, we have no cattle to give.' And the people assembled at Tsate applauded. Shamed and cut to the very quick at the suggestion he was a coward, Sekhukhune hastily reversed his position. With the paramount now in line with the public will, the *pitso* resolved that Clarke should be informed that no fine would be paid.[8]

Clarke refused to negotiate further, and members of the Maroteng royal house and senior councillors debated their next move. Sekhukhune's brothers and sons bitterly complained that 'the English were catching us in a trap ... and were no better than the Boers'. They went on to resolve that 'they will never be subject to the English who compel their subjects to build forts and work for them; that the English are liars, that rather than be in the position of the subject tribes they will fight, that they won't pay taxes before they had a good fight for it'.[9] It speaks to how preconceptions can colour belief, but what encouraged the Pedi notables to resist was their conviction—apparently shared by Sekhukhune himself—that despite all word to the contrary it was inconceivable that the British could really have overthrown the great Zulu power. They could only conclude that the British must be bluffing. Besides, they still held on to the lingering hope that the Boers would stand with them against the British. And, in the short term, they concluded that it was now too late in the season for the British to attack, and that they would hold back until after the horse sickness had died down again in the following year.[10]

They had reckoned without Wolseley who was not the man to shrink from immediately taking up their challenge, even though he hated 'to think of having our men shot down in such a ridiculous contest that can bring no honour or glory'.[11] But it could nevertheless restore the natural order. This time, he promised Hicks Beach from his headquarters in Middelburg, when he attacked the Bapedi the campaign would end with 'the confirmation of the ascendancy of the stronger and the subjugation of the weaker'.[12]

In planning his campaign against Sekhukhune, Wolseley sought to deliver a knock-out blow. The indirect methods of siege, containment and raid unsuccessfully espoused in 1876 and 1878 were not for him. Nothing would do except to storm Tsate itself. Only the capture of the Maroteng capital which had previously withstood the amaSwazi, Boers and British alike would conclusively signal the final overthrow of the Pedi state. Not that Wolseley did not appreciate that Tsate would be a very difficult nut to crack. He heeded Captain Clarke's almost 'superstitious awe' of the Fighting Kopje, or Ntswaneng (see chapter 5), and certainly understood how its Pedi defenders could be 'very nasty customers'. He therefore needed expendable African auxiliaries to undertake essential hand-to-hand fighting and to support his white troops in the rocky terrain where they would be vulnerable to Pedi gunfire. In his estimation the amaSwazi fitted this bill better than any other African auxiliaries he might also recruit.[13]

Accordingly, in early November Wolseley instructed Captain Norman MacLeod, the Swazi Political Agent, to raise about five hundred Swazi *emajaha* to join the forces he was marshalling and, as a sweetener, to promise them a good share of any booty. King Mbandzeni proved cooperative, for after his prevaricating role during the Anglo-Zulu War, and faced with the indubitable evidence of British military predominance in the region, he was anxious to make amends. So, to MacLeod's astonishment—for he had become accustomed to the interminable Swazi foot-dragging over their eventual participation in the Zulu campaign—within only a couple of weeks the amaSwazi mustered an army more than twenty times bigger than the small force he was asking for. When the Swazi *emabutfo* poured into Lydenburg on 18 November, they numbered over eight thousand *emajaha*, and five hundred of these were even carrying firearms of one sort or another.[14] Significantly, Mampuru, Sekhukhune's exiled half-brother and undying rival, marched with them, hitching his fortunes to the British.

The assembled Transvaal Field Force set off on 20 November divided into two columns with a striking force of British regulars who were all veterans of the Anglo-Zulu War. The eastern column, or Lydenburg Column, was under the command of Major Henry Bushman and consisted of the Swazi *emabutfo*, two companies of the 80th Regiment and two more of the 94th, some local mounted rifles and about four hundred local African levies wearing red puggarees to distinguish them from Sekhukhune's men. Wolseley was 'very much put out' that the local chiefs had failed to come up with more men, but they were understandably nervous of the amaSwazi and wanted to defend their homes.[15] The main column was commanded by Lieutenant-Colonel Baker Creed Russell, a close associate of Wolseley's who had accompanied him to Zululand on his staff, and who had commanded the north-western columns engaged in the final pacification of Zululand. His division consisted of six companies each from the 2/21st

Regiment (Royal Scots Fusiliers) and the 94th, five units of mounted irregular horse, the Rustenburg and Zoutpansberg Contingents of African levies drawn from the chiefdoms in the northern Transvaal, another contingent from the Ndzundza Ndebele closer by, and two 4-pounder Krupp guns and two 7-pounder mountain guns. In total, the Transvaal Field Force numbered 1,400 British infantry, their uniforms all ragged and faded from months on previous campaigns, four hundred mounted volunteers, and some eleven thousand African allies and levies outnumbering the white troops by six to one.[16]

This was an army many times larger than in either of the two previous Pedi campaigns, but the Bapedi never contemplated capitulation, even against such formidable odds. They were a warrior people and, like the amaZulu, would go down fighting to the last. Unhappily for them, the cocksure Wolseley was one of those generals whom fortune seemed always to favour. Even nature, that had served the Bapedi so well in previous campaigns, abandoned them. In 1878 Rowlands had had to abort his campaign for lack of water and forage, but in 1879 the heavy rains earlier that year meant that both were plentifully available for Wolseley's forces. Moreover, it was a mild season for horse sickness, and even though Wolseley lost dozens of horses to the disease, this was not enough to force his mounted men out of the field.[17]

Wolseley's strategy was to catch Tsate in a vice. The main column under Russell struggled up the valley of the Lepelle River from Fort Weeber. The narrow tracks were overgrown by thick bush and the column was assailed by violent thunderstorms and hail. It finally swung around the northern tip of the Leolo Mountains and descended southwards down the twenty-mile-long valley towards Tsate. At dawn on 25 November Russell's troops seized the Water Kopje within three miles of Tsate and fortified it. Meanwhile, the Lydenburg Column advanced from Fort Burgers along the eastern slopes of the Leolo Mountains. By 25 November it halted at an entrenched post about five miles from the base of the rugged mountains which overlooked Tsate from the south. That evening, Wolseley grimly scrawled in his journal: 'If I can only manage to kill most of Silukuni's men or even a couple of thousand of them, the effect will be excellent in all this region & it will go far towards settling this hitherto most disturbed District.'[18]

While on the march the British columns encountered far less Pedi resistance than had previous invaders, and Lieutenant Charles Commeline, RE, described the warriors 'making a great noise on the hills, blowing horns and chaffing our fellows' but firing only 'few harmless shots'.[19] It also appears that the Pedi forces defending Tsate were much smaller than in the past, and probably numbered no more than four thousand men. In his memoirs, the missionary Merensky surmises that the reason was that subordinate chiefs, fearing that the numerous Swazi forces would thoroughly ravage Bopedi as they advanced, kept part of their regiments back to defend their own turf. In any case, the preceding couple of years of invasion, dearth and the partial political unravelling of the Maroteng paramountcy meant that many former tributaries prudently withheld their support and awaited the final outcome.[20]

Wolseley, who had himself been reconnoitring assiduously as was his wont, decided to launch his assault on the morning of 28 November. But long before dawn broke, Sekhukhune and his retinue had left Tsate to occupy a cave high up the mountainside behind the town from which to survey the battle. This was the cave he always repaired to in time of danger, but he had no presentiment that the town would actually fall, and optimistically continued to believe that it would hold out as it always had in the past.[21]

The British troops were under arms by 3 a.m. in the pre-dawn of 28 November and struck their tents ahead of the coming battle.[22] Wolseley and his staff seated themselves under a convenient tree to watch and direct the attack as it unfolded. At about 4.15 a.m. the British opened the fighting by firing the first shells at Ntswaneng or the Fighting Kopje, Sekhukhune's rocky citadel in the plain to the north of the town. The Bapedi defenders immediately opened fire in response, sounded their whooping war horns and uttered their shrill war-cries. As Russell's force advanced south down the valley, it encountered a long line of rifle pits the Bapedi had dug to protect Tsate. The town consisted of three thousand round, white thatched huts that straggled for two miles along the flat valley floor and up the lower slopes of the mountains that embraced it to its rear. Besides the men stationed in the rifle pits, Pedi marksmen were also positioned behind rocky outcrops on the mountainside above the town and in the shelter of the thick bush. Lieutenant-Colonel John Murray commanded the regular troops in the British centre, but Wolseley was not prepared to sacrifice them in a frontal attack on Tsate and its prepared positions. So while he held them back in reserve, he sent in two flanking attacks. Some of the dismounted volunteers, along with the Rustenburg and Ndzundza Ndebele contingents, attacked from the right. They were under the command of Commandant Ignatius Ferreira of whom Wolseley privately had a very low opinion. He noted in his journal that Ferreira 'did not regard killing a native as killing a human being', and (even more revealingly) that he was 'most anxious that the town should not be burnt until it is well looted'.[23] Major Fred Carrington led the attack on the town from the left with the balance of the mounted volunteers and African levies.

As Ferreira and Carrington discovered to their cost when they launched their assaults under a sketchy covering fire from the British regulars and artillery, the Pedi defenders were very well positioned. On the western flank Ferreira advanced his force from boulder to boulder under hot Pedi fire. He and some of his men at last gained a krantz overlooking Tsate, but could go no further. They were without the Ndzundza Ndebele contingent who had found the going far too dangerous and deserted, peeling off to raid instead. On the eastern flank Carrington's African levies and dismounted volunteers came under sustained Pedi fire as they tried to advance and flung themselves down and took cover.

With both flanking attacks pinned down, Wolseley and his staff anxiously scanned the mountainside behind Tsate. Major Bushman and the Swazi *emabutfo* of the Lydenburg Column at Fort George had their orders to advance over the mountains behind Tsate and swoop down on the town from the rear in support of Ferreira and Carrington. Wolseley's strategy depended on their arrival, but they were late. The amaSwazi in their towering headdresses of black ostrich plumes had set out in full moonlight four hours before dawn, and were in position in good time on the reverse slope of the mountain. But, remembering how the Boers had left them in the lurch during their attack on Mafolofolo in 1876, they were determined to delay their attack until it was light enough to receive effective covering fire from the British in the valley. Finally, when they appeared on the heights at 6.30 a.m.

silhouetted dramatically against the lightening skyline, the troops stalled on the far side of the Pedi town below greeted them with deafening cheers and Wolseley let out a long, deep sigh of relief.

With their fierce, roaring battle-cry the Swazi *emabutfo* then swept down the hillside behind the Pedi defenders. Lieutenant-Colonel Philip Anstruther was appalled yet awed by the ferocity of these allies, 'fearful demons' who 'don't spare any living thing—man, woman, child, dog, fowl or anything living'.[24] The Bapedi were not in the least expecting to be attacked from that quarter but, even so, they resisted fiercely in hand-to-hand fighting as the amaSwazi flushed them from their rocks and caves. Despite sustaining heavy casualties the *emabutfo* finally drove the outnumbered Bapedi down the mountainside towards the town. Ferreira's men took advantage of the mayhem to scramble down from their krantz to set the thatched huts on fire, while Carrington's force was at last able to advance as the Bapedi fell back from their rifle pits. Trapped as Wolseley had intended they would be between the hammer and the anvil, those Bapedi who were unable to break out fought on grimly to the death. By 9.30 a.m. the struggle in the burning town was over, and the sides of the valley clear of escaping Bapedi warriors. Bodies lay everywhere, stabbed, bludgeoned and shot.

The Bapedi still occupied Ntswaneng even though the light-calibre British guns had been shelling it rather ineffectually since early morning. Commeline described how sometimes 'shells burst right inside the caves and such was the hollowness of the hill smoke was seen to emerge from holes on the far side of it'.[25] Brisk musketry fire from British skirmishers had been successfully suppressing the fire from the defenders within Ntswaneng, but now, with the town captured and in flames, Russell assembled all the British forces in the plain for a final, combined assault. It was with undeniable trepidation that they eyed the great, creviced mound of boulders, honeycombed with caves whose entrances were defended with stone breastworks. The British officers understood that it was required of them to lead by example. So when two rockets were fired to signal the attack on all four sides of Ntswaneng, Russell himself (whom Wolseley indulgently described as 'over-excited')[26] led the charge brandishing his drawn sword, and the officers of Wolseley's staff loped close behind, followed by the British troops. The Swazi *emajaha* held prudently back until they saw they would not be left to bear the brunt alone and that the whites were fully committed to the assault. Then, uttering their terrible battle-roar, pounding their shields against their knees and rhythmically beating the ground with their feet, they too charged Ntswaneng.

The lowing Pedi horns defiantly answered the provocative skirling of the pipe band of the Royal Scots Fusiliers, and the defenders opened a heavy fire from behind the rocks at the attackers. 'Strange to say,' as Commeline wrote to his father, 'as we doubled over the open, though the bullets came very close no one fell, and the men were soon swarming up the rocks like bees.'[27] When the British forces closed in the Bapedi fell back towards their caves. After ferocious hand-to-hand fighting in which most wounds were inflicted by spear or bayonet, at about 10.30 a.m. some Swazi *emajaha* dashed past the white troops and seized the summit. After that the fighting died down, and in the early afternoon the Royal Engineers placed large charges of gun cotton at the cave entrances to destroy the stone defences and to terrify the occupants into submission. However, the Bapedi, many of whom had worked at the diamond diggings and were familiar with explosives, cut the fuses to the charges. Even when they did explode, they did not have the desired effect and no Bapedi surrendered although (as Commeline later discovered) the charges he had helped place had 'wounded many and from the dust and smoke produced terrible thirst, and reduced the garrison to a most pitiable condition'.[28]

Foiled, Wolseley decided to surround Ntswaneng and starve the determined defenders out. He formed a cordon of British regulars, Ferreira's Horse and the Ndzundza Ndebele who had returned from their detour during the battle to raid cattle. Night fell, a thunderstorm with heavy rain rolled in and some of the blockaded defenders seized their chance. Firing and stabbing, they suddenly pushed past the drenched picket lines and made their escape. Most of those who had not broken out (some two hundred in all) surrendered in the following days and emerged 'in the most awful state . . . many of them terribly wounded'.[29] Wolseley made the amaSwazi surrounding Ntswaneng in their hundreds 'very angry' because he 'would not allow them to kill all the prisoners'.[30] The few remaining defenders in Ntswaneng resolved to die of thirst and starvation in the cave and galleries rather than ever give up. Before long an unbearable stench began to seep out of the caves, and the Royal Engineers finally sealed what had become the tomb of the last defenders.

Wolseley had his victory, but at a considerable price. Thirteen whites were killed and thirty-five wounded—a substantial tally for a small colonial campaign. Wolseley ruefully admitted that 'the loss is greater than that at Ulundi', but went on to justify it by noting in his journal that 'Chelmsford stood on the defensive whereas I had to attack in every direction over the open.'[31] The real brunt fell on the amaSwazi. Between five and six hundred *emajaha* lost their lives in the fighting, and as many again were wounded. But they could at least say that they were at last fully revenged for their catastrophic defeat in the Tsate valley in 1869. It is difficult to establish the extent of Pedi casualties, but conservatively more than a thousand must have perished, or a good quarter of the Bapedi engaged, an extremely high casualty rate. Perhaps it is an indication of the extent of the carnage that three of Sekhukhune's brothers fell, as well as nine of his children. One of these was Morwamotse, his designated heir, who, at bay with a rock to his back, died fighting valiantly as became a warrior.

The Swazi assault had swept over Sekhukhune and his entourage hidden undetected in their cave high up on the mountain behind Tsate. They remained holed up there until late in the afternoon the day after the battle, when they made a run for it. With ill luck they were spotted and recognized as they clambered over the top of the mountain. The hunt was now on, and early the following day (30 November) eighty-five mounted men under Captain Clarke and Commandant Ferreira, along with a pack of Swazi *emajaha*, set out in pursuit. More than an hour before the mounted men caught up with the fugitives, the *emajaha* had tracked Sekhukhune to a cave about nine miles away. The pursuers decided his refuge was too inaccessible to risk attacking, but learning that there was scant water in the cave, resolved instead to blockade it and force Sekhukhune to surrender. Appreciating that he doubtless feared the amaSwazi would kill him out of hand if he gave himself up, the British sent the *emajaha* away and kept guard without them. Finally, when Clarke gave his word that he would be taken alive, Sekhukhune surrendered at 6 a.m. on 2 December. He was brought back to the British camp, 'really ill & very hungry' as Wolseley could not help noting, along with about five hundred of his people, mostly women and children. There was 'great rejoicing in camp over the capture', Wolseley added, 'the natives mad with delight and rushing from all quarters to see him'.[32]

His mission satisfactorily accomplished (which was no less than he had come to expect of himself), Wolseley immediately broke up the Transvaal Field Force and turned the settlement of the conquered Pedi territory over to Captain Clarke. As he complacently wrote, 'I expect great things from them as these Basutos, unlike the Zulus, take quickly and naturally to civilization, ploughs, breeches and the singing of psalms. In one or two generations more they will all be Christians. In all I think I may describe the campaign as sharp, short and decisive.'[33]

When he left for Pretoria, Wolseley took the captive Sekhukhune off with him on an ox-wagon, along with his wife, two daughters, a baby son, a young brother and two attendants. As Wolseley doubtless intended, it was a deeply humiliating journey for the defeated Maroteng paramount. At Fort Albert Edward the African levies—old foes and former tributaries—jubilantly 'turned out and danced a war dance round the wagon'.[34] When he entered Pretoria on 9 December, Wolseley paraded Sekhukhune in triumph through the broad, partly built-up streets, the fallen paramount's open, blue-painted ox-wagon with its red wheels flashily escorted by a squadron of King's Dragoon Guards in their scarlet tunics and white helmets. The small clumps of spectators—Africans, settlers and soldiers—who watched the procession pass were not quite sure what to make of it all, many debating whether the skinny captive was actually Sekhukhune or not. Richard Harrison, a young officer, was distinctly disappointed by what he saw. He later recalled that Sekhukhune, 'who had a wretched worn-out look, sat on a box in the centre of the waggon [sic] with a skin round him. His appearance was hardly up to expectation, for he was supposed to be the cleverest native in South Africa.'[35]

Wolseley was assailed by no doubts about the identity of his woebegone captive, and locked the paramount up in the Pretoria jail. The next question was: what to do with him? Wolseley intended that he be sent off to the Cape to join Cetshwayo in exile, along with Langalibalele, the Hlubi chief who was also incarcerated there for his so-called 'rebellion' against the Natal authorities in 1873. Wolseley's argument was that in the Transvaal Sekhukhune 'enjoyed a fame as a Chief of dignity and importance hardly inferior to the fame of Ketchwayo among the Zulus' and that for the same reason it was advisable to remove him as far from his former domain as possible. Nor should he be allowed to return. Any illusory idea that Sekhukhune might soon be released would, Wolseley believed, have a disturbing effect 'among a people we are attempting to wean from the ways of savage life into complete subordination to a civilized sovereignty'.[36] Even so, as was the way with imperial bureaucrats, British officials continued to dither over where Sekhukhune should eventually be held, and he continued for the time being to languish in the Pretoria jail. Meanwhile, Captain Clarke was busy reconfiguring his former paramountcy.

The capture of previously invincible Tsate was without doubt a crushing blow to a people who for decades had withstood both African foes and colonial rule. Not only that, Wolseley had deliberately allowed the Swazi *emabutfo* free rein for ten days after the fall of Tsate to raid the Pedi heartland for cattle and captives. As he callously wrote in his journal, 'my object is to strike terror into the hearts of the surrounding tribes by the utter destruction of Sikukuni, root and branch, so the more the Swazi raid and destroy, the better my purpose is effected'.[37] And it turned out as Wolseley intended. The crushed Bapedi had indeed lost their will to resist. They were willing to agree to the terms Wolseley instructed Clarke to offer them, terms which mirrored those which the Zulu chiefs had accepted three months before. The Pedi chiefs (like the Zulu notables) were promised that they would retain their local power and influence, and were assured that all that was being abolished was the central authority of the Maroteng paramounts. In place of the Maroteng, there would be a British resident magistrate. And as had been the case in Zululand, Clarke stipulated that the royal cattle, which had been pastured with Sekhukhune's tributaries, must be surrendered. Above all, the Bapedi were required to hand over their firearms.[38]

But with surrender, real subjugation followed. Almost before they knew it, the Bapedi were paying taxes and Bopedi itself was being carved up into crown and mission lands and sold off as farms to land companies and settlers.[39] People who once had lived in Tsate were resettled far away so there would be no place where loyalty to the dethroned paramount might be concentrated. And Clarke instructed his magistrates to ensure that in future the Bapedi settled at least a thousand yards from any hills, and that they did not build their huts on hills or among rocks. In other words, the Bapedi were to have no potential fastnesses from which they might again defy the colonial authorities.[40]

CONCLUSION

CHAPTER 23

Paying the Price

————·•·————

ARMY General Order No. 134 of October 1880 authorized the distribution of the South Africa Medal with its golden yellow ribbon with dark blue vertical stripes to all soldiers and other personnel involved in the campaigns fought between 25 September 1877 and 2 December 1879.

A medal bar was attached to the suspender of the silver medal (which depicted Queen Victoria in profile) bearing the dates during which the recipient had served in one or several of these campaigns: 1877, 1877–8, 1879 or 1877–8–9.[1] Of these campaigns only one—the Anglo-Zulu War—was included in the list the War Office drew up in December 1902 identifying those fifteen wars between 1857 and 1899 in which three thousand or more British troops had served.[2] All the others fought in South Africa between 1877 and 1879 were relatively small beer in terms of Britain's many nineteenth-century colonial wars. Yet each one had an enormous, detrimental impact on the Africans attempting to resist the British drive to confederate South Africa by force of arms. Defeat for the amaXhosa, Griqua, Batlhaping, Prieska amaXhosa, Korana, Khoesan, amaZulu and Bapedi meant the overturning of the old order for these peoples and their forced integration on the conqueror's terms into a British-dominated subcontinent. The blood so honourably spilt by their warriors and the sufferings of their non-combatants seemed to have been offered up in vain.

Nor did the sacrifices made by the thousands of African auxiliaries and levies who fought for the British alleviate their increasingly subservient station in the domineering colonial order. Certainly, they had proved useful in a military emergency. Colonial officials were prepared to praise them for their warlike qualities and express their gratitude for their loyalty in fighting beside the white subjects of the Great Queen. Some colonial Africans, such as *iNkosi* Mqawe of the amaQadi who had served in the 5th Battalion NNC, played along and dutifully declared on the disbandment of his men on 1 October 1879: 'War came; we told the government that we were their children. We have now proved it in battle, and are going home.'[3] However, the very next day the same *iNkosi* Mqawe revealed he understood well enough that his loyalty had been cynically exploited. Angered when he discovered that he and his men were not going to receive their promised share of captured Zulu cattle, he exploded:

> Never more will I fight for the white man. Why should I? . . . Here have I, the son of Dabeju, of royal race, been lying in ditches and in mud, ripped by frost by night, drenched by rain and scorched by noon-day marches. I have stood out in the fight with my men; I have seen my favourite councillors, my relatives, my head men and my young men drop by my side shot . . . and now I find we have been fighting for nothing, for a shadow. . . . I come out of the fight unrequited in any sense. . . . My heart is angry, and never again will I respond to the call of your Government.[4]

Ironically for the British, their victories in the wars of 1877–1879 were negated by the almost immediate collapse of the structure of confederation raised through such diplomatic ingenuity, expenditure of treasure and military sacrifice. The first cracks appeared in Basutoland. In 1868 the rulers of the independent kingdom of Lesotho had placed themselves under British protection to prevent the Boers of the neighbouring Orange Free State from seizing more of their land. In 1871 the British passed the administration of Basutoland over to the self-governing Cape Colony whose magistrates challenged chiefly power and attempted to enforce the Cape's hugely resented policy of disarmament. There were warnings of serious trouble when Chief Moorosi of the Phuthi revolted in February 1879, and it required an eight months' siege by Cape forces to reduce his mountain stronghold.[5] Then, in September 1880 the Basotho broke out in a full-scale rebellion, known

as the Gun War, in which they took every advantage of their mountainous terrain and used their now illegal firearms to deadly effect. In
February 1881 the Basotho and Cape forces concluded a ceasefire
which marked the first step towards the dismantling of colonial rule in
Basutoland. In 1884 the Crown Colony of Basutoland became the first
of the High Commission Territories with considerable internal
autonomy under its own chiefs.[6]

Yet if the Gun War of 1880 to 1881 was the sole instance of a
successful African revolt against colonial rule in nineteenth-century
South Africa, it did not throw down the edifice of confederation
because Basutoland remained a loosely connected part of the building.
The real responsibility for the demolition of confederation lay with the
irreconcilably disaffected Boers of the Transvaal Territory. Rebellion
broke out in December 1880 while the Gun War was occupying British
military attention. Culminating in the battle of Majuba on 27 February
1881, the Boers bloodily repulsed several attempts by British forces to
break through from Natal to relieve their besieged Transvaal garrisons.[7]
By the complex Pretoria Convention of 3 August 1881 (agreed to in
the very same room where Shepstone had signed the Annexation
Proclamation four years before) the British ceded to the Transvaal
the substance of independence. Gladstone's Liberal administration
(his party had defeated Beaconsfield's Tories in the general election of
1880) feared that if the Transvaal War continued it could lead to a
pan-Afrikaner uprising throughout southern Africa which might be
the signal for a general African revolt. So the Liberal strategy was to
replace the formal confederation of Tory conception with a looser,
more informal British paramountcy in southern Africa. The Boers had
their part to play in this new scenario by acting as partners to the
British in suppressing the African majority and exercising white rule.[8]

The Liberals may have insouciantly killed off confederation by late
1881, but those imperial agents who had been closely involved in
implementing the project believed Gladstone had dealt a shameful and
critical blow to Britain's position in southern Africa. Frere, who had
finally been recalled in August 1880 from his mortifying half-life as
Governor of the Cape, was bitterly resentful at seeing his work on
confederation undone—work, indeed, which had cost him his career.
Still, he was altogether too resilient to have died of a broken heart as

was said of him at his death in 1884.[9] Wolseley (never one to soft-pedal his opinions) feared that discredited British military power in South Africa would no longer act as a deterrent upon the Boers or upon 'the bellicose instincts and proclivities' of the Africans.[10] In 1899, on the eve of the terrible Anglo-Boer War with its over a hundred thousand casualties, Sir Henry Rider Haggard saw clearly that Britain was paying the bill for abandoning confederation in 1881, and was again being forced 'to assert its dominion even at the price of war'.[11]

The sacrifices Africans had made resisting British imperialism in the wars of 1877 to 1879 were therefore cruelly skewed by the abandonment of the confederation project only two years later. While Sekhukhune fretted in jail in Pretoria after his capture in 1879, the British had rewarded Mampuru, his brother and bitterly envious rival, for expediently joining their side in the Second Anglo-Pedi War. They permitted him to return to Bopedi and to build up his support among the crushed Bapedi. However, Mampuru's regional ambitions were derailed by the Transvaal Rebellion. Article 23 of the Pretoria Convention released Sekhukhune and allowed him to return to his former territory, now in the Boer-ruled, resuscitated ZAR.[12] Over the course of the next year he and Mampuru irreconcilably jockeyed for position. Mampuru decided at length to have done, and assigned a band of assassins to kill Sekhukhune. During the stiflingly hot night of 13 August 1882 they stabbed the one-time Maroteng paramount to death as he slept in a shelter in front of his hut—a poor reward, one might think, for heroically spearheading Pedi resistance to colonial conquest over so many years. Yet butchering him gained Mampuru nothing. He fled ZAR justice to the Ndzundza Ndebele with whom he had taken refuge back in 1868 when first he had unsuccessfully challenged Sekhukhune for the Maroteng succession (see chapter 4). When the forces of the ZAR suppressed the Ndzundza Ndebele chiefdom in 1883, they captured Mampuru and tried and convicted him for Sekhukhune's murder. The Boers bungled his hanging on 22 November 1883, and it was only on the second attempt that Mampuru died at the end of the rope.[13]

In Zululand, Wolseley's settlement soon broke down. Growing strife between the thirteen appointed chiefs was compounded by their deliberate victimization of the royalist party—known as the uSuthu—and threatened to spill over into Natal. Alarmed, Gladstone's government began to rethink the Zululand settlement it had inherited from the Tories. The Anglo-Zulu War was now widely regarded as ill-advised and unfortunate, and the Colonial Secretary, Lord Kimberley, believed that the exiled King Cetshwayo had been 'most villainously used'.[14] In February 1881 the exiled king was transferred to civil custody and moved to the farm Oude Molen in the Cape Flats, where he had Langalibalele on the adjoining farm Uitvlugt as his neighbour.[15] This was a proximity not entirely welcomed by Cetshwayo who, at the time of his capture, had declared that it was 'not fair that he should be sent down with treatment very much like that of Langalibalele, who was an insurgent, whilst he is a king'.[16] It seemed that in the end the British government was willing to accept this fine distinction, for while Langalibalele was never restored to his chiefdom, the cabinet decided to allow Cetshwayo to travel to England to negotiate his restoration to his kingdom.

Cetshwayo arrived in England on 5 August 1882. The Colonial Office believed it should treat even a defeated indigenous ruler with official decorum, and in London rented a pleasant house for him at 18 Melbury Road overlooking Holland Park.[17] Cetshwayo was shown the sights of the great metropolis and charmed the crowds with his exemplary natural dignity and royal ease of manner.[18] The newspapers now referred to the 'unfortunate King of the Zulu nation' as a 'brave and honourable Native African Prince who was maligned and unfairly treated', one who had defended his country 'against the invading British army with admirable courage'.[19] Only once in public did Cetshwayo permit his diplomatic mask to slip when he declared 'in most emphatic tones, that there never ought to have been any war, and ascribed the fact there was war to "the little grey-headed man" [meaning Sir Bartle Frere]'.[20]

On 14 August Queen Victoria granted Cetshwayo a brief, ten-minute audience at Osborne House on the Isle of Wight. In her journal, the Queen wrote that through the interpreter she told the Zulu king that 'I recognized in him a great warrior, who had fought against us, but rejoiced we were now friends.'[21] The meetings Cetshwayo held with the Queen's ministers went less cordially. It was with heavy disappointment that he finally agreed on 11 December to his restoration only to the central part of his former kingdom, and accepted with foreboding that he would be snugly hemmed in to the south by British-controlled territory, and to the north by Zibhebhu, the only one of the former thirteen chiefs favoured with an independent territory.

Cetshwayo set foot once more in Zululand on 10 January 1883 and went about rebuilding his oNdini *ikhanda* a mile east of the one burned by the British in 1879. Very soon he was at war with Zibhebhu and his main ally, the ever-irreconcilable *uMntwana* Hamu.[22] Zibhebhu confirmed his reputation as the very best Zulu general of his generation by a string of victories over the uSuthu. On 21 July 1883 Zibhebhu utterly crushed Cetshwayo's poorly led uSuthu forces in a lightning thrust at oNdini itself. The list of eminent men who were cut down that day reads like a roll-call of the elite of the old Zulu kingdom. Jeff Guy is surely right to conclude that this slaughter marked the true end of the old Zulu order.[23] Cetshwayo, a fugitive once more, fled south to British territory where the authorities allocated him a small house outside the tiny village of Eshowe. There he anguished over the destruction of all his hopes until on the afternoon of 8 February 1884, having just eaten, he was overtaken by convulsions and died. The British declared he had succumbed to heart disease, but the uSuthu were convinced that Zibhebhu had arranged to have him poisoned.

Fighting continued furiously after Cetshwayo's death between his heir, Dinuzulu, and Zibhebhu and his allies.[24] Land-grabbing Boer adventurers opportunistically intervened on Dinuzulu's side and helped him defeat Zibhebhu. In return, they exacted a vast grant of land in north-western Zululand that encompassed a full third of the former kingdom. The British recognized this territory on 22 October 1886 as the independent New Republic but, alarmed by continuing turmoil and Boer and German aspirations in the region, annexed what remained of Zululand on 19 May 1887 as a colony. It had taken years of increasingly destructive civil war and the division of the spoils between the Boers and British, but nearly eight years after the British invasion of 1879 all vestiges of an independent Zulu kingdom were finally extinguished.

What then of the warriors across South Africa who had waged their heroic but futile wars of resistance between 1877 and 1879 against the British, and what of their disarmed and disinherited heirs? After that clanging closure of the frontier how could they maintain their deep-seated warrior traditions and keep their sense of honour alive in what

was now the white man's country, and in which they were being transformed into wage labourers?

It is true that with conquest Africans did not immediately lose all
their traditional institutions. Yet, as Aran MacKinnon has pointed out,
all features of African society were relentlessly 'corrupted, reconfigured,
and made compliant with the demands of the white state and capitalism'.[25] The erosion under colonial rule of the authority held by the
male head of a household over the women and young men of the
homesteads deeply offended men's honour, as did the loss of respect
due to rank and lineage. Alternative routes to honour, and ways to salve
their wounded warrior ethos, had to be explored. These could be found
most naturally through warrior-like service in the colonial police or in
the army and, later, in armed insurgency against the apartheid state.
Also, from the days when first they had made the arduous journey to
the diamond diggings, migrant labourers continued to regard such
work as a form of heroic warfare. In time this morphed into the hard-
bitten proletarian ethic essential for survival in industrial, urban work-
places.[26] Unsurprisingly, it was in the dangerous environment of the
deep-level mines that the age-old heroic culture survived most strongly.
As the Sotho proverb has it, 'Manhood is hard, it is dug from out of
the rocks'.[27] And this reminds us that self-mastery, endurance in the
face of pain and adversity, is as much part of the culture of masculinity
inherited from warrior traditions as is its belligerent component. Both
elements survive into the present day, although aggressiveness is by far
the more apparent. Warrior culture is consciously to be found in
competitive sports from the team-dancing competitions in the labour
and mining compounds to soccer matches, in the possession and
display of firearms, in criminal gangs and gang warfare, in the cut-
throat tactics of the boardroom, in male dominance over women. It is
even found in the widespread expense or flamboyance of personal dress,
for in warrior societies a fine appearance has always been an essential
expression of identity, self-respect and personal honour.[28]

Indeed, when all is said and done, to an alienated worker in an indus-
trialized world, it is that conscious connection to a worthy—if idealized—
warrior heritage that imparts a degree of dignity and worth. Perhaps, in
that way, the sacrifice of those who fought against British conquest in
1877–1879 continues to have value and meaning, even to the present day.

NOTES

Chapter 1 The Shadow of Isandlwana

1. Norman Etherington, Patrick Harries and Bernard K. Mbenga make this suggestion in 'From Colonial Hegemonies to Imperial Conquest, 1840–1880' in Carolyn Hamilton, Bernard K. Mbenga and Robert Ross (eds), *The Cambridge History of South Africa*, vol. 1, *From Early Times to 1885*, Cambridge: Cambridge University Press, 2009, 2012 pb edn, p. 383. The Second War for South African Unification was the Anglo-Boer (South African) War of 1899–1902. To put these wars into their wider military context, see Richard J. Reid, *Warfare in African History*, Cambridge: Cambridge University Press, 2012, chapter 5.

2. During 1880–1881 the Transvaal Rebellion, which overthrew British rule, and the limited success of the Basotho in the Gun War against the Cape administration, combined to unravel the fabric of confederation woven at gun-point during 1877–1879. But that is another story. See the concluding chapter to this book.

3. For a discussion on the South African frontier and the fragmented nature of African resistance, see Christopher Saunders, 'Political Processes in the Southern African Frontier Zones' in Howard Lamar and Leonard Thompson (eds), *The Frontier in History: North America and Southern Africa Compared*, New Haven, CT, and London: Yale University Press, 1981, esp. pp. 150, 156, 162, 164–8.

4. See J.B. Peires, 'Ngqika c. 1779–1829' in Christopher Saunders (ed.), *Black Leaders in Southern African History*, London: Heinemann, 1979, pp. 22–6, and John Laband, *The Rise and Fall of the Zulu Nation*, London: Arms and Armour Press, 1997, pp. 135–46, for examples of civil strife in Xhosa and Zulu society respectively.

5. For the example of the defection of *uMntwana* (Prince) Hamu kaNzibe and his Ngenetsheni in the Anglo-Zulu War, see Laband, *Zulu Nation*, pp. 258–9, 328, 332.

6. For the case of the exiled iziGqoza under *uMntwana* Sikhota kaMpande who joined the British invasion of Zululand, see P.S. Thompson, *Black Soldiers of the Queen: The Natal Native Contingent in the Anglo-Zulu War*, revised edn, Tuscaloosa: University of Alabama Press, 2006, pp. 31–2.

7. John Laband (ed.), *Lord Chelmsford's Zululand Campaign 1878–1879*, Stroud: Alan Sutton Publishing for the Army Records Society, 1994, p. xv.

8. Tim Stapleton, '"Valuable, Gallant and Faithful Assistants": The Fingo (Mfengu) as Colonial Military Allies during the Cape-Xhosa Wars, 1835–1881' in Stephen M. Miller (ed.), *Soldiers and Settlers in Africa, 1850–1918*, Leiden and Boston: Brill, 2009, pp. 15–47.

9. See Shula Marks and Anthony Atmore, 'Firearms in Southern Africa: A Survey', *Journal of African History*, 12, 4 (1971), pp. 517–30, for a discussion on firearms in African societies between the seventeenth and late nineteenth centuries.

10. Michael Howard, *The Causes of Wars and Other Essays*, London: Temple Smith, 1983, pp. 216–17.
11. Jay Winter and Antoine Prost, *The Great War in History: Debates and Controversies 1914 to the Present*, Cambridge: Cambridge University Press, 2005, pp. 28–31.
12. For an illuminating discussion on military culture, consult John A. Lynn, *Battle: A History of Combat and Culture from Ancient Greece to Modern America*, Boulder, CO, and Oxford: Westview Press, 2003, esp. pp. xx–xxi, xvi–xviii, 115, 121, 124, 232, 245, 249, 280, 303, 306, 314.
13. Connell borrowed the concept of 'hegemony' from the writings of Antonio Gramsci (1891–1937), the Italian Marxist political theorist and sociologist, who used the term in his analysis of class relations to describe forms of social ascendancy based not simply on brute force, but on cultural acquiescence.
14. See Robert Morrell, 'The Times of Change: Men and Masculinity in South Africa' in Robert Morrell (ed.), *Changing Men in Southern Africa*, Pietermaritzburg: University of Natal Press; London: Zed Books, 2001, pp. 6–10; R.W. Connell, *Gender and Power: Society, the Person and Sexual Politics*, Stanford, CA: Stanford University Press, 1987, pp. 183–7; Connell, *Masculinities*, Berkeley and Los Angeles, CA: University of California Press, 1995, pp. 67–86; and Connell, *The Men and the Boys*, Berkeley and Los Angeles, CA: University of California Press, 2000, pp. 10–11, 23, 69, 84, 209, 216–17.
15. For a masterly discussion on honour in black societies in southern African during the nineteenth century, see John Iliffe, *Honour in African History*, Cambridge: Cambridge University Press, 2005, pp. 140–60.
16. Benedict Carton and Robert Morrell, 'Zulu Masculinities, Warrior Culture and Stick Fighting: Reassessing Male Violence and Virtue in South Africa', *Journal of Southern African Studies*, 38, 1 (March 2012), pp. 32–4.
17. For a discussion on how in nineteenth-century Zulu society youths were organized to serve patriarchy, see Benedict Carton, *Blood from Your Children: The Colonial Origins of Generational Conflict in South Africa*, Pietermaritzburg: University of Natal Press, 2000, pp. 16–25, and Michael R. Mahoney, *The Other Zulus: The Spread of Zulu Ethnicity in Colonial South Africa*, Durham, NC, and London: Duke University Press, 2012, pp. 90–5.
18. Connell, *Gender and Power*, p. 185.
19. For a challenging discussion on the role of Zulu women in warfare, see Sifiso Ndlovu, 'A Reassessment of Women's Power in the Zulu Kingdom', in Benedict Carton, John Laband and Jabulani Sithole (eds), *Zulu Identities: Being Zulu, Past and Present*, New York: Columbia University Press, 2009, pp. 111–13.
20. *British Parliamentary Papers* [henceforth *BPP*] C. 1748, enc. 1 in no. 165: statement of Barjeni and Mansthonga, messengers sent by the Lieutenant-Governor of Natal to King Cetshwayo, forwarded by F. Bernard Fynney, 2 November 1876. The occasion was Cetshwayo's execution of girls of the iNgcugce *ibutho* (or age-grade regiment) who disobeyed his orders to marry the much older men of the iNdlondlo *ibutho* and tried to flee to Natal with their current lovers. This was a direct challenge to Cetshwayo's royal authority that he could not condone.
21. John Laband and Paul Thompson, 'African Levies in Natal and Zululand, 1838–1906' in Miller (ed.), *Soldiers and Settlers*, pp. 59–60.

Chapter 2 Bushman's River Pass

1. John Laband, 'Durnford, Anthony William (1830–1879)', *Oxford Dictionary of National Biography*, Oxford: Oxford University Press, <http://www.oxforddnb.com/view/article/8325> (accessed 14 August 2013).
2. The Bushman's River is known as the Mtshezi in isiZulu.
3. The District of Port Natal was annexed as a British dependency in 1843, and annexed to the Cape Colony as a District in 1844. The next year Natal became a separate District under a lieutenant-governor, and finally in 1856 Natal was established as a separate British colony.

4. For the most recent and fullest study of the Shepstone System and how it affected the amaHlubi, see Jeff Guy, *Theophilus Shepstone and the Forging of Natal*, Pietermaritzburg, University of KwaZulu-Natal Press, 2013, Parts 2–7. See also Thomas V. McClendon, *White Chief, Black Lords: Shepstone and the Colonial State in Natal, South Africa 1845–1878*, Rochester, NY: Rochester University Press, 2010, pp. 84, 94–5, 101–4, 145–7; Bill Guest, 'Colonists, Confederation and Constitutional Change' in Andrew Duminy and Bill Guest (eds), *Natal and Zululand from Earliest Times to 1910: A New History*, Pietermaritzburg: University of Natal Press and Shuter & Shooter, 1989, pp. 151–4; Norman Etherington, 'Shepstone, Sir Theophilus (1817–1893)', *Oxford Dictionary of National Biography*, Oxford: Oxford University Press, <http://www.oxforddnb.com/view/article/25353> (accessed 14 August 2013); William Kelleher Storey, *Guns, Race, and Power in Colonial South Africa*, Cambridge: Cambridge University Press, 2008, pp. 145, 147; Edgar H. Brookes and Colin de B. Webb, *A History of Natal*, Pietermaritzburg: University of Natal Press, 1965, p. 113; Laband, *Zulu Nation*, pp. 131–2; Graham Dominy, 'Thomas Baines and the Langalibalele Rebellion: A Critique of an Unrecorded Sketch of the Action at "Bushman's Pass", 1873', *Natal Museum Journal of Humanities*, 3 (October 1991), pp. 48–9.
5. Leonard Thompson, *A History of South Africa*, New Haven, CT, and London: Yale University Press, 1990, p. 115; Etherington et al., 'Colonial Hegemonies', pp. 370–1.
6. Aran S. MacKinnon, *The Making of South Africa: Culture and Politics*, Upper Saddle River, NJ: Pearson Prentice Hall, 2004, pp. 132–8; H. Houghton, 'Economic Development, 1865–1965' in Monica Wilson and Leonard Thompson (eds), *Oxford History of the British Empire*, vol. 2, *South Africa 1870–1966*, Oxford: Oxford University Press, 1971, pp. 10–12.
7. William H. Worger, *South Africa's City of Diamonds: Mine Workers and Monopoly Capitalism in Kimberley, 1867–1895*, New Haven, CT: Yale University Press, 1987, p. 75.
8. When young men were tied into a military system, such as in Zululand, they were obliged to serve their ruler and were not free to offer their labour in the colonial market. It therefore became a British objective to 'unlock' their economic potential.
9. Anthony Atmore, J.M. Chirenje and S.I. Mudenge, 'Firearms in South Central Africa', *Journal of African History*, 12, 4 (1971), pp. 546–7; Sue Miers, 'Notes on the Arms Trade and Government Policy in Southern Africa between 1870 and 1890', *Journal of African History*, 12, 4 (1971), pp. 571–2, 577.
10. For the various types of firearms in Pedi hands by the 1870s, see Storey, *Guns*, pp. 133–40; John Laband, *Historical Dictionary of the Zulu Wars*, Lanham, MD: The Scarecrow Press, 2009, pp. 172, 214, 238.
11. Gavin White, 'Firearms in Africa: An Introduction', *Journal of African History*, 12, 2 (1971), p. 81.
12. Atmore et al., 'Firearms', pp. 549–50.
13. Laband, *Historical Dictionary*, p. 151.
14. White, 'Firearms', pp. 177–8. Magazine rifles, firing a succession of cartridges without reloading, were not in common use until the mid-1880s.
15. Storey, *Guns*, pp. 131–2.
16. For the build-up to the Langalibalele Rebellion, see Guy, *Shepstone*, pp. 362–90; McClendon, *White Chief*, pp. 82, 84, 93–9, 131–2; Brookes and Webb, *Natal*, pp. 114–16; Storey, *Guns*, pp. 145, 148–9, 151–5, 157. The Brussels Act of 1892 finally bound the signatories to control the African arms trade and not to deal in 'precision arms' such as rifled breech-loaders with magazines.
17. Anthony Trollope, *South Africa*, reprint of the 1878 edition with an introduction and notes by J.H. Davidson, Cape Town: A.A. Balkema, 1973, pp. 238–9, 241.
18. The British established Fort Napier in 1843 and steadily improved its fortifications over the years. A garrison remained there until finally withdrawn in August 1914. See Graham Dominy and Hamish Paterson, 'Fort Napier: The Imperial Base that Shaped the City' in John Laband and Robert Haswell (eds), *Pietermaritzburg 1838–1988: A*

New Portrait of an African City, Pietermaritzburg: University of Natal Press and Shuter & Shooter, 1988, pp. 102–9.

19. For the skirmish at the Bushman's River Pass, see R.W.F. Droogleever, *The Road to Isandhlwana: Colonel Anthony Durnford in Natal and Zululand*, London: Greenhill Books, 1992, pp. 38–57, 70–74; Mark Coghlan, *Pro Patria: Another 50 Natal Carbineer Years 1945 to 1995*, Pietermaritzburg: The Natal Carbineer Trust, 2000, pp. 5–7; Dominy, 'Langalibalele Rebellion', pp. 49–51; McClendon, *White Chief*, pp. 100–1.

20. For the destruction of the amaHlubi and Langalibalele's fate, see Guy, *Shepstone*, pp. 391–400; Storey, *Guns*, pp. 156–80; McClendon, *White Chief*, pp. 82, 99, 101, 103, 105, 132; Brookes and Webb, *Natal*, pp. 115–17; Guest, 'Colonists', p. 155.

21. Trollope, *South Africa*, p. 237.

22. Storey, *Guns*, pp. 125, 131–2 and 180. For Storey's discussion on confederation, frontier control and gun control, see pp. 182–99, 231–42. See also Marks and Atmore, 'Firearms', p. 524, and C.F. Goodfellow, *Great Britain and South African Confederation (1870–1881)*, Cape Town: Oxford University Press, 1966, p. 113.

23. *BPP* C. 2144, no. 111: Sir Theophilus Shepstone to Hicks Beach, 10 June 1878.

Chapter 3 Bopedi

1. This discussion of the Great Trek is based on Martin Legassik, 'The Great Treks: The Evidence', *South African Historical Journal*, 46 (May 2002), pp. 282–9, Christopher Saunders, 'Great Treks?' in ibid., pp. 300–7, and Norman Parsons, 'Reviving the Trek Debates', in ibid., pp. 308–12. See also Tim Keegan, *Colonial South Africa and the Origins of the Racial Order*, Cape Town: David Philip, 1996, pp. 184–96, and Leonard Thompson, 'Co-operation and Conflict: the High Veld' in Monica Wilson and Leonard Thompson (eds), *The Oxford History of South Africa*, vol. 1, *South Africa to 1870*, Oxford: Oxford University Press, 1969, pp. 405–8. Norman Etherington, *The Great Treks: The Transformation of Southern Africa, 1815–1854*, London: Longman Pearson, 2001, pp. xix–xxv, 1–9, 340–4, makes the vital point that the Boer exodus was not unique and but one of many 'treks' during the early nineteenth century by other indigenous peoples in southern Africa.

2. Rodney Davenport and Christopher Saunders, *South Africa: A Modern History*, London: Macmillan, 5th edn, 2000, pp. 194–5. See also Nigel Worden, *The Making of Modern South Africa*, Oxford: Wiley-Blackwell, 4th edn, 2007, pp. 22–3.

3. The Portuguese were confined to the environs of Delagoa Bay. South West Africa (now Namibia) did not become a German colony until 1884.

4. Christopher Saunders and Iain R. Smith, 'Southern Africa, 1795–1910' in Andrew Porter (ed.), *The Oxford History of the British Empire*, vol. 3, *The Nineteenth Century*, Oxford: Oxford University Press, 2001, p. 602.

5. Thompson, 'High Veld', pp. 412–13.

6. See G.W. Eybers (ed.), *Select Constitutional Documents Illustrating South African History 1795–1910*, London: Routledge, 1918, pp. 358–9, for the text of the Sand River Convention.

7. Ibid, pp. 282–5, for the text of the Bloemfontein Convention.

8. Davenport and Saunders, *South Africa*, pp. 195–9.

9. Thompson, 'High Veld', pp. 424–35.

10. D.H. Heydenrych, 'The Boer Republics, 1852–1881' in T. Cameron and S.B. Spies (eds), *An Illustrated History of South Africa*, Johannesburg: Jonathan Ball, 1986, p. 150.

11. Timothy J. Stapleton, *A Military History of South Africa from the Dutch-Khoi Wars to the End of Apartheid*, Santa Barbara, CA: Praeger, 2010, p. 46.

12. For a detailed description of Boer society in the Transvaal, see John Laband, *The Transvaal Rebellion: The First Boer War 1880–1881*, Harlow, Essex: Pearson Longman, 2005, pp. 26–40.

13. Peter Delius, *The Land Belongs to Us: The Pedi Polity, the Boers and the British in the Nineteenth-Century Transvaal*, Berkeley, CA: University of California Press, 1984,

pp. 11–12; Peter Delius, *A Lion Amongst the Cattle: Reconstruction and Resistance in the Northern Transvaal*, Oxford: James Currey, 1996, p. 10.

14. Delius, *Northern Transvaal*, p. 45, note 1.

15. For the methodological challenges confronting historians of Africa, see John Edward Philip (ed.), *Writing African History*, Rochester, NY: Rochester University Press, 2006, Part II: 'Sources of Data'.

16. The following account of Pedi origins and vicissitudes during the *Mfecane* is based on Delius, *Pedi Polity*, pp. 12–27; Etherington, *Great Treks*, 123, 161–3; Paul Maylam, *A History of the African People of South Africa: From the Early Iron Age to the 1970s*, London: Croom Helm, 1986, pp. 127–8; Hermann Giliomee and Bernard Mbenga (eds), *New History of South Africa*, Cape Town: Tafelberg, 2008, pp. 36–7; John Wright, 'Turbulent Times: Political Transformations in the North and East, 1760s–1830s' in Hamilton, et al. (eds), *South Africa*, pp. 216, 218, 220, 231, 235–7, 239–41, 248–50.

17. See Wright, 'Turbulent Times', pp. 212–13, 218–19, 249–50; John Laband, 'Mfecane (1815–1840)' in Gordon Martel (ed.), *The Encyclopedia of War*, Oxford: Wiley-Blackwell, 2011, <http://onlinelibrary.wiley.com/doi/10.1002/9781444338232. wbeow400/abstract> (accessed 7 August 2013).

18. Laband, *Zulu Nation*, pp. 15–21; Wright, 'Turbulent Times', pp. 225–6.

19. Wright, 'Turbulent Times, pp. 239–41.

20. Ibid, pp. 223–5. Although the British had abolished the slave trade in 1807, the Anglo-Portuguese treaty of 1810 permitted the Portuguese to buy slaves in their own colonies. The slaves obtained at Delagoa Bay from African traders were shipped mainly to Portuguese Brazil. See David Eltis and David Richardson, *Atlas of the Transatlantic Slave Trade*, New Haven, CT, and London: Yale University Press, 2010, pp. 278 (map 182), 280 (map 183).

21. Etherington, *Great Treks*, pp. 123, 161–3.

22. Laband, *Zulu Nation*, pp. 31–41; Wright, 'Turbulent Times', pp. 226–7, 231, 236.

23. Laband, *Zulu Nation*, pp. 79–80.

24. Delius, *Pedi Polity*, pp. 27–8; Wright, 'Turbulent Times', p. 248; Giliomee and Mbenga, *South Africa*, pp. 13–17.

25. For the Pedi way of life, see Delius, *Pedi Polity*, pp. 48–53, 68, and David Hammond-Tooke, *The Roots of Black South Africa*, Johannesburg: Jonathan Ball, 1993, pp. 51, 58–9, 62.

26. For the powers of the Pedi paramount, see Delius, *Pedi Polity*, pp. 27–8, 53–9; Hammond-Tooke, *Roots*, pp. 6, 81–3, 85, 87, 151, 153–4, 167; Giliomee and Mbenga, *South Africa*, pp. 136–7.

27. Wright, 'Turbulent Times', pp. 218–19, 250–2.

28. Delius, *Pedi Polity*, p. 53; Hammond-Tooke, *Roots*, pp. 81–2, 151, 153–4, 167.

29. Wright, 'Turbulent Times', pp. 250–52.

30. Delius, *Pedi Polity*, pp. 50–53; Hammond-Tooke, *Roots*, pp. 79, 138–43.

31. Women's age-grade regiments were likewise placed under the leadership of a daughter of the chief.

32. Maylam, *African People*, pp. 278–9; Delius, *Pedi Polity*, pp. 28–30, 53–4.

33. Ibid., pp. 53–4.

34. H.W. Kinsey, 'The Sekukuni Wars', *Military History Journal*, 2, 5 (June 1973), <samilitaryhistory.org/journal.html> (accessed 10 March 2013).

35. Atmore et al., 'Firearms', p. 556.

36. Marks and Atmore, 'Firearms', p. 527. For a discussion on the Bapedi and firearms, see Delius, *Pedi Polity*, pp. 63, 68–9, 72–3, 75.

37. For Pedi migrant labour, see Delius, *Pedi Polity*, pp. 62–79.

38. For the various types of firearms in Pedi hands by the 1870s, see Storey, *Guns*, pp. 133–40; Laband, *Historical Dictionary*, pp. 172, 214, 238.

39. It was only with the uncovering of a vast seam of gold-bearing ore on the Witwatersrand in 1886 that the Transvaal was set to become the world's biggest gold producer by the

late 1890s. See Albert M. Grundlingh, 'Prelude to the Anglo-Boer War, 1881–1899' in Cameron and Spies (eds), *South Africa*, p. 184.

40. Laband, *Transvaal Rebellion*, pp. 35, 43. Most 'Outsiders' were of British stock, although there was a sprinkling of Jews (mainly from Eastern Europe and Russia), Americans, Dutch, Germans, Belgians and Portuguese.

41. Laband, *Transvaal Rebellion*, p. 15; K.W. Smith, 'The Fall of the Bapedi of the North-Eastern Transvaal', *Journal of African History*, 10, 2 (1969), pp. 240–1.

42. T. Dunbar Moodie, 'Black Migrant Mine Labourers and the Vicissitudes of Male Desire' in Morrell (ed.), *Changing Men*, pp. 299–303.

43. Atmore et al., 'Firearms', p. 550.

Chapter 4 Sobhuza's Dream

1. Delius, *Pedi Polity*, pp. 30, 99; Smith, 'Bapedi', p. 237.

2. This description of the Swazi military system is drawn from Hilda Kuper, *The Swazi: A South African Kingdom*, 2nd edn, New York: Holt, Rinehart and Winston, 1986, pp. 50–3; Hilda Kuper, *An African Aristocracy: Rank among the Swazi*, London: Oxford University Press for the International African Institute, 1969, pp. 14–15, 17, 43–4, 54–8, 77, 117–28; Brian Allan Marwick, *The Swazi: An Ethnographic Account of the Natives of the Swaziland Protectorate*, London: Frank Cass, 1966, pp. 256, 263–5, 271–9; Hilda Beemer, 'The Development of the Military Organization in Swaziland', *Africa*, 10, 1 (January 1937), pp. 57, 61–4, 67–74, and *Africa*, 10, 2 (April 1937), pp. 176–8, 180, 184–5, 187–8, 191, 193; Philip Bonner, *Kings, Commoners and Concessionaires: The Evolution and Dissolution of the Nineteenth-Century Swazi State*, Johannesburg: Ravan Press, 1983, pp. 49, 87–8.

3. For a full description of the *Ncwala* ceremony, see Kuper, *Swazi*, pp. 71–6, and *African Aristocracy*, pp. 202–25; Marwick, *Swazi*, pp. 182–95; Bonner, *Swazi State*, p. 49.

4. Kuper, *African Aristocracy*, p. 126.

5. For doctoring, see ibid, p. 125, and Marwick, *Swazi*, pp. 278–9.

6. The amaSwazi also possessed a much smaller shield for use when walking, courting or dancing.

7. *BPP* C. 1748, enc. 2 in no. 42: To the editor of the *Cape Times*, 18 June 1876.

8. Beemer, 'Military Organization', p. 193.

9. The amaZulu awarded a similar necklace with an identical purpose, known as *iziqu*.

10. Today, we would understand these cleansing rituals after combat as an effective way of minimizing post-traumatic stress disorder.

11. Marks and Atmore, 'Firearms', p. 526.

12. Delius, *Pedi Polity*, pp. 30–7; Giliomee and Mbenga (eds), *South Africa*, pp. 155–6.

13. Quoted in Etherington, *Great Treks*, p. 297.

14. F. Morton, 'Slavery and South African Historiography' and 'Slavery' in Elizabeth A. Eldredge and Fred Morton (eds), *Slavery in South Africa: Captive Labour on the Dutch Frontier*, Boulder, CO: Westview Press and Pietermaritzburg: University of Natal Press, 1994, pp. 1–2, 262; Etherington et al., 'Colonial Hegemonies', pp. 347–9, 355.

15. Kuper, *African Aristocracy*, p. 19: Kuper's informants.

16. For the text of the treaty, see *BPP* C. 1748, annexure A in enc. 1 in no. 178: Masoas [Mswati] his mark, 25 July 1846.

17. Delius, *Pedi Polity*, pp. 38–9.

18. Ibid, p. 40.

19. Thompson, 'Co-operation and Conflict', pp. 412–13; Etherington et al., 'Colonial Hegemonies', pp. 33–8.

20. See *BPP* C. 1748, no. 160: Barkly to Carnarvon, 6 November 1876, for details of the treaty. For the text, see annexure B in enc. 1 in no. 178: Agreement between the Commission appointed by the Honourable Volksraad of the Republic of Lydenburg and the Mattatees of Captain Sequati, 17 November 1857.

21. Etherington et al., 'Colonial Hegemonies', p. 375.

22. The Berlin Missionary Society, or The Society for the Propagation of the Gospel among the Heathen, was founded in 1824 and catered to pious and patriotic young Prussians who were zealous that their kingdom shoulder its burden in evangelizing the heathen outside Europe. For missionaries in Bopedi, see Delius, *Pedi Polity*, pp. 108–20.
23. Ibid, pp. 83–9.
24. Ibid, pp. 90–4, 99–100, 104.
25. Etherington et al., 'Colonial Hegemonies', pp. 355–7.
26. Delius, *Pedi Polity*, pp. 121–3, 158–70.
27. Adrian Preston (ed.), *The South African Journal of Sir Garnet Wolseley 1879–1880*, Cape Town: A.A. Balkema, 1973, pp. 144–6: entry of 23 October 1879.
28. Delius, *Pedi Polity*, pp. 99–101. The first major Swazi raid into Pedi territory was in about 1838 when the fortifications at Phiring held, and the amaSwazi retired after a failed night attack (ibid, pp. 29–30).
29. Maylam, *African People*, pp. 278–9.
30. Preston (ed.), *Wolseley's Journal*, p. 153: entry of 30 October 1879.
31. *BPP* C. 1748, enc. 2 in no. 42: To the editor of the *Cape Times*, 10 July 1876.
32. Delius, *Pedi Polity*, p. 100.
33. Ibid, pp. 110–14.

Chapter 5 'The Boers Are Killing Me'

1. Delius, *Pedi Polity*, pp. 126–53; Maylam, *African People*, p. 129; Etherington et al., 'Colonial Hegemonies', pp. 352–3.
2. Delius, *Pedi Polity*, pp. 170–8.
3. *BPP* C. 1748, enc. 3 in no. 118: Rev. Merensky to the *Natal Mercury*, 18 September 1876.
4. Bonner, *Swazi State*, pp. 135–7, 160–2. In 1876 Mbandzeni was induced to make enormous land concessions to Boer farmers.
5. *BPP* C. 1748, enc. 1 in no. 21: J.L. Vivian to Sir H.E. Bulwer, 21 April 1876.
6. Although it should be noted that local rich and politically prominent farmers were usually elected as officers. See also Stanley Trapido, 'Reflections on Land, Office and Wealth in the South African Republic, 1850–1900' in Shula Marks and Anthony Atmore (eds), *Economy and Society in Pre-Industrial South Africa*, Harlow, Essex: Longman, 1980, particularly pp. 352, 356, 361. The following description of the commando system is based on Tim Stapleton, 'South Africa' in Ian F.W. Beckett (ed.), *Citizen Soldiers and the British Empire, 1837–1902*, London: Pickering & Chatto, 2012, pp. 139–43; Ian van der Waag, 'South Africa and the Boer Military System' in Peter Dennis and Jeffrey Grey (eds), *The Boer War: Arms, Nation and Empire*, Canberra: Army History Unit, Department of Defence, 2000, pp. 49–51, 53–62, 64, 67; George Tylden, 'The Development of the Commando System in South Africa, 1715 to 1922', *Africana Notes and News*, 13 (March 1958–December 1959), pp. 303–13.
7. Laband, *Historical Dictionary*, pp. 119–20.
8. Pieter Labuschange, *Ghostriders of the Anglo-Boer War (1899–1902): The Role and Contribution of Agterryers*, Pretoria: University of South Africa Press 1999, pp. ix, 4–5, 7–9, 14, 25–6; Peter Warwick, *Black People and the South African War 1899–1902*, Johannesburg: Ravan Press, 1983, pp. 11, 25–6.
9. 'Kafir' ('kaffer' in Dutch) is a very problematic term, although in wide colonial use during the time-period of this book. 'Kafir' is an Arabic word originally employed in the Islamic sense to mean a disbeliever. By the fifteenth century Muslims in Africa were using it to denote non-Muslim Africans. The term was picked up by Europeans in Africa and applied to Sub-Saharan blacks. By the end of the nineteenth century it was becoming a racial slur applied offensively to Africans. Nowadays it is regarded as an unforgivable insult.
10. *BPP* C. 2584, enc. in no. 20: Sikukuni's statement to H.C. Shepstone, 23 December 1879.

11. For a full discussion on the drift to war, see Delius, *Pedi State*, pp. 181–205.

12. For Boer operations against Sekhukhune, see Great Britain, War Office Intelligence Department, *Précis of Information Concerning South Africa: The Transvaal Territory*, London: Her Majesty's Stationery Office, 1878, pp. 67–74; Smith, 'Bapedi', pp. 241–3; Kinsey, 'Sekukuni Wars', part I; Bonner, *Swazi State*, pp. 14–24; Delius, *Pedi Polity*, pp. 205–12; Stapleton, *Military History*, pp. 53–4; Ian Knight, *The Boer Wars (1) 1836–1898*, London: Osprey Military, 1996, pp. 21–4; T.S. van Rooyen, 'Die Verhouding tussen die Boer, Engelse en Naturelle in die Geskiedenis van die Oos-Transvaal tot 1882', *Archives Year Book for South African History, 14, I*, 1951, Cape Town: Government Printer, 1951, pp. 245–74.

13. Blanche, Lady Bellairs, *The Transvaal War 1880–1*, Edinburgh and London: William Blackwood and Sons, 1885, p. 15.

14. *BPP* C. 1748, enc. in no. 51: *Daily News* (Cape Town), 14 July 1876.

15. Ibid, enc. in no. 72: *Standard and Mail*, 24 August 1876.

16. For a description of Tsate, see ibid, enc. 2 in no. 80: To the editor of the *Gold Fields Mercury*, 26 July 1876; Delius, *Pedi Polity*, pp. 243–4; H.W. Kinsey, 'The Sekukuni Wars', part II, *Military History Journal*, 2, 6 (December 1973), http://samilitaryhistory.org/journal.html (accessed 10 March 2013).

17. Geologically, Ntswaneng was a norite extrusion from the level plain of the Bushveld Igneous Complex.

18. *BPP* C. 1748, enc. in no. 176: Statement of Mahoieza, taken by J.W. Shepstone, 23 October 1976.

19. Ibid, enc. 2 in no. 80: *Cape Times*, 25 August 1876.

20. Kinsey, 'Sekukuni Wars', part I.

21. *BPP* C. 1748, no. 130: Barkly to Carnarvon, 9 October 1876.

22. Ibid., enc. in no. 65: Proclamation by Henry Barkly, High Commissioner, 14 August 1876.

23. Philip Gon, *The Road to Isandlwana: The Years of an Imperial Battalion*, Johannesburg: Ad. Donker, 1979, pp. 37–8, 74.

24. Charles Norris-Newman, *With the Boers in the Transvaal and Orange Free State in 1880–1*, London: W.H. Allen, 1882, p. 71.

25. *BPP* C. 1748, enc. 2 in no. 130: W.V. Phelan, editor, *Gold Fields Mercury*, 4 September 1976.

26. Gon, *Road to Isandlwana*, p. 74; Laband, *Transvaal Rebellion*, p. 184.

27. *BPP* C. 1748, no. 188: Barkly to Carnarvon, 4 December 1876.

28. For the terms of the treaty, see *BPP* C. 1776, enc. in no. 64: report from the *Volksstem*, 7 February 1877. See too *BPP* C. 1748, enc. 5 in no. 111: testimony of Gideon, 19 March 1877, and enc. 6 in no. 111: Report of the proceedings of a Commission sent by the President of the South African Republic to investigate the circumstances attending the signing of a Treaty of Peace dated 15 February 1877, between the Transvaal Government and the Chief Sekukuni, 21 February 1877.

29. *BPP* C. 1776, enc. 7 in no. 111: M. Osborn and M. Clarke to T.S. Shepstone, 28 March 1877: Sikukuni's statement made on 15 February 1877.

30. Peter Gordon, 'Herbert, Henry Howard Molyneux, fourth earl of Carnarvon (1831–1890)', *Oxford Dictionary of National Biography*, Oxford: Oxford University Press, <http://www.oxforddnb.com/view/article/13035> (accessed 14 August 2013).

31. See Richard Cope, *Ploughshare of War: The Origins of the Anglo-Zulu War of 1879*, Pietermaritzburg: University of Natal Press, 1999, pp. 2–8.

32. The following discussion on Carnarvon's confederation scheme is based on ibid, pp. 80–85 and 257–64, and on Goodfellow, *Confederation*, pp. 49–59.

33. Saunders and Smith, 'Southern Africa', p. 605.

34. C.W. de Kiewiet, 'The Establishment of Responsible Government in Cape Colony, 1870–1872' in Eric A. Walker (ed.), *The Cambridge History of the British Empire*, vol. VIII, *South Africa, Rhodesia and the High Commission Territories*, Cambridge: Cambridge University Press, 1963, pp. 452, 455, 458; Davenport and Saunders, *South Africa*, pp. 199–203.

35. In 1875 an international tribunal confirmed Portuguese claims to Delagoa Bay.
36. Laband, *Transvaal Rebellion*, p. 18.
37. Sir Llewellyn Woodward, *The Age of Reform 1815–1870*, 2nd edn, Oxford: Clarendon Press, 1962, pp. 383–4; D.M. Schreuder, *The Scramble for Southern Africa, 1877–1895*, Cambridge: Cambridge University Press, 1980, pp. 61–4; Thompson, *South Africa*, p. 133; Laband, *Transvaal Rebellion*, pp. 17–18.
38. Storey, *Guns*, p. 177.
39. *BPP* C. 1776, enc. 1 in no. 111: Sikukuni to Sir T. Shepstone, 16 February 1876.
40. Laband, *Transvaal Rebellion*, pp. 18–19.

Chapter 6 The 'Black Conspiracy'

1. Great Britain, Intelligence Branch of the War Office, *Narrative of the Field Operations Connected with the Zulu War of 1879*, London: Her Majesty's Stationery Office, 1881, p. 6.
2. *BPP* C. 1883, enc. 1 in no. 21: Melmoth Osborn to Sikukuni, 9 May 1877.
3. Delius, *Pedi Polity*, pp. 222–3.
4. For Shepstone and his policies, see Brookes and Webb, *Natal*, pp. 56–60, Norman Etherington, 'The "Shepstone System" in the Colony of Natal and Beyond the Borders' in Duminy and Guest (eds), *Natal and Zululand*, pp. 170–81.
5. Norris-Newman, *With the Boers*, p. 81.
6. John Benyon, 'Frere, Sir (Henry) Bartle Edward, first baronet (1815–1884)', *Oxford Dictionary of National Biography*, Oxford: Oxford University Press <http://www. oxforddnb.com/view/article/10171> (accessed 14 August 2013); Benyon, *Proconsul*, pp. 144–8; John Benyon, 'Isandlwana and Passing of a Proconsul', *Natalia*, 8 (December 1978), p. 38.
7. Major-General W.C.F. Molyneux, *Campaigning in South Africa and Egypt*, London: Macmillan, 1896, p. 32.
8. Frank Emery, 'Geography and Imperialism: The Role of Sir Bartle Frere 1815–84', *Geographical Journal*, 150, 3 (November 1984), pp. 346–8; D.M. Schreuder, *The Scramble for Southern Africa, 1877–1895*, Cambridge: Cambridge University Press, 1980, pp. 68–9.
9. Colin de B. Webb, 'Lines of Power: The High Commissioner, the Telegraph and the War of 1879', *Natalia*, 8 (December 1978), p. 31; Leonard Thompson, 'Great Britain and the Afrikaner Republics, 1879–1899' in Wilson and Thompson (eds), *Oxford History of the British Empire*, vol. 2, *South Africa 1870–1966*, pp. 289–90.
10. De Kiewiet, 'Responsible Government', pp. 452, 455, 458; John Darwin, 'Britain's Empires' in Sarah Stockwell (ed.), *The British Empire: Themes and Perspectives*, Oxford: Blackwell, 2008, pp. 8, 13.
11. Despite considerable opposition in the Cape, the Permissive Federation Bill would nevertheless receive the royal assent on 10 August 1877 as the South Africa Act of 1877.
12. Laband, *Transvaal Rebellion*, p. 20.
13. Theophilus Shepstone to Frere, 30 April 1878, quoted in J. Martineau, *The Life and Correspondence of the Right Hon. Sir Bartle Frere, Bart., G.C.B., F.R.S., etc.*, London: John Murray, 1895, vol. II, p. 235; Delius, *Pedi Polity*, p. 225.
14. *BPP* C. 2100, enc. 1 in no. 39: A. Nachtigal to G.A. Roth, Landdrost of Lydenburg, 14 January 1878. See Mary Monteith, 'Cetshwayo and Sekhukhune 1875–1879', unpublished M.A. thesis, University of the Witwatersrand, 1978, pp. 170–6.
15. *BPP* C. 2222, no. 5: Sir Bartle Frere to Sir Michael Hicks Beach, 10 December 1878. For Shepstone's identical thoughts about the 'black conspiracy' and the Zulu as the 'root of all evil', see Laband, *Zulu Nation*, p. 190.
16. Frere to Hicks Beach, 28 October 1878, and notes by Frere, 3 February 1879, quoted in Laband, *Zulu Nation*, p. 189.
17. See, for example, *BPP* C. 2222, enc. 2 in no. 38: memorandum by C. Brownlee, Resident Commissioner of Native Affairs, Cape Colony, 12 November 1878.

18. Delius, *Pedi Polity*, p. 227.
19. *BPP* C. 1883, enc. 2 in no. 21: Captain M. Clarke to Shepstone, 13 June 1877.
20. Delius, *Pedi Polity*, pp. 227–31.
21. Laband, *Zulu Nation*, pp. 150, 158–60, 183, 190; Cope, *Ploughshare of War*, p. 161.
22. Shepstone to Herbert, 5 October 1877, quoted in Delius, *Pedi Polity*, p. 229.
23. *BPP* C. 2242, appendix III, no. 1: Shepstone to Carnarvon, 1 December 1877. See Cope, *Ploughshare of War*, pp. 162–6, for an analysis of the meeting. For the contemporary Zulu perspective, see Colin de B. Webb and John B. Wright (eds), *A Zulu King Speaks: Statements Made by Cetshwayo kaMpande on the History and Customs of his People*, Pietermaritzburg: University of Natal Press; Durban: Killie Campbell Africana Library, 1978, pp. 23–4, 48–50.

Chapter 7 EmaXhoseni

1. Noël Mostert, *Frontiers: The Epic of South Africa's Creation and the Tragedy of the Xhosa People*, London: Pimlico, 1993, p. 1249.
2. John Benyon, *Proconsul and Paramountcy in South Africa: The High Commission, British Supremacy and the Sub-Continent 1806–1910*, Pietermaritzburg: University of Natal Press, 1980, p. 149.
3. J.B. Peires, *The House of Phalo: A History of the Xhosa People in the Days of their Independence*, Johannesburg: Ravan Press, 1981, pp. 1–2.
4. Ibid, p. 3; Leo Switzer, *Power and Resistance in an African Society: the Ciskei Xhosa and the Making of South Africa*, Madison: University of Wisconsin Press, 1993, pp. 22–34; Maylam, *African People*, pp. 33–5; Trevor R. Getz, *Cosmopolitan Africa c.1700–1875*, New York and Oxford: Oxford University Press, 2013, p. 7.
5. Switzer, *Ciskei Xhosa*, pp. 33–4.
6. Khoesan is a portmanteau term describing both the pastoralist Khoekhoen and the hunter-gathering San who shared numerous common characteristics distinguishing them from the later, Nguni-speaking settlers.
7. Shula Marks, 'Khoisan Resistance to the Dutch in the Seventeenth and Eighteenth Centuries', *Journal of African History*, 13, 1 (1972), pp. 55–80.
8. Switzer, *Ciskei Xhosa*, pp. 40–2, and Hermann Giliomee, 'The Eastern Frontier, 1777–1812' in Robert Elphick and Hermann Gilliomee (eds), *The Shaping of South African Society, 1652–1820*, London and Cape Town: Maskew Miller Longman, 1987, pp. 294–303, for the Cape open frontier up to 1779.
9. Switzer, *Ciskei Xhosa*, pp. 37–8; John Milton, *The Edges of War: A History of the Frontier Wars, 1702–1878*, Cape Town: Juta, 1983, pp. 11–13; Getz, *Africa*, pp. 7–8, 63; Iliffe, *Honour*, p. 151.
10. Iliffe, *Honour*, pp. 152–3; Peires, *House of Phalo*, chapter 3; Switzer, *Ciskei Xhosa*, pp. 34–6.
11. John Henderson Soga, *The Ama-Xhosa: Life and Customs*, Alice, Eastern Cape: Lovedale Press; London: Kegan Paul, Trench, Trubner, c.1932, pp. 247–60; Switzer, *Ciskei Xhosa*, pp. 34–8; Peires, *House of Phalo*, pp. 20–1; Aubrey Elliott, *The Magic World of the Xhosa*, London: Collins, 1972, pp. 83–95; Ian Knight, *Warrior Chiefs of South Africa*, Poole, Dorset: Firebird Books, 1994, p. 180; Ian Knight, *Queen Victoria's Enemies (1): Southern Africa*, London: Osprey Military, 5th impression, 2005, pp. 8–9.
12. Peires, *House of Phalo*, chapters 2 and 4; Switzer, *Ciskei Xhosa*, pp. 38–42.
13. Giliomee, 'Eastern Frontier', p. 293.
14. Switzer, *Ciskei Xhosa*, pp. 43–58; Peires, *House of Phalo*, pp. 140–2; Stapleton, *Military History*, p. 4.
15. Peires, *House of Phalo*, p. 141.
16. Stapleton, *Military History*, pp. 6–7; Stapleton, 'South Africa', p. 143.
17. Elliott, *Xhosa*, pp. 70, 78–9.
18. Iliffe, *Honour*, pp. 153, 160, 301; Mostert, *Frontiers*, pp. 721–2; Molyneux, *Campaigning*, p. 55.

19. For traditional Xhosa warfare, see Peires, *House of Phalo*, pp. 135–9; Soga, *Ama-Xhosa*, pp. 65–81, 312–13; Knight, *Warrior Chiefs*, pp. 179–86; Knight, *Victoria's Enemies*, pp. 8–10; Milton, *Edges of War*, pp. 13–14; Iliffe, *Honour*, p. 153; Jochen S. Arndt, 'Treacherous Savages & Merciless Barbarians: Knowledge, Discourse and Violence during the Cape Frontier Wars, 1834–1853', *The Journal of Military History*, 74, 3 (July 2010), p. 726.

20. Soga, *Ama-Xhosa*, p. 75.

21. Ibid, pp. 79–81. These were challenges and counter-challenges at the battle of Amalinde in 1818 between Xhosa factions.

22. Stapleton, *Military History*, pp. 5–6; Giliomee, 'Eastern Frontier', pp. 308–26; Martin Legassick and Robert Ross, 'From Slave Economy to Settler Capitalism: The Cape Colony and Its Extensions, 1800–1854' in Hamilton et al. (eds), *South Africa*, pp. 265–6.

23. Storey, *Guns*, pp. 54–5.

24. Between 1851 and 1863 the average number of imperial troops garrisoning British colonies around the world (excluding India) numbered about 43,000. These troops included not only British regulars but small local corps raised in the colonies. See Sir Charles Lucas, *The Empire at War*, vol. 1, London: Humphrey Milford; Oxford: Oxford University Press, 1971, pp. 78–81.

25. Linda Robson and Mark Oranje, 'Strategic Military Colonisation: The Cape Eastern Frontier 1806–1872', *Scientia Militaria, South African Journal of Military Studies*, 49, 2 (2012), pp. 51–9, 68.

Chapter 8 'They Must Be Humbled and Subdued'

1. Stapleton, *Military History*, p. 20; Storey, *Guns*, p. 54.

2. Milton, *Edges of War*, pp. 58–70; Stapleton, *Military History*, pp. 7–9; Legassick and Ross, 'Cape Colony', pp. 266–7.

3. Stapleton, *Military History*, pp. 9–11, 20; Milton, *Edges of War*, pp. 69–97.

4. Legassick and Ross, 'Cape Colony', pp. 269–70.

5. Switzer, *Ciskei Xhosa*, p. 56; Storey, *Guns*, p. 69; Getz, *Africa*, pp. 78–9.

6. Timothy J. Stapleton, *Maqoma: Xhosa Resistance to Colonial Advance 1798–1873*, Johannesburg: Jonathan Ball, 1994, pp. 153–66 and 207; Mostert, *Frontiers*, p. 613; Iliffe, *Honour*, pp. 154–5.

7. Milton, *Edges of War*, pp. 96–144; Stapleton, *Military History*, pp. 22–4; Peires, *House of Phalo*, pp. 145–50; Mostert, *Frontiers*, pp. 689–94; Switzer, *Ciskei Xhosa*, pp. 56–8; Storey, *Guns*, pp. 70–71; Legassick and Ross, 'Cape Colony', pp. 281–5.

8. Molyneux, *Campaigning*, p. 43.

9. Peires, *House of Phalo*, p. 111.

10. Switzer, *Ciskei Xhosa*, pp. 60–1; Storey, *Guns*, p. 71.

11. Robson and Oranje, 'Strategic Military Colonisation', pp. 60–2.

12. Knight, *Warrior Chiefs*, pp. 183–6; Knight, *Victoria's Enemies*, pp. 9–10.

13. Quoted in Knight, *Warrior Chiefs*, p. 185.

14. Storey, *Guns*, pp. 55, 67–70, 72–3; Knight, *Warrior Chiefs*, pp. 183–4; Knight, *Victoria's Enemies*, p. 10.

15. Molyneux, *Campaigning*, p. 36.

16. Xhosa women too were adopting red blankets, described in the 1870s as being 'adorned with a perfect mass of embroidery, consisting of black braid and white buttons; arranged in geometrical patterns' (Helen M. Prichard, *Friends and Foes in the Transkei: An Englishwoman's Experiences during the Cape Frontier War of 1877–8*, London: Sampson Low, Marston, Searle & Rivington, 1880, p. 110). Married women wore a skin kilt; unmarried girls little more than a bunch of beads. All women wore necklaces and bangles (Molyneux, *Campaigning*, p. 35).

17. 'Fingo' appears to be an English corruption of their original name, the amaMfengu, from the Xhosa verb, *ukumfenguza*, meaning 'to seek work'.

18. Stapleton, 'Fingo', pp. 16–18; Stapleton, *Maqoma*, pp. 90–3; Mostert, *Frontiers*, pp. 697–8, 714–15, 722; Richard A. Moyer, 'The Mfengu, Self-Defence and the Cape Frontier Wars' in Christopher Saunders and Robin Derrincourt (eds), *Beyond the Cape Frontier: Studies in the History of the Transkei and Ciskei*, London: Longman, 1974, pp. 107–9; Clifton Crais, *White Supremacy and Black Resistance in Pre-Industrial South Africa: The Making of the Colonial Order in the Eastern Cape, 1770–1865*, Cambridge: Cambridge University Press, 1992, pp. 99, 117, 118, 152; Switzer, *Ciskei Xhosa*, pp. 58–60; Storey, *Guns*, pp. 69–70; Legassick and Ross, 'Cape Colony', pp. 283–4.

19. Iliffe, *Honour*, pp. 246–9.

20. H.S., 'The Kaffir War: By an English Officer in South Africa', *Fraser's Magazine*, February 1878, p. 256. See Stapleton, 'Fingo', pp. 18–19 and Moyer, 'Mfengu', p. 109.

21. Peires, *House of Phalo*, pp. 150–8; Milton, *Edges of War*, pp. 151–76; Mostert, *Frontiers*, pp. 891–935; Stapleton, *Military History*, pp. 24–6; Stapleton, 'Fingo', pp. 19–25; Stapleton, *Maqoma*, pp. 133–41; Moyer, 'Mfengu', pp. 110–11; Switzer, *Ciskei Xhosa*, pp. 61–3; Storey, *Guns*, pp. 73–4; Legassick and Ross, 'Cape Colony', pp. 293–301.

22. Stapleton, 'Fingo', pp. 46–7.

23. Soga, *Ama-Xhosa*, pp. 109–13; J.B. Peires, *The Dead Will Arise: Nongqawuse and the Great Xhosa Cattle-Killing Movement of 1856–7*, Johannesburg: Ravan Press, 1989, p. 82; Mostert, *Frontiers*, p. 1184; Iliffe, *Honour*, pp. 154–5.

24. Basil Le Cordeur and Christopher Saunders (eds), *The War of the Axe, 1847. Correspondence between the Governor of the Cape Colony, Sir Henry Pottinger, and the Commander of the British Forces at the Cape, Sir George Berkeley, and Others*, Johannesburg: Brenthurst Press, 1981, p. 128: Pottinger to Berkeley, 20 June 1847.

25. Peires, *House of Phalo*, pp. 165–9.

26. Quoted in Christopher Saunders, Colin Bundy and Dougie Oakes, *Illustrated History of South Africa: The Real Story*, 3rd edn, Pleasantville, New York: The Readers' Digest Association, 1988, pp. 133, 135.

27. For the War of Mlanjeni, see Milton, *Edges of War*, pp. 177–222; Mostert, *Frontiers*, pp. 1073–1160; Stapleton, *Maqoma*, pp. 143–67; Peires, *Dead Will Arise*, pp. 12–30; Stapleton, *Military History*, pp. 32–8; Crais, *Colonial Order*, pp. 175–88; Switzer, *Ciskei Xhosa*, pp. 63–5; Legassick and Ross, 'Cape Colony', pp. 30–3, 307–11; Etherington et al., 'Colonial Hegemonies', pp. 322–5.

28. Getz, *Africa*, pp. 9–10.

29. Peires, *House of Phalo*, pp. 69–71.

30. Switzer, *Ciskei Xhosa*, p. 68.

31. Stapleton, 'Fingo', 26–36, 46–7; Moyer, 'Mfengu', pp. 104–6, 114, 117–19; Storey, *Guns*, p. 77; Iliffe, *Honour*, p. 244.

32. Michael Carver (ed.), *Letters of a Victorian Army Officer, Edward Wellesley: Major, 73rd Regiment of Foot, 1840–1854*, Stroud, Gloucestershire: Alan Sutton Publishing for the Army Records Society, 1995, p. 29: Major Wellesley to Richard Wellesley, 14 June 1851.

33. Peter Boyden (ed.), *The British Army in Cape Colony: Soldiers' Letters and Dairies, 1806–58*, London: Society for Army Historical Research, Special Publication No. 15, 2001, p. 133: Private John Pine to his father, 9 December 1852.

34. Peires, *Dead Will Arise*, p. 28.

35. Crais, *Colonial Order*, pp. 125–46; Richard Price, *Making Empire: Colonial Encounters and the Creation of Imperial Rule in Nineteenth-Century Africa*, Cambridge: Cambridge University Press, 2008, pp. 127–47.

36. Peires, *Dead Will Arise*, pp. 23–5.

37. Arndt, 'Barbarians', pp. 730–4.

38. Carver, *Letters*, pp. 116–17: Major Wellesley to Richard Wellesley, 30 September 1853.

39. Ibid, p. 30: Major Wellesley to Richard Wellesley, 14 June 1851; Arndt, 'Barbarians', p. 724.

40. 'The kaffirs offered him sum if his Own fless to eat which they ded cut Of him and when they had dunn This they then let the young kaffirs Play at him as they thought fit' (Boyden, *Letters*, p. 113: diary of Private Thomas Scott, 1 November 1851). Arndt, 'Barbarians', pp. 727–9; Mostert, *Frontiers*, p. 900; Iliffe, *Honour*, p. 154.
41. Soga, *Ama-Xhosa*, pp. 74, 76–7.
42. Peires, *Dead Will Arise*, p. 23; Knight, *Warrior Chiefs*, p. 186.
43. Carver, *Letters*, p. 22: Major Wellesley to his wife, 31 May 1851.
44. Arndt, 'Barbarians', pp. 725–6.
45. Carver, *Letters*, p. 90: Major Wellesley to Richard Wellesley, 20 September 1852.
46. For Grey's unsuccessful attempt to plant military settlers along the frontier, see John Laband, 'From Mercenaries to Military Settlers: the British German Legion, 1854–1861' in Miller (ed.), *Soldiers and Settlers*, pp. 85–122.
47. Mostert, *Frontiers*, 1165, 1167–9; Benyon, *Proconsul*, pp. 60–5; Storey, *Guns*, pp. 76–7.
48. For the Cattle Killing, see Peires, *Dead Will Arise*, pp. 81–7, 148–59, passim; Milton, *Edges of War*, pp. 226–45; Mostert, *Frontiers*, pp. 1177–1222; Getz, *Africa*, pp. 61–5; Etherington et al., 'Colonial Hegemonies', pp. 325–6.
49. Etherington et al., 'Colonial Hegemonies', p. 334.
50. H.S., 'Kaffir War', p. 252.
51. Moyer, 'Mfengu', p. 121.
52. Milton, *Edges of War*, pp. 249–50.

Chapter 9 'I Am in a Corner'

1. Mostert, *Frontiers*, p. 1251.
2. Milton, *Edges of War*, pp. 252–6; Mostert, *Frontiers*, p. 1252.
3. Ibid, p. 1249; A.J. Smithers, *The Kaffir Wars 1779–1877*, London: Leo Cooper, 1973, p. 266.
4. Storey, *Guns*, pp. 199–200, 210, 227; J.S. Kotze, 'Counter Insurgency in the Cape Colony, 1872–1881', *Scientia Militaria: South African Journal of Military Studies*, 31, 2 (2003), pp. 42–3.
5. Evidence of E.B. Chalmers, FAMP, 16 September 1876, quoted in ibid, p. 224.
6. Evidence of Frederick Martin, settler, 18 September 1876 and John Hemming, magistrate, 30 September 1876, quoted in ibid.
7. Stapleton, 'Fingo', p. 37.
8. Storey, *Guns*, pp. 213–18, 223.
9. *BPP* C. 1961, no. 30: Frere to Carnarvon, 5 September 1877.
10. Ibid, enc. in no. 83: Col. John Eustace to Charles Brownlee, 18 August 1877.
11. Keith Smith, *The Wedding Feast War: The Final Tragedy of the Xhosa People*, London: Frontline Books, 2012, pp. 107–13.
12. Ibid, pp. 113–15.
13. Milton, *Edges of War*, pp. 257–8; Mostert, *Frontiers*, p. 1249.
14. Switzer, *Ciskei Xhosa*, p. 73.
15. Smithers, *Kaffir Wars*, pp. 265–6.
16. Basil Worsfold, *Sir Bartle Frere: A Footnote to the History of the British Empire*, London: Butterworth, 1923, p. 52.
17. H.S., 'Kaffir War', p. 254.
18. Ian Beckett, *The Victorians at War*, London: Hambledon, 2003, pp. 95–6.
19. Phyllis Lewsen (ed.), *Selections from the Correspondence of J. X. Merriman 1870–1890*, Cape Town: Van Riebeeck Society, 1960, p. 26; Gon, *Road to Isandlwana*, p. 107.
20. For useful summaries of the Ninth Cape Frontier War as they affected the question of command, see Phyllis Lewsen, *John X. Merriman: Paradoxical South African Statesman*, New Haven, CT, and London: Yale University Press, 1982, pp. 65–8; Lewsen (ed.), *Merriman*, pp. 26–7; Chris Hummel (ed.), *The Frontier War Journal of Major John Crealock 1878: A Narrative of the Ninth Frontier War by the Assistant Military Secretary to Lieutenant General Thesiger*, Cape Town: Van Riebeeck Society, 2nd series, no. 19, 1989, pp. 10–11.

21. Gon, *Road to Isandlwana*, pp. 106–7; Philip Gon, 'The Last Frontier War', *Military History Journal*, 5, 6 (December 1982), <http://samilitaryhistory.org/vol056pg.html> (accessed 10 March 2013).
22. H.S., 'Kaffir War', p. 254; Smithers, *Kaffir Wars*, p. 266.
23. Hummel (ed.), *Crealock*, p. 24, note 14; Smith, *Wedding Feast War*, p. 115.
24. In 1878 the FAMP would also appropriate the name of its Khoekhoe predecessor, and become the Cape Mounted Riflemen.
25. Stapleton, 'South Africa', pp. 144–5; Smithers, *Kaffir Wars*, pp. 263, 265; Kotze, 'Counter Insurgency', pp. 41–2.
26. A.T. Cunynghame, *My Command in South Africa, 1874–1878*, London: Macmillan, 1879, p. 307.
27. Stapleton, 'South Africa', pp. 139, 144–8.
28. Hummel (ed.), *Crealock*, p. 45: entry of 21 March 1878.
29. Ibid, p. 27: entry of 14 March 1878.
30. *BPP* C. 1961, enc. 2 in no. 102: Inspector C.B. Chalmer's report, 25 October 1877; H.S., 'Kaffir War', p. 252; Smith, *Wedding Feast War*, pp. 118–20.
31. Prichard, *Englishwoman's Experiences*, p. 183.
32. Ibid, pp. 215, 232.
33. Captain Henry Hallam Parr, *A Sketch of the Kafir and Zulu Wars: Guadana to Isandhlwana*, London: C. Kegan Paul, 1880, p. 35; H.S., 'Kaffir War', p. 253; Milton, *Edges of War*, p. 259.
34. Smithers, *Kaffir Wars*, p. 267.
35. Cunynghame, *Command*, p. 321.
36. *BPP* C. 1961, enc. in no. 61, Commandant C. Griffith to Military Secretary, 17 October 1877; H.S., 'Kaffir War', p. 253; Milton, *Edges of War*, p. 259; Stapleton, 'Fingo', pp. 37–8; Smith, *Wedding Feast War*, pp. 121–4.
37. Gon, *Road to Isandlwana*, p. 106.
38. *BPP* C. 1961, enc. in no. 51: Proclamation of His Excellency the Governor, 5 October 1877.
39. Milton, *Edges of War*, p. 261; Storey, *Guns*, p. 239.
40. Hallam Parr, *Wars*, p. 39.
41. H.S., 'Kaffir War', p. 254.
42. Hallam Parr, *Wars*, pp. 42–3. According to Hallam Parr, the Mfengu disliked leaving a charge in their gun for more than a day, and because they never went about with it unloaded, this required firing it off unnecessarily.
43. Smith, *Wedding Feast War*, pp. 128–35; Stapleton, 'Fingo', pp. 38–9.
44. H.S., 'Kaffir War', p. 256.
45. Hummel (ed.), *Crealock*, p. 24, note 14.
46. *BPP* C. 2000, enc. in no. 10: Griffith to Deputy Adjutant-General, 29 November 1877.
47. Ibid, C. 1961, enc. 3 in no. 102: Proclamation by Sir Bartle Frere, 21 November 1877; Milton, *Edges of War*, pp. 261–2.

Chapter 10 Calling in the 'amaJohnnies'

1. This was the chiefdom founded by Ndlambe who had been regent of the Rharhabe amaXhosa during his nephew Ngqika's minority.
2. Gon, *Road to Isandlwana*, pp. 116–17; Gon, 'Frontier War'.
3. Mostert, *Frontiers*, p. 1250; Smith, *Wedding Feast War*, pp. 138–41.
4. Milton, *Edges of War*, p. 264.
5. *BPP* C. 2000, enc. 1 in no. 22: Inspector J.H.W. Bourne's report, 3 December 1878; Gon, *Road to Isandlwana*, pp. 117–19; Milton, *Edges of War*, pp. 262–4; Smith, *Wedding Feast War*, pp. 141–4.
6. Smithers, *Kaffir Wars*, p. 267.
7. Hummel (ed.), *Crealock*, p. 77: entry of 30 April 1878; p. 77, note 143.

8. The discussion below on the British Army in the late 1870s is based on Laband, *Transvaal Rebellion*, pp. 67–82; Laband, *Historical Dictionary*, pp. 1, 7–9, 12–13, 30–2, 39–40, 48, 53, 70–2, 102, 140–1, 151, 163, 166–7, 210, 241, 258–9, 278–80, 283, 288; Edward M. Spiers, *The Late Victorian Army 1868–1902*, Manchester: Manchester University Press, 1992, pp. 272–304; Hew Strachan, *European Armies and the Conduct of War*, London: G. Allen & Unwin, 1983, pp. 6–89; Philip J. Haythornthwaite, *The Colonial Wars Source Book*, London: Caxton Editions, 2000, pp. 17–45, 48–60; Ian Knight, *Go to Your God like a Soldier: The British Soldier Fighting for Empire, 1837–1902*, London: Greenhill Books, 1996, pp. 12–32, 132, 138–52, 155–72, 182–202, 204–6, 247–9.

9. Beckett, *Victorians at War*, pp. 179–90.

10. Wolseley's 'ring' was first formed for the Ashanti expedition of 1873–4, and was made up of ambitious officers who were either decorated veterans of distinguished service, or Staff College graduates who showed promise. See Ian W.F. Beckett, 'Wolseley, Garnet Joseph, first Viscount Wolseley (1833–1913)', *Oxford Dictionary of National Biography*, Oxford: Oxford University Press, <http://www.oxforddnb.com> (accessed 14 August 2013); Beckett, 'Military High Command in South Africa, 1854–1914' in Peter Boyden, Alan Guy and Marion Harding (eds), *'Ashes and Blood': The British Army in South Africa 1795–1914*, London: National Army Museum, 1999, pp. 60–63; Beckett, *Victorians at War*, pp. 6–7; Steven J. Corvi, 'Garnet Wolseley' in Steven J. Corvi and Ian F.W. Beckett (eds), *Victoria's Generals*, Barnsley: Pen & Sword Military, 2009, pp. 12–14.

11. For his definition, see Charles Callwell, *Small Wars: Their Principles and Practice*, 3rd edn, London: His Majesty's Stationery Office, 1906, pp. 21–2.

12. Paul H. Butterfield, *War and Peace in South Africa 1879–1881: The Writings of Philip Anstruther and Edward Essex*, Melville, South Africa: Scripta Africana, 1987, p. 67: Lt-Col Anstruther to his wife, Zaida, 20 October 1878.

13. Some experts nevertheless preferred the older Snider rifle for bush fighting because its bullet penetrated a body less cleanly than a Martini-Henry's, making an appalling exit wound that had greater stopping-power. See Molyneux, *Campaigning*, pp. 69–70.

14. Ibid, p. 207.

15. Great Britain, War Office, *Field Exercise and Evolution of Infantry*, London: Her Majesty's Stationery Office, pocket edition, 1877, pp. 53–4.

16. Ibid, pp. 93–4, 96–9, 210–41.

17. Ian Knight, *Zulu Rising: The Epic Story of Isandlwana and Rorke's Drift*, London: Macmillan, 2010, p. 353.

18. Gon, 'Frontier War'.

19. Fleet Surgeon Henry F. Norbury, *The Naval Brigade in South Africa during the Years 1877–78–79*, London: Sampson Low, Marston, Searle & Rivington, 1880, p. 88. The Naval Brigade left its six 12-pounder guns on board.

20. Milton, *Edges of War*, p. 264. For lurid memories of trying to discipline these roughs, see Colonel G. Hamilton-Browne, *A Lost Legionary in South Africa*, London: T. Werner Laurie, 1912, pp. 36–42.

21. Laband, *Historical Dictionary*, p. 100. The FLH was finally disbanded in December 1879 after service against the amaZulu and Bapedi as well as the amaXhosa.

22. Ian W.F. Beckett, 'Buller, Sir Redvers Henry (1839–1908)', Oxford *Dictionary of National Biography*, Oxford: Oxford University Press, <http://www.oxforddnb.com> (accessed 14 August 2013).

Chapter 11 Not the 'White Man's Dogs'

1. *BPP* C. 1961, enc. in no. 43: report by West Fynn, clerk and interpreter to Colonel Eustace, Resident with Kreli, to Frere, 29 September 1877.

2. Milton, *Edges of War*, pp. 265–6; Gon, 'Frontier War'; Smith, *Wedding Feast War*, pp. 148–50, 155.

3. *Illustrated London News*, 16 February 1878, p. 139; Milton, *Edges of War*, p. 266; Smith, *Wedding Feast War*, pp. 151–5.

4. Gon, *Road to Isandlwana*, pp. 124–6; Gon, 'Frontier War'; Milton, *Edges of War*, p. 266; Smith, *Wedding Feast War*, pp. 196–201.

5. Phyllis Lewsen, 'The First Crisis in Responsible Government in the Cape Colony', *Archives Year Book for South African History, 1943 (2)*, Pretoria: Archives Year Book, V, 2 (1943), pp. 242–5; Lewsen, *Merriman*, p. 66; Hummel (ed.), *Crealock*, p. 12.

6. *BPP* C. 2000, enc. 6 in no. 78: Cunynghame to Frere, Ibeka, 29 December 1877; ibid, no. 78: Frere to Carnarvon, 31 December 1878 (received 5 February 1878); Cape of Good Hope, *Copy of Despatches which have Passed between the Right Honourable the Secretary of State for the Colonies and His Excellency the Governor since January Last*, Cape Town: Printed by Order of the House of Assembly, 1878, pp. 11–12: Cape of Good Hope No. 482: Carnarvon to Frere, 30 January 1878.

7. *BPP* C. 2079, no. 9: Frere to Carnarvon, 16 January 1878 (received 16 February 1878).

8. Ibid, no. 42: Frere to Carnarvon, 24 January 1878 (received 1 March 1878); Smith, *Wedding Feast War*, p. 162.

9. For the engagement at Nyumaga, see Smith, *Wedding Feast War*, pp. 201–4; Smithers, *Kaffir Wars*, pp. 270–1; Gon, *Road to Isandlwana*, pp. 131–2; Milton, *Edges of War*, pp. 266–7; Stapleton, *Military History*, pp. 59–60.

10. Edward M. Spiers, *The Victorian Soldier in Africa*, Manchester and New York: Manchester University Press, 2004, p. 36: 'Recollections of Lt. Thomas Ryder Main', n.d., p. 108.

11. Smith, *Wedding Feast War*, pp. 204–6.

12. *BPP* C. 2079, enc. 4 in no. 46: Cmdt J. Frost to Merriman, 23 January 1878; ibid, no. 10: telegram, Frere to Carnarvon, 29 January 1878; Milton, *Edges of War*, p. 270; Smith, *Wedding Feast War*, pp. 181–3.

13. Smith, *Wedding Feast War*, pp. 183–9. For operations by the colonial forces in the 'Tambookie Location', see *BPP* C. 2079, no. 80: Frere to Carnarvon, 16 February 1878, and enclosure.

14. *BPP* C. 2079, no. 86: Frere to Sir Michael Hicks Beach, 21 May 1878 (received 14 June 1878); Benyon, *Proconsul*, p. 151.

15. Lewsen, *Merriman*, pp. 69, 73; Lewsen, Responsible Government, p. 250.

16. *BPP* C. 2079: enc. in no. 86: Minutes of Executive Council, King William's Town, 2 February 1878; ibid, no. 54: Frere to Carnarvon, 5 February 1878 (received 11 March 1878); ibid, encs in no. 63: Frere to Molteno and Merriman, 6 February 1878; ibid, no. 63: Frere to Secretary of State for Colonies, 12 February 1878 (received 15 March 1878).

17. For the battle of Kentani, see ibid, no. 81: Frere to Carnarvon, 20 February 1878 and ibid, enc. 1 with official dispatches and reports of the engagement; Hallam Parr, *Wars*, pp. 83–5; Smithers, *Kaffir Wars*, pp. 268–70; Gon, *Road to Isandlwana*, pp. 134–40, 145–6; Milton, *Edges of War*, pp. 267–9; Stapleton, 'Fingo', p. 40; Switzer, *Ciskei Xhosa*, p. 74; Smith, *Wedding Feast War*, pp. 207–13.

18. Hallam Parr, *Wars*, p. 86: report by 'Gaika warrior'.

19. Ibid, p. 87: report by 'Gaika warrior'.

20. Milton, *Edges of War*, pp. 267–9; Gon, 'Frontier War'.

21. Smithers, *Kaffir Wars*, p. 271.

22. Hummel (ed.), *Crealock*, p. 20: entry of 4 March 1878.

23. Storey, *Guns*, pp. 239–40.

24. *BPP* C. 2144, no. 101: Frere to Hicks Beach, 18 June 1878.

25. Ibid, C. 2100, no. 56: Frere to Hicks Beach, 16 March 1878, quoting from Sprigg's 'demi-official', letter of 27 February 1878.

26. Ibid, C. 2144, enc. 1 in no. 102: Memorandum by Cunynghame, HMS *Hamalaya*, at sea, 4 April 1878.

27. Goodfellow, *Confederation*, p. 155.

28. *BPP* C. 2100, no. 56: General Order King William's Town, 11 March 1878, Col Bellairs.
29. Ibid, enc. in no. 43: Gen. Thesiger to Secretary of State for War, 12 March 1878.

Chapter 12 'Rather Like a Rat Hunt'

1. Jeffrey Mathews, 'Lord Chelmsford: British General in Southern Africa', unpublished D. Litt. et Phil. thesis, University of South Africa, 1986, pp. 41–2: Mitchell to Thesiger, 28 January 1878, pp. 41–2.
2. Spiers, *Victorian Army*, p. 272.
3. John Laband, 'Lord Chelmsford' in Corvi and Beckett (eds), *Victoria's Generals*, pp. 96, 98.
4. Smithers, *Kaffir Wars*, p. 271; Mathews, 'Chelmsford', p. 42.
5. Smith, *Wedding Feast War*, p. 217.
6. Molyneux, *Campaigning*, p. 43.
7. Milton, *Edges of War*, pp. 271–2; Gon, *Road to Isandlwana*, p. 151; Mostert, *Frontiers*, p. 1252; Stapleton, *Military History*, p. 62.
8. Milton, *Edges of War*, p. 272.
9. Hallam Parr, *Wars*, pp. 87–8.
10. Smithers, *Kaffir Wars*, p. 271; Stephen Manning, 'Evelyn Wood' in Corvi and Beckett (eds), *Victoria's Generals*, p. 39.
11. See *BPP* C. 2144, enc. in no. 20: Thesiger's diary of operations, 12 to 22 March 1878.
12. Mathews, 'Chelmsford', pp. 43–4; Gon, *Road to Isandlwana*, pp. 153–5; Gon, 'Frontier War'; Milton, *Edges of War*, p. 274; Smith, *Wedding Feast War*, pp. 218–22.
13. Hummel (ed.), *Crealock*, pp. 37–8: entry of 18 March 1878.
14. For this offensive, see *BPP* C. 2144, enc. in no. 29: Thesiger to Secretary of State for War, 10 April 1878.
15. Smith, *Wedding Feast War*, pp. 224–5; Stapelton, 'Fingo', p. 41; Gon, *Road to Isandlwana*, pp. 153–5; Milton, *Edges of War*, pp. 274–5.
16. Frank Emery, *Marching over Africa: Letters from Victorian Soldiers*, London: Hodder and Stoughton, 1986, pp. 54–5: Private George Morris to his father, March 1878.
17. Mathews, 'Chelmsford', pp. 44, 46.
18. Gon, *Road to Isandlwana*, p. 156; Stapleton, *Military History*, p. 62.
19. Hummel (ed.), *Crealock*, p. 57: entry of 5 April 1878; ibid, p. 65: entry of 6 April 1878.
20. Milton, *Edges of War*, p. 275; Smith, *Wedding Feast War*, pp. 189–92.
21. See *BPP* C. 2144, enc. in no. 11: Thesiger's diary of operations, 10 to 17 April 1878; ibid, enc. in no. 31: Thesiger to Secretary of State for War, 24 April 1878.
22. Stapleton, 'Fingo', pp. 41–2; Milton, *Edges of War*, p. 275; Mathew, 'Chelmsford', p. 46; Gon, *Road to Isandlwana*, p. 158; Smith, *Wedding Feast War*, pp. 226–8.
23. For these operations, see *BPP* C. 2144, enc. in no. 46: Thesiger to Secretary of State for War, 5 May 1878; ibid, enc. in no. 47: diary of Quartermaster-General's Department, 8 May 1878; ibid, enc. in no. 55: Thesiger to Secretary of State for War, 15 May 1878.
24. Molyneux, *Campaigning*, p. 81.
25. Mathews, 'Chelmsford', p. 47; Smithers, *Kaffir Wars*, p. 272; Milton, *Edges of War*, p. 276; Stapleton, *Military History*, p. 62; Smith, *Wedding Feast War*, pp. 226–32.
26. Mathews, 'Chelmsford', pp. 47–8; Milton, *Edges of War*, p. 276; Smith, *Wedding Feast War*, pp. 232–6.
27. Hummel (ed.), *Crealock*, p. 81: entry of 3 May 1878.
28. Gon, *Road to Isandlwana*, p. 163; Mathews, 'Chelmsford', p. 49; Stapleton, *Military History*, p. 62.
29. *BPP* C. 2144, enc. in no. 47: diary of Quartermaster-General's Department, 8 May 1878; ibid, enc. in no. 55: Thesiger to Secretary of State for War, 15 May 1878; ibid, enc. in no. 56: diary of Quartermaster-General's Department, 15 May 1878; ibid, encs

1, 2 and 3 in no. 77: Thesiger's reports to Frere, 22 May, 29 May, 2 June 1878; ibid, encs 1 and 2 in no. 91: operations from 29 May to 5 June 1878.
30. Ibid, no. 32: Frere to Hicks Beach, 30 April 1878.
31. Hallam Parr, *Wars*, p. 94; Mathews, 'Chelmsford', p. 48; Milton, *Edges of War*, pp. 274, 276–8; Smith, *Wedding Feast War*, pp. 236–7; Stapleton, *Military History*, pp. 60–1.
32. Jennifer Crwys-Williams (ed.), *South African Despatches: Two Centuries of the Best in South African Journalism*, Johannesburg: Ashanti, 1989, pp. 35–9: *The Eastern Star*, 14 June 1878; Motert, *Frontiers*, p. 1252; Milton, *Edges of War*, pp. 278–9; Smith, *Wedding Feast War*, pp. 237–9.
33. For Thesiger's detailed report on his conduct of operations from March 1878, see *BPP* C. 2144, enc. 1 in no. 126: Thesiger to Secretary of State for War, 26 June 1878.
34. Milton, *Edges of War*, pp. 280–1; Gon, *Road to Isandlwana*, p. 166; Gon, 'Frontier War'; Stapleton, 'Fingo', pp. 42–3; Smith, *Wedding Feast War*, p. 245.
35. Soga, *Ama-Xhosa*, pp. 118–23; Mostert, *Frontiers*, p. 1254; Smith, *Wedding Feast War*, pp. 239–40.
36. *BPP* C. 2144, enc. 3 in no. 110: D.A.G. to Military Secretary, 21 June 1878; Milton, *Edges of War*, p. 274; Motert, *Frontiers*, pp. 1254, 1281; Switzer, *Ciskei Xhosa*, p. 74.
37. Crwys-Williams (ed.), *Despatches*, p. 39: *The Eastern Star*, 14 June 1878.
38. Switzer, *Ciskei Xhosa*, pp. 74–5; Milton, *Edges of War*, p. 282; Mostert, *Frontiers*, pp. 1252–3; Smith, *Wedding Feast War*, pp. 241–4.
39. Milton, *Edges of War*, p. 281; Storey, *Guns*, pp. 240–2.
40. *Cape Argus*, 12 May 1878, quoted in Storey, *Guns*, p. 241.
41. Although the Transkei was not formally annexed to the Cape until 1885, Frere invoked his powers as High Commissioner to disarm the Africans living there.
42. Storey, *Guns*, pp. 246–52.
43. W.G. Cumming of Xalanga District, quoted in Storey, *Guns*, pp. 246–7.
44. Stapleton, 'Fingo', pp. 43, 47.
45. Carnarvon resigned over the Eastern Question. By advocating neutrality, he crossed the prime minster, Lord Beaconsfield, who was contemplating war against Russia to maintain Ottoman control over the Dardanelles and so keep the Russian Black Sea fleet out of the Mediterranean where it might threaten the British route to India. See Gordon, 'Herbert, Henry Howard Molyneux'.
46. Martin Pugh, 'Beach, Michael Edward Hicks, first Earl St Aldwyn (1837–1916)', *Oxford Dictionary of National Biography*, Oxford: Oxford University Press, <http://www.oxforddnb.com/view/article/33859> (accessed 14 August 2013).
47. Cope, *Ploughshare of War*, pp. 217–18; Storey, *Guns*, p. 240.
48. H.S., 'Kaffir War', p. 258.
49. Hallam Parr, *Wars*, p. 101.
50. Ibid, pp. 101–2.

Chapter 13 A 'Hideous and Disgusting Place'

1. For the discovery of diamonds, see John Benyon, 'The Cape Colony, 1854–1881' in T. Cameron and S.B. Spies (eds), *An Illustrated History of South Africa*, Johannesburg: Jonathan Ball, 1986, pp. 167–8; Storey, *Guns*, pp. 119–20; Kevin Shillington, *Luka Jantjie: Resistance Hero of the South African Frontier*, London: Aldridge Press, 2011, pp. 42–4, 48, 51–2, 54.
2. W. Crisp to Father, Whitsun Tuesday, 1872, quoted in Paul S. Landau, *Popular Politics in the History of South Africa, 1400–1948*, Cambridge: Cambridge University Press, 2010, p. 138.
3. Ibid, p. 22.
4. Ibid, pp. 22, 26; Maylam, *African People*, pp. 42–4.
5. Maylam, *African People*, pp. 44–8; Shillington, *Luka*, p. 2.
6. Robert Ross, 'The !Kora Wars on the Orange River, 1830–1888', *Journal of African History*, 16, 4 (1975), pp. 561–3 and 575.

7. For the early history of the Griqua, see Giliomee and Mbenga (eds), *South Africa*, pp. 68–9; Legassick and Ross, 'Cape Colony', p. 264; Nigel Penn, *The Forgotten Frontier: Colonists and Khoisan on the Cape's Northern Frontier in the 18th Century*, Athens, OH: Ohio University Press; Cape Town: Double Story Books, 2006, pp. 157–69; Robert Ross, 'Khoesan and Immigrants: The Emergence of Colonial Society in the Cape, 1500–1800' in Hamilton, et al. (eds), *South Africa*, p. 206; Shillington, *Luka*, p. 4–5, 8–9, 92; Storey, *Guns*, pp. 89–93.

8. Landau, *Popular Politics*, pp. 4, notes 8, 5, 17, 145.

9. The name Griqua was derived from the Khoesan Cha-guriqua clan from which the former Basters were partly descended through Adam Kok I's marriage in the 1750s (Shillington, *Luka*, p. 9, note 9; Landau, *Popular Politics*, pp. 4, 13; J.T. du Bruyn, 'The Great Trek' in Cameron and Spies (eds), *South Africa*, p. 128; Heydenrych, 'Boer Republics', pp. 144–5).

10. Heydenrych, 'Boer Republics', pp. 144–5; Benyon, 'Cape Colony', p. 166; Landau, *Popular Politics*, p. 200; Du Bruyn, 'Great Trek', p. 128; Etherington et al., 'Colonial Hegemonies', p. 369; Giliomee and Mbenga (eds), *South Africa*, pp. 143–4; Legassick and Ross, 'Cape Colony', p. 265. Griqualand East came under British rule in 1874. It passed under the control of the Cape in 1877, but the annexation act was only promulgated in September 1879.

11. Shillington, *Luka*, p. 9.

12. Ibid, pp. 5–6 and 11–13; Knight, *Warrior Chiefs*, pp. 61, 65, 70–1.

13. The identity of the raiders in the battle of Dithakong has raised considerable controversy, as has the impact of the *Difaqane* generally in the western highveld. I have followed the conclusions of Margaret Kinsman, ' "Hungry Wolves": The Impact of Violence on Rolong Life 1823–1836', and Guy Hartley, 'The Battle of Dithakong and "Mfecane" Theory', in Carolyn Hamilton (ed.), *The Mfecane Aftermath: Reconstructive Debates in Southern African History*, Johannesburg: Witwatersrand University Press; Pietermaritzburg: University of Natal Press, 1995, pp. 363–416. See also Giliomee and Mbenga (eds), *South Africa*, p. 130; Shillington, *Luka*, p. 11; Wright, 'Turbulent Times', p. 235, and Maylam, *African People*, pp. 59–60.

14. Maylam, *African People*, p. 121; Shillington, *Luka*, p. 11–13.

15. Shillington, *Luka*, pp. 2–4, 13–15, 17, 20–3, 26; Maylam, *African People*, pp. 120–1.

16. Maylam, *African People*, pp. 121–2; Shillington, *Luka*, pp. 24–5, 42–3.

17. Etherington et al., 'Colonial Hegemonies', pp. 354–5; Maylam, *African People*, pp. 122–3.

18. Shillington, *Luka*, pp. 31–5, 37.

19. For the diamond fields dispute, the Keate Award and the splitting of the Batlhaping *merafe*, see Benyon, 'Cape Colony', p. 166; De Kiewiet, 'Responsible Government', pp. 440–58; Cecil Headlam, 'The Failure of Confederation, 1871–1881' in Walker (ed.), *South Africa*, pp. 461–3; Giliomee and Mbenga (eds), *South Africa*, pp. 159–60; Gon, *Road to Isandlwana*, p. 32; Heydenrych, 'Boer Republics', p. 148; Shillington, *Luka*, pp. 57, 59–64, 73, 75–6.

20. Etherington, 'Colonial Hegemonies', p. 372; Gon, *Road to Isandlwana*, pp. 3–49, 60; Storey, *Guns*, p. 121; Roger T. Stearn, 'Lanyon, Sir (William) Owen (1842–1887)', *Oxford Dictionary of National Biography*, Oxford: Oxford University Press, <http://www.oxforddnb.com/> (accessed 6 October 2004).

21. Lanyon was very swarthy, and when in March 1879 he became Administrator of the Transvaal, the Boers put out that he had African blood and that they were being oppressed by a 'kaffer'. See Stearn, 'Lanyon'.

22. Owen Lanyon to Charles Lanyon, 22 January 1877, quoted in Bridget M. Theron-Bushell, 'Puppet on an Imperial String: Owen Lanyon in South Africa, 1875–1881', unpublished D. Litt. et Phil. thesis, University of South Africa, 2002, p. 91.

23. *BPP* C. 2585, enc. in no. 23: minute by J. Gordon Sprigg, 15 December 1879; Theron-Bushell, 'Lanyon', pp. 92, 101, 103–4, 112, 125. In the interim, Lanyon was addressed as the Lieutenant-Governor of the Province of Griqualand West.

24. Theron-Bushell, 'Lanyon', p. 130; Shillington, *Luka*, pp. 89–90; J.B. Sutton, 'The 1878 Rebellion in Griqualand West and Adjacent Territories', unpublished Ph.D. thesis, School of Oriental and African Studies, University of London, 1975, pp. 176, 229.
25. Sutton, '1878 Rebellion', pp. 126–7; Gon, *Road to Isandlwana*, p. 171; Maylam, *African People*, p. 123; Shillington, *Luka*, pp. 64, 78–81.
26. Lanyon to Frere, 19 September 1878, quoted in Theron-Bushell, 'Lanyon', pp. 118–19.
27. *BPP* C. 2100, no. 63: Hicks Beach to Shepstone, 26 April 1878; Theron-Bushell, 'Lanyon', pp. 118–21.

Chapter 14 Resisting with 'Fixity of Purpose'

1. *BPP* C. 2100, enc. in no. 14: Jappie Ginga on oath to James Buchanan, 12 February 1878.
2. Shillington, *Luka*, pp. 81–2, 85–6.
3. Stapleton, 'South Africa', p. 148.
4. Theron-Bushell, 'Lanyon', pp. 109, 115, 117.
5. For the campaign against Botlasitse, see *BPP* C. 2100, enc. in no. 7: Frere to Carnarvon, 12 February 1878; Theron-Bushell, 'Lanyon', pp. 127, 129; Shillington, *Luka*, p. 87–8.
6. Shillington, *Luka*, pp. 89–90.
7. *BPP* C. 2220, enc. 3 in no. 110: minutes of a meeting between Lanyon and Griqua leaders who had taken no part in the rebellion, 28 June 1878.
8. Cape of Good Hope, *Copy of Further Correspondence on the Subject of the Recent Native Disturbances in Griqualand West (2)*, Cape Town: printed by Order of the House of Assembly, 1878: Lanyon to Frere, 15 June 1878 and five enclosures.
9. Ross, '!Kora Wars', p. 575.
10. Cape of Good Hope, *Copy of a Despatch Addressed to His Excellency the Governor by the Lieutenant-Governor of the Province of Griqualand West, on the Subject of Native Disturbances in that Province*, Cape Town: printed by Order of the House of Assembly, 1878: H.B. Roper, Resident Magistrate, Hay, to Francis Villiers, Acting Colonial Secretary, 19 April 1878.
11. For operations in southern Griqualand West between April and July 1878, see *BPP* C. 2220, enc. 2 in no. 28: *précis* of operations in Griqualand West, April through July 1878 compiled by Lt.-Gen. Thesiger, 30 July 1878; ibid, enc. 1 in no. 110: Lanyon to Frere, 6 July 1878; ibid, enc. 4 in no. 110: Warren to Lanyon, 2 July 1878.
12. Cape, *Copy of Despatch*: Lanyon to Frere, 12 May 1878.
13. Cape, *Griqualand West (2)*, enc. 2 to no. 48: report by H.B. Roper, 15 June 1878.
14. *BPP* C. 2220, enc. 2 in no. 110: Warren to Lanyon, 28 June 1878.
15. Cape of Good Hope, *Copy of Further Correspondence on the Subject of the Recent Native Disturbances in Griqualand West*, Cape Town: printed by Order of the House of Assembly, 1878: Lanyon to J.D. Barry, 28 May 1878.
16. Laband, *Historical Dictionary*, pp. 8–9.
17. Cape, *Griqualand West*: Lanyon to J.D. Barry, 28 May 1878.
18. Ibid, R.E. Nesbitt to Lanyon, 1 June 1878.
19. Ibid, Warren to Colonial Secretary, Kimberley, 10 June 1878.
20. For the battle of Paarde Kloof, see *BPP* C. 2220, enc. 2 in no. 110: Warren to Lanyon, 28 June 1878.
21. For the battle of Witsand, see ibid, sub-enc. 3. in enc. in no. 127: Warren to Colonial Secretary, Kimberley, 19 September 1878.
22. For the Burness incident and its immediate aftermath, see Theron-Bushell, 'Lanyon', p. 132; Shillington, *Luka*, pp. 91–9.
23. Cape, *Griqualand West*: Lanyon to J.D. Barry, 28 May 1878.
24. This new-found punctiliousness had its roots in the embarrassing enquiry F.W. Chesson of the Aborigines' Protection Society in London had made into Lanyon's

punitive raid to Phokwani in January 1878. Not without reason, Chesson wondered what Lanyon thought he was doing conducting military operations in the territory of an independent chief (*BPP* C. 2100, no. 28: F.W. Chesson to Hicks Beach, 6 April 1878).

25. Ibid, enc. in no. 61: Lanyon to Frere, 24 August 1878: extract from instructions given to Mr Ford.

26. For the skirmish at Kho, see Shillington, *Luka*, pp. 99–105.

27. See ibid, p. 103, note 18, for Shillington's interview with Molehabangwe Jantjie, grandson of Olebile Devolk Jantjie, at Manyeding in March 1978.

28. Lanyon's combined forces at Kuruman numbered 482 (Cape, *Griqualand West*: Lanyon to J.D. Barry, 1 June 1878).

29. For the attack on Gamopedi, see *BPP* C. 2220, enc. in no. 61: Lanyon to Frere, 24 August 1878; Theron-Bushell, 'Lanyon', p. 132; Shillington, *Luka*, pp. 106–8.

30. For the battle of Dithakong, see *BPP* C. 2220, enc. in no. 32: memorandum by Lanyon, 30 July 1878; enc. in no. 61: Lanyon to Frere, 24 August 1878; Shillington, *Luka*, pp. 106, 109–13.

31. *BPP* C. 2220, enc. in no. 61: Lanyon to Frere, 24 August 1878.

32. See the image of the advertisement in Shillington, *Luka*, p. 113.

33. *BPP* C. 2220, enc. 2 in no. 62: Mankoroane Motihubanwe to Lanyon, 1 August 1878.

34. Ibid, enc. in no. 61: Lanyon to Frere, 24 August 1878; Theron-Bushell, 'Lanyon', pp. 132–3; Shillington, *Luka*, pp. 113–15.

35. Gon, *Road to Isandlwana*, pp. 171, 173.

36. For the engagement of the Gobatse Heights, see *BPP* C. 2252, enc. 1 in no. 1: extract from letter from Colonel Warren, Commanding troops during final operations on Desert Border, n.d.; Gon, *Road to Isandlwana*, pp. 171, 173–5.

37. Quoted in ibid., p. 175.

38. *BPP* C. 2367, enc. 4 in no. 30, telegram, Civil Commissioner, Victoria West, to the Colonial Secretary, Cape Town, 7 November 1878. During the autumn of 1880 Cape colonial forces finally expelled the Korana from their island fastness in the Orange River, drove them into the desert and gave their lands to settlers (Ross, '!Kora Wars', p. 575).

39. *BPP* C. 2220, enc. in no. 127: Lanyon to Frere, 24 September 1878.

40. Ibid, sub-enc. 3 in no. 127: Warren to Colonial Secretary, Kimberley, 19 September 1878.

41. Warren's military tour was intended as a preliminary to taking over the region as a protectorate and including it in the projected South African confederation. However, the territory between Griqualand West and the Molopo River was annexed as the Colony of British Bechuanaland only in 1885, long after confederation had become a dead letter, in order to keep open the 'road to the north'. In 1895 British Bechuanaland was incorporated into the Cape Colony, just as Griqualand West had been in 1880.

42. *BPP* C. 2222, sub-enc. in enc. in no. 37: proclamation, 13 November 1878; Theron-Bushell, 'Lanyon', p. 116.

43. *BPP* C. 2308, enc. 2 in no. 1: C. Warren to Lanyon, 26 November 1878; Theron-Bushell, 'Lanyon', pp. 132 and 134; Shillington, *Luka*, pp. 115–17.

44. Shillington, *Luka*, pp. 119–22.

45. Thesiger had succeeded his father on 5 October 1878 as the Second Baron Chelmsford.

46. *BPP* C. 2252, enc. in no. 3: minute by Chelmsford, 25 November 1878.

47. Shillington, *Luka*, pp. 118–19. Resistance to colonial rule broke out again in 1897 among the Batswana soon after British Bechuanaland became part of the Cape. The rebels (including Luka) made their last stand in the northern Langeberg where they were defeated by the colonial police (Shillington, *Luka*, pp. 182–262).

48. Quoted in Theron-Bushell, 'Lanyon', p. 145.

49. *BPP* C. 2220, no. 112: Hicks Beach to Frere, 13 November 1878; Theron-Bushell, 'Lanyon', pp. 89, 125, 135, 137–8.

50. *BPP* C. 2222, enc. in no. 36: Lanyon to Frere, 19 November 1878.

Chapter 15 'The Ground Was His'

1. Shepstone to Carnarvon, 11 December 1877, quoted in Delius, *Pedi Polity*, p. 232.
2. See *BPP* C. 2100: Shepstone to Carnarvon, 23 February 1878.
3. See Delius, *Pedi Polity*, p. 232.
4. Smith, 'Bapedi', p. 244.
5. Great Britain, *Zulu War*, p. 6; Laband, *Transvaal Rebellion*, p. 20.
6. Great Britain, *Zulu War*, p. 6.
7. *BPP* C. 2100, enc. 3 in no. 39: Shepstone to Clarke, 23 February 1878.
8. Delius, *Pedi Polity*, pp. 210, 233–4; Norris-Newman, *With the Boers*, p. 79; Kinsey, 'Sekukuni Wars', part II.
9. *BPP* C. 2100, no. 72: message from Sikukuni to G.A. Roth, Landdrost of Lydenburg, 2 March 1878.
10. Ibid, no. 72: Clarke to Melmoth Osborn, 8 March 1878.
11. Smith, 'Bapedi', pp. 245–6; Delius, *Pedi Polity*, pp. 234–5.
12. Smith, 'Bapedi', p. 245; Delius, *Pedi Polity*, pp. 236–8.
13. *BPP* C. 2505, no. 19: declaration of Chief Sekukuni to H.C. Shepstone, 10 December 1879.
14. Ibid., C. 2100, no. 39: Shepstone to Carnarvon, 23 February 1878.
15. Shepstone to Bulwer, 30 March 1878, quoted in Delius, *Pedi Polity*, p. 239.
16. Great Britain, *Zulu War*, p. 7; Kinsey, 'Sekukuni Wars', part II.
17. *BPP* C. 2144, enc. 2 in no. 27: Clarke to Melmoth Osborn, 7 April 1878 and memorandum by Osborn, 15 April 1878; Great Britain, *Zulu War*, p. 7; Kinsey, 'Sekukuni Wars', part II.
18. Losses were four Zulu Police and six African levies killed, five white troops and seven Zulu Police wounded. The defenders' losses are unknown.
19. *BPP* C. 2144, enc. 2 in no. 25: memorandum by Captain Clarke, received 14 June 1878.
20. Great Britain, *Zulu War*, p. 7; Delius, *Pedi Polity*, p. 239; Smith, 'Bapedi', p. 246; Kinsey, 'Sekukuni Wars', part II.
21. *BPP* C. 2220, enc. in no. 48: Capt. Ramsay Steuart, DFH, to Clarke, 8 August 1878; ibid, enc. in no. 73: operations against Sikukuni, Capt. E. Woodgate, 19 August 1878; Great Britain, *Zulu War*, pp. 7–8; Kinsey, 'Sekukuni Wars', part II.
22. For Rowlands's campaign, see *BPP* C. 2220, sub-enc. 1 in enc. in no. 131: report by Col Hugh Rowlands, 9 October, 1878; Great Britain, *Zulu War*, pp. 8–10; Kinsey, 'Sekukuni Wars', part II; Delius, *Pedi Polity*, pp. 239–40; Smith, 'Bapedi', p. 246; Stapleton, *Military History*, p. 55.
23. Preston (ed.), *Wolseley's Journal*, p. 149: entry of 26 October 1879. It was not until 1899 that the trypanosome parasite carried by tsetse flies was identified as causing horse sickness. See Mary Dobson, *Disease: The Extraordinary Stories behind History's Deadliest Killers*, London: Quercus, 2007, pp. 94–7.
24. *BPP* C. 2222, enc. 1 in no. 12: Gen. Thesiger to the Secretary of State for War, 11 November 1878.
25. *Blue Book for the Transvaal Province. 1879*, Pretoria: Coppen, Deeker, Government Printers, 1879, p. 6.
26. Quoted in Monteith, 'Cetshwayo and Sekhukhune', p. 166.

Chapter 16 Preparing to 'Draw the Monster's Teeth and Claws'

1. Laband, *Zulu Nation*, pp. 173–4.
2. *Natal Witness*, 2 August 1878, quoted in ibid, p. 186.
3. Laband, 'Chelmsford', p. 98.
4. For succinct accounts of the political build-up to the Anglo-Zulu War, see John Laband, *Kingdom in Crisis: The Zulu Response to the British Invasion of 1879*, Manchester: Manchester University Press, 1992; Barnsley: Pen & Sword Military,

2007, pp. 10–14; John Laband and Paul Thompson, *The Illustrated Guide to the Anglo-Zulu War*, Pietermaritzburg: University of Natal Press, 2000, pp. 5–7. See also Cope, *Ploughshare of War*, chapters 7–9.

5. Frere to Hicks Beach, 8 December 1878, quoted in Martineau, *Frere*, vol. II, p. 253.

6. Frere to Shepstone, 30 November 1878, quoted in Laband, *Kingdom in Crisis*, p. 12.

7. It took five weeks for a dispatch to travel between Frere and the Colonial Office, and sixteen days for a telegram, because there was no direct cable link (see chapter 6).

8. Frere to Hicks Beach, 28 October 1878, quoted in Martineau, *Frere*, vol. II, pp. 259–60; *BPP* C. 2222, no. 54: Frere to Hicks Beach, 14 December 1878.

9. Laband, 'Chelmsford', pp. 100–5.

10. Laband (ed.), *Chelmsford's Zululand Campaign*, p. 158: Chelmsford to Brig.-Gen. H.E. Wood, 22 April 1879.

11. In 1879 a further force of African levies raised in southern Natal was called the Ixopo Native Contingent and wore grey armbands with an orange stripe. The fullest treatment of the NNC is to be found in Thompson, *Black Soldiers*, and in Ingrid Machin, *Antbears and Targets for Zulu Assegais*, Howick: Brevitas, 2002.

12. The 1st Battalion of Wood's Irregulars wore red and white cloths around their heads and the 2nd Battalion wore blue and white ones.

13. For succinct accounts of the formation of the NNC and related units, see John Laband and Paul Thompson, 'African Levies', pp. 53–5; and Laband and Thompson, *Anglo-Zulu War*, pp. 22–3. For Transvaal and Swazi levies, see John Laband, 'Mbilini, Manyonyoba and the Phongolo River Frontier: A Neglected Sector of the Anglo-Zulu War of 1879' in John Laband and Paul Thompson, *Kingdom and Colony at War: Sixteen Studies on the Anglo-Zulu War of 1879*, Pietermaritzburg: University of Natal Press; Cape Town: N & S Press, 1990, pp. 194, 197; and Huw M. Jones, *The Boiling Cauldron: Utrecht District and the Anglo-Zulu War, 1879*, Bisley, Gloucestershire: Shermershill Press, 2006, pp. 188–90, 202–3, 224–5.

14. Charles E. Fripp, 'Reminiscences of the Zulu War, 1879', *Pall Mall Magazine*, 20 (1900), p. 549.

15. For the service of the Mounted Basutos between 1874 and 1888, see John Laband, *The Atlas of the Later Zulu Wars 1883–1888*, Pietermaritzburg: University of Natal Press, 2001, pp. 14–15.

16. For details of the Natal Volunteer Corps, see Stapleton, 'South Africa', pp. 145–7, 149; Laband and Thompson, *Anglo-Zulu War*, pp. 22–3, 36.

17. A.W.A. Pollock, quoted in Stapleton, 'South Africa', p. 151.

18. Major Ashe and Captain E.V. Wyatt-Edgell, *The Story of the Zulu Campaign*, London: Sampson Low, Marston, Searle & Rivington, 1880), p. 189.

19. Laband, 'Chelmsford', pp. 101–2.

20. Ibid, p. 102.

21. Sonia Clarke (ed.), *Zululand at War, 1879: The Conduct of the Anglo-Zulu War*, Houghton, South Africa: Brenthurst Press, 1984, p. 126: Major Clery to General Alison, 13 April 1879.

22. Ibid, p. 122: Clery to Alison, 18 March 1879.

23. John Laband, 'Bulwer, Chelmsford and the Border Levies: The Dispute over the Defence of Natal, 1879' in Laband and Thompson, *Kingdom and Colony*, pp. 150–3; Laband and Thompson, 'African Levies', pp. 57–8.

24. Laband, 'Chelmsford', pp. 102–3.

25. Great Britain, Intelligence Division of the War Office, *Précis of Information Concerning Zululand, Corrected to December, 1894*, London: Her Majesty's Stationery Office, 1895, p. 58.

26. See Mathews, 'Chelmsford', pp. 71–84, 111–12, 243–4, 344.

27. Arthur Harness, 'The Zulu Campaign from a Military Point of View', *Fraser's Magazine*, new series 21, 101 (April 1880), pp. 478–9; Laband and Thompson, 'African Levies', p. 55.

28. John Laband, 'The Cohesion of the Zulu Polity and the Impact of the Anglo-Zulu War: A Reassessment' in Laband and Thompson, *Kingdom and Colony*, pp. 3–7.
29. Laband, 'Chelmsford', pp. 104–5.

Chapter 17 The Meat of Heroes

1. For the Zulu handling of the ultimatum crisis, see Laband, *Zulu Nation*, pp. 196–205.
2. Cornelius Vijn, *Cetshwayo's Dutchman. Being the Private Journal of a White Trader in Zululand during the British Invasion*, ed. Bishop J.W. Colenso, London: Longmans, Green and Co., 1880, p. 15: entry of 24 November 1878.
3. Colin de B. Webb and John B. Wright (eds), *The James Stuart Archive of Recorded Oral Evidence Relating to the History of the Zulu and Neighbouring Peoples*, Pietermaritzburg: University of Natal Press; Durban: Killie Campbell Africana Library, vol. 5, 2001, p. 57: Ngidi ka Mcikaziswa, 6 November 1904.
4. For a chronology of the Zulu kingdom from its foundation up to the outbreak of the Anglo-Zulu War, and for a short account of its history in this period, see Laband, *Historical Dictionary*, pp. xxiii–xxix, xliv–xlix.
5. For the pre-colonial Zulu way of life and homestead economy, see Laband, *Zulu Nation*, pp. 4–10, 58–61.
6. For calculations of the number of *imizi* in the Zulu kingdom and its populations, see John Laband, ' "War Can't Be Made with Kid Gloves": The Impact of the Anglo-Zulu War of 1879 on the Fabric of Zulu Society', *South African Historical Journal*, 43 (November 2000), pp. 184–5.
7. Magema M. Fuze, *The Black People and Whence They Came: A Zulu View*, translated by H.C. Lugg and edited by A.T. Cope, Pietermaritzburg: University of Natal Press; Durban: Killie Campbell Africana Library, 1979, p. 53.
8. For detailed descriptions of the Zulu military system, see Ian Knight, *The Anatomy of the Zulu Army from Shaka to Cetshwayo 1818–1879*, London: Greenhill Books, 1995, pp. 46–90, and Laband and Thompson, *Anglo-Zulu War*, pp. 9–19.
9. The following discussion is based on John Laband, 'The War-Readiness and Military Effectiveness of the Zulu Forces in the 1879 Anglo-Zulu War', *Natalia*, 39 (December 2009), pp. 37–41.
10. For Ndondakusuka, see Laband, *Zulu Nation*, pp. 142–6.
11. Webb and Wright (eds), *Stuart Archive*, vol. 5, p. 344: Singcofela ka Mtshungu, 2 April 1910.
12. Iliffe, *Honour*, p. 142.
13. Webb and Wright (eds), *Stuart Archive*, vol. 4, p. 88: Mtshapi ka Noradu, 9 May 1918.
14. For a discussion on Zulu battle tactics, see Laband, *Zulu Nation*, pp. 39–41; Knight, *Zulu Army*, pp. 192–223.
15. Ian Knight, *A Companion to the Anglo-Zulu War*, Barnsley: Pen & Sword Military, 2008, p. 96. See also Jeff Guy, 'Imperial Appropriations: Baden-Powell, the Wood Badge and the Zulu *Iziqu*' in Carton et al. (eds), *Zulu Identities*, pp. 193–7.
16. Webb and Wright (eds), *Stuart Archive*, vol. 4, p. 88: Mtshapi ka Noradu, 9 May 1918.
17. For the campaign of 1838, see Laband, *Zulu Nation*, pp. 89–105.
18. Webb and Wright (eds), *Stuart Archive*, vol. 5, p. 77: Ngidi ka Mcikaziswa, 18 October 1905.
19. The ensuing discussion on the Zulu import of firearms in the 1870s is based on the research of Jeff Guy in 'A Note on Firearms in the Zulu Kingdom with Special Reference to the Anglo-Zulu War, 1879', *Journal of African History*, 12, 4 (1971), pp. 559–60.
20. In February 1878 the British pressured the Portuguese to halt the sale of guns and ammunition to Africans through Delagoa Bay, although it took until August that year to make the ban effective.

21. Charles Ballard, *John Dunn: The White Chief of Zululand*, Craighall: Ad. Donker, 1985, pp. 112–22.
22. See Guy, 'Firearms', p. 560; Storey, *Guns*, pp. 270–2; Knight, *Zulu Army*, pp. 167–9.
23. Webb and Wright (eds), *Stuart Archive*, vol. 3, p. 305: Mpatshana ka Sodondo, 24 May 1912.
24. Chris Peers, *The African Wars: Warriors and Soldiers of the Colonial Campaigns*, Barnsley: Pen & Sword Military, 2010, pp. 10–13; Laband and Thompson, *Anglo-Zulu War*, pp. 14–15; Laband, *Historical Dictionary*, p. 86.
25. Webb and Wright (eds), *Stuart Archive*, vol. 3, p. 328: Mpatshana ka Sodondo, 2 June 1912.
26. Ibid, vol. 2, p. 144: Mahungane, 20 November 1900. See also Julie Pridmore, 'Introduction' to John Laband (ed.), *The Journal of William Clayton Humphreys . . . Trader and Hunter in the Zulu Country during the Months July–October 1851*, No. 6, Colin Webb Natal and Zululand Series, Durban: Killie Campbell Africana Library and Pietermaritzburg: University of Natal Press, 1993, pp. vii–x.
27. *BPP* C. 2482, enc. D in enc. in no. 32: Statement by Ungungungunga taken by T. Shepstone, Jnr., 4 July 1879. He was taken prisoner at the battle of Ulundi on 4 July 1879.

Chapter 18 'We Shall Go and Eat Up the White Men'

1. Webb and Wright (eds), *Zulu King*, p. 30.
2. Laband, *Kingdom in Crisis*, p. 54.
3. Saunders, 'Frontier Zones', p. 162.
4. John Laband, 'Zulu Strategic and Tactical Options in the Face of the British Invasion of January 1879', *Scientia Militaria: South African Journal of Military Studies*, 28, 1 (1998), pp. 5–7.
5. The amaPondo would be annexed by the Cape in 1884.
6. Monteith, 'Cetshwayo and Sekhukhune', pp. 173–6; Delius, *Pedi Polity*, pp. 236, 238.
7. John Laband, 'Zulu Civilians during the Rise and Fall of the Zulu Kingdom, *c.*1817–1879' in John Laband (ed.), *Daily Lives of Civilians in Wartime Africa from Slavery Days to Rwandan Genocide*, Westport, CT: Greenwood Press, 2007, p. 64.
8. Vijn, *Cetshwayo's Dutchman*, p. 31. For a reiteration just before the battle of Ulundi, see ibid, p. 48.
9. Webb and Wright (eds), *Zulu King*, pp. 29–31, 55–6; Bridget Theron, 'King Cetshwayo and Victorian England: A Cameo of Imperial Interaction', *South African Historical Journal*, 56 (2006), p. 71.
10. Laband, 'Zulu Civilians', p. 65; Laband, 'Zulu Options', p. 5.
11. For Cetshwayo's strategic calculations, see Webb and Wright (eds), *Zulu King*, pp. 30–2, 55.
12. Norbury, *Naval Brigade*, p. 219.
13. Laband, *Kingdom in Crisis*, pp. 59–60.
14. Laband, 'Zulu Options', p. 8.
15. Kumbeka Gwabe, 'Supplement', *Natal Mercury*, 22 January 1929.
16. See John Laband, 'Zulu (amaZulu) War Rituals' in Bron R. Taylor and Jeffrey Kaplan (eds), *The Encyclopedia of Religion and Nature*, London and New York: Thoemmes Continuum, 2005, pp. 1824–5.
17. Webb and Wright (eds), *Stuart Archive*, vol. 3, p. 324: Mpatshana ka Sodondo, 31 May 1912.
18. Ibid, pp. 296–7, 313: Mpatshana ka Sodondo, 24 and 28 May 1912.
19. Ibid, p. 306: Mpatshana ka Sodondo, 25 May 1912.
20. Vijn, *Cetshwayo's Dutchman*, p. 39.
21. Nzuzi, 'Supplement', *Natal Mercury*, 22 January 1929.
22. Ibid.

Chapter 19 'How Can We Give You Mercy?'

1. Great Britain, *Zulu War*, pp. 22–138, presents a detailed narrative of the campaign from a British perspective based on the war diaries of the various invading columns. A succinct account of field operations with detailed maps can be found in Laband and Thompson, *Anglo-Zulu War*, pp. 48–65. For a critical bibliography of works published on the Anglo-Zulu War, see John Laband, 'Zulu Wars' in Dennis Showalter (ed.), *Oxford Bibliographies Online: Military History*, New York: Oxford University Press, 2012.
2. Hallam Parr, *Wars*, p. 183.
3. Daphne Child (ed.), *The Zulu War Journal of Colonel Henry Harford, C.B.*, Pietermaritzburg: Shuter & Shooter, 1978, pp. 18–21.
4. Clarke (ed.), *Conduct*, p. 126: Clery to Alison, 13 April 1879.
5. Laband, 'Chelmsford', pp. 105–6.
6. Knight, *Zulu Rising*, p. 431.
7. There is an excellent discussion of the Isandlwana campaign in Ian Beckett, *Battles in Focus: Isandlwana 1879*, London: Brassey's, 2003, pp. 47–91, but the most authoritative narrative is in Knight, *Zulu Rising*, pp. 233–473. See Laband and Thompson, *Anglo-Zulu War*, pp. 99–108 for a succinct account.
8. Thompson, *Black Soldiers*, pp. 41–3.
9. Clarke (ed.) *Conduct*, p. 84: Clery to Harman, 17 February 1878 [*should read* 1879].
10. Child (ed.), *Harford*, p. 23.
11. Adrian Greaves and Brian Best (eds), *The Curling Letters of the Zulu War: 'There Was Awful Slaughter'*, Barnsley: Leo Cooper, 2001, pp. 91–2: Henry Curling to his Mother, 2 February 1879.
12. Clarke (ed.), *Conduct*, p. 84: Clery to Harman, 17 February 1878 [*should read* 1879].
13. Ibid, p. 122: Clery to Alison, 18 March 1879.
14. Ibid, p. 85: Clery to Harman, 17 February 1878 [*should read* 1879].
15. Spiers, *Victorian Soldier*, p. 42: 'Letter from an Abergavenny Man', *Abergavenny Chronicle*, 29 March 1879.
16. Clarke (ed.), *Conduct*, p. 85: Clery to Harman, 17 February 1878 [*should read* 1879].
17. Laband (ed.), *Chelmsford's Zululand Campaign*, p. 77: Chelmsford to Frere, 23 January 1879.
18. Webb and Wright (eds), *Stuart Archive*, vol. 3, pp. 301: Mpatshana ka Sodondo, 24 May 1912.
19. 'Zulu Deserter', quoted in John Laband, *Fight Us in the Open: The Anglo-Zulu War through Zulu Eyes*, Pietermaritzburg: Shuter & Shooter; Ulundi: KwaZulu Monuments Council, 1985, p. 14.
20. Webb and Wright (eds), *Stuart Archive*, vol. 3, p. 304: Mpatshana ka Sodondo, 24 May 1912.
21. Ibid, p. 307: Mpatshana ka Sodondo, 25 May 1912.
22. G.H. Swinny, *A Zulu Boy's Recollections of the Zulu War* (1884), edited by C. de B. Webb, *Natalia* 8 (December 1978), p. 11.
23. Bertram Mitford, *Through the Zulu Country: Its Battlefields and Its People*, London: Kegan Paul, Trench, 1883, p. 91.
24. Thompson, *Black Soldiers*, pp. 53–8; Laband, 'Chelmsford', p. 111.
25. Charles Norris-Newman, *In Zululand with the British*, London: W.H. Allen, 1880, p. 81: Mehlokazulu kaSihayo's account.
26. Nzuzi, 'Supplement', *Natal Mercury*, 22 January 1929.
27. Webb and Wright (eds), *Stuart Archive*, vol. 3, p. 301: Mpatshana ka Sodondo, 24 May 1912.
28. Laband, *Kingdom in Crisis*, pp. 88, 109.
29. Laband, 'War Rituals', p. 1825.
30. The eclipse reached its greatest phase at 2.29 p.m.

31. Webb and Wright (eds), *Stuart Archive*, vol. 3, p. 318: Mpatshana ka Sodondo, 29 May 1912.
32. Knight, *Zulu Rising*, pp. 47–535, has a full and authoritative account of the battle of Rorke's Drift, but see also Edmund Yorke, *Rorke's Drift 1879: Anatomy of an Epic Zulu War Siege*, Stroud, Glos.: Tempus Publishing, 2001, pp. 77–149, and Laband, *Zulu Nation*, pp. 230–41. For a succinct account, see Laband and Thompson, *Anglo-Zulu War*, pp. 109–13.
33. Swinny, *Zulu Boy*, p. 12.
34. Mitford, *Zulu Country*, p. 97.
35. Swinny, *Zulu Boy*, pp. 12–13.
36. Hamilton-Browne, *Lost Legionary*, p. 152.
37. Clarke (ed.), *Conduct*, p. 129: Clery to Alison, 28 April 1879.
38. For the fullest account of the battle of Nyezane, see Ian Castle and Ian Knight, *Fearful Hard Times: The Siege and Relief of Eshowe, 1879*, London: Greenhill, 1994, pp. 49–73. See also Laband, *Zulu Nation*, pp. 24–47; Laband and Thompson, *Anglo-Zulu War*, pp. 82–5; Thompson, *Black Soldiers*, pp. 79–80.
39. *BPP* C. 2454, sub-enc. in enc. 1 in no. 34: Statement of Sihlahla taken by J.W. Shespstone, 3 June 1879.
40. Laband, *Zulu Nation*, p. 28.
41. Swinny, *Zulu Boy*, p. 13.
42. Vijn, *Cetshwayo's Dutchman*, p. 28.

Chapter 20 'No Quarter, Boys!'

1. Laband, 'War Rituals', p. 1825.
2. Laband, 'Chelmsford', p. 110.
3. For this 'cover-up' see Ron Lock and Peter Quantrill, *Zulu Victory: The Epic of Isandlwana and the Cover-Up*, London: Greenhill Books, 2002, pp. 236–46, 251–7.
4. Laband, 'Chelmsford', pp. 110–12.
5. Thompson, *Black Soldiers*, pp. 74–7, 82–3, 85–9, 105–6; Laband, *Historical Dictionary*, pp. 177–9.
6. For the siege of Eshowe, see Castle and Knight, *Eshowe*, pp. 74–188.
7. Laband, *Chelmsford's Zululand Campaign*, p. 92: Chelmsford to Wood, 3 February 1879.
8. Jones, *Boiling Cauldron*, pp. 215–36; Laband, 'Mbilini', pp. 194–8.
9. John Laband, 'Humbugging the General? King Cetshwayo's Peace Overtures during the Anglo-Zulu War' in Laband and Thompson, *Kingdom and Colony*, pp. 49–51.
10. Laband, *Zulu Nation*, pp. 258–62.
11. Laband and Thompson, *Anglo-Zulu War*, pp. 138–41; Laband, 'Mbilini', pp. 198–9.
12. For the battle of Hlobane, see Jones, *Boiling Cauldron*, pp. 252–82; Laband and Thompson, *Anglo-Zulu War*, pp. 176–9.
13. Vijn, *Cetshwayo's Dutchman*, p. 127, Bishop Colenso's notes: Magema M. Fuze.
14. Ian Knight, 'Kill Me in the Shadows', *Soldiers of the Queen*, 74 (September 1993), p. 12: statement of Mgelija Ngema.
15. Mehlokazulu kaSihayo, quoted in Norris-Newman, *In Zululand*, p. 85.
16. Webb and Wright (eds), *Zulu King*, pp. 33–4.
17. British infantryman quoted in Frank Emery, *The Red Soldier: Letters from the Zulu War, 1879*, London: Hodder and Stoughton, 1977, p. 171.
18. For the battle Khambula, see Laband, *Zulu Nation*, pp. 268–77; Jones, *Boiling Cauldron*, pp. 283–92; Laband and Thompson, *Anglo-Zulu War*, pp. 180–3.
19. Mehlokazulu kaSihayo, quoted in Norris-Newman, *In Zululand*, p. 85.
20. Captain Cecil D'Arcy, quoted in Emery, *Red Soldier*, p. 169.
21. *BPP* C. 2454, sub-enc. in enc. 1 in no. 34: statement of Sihlahla taken by J.W. Shepstone, 3 June 1879.
22. Ibid.

23. Laband (ed.), *Zululand Campaign*, pp. 150–51: Chelmsford to Wood, [?15] April 1879.
24. For the battle of Gingindlovu, see Castle and Knight, *Eshowe*, pp. 189–214; Laband, *Zulu Nation*, pp. 279–84; Thompson, *Black Soldiers*, pp. 91–5; Laband and Thompson, *Anglo-Zulu War*, pp. 86–9.
25. Letter to the *Daily News*, 27 June 1879, quoted in Michael Lieven, ' "Butchering the Brutes All over the Place": Total War and Massacre in Zululand, 1879', *History*, 84, 276 (October 1999), p. 626.
26. See Norris-Newman, *In Zululand*, p. 140, for an eye-witness account; also Thompson, *Black Soldiers*, pp. 91–5.
27. Mitford, *Zulu Country*, p. 279: warrior of the uThulwana.
28. Vijn, *Cetshwayo's Dutchman*, pp. 40–41.
29. See Laband, 'Border Levies', pp. 150–65.
30. *BPP* C. 2318, no. 18: Chelmsford to Bulwer, 18 April 1879.
31. Ibid, enc. 10 in no. 1: minute by Frere, 11 February 1879.
32. Laband, *Transvaal Rebellion*, pp. 20–2.
33. Laband, 'Chelmsford', p.114. The cost of the war was eventually put at £5,230,328, considerably more than the government was willing to countenance for a colonial campaign.
34. *BPP* C. 2318, no. 11: telegram, Hicks Beach to Bulwer, 19 May 1879.
35. Ibid, Appendix: Commission issued to Sir Garnet Wolseley, 28 May 1879.
36. Chelmsford would receive formal notice of his supersession only on 9 July.
37. Laband, 'Chelmsford', p. 114.

Chapter 21 'The Army Is Now Thoroughly Beaten'

1. *BPP* C. 2454, sub-enc. in enc. 1 of no. 32: statement of Sibalo taken by J.W. Shepstone, 1 June 1879.
2. Laband, 'Chelmsford', p. 113.
3. Laband and Thompson, *Anglo-Zulu War*, pp. 60–1.
4. Laband (ed.), *Chelmsford's Zululand Campaign*, p. 174: Chelmsford to Wood, 19 May 1879. Chelmsford quoted the proverb (which he considered 'good') in Italian: 'Chi va piano, va sano e va lontano.'
5. See Beckett, *Victorians at War*, pp. 122–7.
6. Laband, 'Chelmsford', p. 113.
7. Laband and Thompson, 'African Levies', p. 59.
8. Webb and Wright (eds), *Stuart Archive*, vol. 3, p. 320: Mpatshana ka Sodondo, in 30 May 1912.
9. Laband and Thompson, *Anglo-Zulu War*, pp. 154–7. For the authoritative account of the Prince Imperial in Zululand, his death and the aftermath, see Ian Knight, *With His Face to the Foe: The Life and Death of Louis Napoleon, the Prince Imperial: Zululand 1879*, Staplehurst: Spellmount, 2001, pp. 120–271.
10. Laband and Thompson, *Anglo-Zulu War*, pp. 158–60.
11. Laband (ed.), *Chelmsford's Zululand Campaign*, p. 51: Chelmsford to Col W. Bellairs, 31 December 1878.
12. Clarke (ed.), *Conduct*, p. 229: Crealock to Alison, 28 June 1879.
13. Norris-Newman, *In Zululand*, p. 47.
14. John Laband, 'Impact of the Anglo-Zulu War', pp. 183, 195–6.
15. Peevan correspondent, 5 June 1879, *Natal Mercury*, 17 June 1879, quoted in Ron Lock and Peter Quantrill (eds), *The Red Book: Natal Press Reports, Anglo-Zulu War 1879*, privately printed, n.d., p. 249.
16. Ulundi correspondent, *Natal Witness*, 23 August 1879, quoted in John Laband and Ian Knight, *The War Correspondents: The Anglo-Zulu War*, Stroud, Glos: Sutton Publishing, 1996, p. 156.
17. Correspondent with General Hope Crealock's Division, *Illustrated London News*, 23 August 1879, quoted in ibid, p. 147.

18. Laband, 'Mbilini', pp. 206–7.
19. Webb and Wright (eds), *Zulu King*, p. 34.
20. See Preston (ed.), *Wolseley's Journal*, pp. 43–52: entries of 24 June to 7 July 1879. Between 2 and 4 July Wolseley was prevented by heavy surf from landing at Port Durnford and had to enter Zululand overland instead.
21. See Laband, 'Humbugging the General', pp. 52–9.
22. Webb and Wright (eds), *Zulu King*, p. 58. See also Vijn, *Cetshwayo's Dutchman*, pp. 50–1, 142.
23. Quoted in Iliffe, *Honour*, p. 190.
24. Laband and Thompson, *Anglo-Zulu War*, pp. 161–4.
25. Guy C. Dawnay, *Campaigns: Zulu 1879, Egypt 1882, Suakim 1885*, privately printed *c.* 1886, Cambridge: Ken Trotman, 1989, p. 65.
26. Laband and Thomspon, *Anglo-Zulu War*, pp. 166–9. See Laband, *Kingdom in Crisis*, pp. 206–36, for a description of the battle of Ulundi and its decisive impact.
27. Mehlokazulu kaSihayo, quoted in Norris-Newman, *In Zululand*, p. 85.
28. Quoted in Ian Knight, *The National Army Museum Book of the Zulu War*, London: Sidgewick & Jackson in association with The National Army Museum, 2003, p. 255.
29. *BPP* C. 2482, enc. D in enc. in no. 32: statement of Ungungungunga taken by T. Shepstone, Jnr, 4 July 1879.
30. Laband, *Zulu Nation*, p. 325.
31. Magema Fuze, quoted in Vijn, *Cetshwayo's Dutchman*, p. 143.
32. Mfunzi, quoted in ibid, p. 149.
33. Laband, 'Chelmsford', pp. 116–18.
34. See Laband, 'Cohesion of the Zulu Polity', pp. 15–19.
35. Through the practice of *ukusisa* the king pastured his huge herds in the care of subordinate chiefs.
36. Quoted in Knight, *Zulu War*, p. 266.
37. Wolseley to Lady Wolseley, 10 July 1879, quoted in Laband, *Zulu Nation*, p. 327.
38. Laband, 'Mbilini', pp. 204–5.
39. See Special Reporter of the 'Cape Times' [R.W. Murray], *Cetywayo, from the Battle of Ulundi to the Cape of Good Hope*, Cape Town: Murray & St Leger, 1879, pp. 6–16.
40. Laband, *Zulu Nation*, pp. 333–4.
41. Ibid, p. 343.
42. John Laband and Paul Thompson, 'The Reduction of Zululand, 1878–1904' in Duminy and Guest (eds), *Natal and Zululand*, pp. 202–7; Laband, *Zulu Nation*, pp. 334–9.
43. Thompson, *Black Soldiers*, pp. 166–72; Laband and Thompson, *Anglo-Zulu War*, p. 39
44. Jeff Guy, *The Destruction of the Zulu Kingdom: The Civil War in Zululand, 1879–1884*, London: Longman, 1979, pp. 58–9, 92.
45. Port Durnford correspondent, *Natal Witness*, 29 July 1879, quoted in Laband and Knight, *War Correspondent*, p. 150.
46. The official figures for British casualties were 76 officers killed and 37 wounded; 1,007 NCOs and men killed and 206 wounded; 17 officers and 330 men dead of disease. The doubtless incomplete total for African troops was 661. See Great Britain, *Zulu War*, p. 167. For a discussion on relative casualty rates, see Laband, 'Impact of the Anglo-Zulu War', pp. 185–7.
47. Spiers, *Victorian Army*, p. 296.

Chapter 22 'Short, Sharp and Decisive'

1. Delius, *Pedi Polity*, p. 240; Smith, 'Bapedi', pp. 246–7.
2. Laband, *Transvaal Rebellion*, p. 23; Theron-Bushell, 'Lanyon', p. 144.
3. *BPP* C. 2482, enc. in no. 35: Lanyon to Wolseley, 14 July 1879.
4. Ibid, C. 2318, no. 20: Hicks Beach to Lanyon, 28 May 1879; ibid, C. 2482, no. 20: Wolseley to Hicks Beach, 29 June 1879; Theron-Bushell, 'Lanyon', pp. 205–7.

5. Theron-Bushell, 'Lanyon', pp. 183, 193.
6. Smith, 'Bapedi', p. 247.
7. *BPP* C. 2482, no. 158: Wolseley to Hicks Beach, 30 September 1879. See also Preston (ed.), *Wolseley's Journal*, p. 131: entry of 9 October 1879.
8. *BPP* C. 2482, no. 158: statement of Tamakana before Clarke, 26 October 1879.
9. Ibid: Nopatula's statement, 25 October 1879.
10. *BPP* C. 2505, no. 19: statement of Sekukuni to H.C. Shepstone, 10 December 1879; Smith, 'Bapedi', p. 247.
11. Preston (ed.), *Wolseley's Journal*, p. 136: entry of 15 October 1879.
12. *BPP* C. 2482, no. 158: Wolseley to Hicks Beach, 28 October 1879.
13. Preston (ed.), *Wolseley's Journal*, p. 151: entry of 29 October 1879.
14. Bonner, *Swazi State*, pp. 154–5.
15. Preston (ed.), *Wolseley's Journal*, pp. 172–3: entry of 22 November 1879.
16. Kinsey, 'Sekukuni Wars', part II.
17. See, for example, Preston (ed.), *Wolseley's Journal*, p. 156: entry of 3 November 1879. Wolseley recorded that in October fifty-eight horses died at Fort Burgers alone.
18. Preston (ed.), *Wolseley's Journal*, p. 174: entry of 25 November 1879.
19. Emery, *Marching over Africa*, p. 93: Lt Charles Commeline to his father, 29 November 1879.
20. D.A. Merensky, *Erinnerungen aus dem Missionsleben in Transvaal 1859–1882*, 2nd edn, Berlin: Buchhandlung der Berliner evangel. Missionsgesellschaft, 1882, pp. 338–43.
21. *BPP* C. 2505, enc. in no. 19: statement of Sekukuni to H.C. Shepstone, 10 December 1879.
22. For accounts of the battle of Tsate and its immediate aftermath, see Preston (ed.), *Wolseley's Journal* pp. 176–81: entries of 28 November–2 December 1879; Delius, *Pedi Polity*, pp. 244–5; Bonner, *Swazi State*, p. 155; Smith, 'Bapedi', pp. 249–51.
23. Preston (ed.), *Wolseley's Journal*, pp. 162–3: entry of 10 November 1879.
24. Butterfield, *Anstruther and Essex*, p. 76: Anstruther to his wife, 30 November 1879.
25. Emery, *Marching over Africa*, p. 94: Commeline to his father, 29 November 1879.
26. Preston (ed.), *Wolseley's Journal*, p. 177: entry of 28 November 1979.
27. Emery, *Marching over Africa*, p. 95: Commeline to his father, 29 November 1879.
28. Ibid.
29. Ibid, p. 96: Commeline to his father, 29 November 1879.
30. Preston (ed.), *Wolseley's Journal*, p. 179: entry of 29 November 1879.
31. Ibid, p. 180: entry of 1 December 1879.
32. Ibid, pp. 180–1: entry of 2 December 1879.
33. Emery, *Marching over Africa*, p. 97: Wolseley to a member of parliament, 22 December 1879.
34. Preston (ed.), *Wolseley's Journal*, p. 183: entry of 3 December 1979.
35. General Sir Richard Harrison, *Recollections of a Life in the British Army during the Latter Half of the Nineteenth Century*, London: John Murray, 1908, p. 228.
36. *BPP* C. 2584, no. 19: Wolseley to Hicks Beach, 13 September 1880.
37. Preston (ed.), *Wolseley's Journal*, p. 179: entry of 30 November 1879.
38. At Tsate *BPP* C. 2505, no. 18: Wolseley to Hicks Beach, 12 December 1879; ibid, C. 2584, enc. 1 in no. 21: memorandum by Clarke, 2 January 1880. At Tsate 2,041 guns were captured, and by early January 1880 a further 1,349 had been handed over. See ibid, C. 2584, enc. in no. 48: return of fire-arms, 14 January 1880.
39. Delius, *Pedi Polity*, p. 246; Delius, *Northern Transvaal*, p. 10.
40. *BPP* C. 2505, enc. 1 in no. 39: Clarke to Schultz, 19 December 1879 and instructions to magistrates, Lulu mountains, 16 December 1879; ibid, C. 2584, enc. 1 in no. 21: Clarke's memorandum on the consequences of the defeat and capture of Sikukuni, and the settlement of the district claimed by him, 2 January 1880.

Chapter 23 Paying the Price

1. Brian Best, 'Zulu War Medals', *Journal of the Anglo Zulu War Historical Society*, 3 (June 1998), pp. 35–8.
2. John Darwin, *Unfinished Empire: The Global Expansion of Britain*, London: Allen Lane, 2012, p. 117.
3. Quoted in Thompson, *Black Soldiers*, p. 168.
4. 'Zululand. Extraordinary statement by Umqawe', *Natal Witness*, 2 October 1879, quoted in ibid, p. 169.
5. For Moorosi's revolt, see Anthony Atmore, 'The Moorosi Rebellion: Lesotho, 1879' in Robert I. Rotberg and Ali A. Mazrui (eds), *Protest and Power in Black Africa*, New York: Oxford University Press, 1970, pp. 2–35; Sandra Burman, *Chiefdom Politics and Alien Law: Basutoland under Cape Rule, 1881–1884*, New York: Africana Publishing Company, 1981, pp. 108–131; Elizabeth A. Eldredge, *Power in Colonial Africa: Conflict and Discourse in Lesotho, 1870–1960*, Madison: University of Wisconsin Press, 2007, pp. 55–70. Called by the British the Moirosi Mountain campaign, the Cape troops who fought in it were eligible for the South Africa Medal. However, the campaign has not been treated in this book because it was a curtain-raiser to the Gun War which falls beyond its scope.
6. For the Gun War, see Eldredge, *Lesotho*, pp. 71–117; Burman, *Basutoland*, pp. 132–91; Storey, *Guns*, pp. 287–318.
7. For the campaign and concluding negotiations, see Laband, *Transvaal Rebellion*, pp. 86–223.
8. Schreuder, *Gladstone and Kruger*, pp. 212–14, 222–4, 465–9; Goodfellow, *Confederation*, pp. 201–3.
9. Worsfold, *Frere*, p. 335. For the last twenty months of Frere's tenure in South Africa, see John Benyon, 'Isandlwana and the Passing of a Proconsul', *Natalia* 8 (December 1978), pp. 39–44.
10. Confidential memorandum by Wolseley, 31 October 1881, quoted in Laband, *Transvaal Rebellion*, p. 237.
11. Sir H. Rider Haggard, *The Last Boer War*, London: Kegan Paul, Trench and Trubner, 1899, p. xxiii.
12. Laband, *Transvaal Rebellion*, pp. 221–2.
13. Merensky, *Erinnerungen*, pp. 400–4; Delius, *Pedi Polity*, pp. 251–2.
14. Guy, *Zulu Kingdom*, p. 131.
15. Webb and Wright, *Zulu King*, pp. xviii–xix.
16. Special Reporter, 'Cetywayo', p. 17.
17. On 25 October 2006 English Heritage put up a blue plaque on the house commemorating Cetshwayo's stay.
18. For Cetshwayo in England, see Guy, *Zulu Kingdom*, pp. 148–64; Theron, 'Cetshwayo and England', pp. 76–84.
19. *Illustrated London News*, 12 and 19 August 1882.
20. Ibid, 12 August 1882.
21. Quoted in Theron, 'Cetshwayo and England', p. 84.
22. For Zululand between January 1883 and May 1887, see Laband, *Zulu Nation*, pp. 355–77; Laband, *Later Zulu Wars*, pp. 42–83; Guy, *Zulu Kingdom*, pp. 167–209.
23. Ibid, p. 204.
24. For a detailed account of the period between April 1884 and July 1887, see Jeff Guy, *The View across the River: Harriette Colenso and the Zulu Struggle against Imperialism*, Charlottesville: University Press of Virginia, 2002, pp. 87–114, 125–35, 138–78.
25. MacKinnon, *South Africa*, p. 146.
26. Iris Berger, *South Africa in World History*, Oxford: Oxford University Press, 2009, pp. 71–2.

27. Quoted in Iliffe, *Honour*, p. 287.
28. See ibid, pp. 6, 140–1, 202–4, 223–4, 281, 287, 297–305, 312–13; Carton and Morrell, 'Zulu Masculinities', pp. 39–40, 47–8, 50–51. Also see a number of essays in Morrell (ed.), *Changing Men*, especially chapters 1, 2, 5, 6, 10, 17, 18, and Carton, et al. (eds), *Zulu Identities*, especially chapters 22, 31, 48, 51.

BIBLIOGRAPHY
of Printed Works Cited in the Notes

Arndt, Jochen S. 'Treacherous Savages & Merciless Barbarians: Knowledge, Discourse and Violence during the Cape Frontier Wars, 1834–1853', *Journal of Military History*, 74, 3 (July 2010), pp. 709–35

Ashe, Major and Captain E.V. Wyatt-Edgell. *The Story of the Zulu Campaign*, London: Sampson Low, Marston, Searle & Rivington, 1880

Atmore, Anthony. 'The Moorosi Rebellion: Lesotho, 1879' in Robert I. Rotberg and Ali A. Mazrui (eds), *Protest and Power in Black Africa*, New York: Oxford University Press, 1970

Atmore, Anthony, J.M. Chirenje and S.I. Mudenge. 'Firearms in South Central Africa', *Journal of African History*, 12, 4 (1971), pp. 545–56

Ballard, Charles. *John Dunn: The White Chief of Zululand*, Craighall, South Africa: Ad. Donker, 1985

Beckett, Ian F.W. *Battles in Focus: Isandlwana 1879*, London: Brassey's, 2003

—— 'Buller, Sir Redvers Henry (1839–1908)', *Oxford Dictionary of National Biography*, Oxford: Oxford University Press, online edn, 2008, <http://www.oxforddnb.com/view/article/32165> (accessed 14 August 2013)

—— 'Military High Command in South Africa, 1854–1914' in Peter Boyden, Alan Guy and Marion Harding (eds), *'Ashes and Blood': The British Army in South Africa 1795–1914*, London: National Army Museum, 1999

—— *The Victorians at War*, London: Hambledon, 2003

—— 'Wolseley, Garnet Joseph, first Viscount Wolseley (1833–1913)', *Oxford Dictionary of National Biography*, Oxford: Oxford University Press, online edn, 2008, <http://www.oxforddnb.com/view/article/36995> (accessed 14 August 2013)

Beemer, Hilda. 'The Development of the Military Organization in Swaziland', *Africa*, 10, 1 (January 1937), pp. 55–74; *Africa*, 10, 2 (April 1937), pp. 176–205

Bellairs, [Blanche], Lady. *The Transvaal War 1880–1*, Edinburgh and London: William Blackwood and Sons, 1885

Benyon, John. 'The Cape Colony, 1854–1881' in T. Cameron and S.B. Spies (eds), *An Illustrated History of South Africa*, Johannesburg: Jonathan Ball, 1986

—— 'Frere, Sir (Henry) Bartle Edward, first baronet (1815–1884)', *Oxford Dictionary of National Biography*, Oxford: Oxford University Press, online edn, 2008, <http://www.oxforddnb.com/view/article/10171> (accessed 14 August 2013)

—— 'Isandlwana and the Passing of a Proconsul', *Natalia*, 8 (December 1978), pp. 38–45

—— *Proconsul and Paramountcy in South Africa: The High Commission, British Supremacy and the Sub-Continent 1806–1910*, Pietermaritzburg: University of Natal Press, 1980

Berger, Iris. *South Africa in World History*, Oxford: Oxford University Press, 2009

Best, Brian. 'Zulu War Medals', *Journal of the Anglo Zulu War Historical Society*, 3 (June 1998), pp. 35–8

Blue Book for the Transvaal Province, 1879, Pretoria: Coppen, Deeker; Government Printers, 1879

Bonner, Philip. *Kings, Commoners and Concessionaires: The Evolution and Dissolution of the Nineteenth-Century Swazi State*, Johannesburg: Ravan Press, 1983

Boyden, Peter (ed.). *The British Army in Cape Colony: Soldiers' Letters and Diaries, 1806–58*, London: Society for Army Historical Research, Special Publication No. 15, 2001

Boyden, Peter, Alan Guy and Marion Harding (eds). *'Ashes and Blood': The British Army in South Africa 1795–1914*, London: National Army Museum, 1999

British Parliamentary Papers (BPP). C. 1748, C. 1776, C. 1883, C. 1961, C. 2000, C. 2079, C. 2100, C. 2144, C. 2220, C. 2222, C. 2242, C. 2318, C. 2454, C. 2482, C. 2505, C. 2584, C. 2585

Brookes, Edgar H. and Colin de B. Webb. *A History of Natal*, Pietermaritzburg: University of Natal Press, 1965

Burman, Sandra. *Chiefdom Politics and Alien Law: Basutoland under Cape Rule, 1881–1884*, New York: Africana Publishing Company, 1981

Butterfield, Paul H. *War and Peace in South Africa 1879–1881: The Writings of Philip Anstruther and Edward Essex*, Melville, South Africa: Scripta Africana, 1987

Callwell, Charles. *Small Wars: Their Principles and Practice*, 3rd edn, London: His Majesty's Stationery Office, 1906

Cameron, T. and S.B. Spies (eds). *An Illustrated History of South Africa*, Johannesburg: Jonathan Ball, 1986

Cape of Good Hope. *Copy of a Despatch Addressed to His Excellency the Governor by the Lieutenant-Governor of the Province of Griqualand West, on the Subject of Native Disturbances in that Province*, Cape Town: Printed by Order of the House of Assembly, 1878

—— *Copy of Despatches which have Passed between the Right Honourable the Secretary of State for the Colonies and His Excellency the Governor since January Last*, Cape Town: Printed by Order of the House of Assembly, 1878

—— *Copy of Further Correspondence on the Subject of the Recent Native Disturbances in Griqualand West*, Cape Town: Printed by Order of the House of Assembly, 1878

—— *Copy of Further Correspondence on the Subject of the Recent Native Disturbances in Griqualand West (2)*, Cape Town: Printed by Order of the House of Assembly, 1878

Carton, Benedict. *Blood from Your Children: The Colonial Origins of Generational Conflict in South Africa*, Pietermaritzburg: University of Natal Press, 2000

Carton, Benedict, John Laband and Jabulani Sithole (eds). *Zulu Identities: Being Zulu, Past and Present*, New York: Columbia University Press, 2009

Carton, Benedict and Robert Morrell. 'Zulu Masculinities, Warrior Culture and Stick Fighting: Reassessing Male Violence and Virtue in South Africa', *Journal of Southern African Studies*, 38, 1 (March 2012), pp. 31–53

Carver, Michael (ed.). *Letters of a Victorian Army Officer, Edward Wellesley: Major, 73rd Regiment of Foot, 1840–1854*, Stroud, Glos: Alan Sutton Publishing for the Army Records Society, 1995

Castle, Ian and Ian Knight. *Fearful Hard Times: The Siege and Relief of Eshowe, 1879*, London: Greenhill, 1994

Child, Daphne (ed.). *The Zulu War Journal of Colonel Henry Harford, C.B.*, Pietermaritzburg: Shuter & Shooter, 1978

Clarke, Sonia (ed.). *Zululand at War, 1879: The Conduct of the Anglo-Zulu War*, Houghton, South Africa: Brenthurst Press, 1984

Coghlan, Mark. *Pro Patria: Another 50 Natal Carbineer Years 1945 to 1995*, Pietermaritzburg: The Natal Carbineer Trust, 2000

Connell, R.W. *Gender and Power: Society, the Person and Sexual Politics*, Stanford, CA: Stanford University Press, 1987

—— *Masculinities*, Berkeley and Los Angeles, CA: University of California Press, 1995

—— *The Men and the Boys*, Berkeley and Los Angeles, CA: University of California Press, 2000

Cope, Richard. *Ploughshare of War: The Origins of the Anglo-Zulu War of 1879*, Pietermaritzburg: University of Natal Press, 1999

Corvi, Steven J. 'Garnet Wolseley' in Corvi and Beckett (eds), *Victoria's Generals*

Corvi, Steven J. and Ian F.W. Beckett (eds). *Victoria's Generals*, Barnsley: Pen & Sword Military, 2009

Crais, Clifton. *White Supremacy and Black Resistance in Pre-Industrial South Africa: The Making of the Colonial Order in the Eastern Cape, 1770–1865*, Cambridge: Cambridge University Press, 1992

Crwys-Williams, Jennifer (ed.). *South African Despatches: Two Centuries of the Best in South African Journalism*, Johannesburg: Ashanti, 1989

Cunynghame, A.T. *My Command in South Africa, 1874–1878*, London: Macmillan, 1879

Darwin, John. 'Britain's Empires' in Sarah Stockwell (ed.), *The British Empire: Themes and Perspectives*, Oxford: Blackwell, 2008

—— *Unfinished Empire: the Global Expansion of Britain*, London: Allen Lane, 2012

Davenport, Rodney and Christopher Saunders. *South Africa: A Modern History*, London: Macmillan, 5th edn, 2000

Dawnay, Guy C. *Campaigns: Zulu 1879, Egypt 1882, Suakim 1885*, privately printed *c*. 1886, Cambridge: Ken Trotman, 1989

De Kiewiet, C.W. 'The Establishment of Responsible Government in Cape Colony, 1870–1872' in Eric A. Walker (ed.), *The Cambridge History of the British Empire*, vol. VIII, *South Africa, Rhodesia and the High Commission Territories*, Cambridge: Cambridge University Press, 1963

Delius, Peter. *The Land Belongs to Us: The Pedi Polity, the Boers and the British in the Nineteenth-Century Transvaal*, Berkeley, CA: University of California Press, 1984

—— *A Lion amongst the Cattle. Reconstruction and Resistance in the Northern Transvaal*, Oxford: James Currey, 1996

Dobson, Mary. *Disease: The Extraordinary Stories behind History's Deadliest Killers*, London: Quercus, 2007

Dominy, Graham. 'Thomas Baines and the Langalibalele Rebellion: A Critique of an Unrecorded Sketch of the Action at "Bushman's Pass", 1873', *Natal Museum Journal of Humanities*, 3 (October 1991), pp. 41–55

Dominy, Graham and Hamish Paterson, 'Fort Napier: The Imperial Base that Shaped the City' in John Laband and Robert Haswell (eds), *Pietermaritzburg 1838–1988: A New Portrait of an African City*, Pietermaritzburg: University of Natal Press and Shuter & Shooter, 1988

Droogleever, R.W.F. *The Road to Isandlwana: Colonel Anthony Durnford in Natal and Zululand*, London: Greenhill Books, 1992

Du Bruyn, J.T. 'The Great Trek' in T. Cameron and S.B. Spies (eds), *An Illustrated History of South Africa*, Johannesburg: Jonathan Ball, 1986

Duminy, Andrew and Bill Guest (eds). *Natal and Zululand from Earliest Times to 1910: A New History*, Pietermaritzburg: University of Natal Press and Shuter & Shooter, 1989

Eldredge, Elizabeth A. *Power in Colonial Africa: Conflict and Discourse in Lesotho, 1870–1960*, Madison: University of Wisconsin Press, 2007

Eldredge, Elizabeth A. and Fred Morton (eds). *Slavery in South Africa: Captive Labour on the Dutch Frontier*, Boulder, CO: Westview Press; Pietermaritzburg: University of Natal Press, 1994

Elliott, Aubrey. *The Magic World of the Xhosa*, London: Collins, 1972

Elphick, Robert and Hermann Gilliomee (eds). *The Shaping of South African Society, 1652–1820*, London and Cape Town: Maskew Miller Longman, 1987

Eltis, David and David Richardson. *Atlas of the Transatlantic Slave Trade*, New Haven, CT, and London: Yale University Press, 2010

Emery, Frank. 'Geography and Imperialism: The Role of Sir Bartle Frere 1815–84', *Geographical Journal*, 150, 3 (November 1984), pp. 342–50

—— *Marching over Africa: Letters from Victorian Soldiers*, London: Hodder and Stoughton, 1986

—— *The Red Soldier: Letters from the Zulu War, 1879*, London: Hodder and Stoughton, 1977

Etherington, Norman. *The Great Treks: The Transformation of Southern Africa, 1815–1854*, Harlow, Essex: Longman Pearson, 2001

—— 'Shepstone, Sir Theophilus (1817–1893)', *Oxford Dictionary of National Biography*, Oxford: Oxford University Press, online edn, 2008, <http://www.oxforddnb.com/view/article/25353> (accessed 14 August 2013)

—— 'The "Shepstone System" in the Colony of Natal and Beyond the Borders' in Andrew Duminy and Bill Guest (eds), *Natal and Zululand from Earliest Times to 1910: A New History*, Pietermaritzburg: University of Natal Press and Shuter & Shooter, 1989

Etherington, Norman, Patrick Harries and Bernard K. Mbenga. 'From Colonial Hegemonies to Imperial Conquest, 1840–1880' in Carolyn Hamilton, Bernard K. Mbenga and Robert Ross (eds), *The Cambridge History of South Africa*, vol. 1, *From Early Times to 1885*, Cambridge: Cambridge University Press, 2010

Eybers, G.W. (ed.). *Select Constitutional Documents Illustrating South African History 1795–1910*, London: Routledge, 1918

Fripp, Charles E. 'Reminiscences of the Zulu War, 1879', *Pall Mall Magazine*, 20 (1900), pp. 547–62

Fuze, Magema M. *The Black People and Whence They Came: A Zulu View*, translated by H.C. Lugg and edited by A.T. Cope, Pietermaritzburg: University of Natal Press; Durban: Killie Campbell Africana Library, 1979

Getz, Trevor R. *Cosmopolitan Africa c.1700–1875*, New York and Oxford: Oxford University Press, 2013

Giliomee, Hermann. 'The Eastern Frontier, 1777–1812' in Robert Elphick and Hermann Giliomee (eds), *The Shaping of South African Society, 1652–1820*, London and Cape Town: Maskew Miller Longman, 1987

Giliomee, Hermann and Bernard Mbenga (eds). *New History of South Africa*, Cape Town: Tafelberg, 2008

Gon, Philip. 'The Last Frontier War', *Military History Journal*, 5, 6 (December 1982), <http://samilitaryhistory.org> (accessed 14 August 2013)

—— *The Road to Isandlwana: The Years of an Imperial Battalion*, Johannesburg: Ad. Donker, 1979

Goodfellow, C.F. *Great Britain and South African Confederation (1870–1881)*, Cape Town: Oxford University Press, 1966

Gordon, Peter. 'Herbert, Henry Howard Molyneux, fourth earl of Carnarvon (1831–1890)', *Oxford Dictionary of National Biography*, Oxford: Oxford University Press, online edn, 2008, <http://www.oxforddnb.com/view/article/13035> (14 August 2013)

Great Britain. Intelligence Branch of the War Office. *Narrative of the Field Operations Connected with the Zulu War of 1879*, London: Her Majesty's Stationery Office, 1881

—— Intelligence Division of the War Office. *Précis of Information Concerning Zululand, Corrected to December, 1894*, London: Her Majesty's Stationery Office, 1895

—— War Office. *Field Exercise and Evolution of Infantry*, London: Her Majesty's Stationery Office, pocket edition, 1877

—— War Office Intelligence Department. *Précis of Information Concerning South Africa: The Transvaal Territory*, London: Her Majesty's Stationery Office, 1878

Greaves, Adrian and Brian Best (eds). *The Curling Letters of the Zulu War: 'There Was Awful Slaughter'*, Barnsley: Leo Cooper, 2001

Grundlingh, Albert M. 'Prelude to the Anglo-Boer War, 1881–1899' in T. Cameron and S.B. Spies (eds), *An Illustrated History of South Africa*, Johannesburg: Jonathan Ball, 1986

Guest, Bill. 'Colonists, Confederation and Constitutional Change' in Andrew Duminy and Bill Guest (eds), *Natal and Zululand from Earliest Times to 1910: A New History*, Pietermaritzburg: University of Natal Press and Shuter & Shooter, 1989

Guy, Jeff. *The Destruction of the Zulu Kingdom: The Civil War in Zululand, 1879–1884*, London: Longman, 1979

—— 'Imperial Appropriations. Baden-Powell, the Wood Badge and the Zulu *Iziqu*' in Benedict Carton, John Laband and Jabulani Sithole (eds), *Zulu Identities: Being Zulu, Past and Present*, New York: Columbia University Press, 2009

—— 'A Note on Firearms in the Zulu Kingdom with Special Reference to the Anglo-Zulu War, 1879', *Journal of African History*, 12, 4 (1971), pp. 557–70

—— *Theophilus Shepstone and the Forging of Natal*, Pietermaritzburg: University of KwaZulu-Natal Press, 2012

—— *The View across the River: Harriette Colenso and the Zulu Struggle against Imperialism*, Charlottesville, VA: University Press of Virginia, 2002

Hallam Parr, Captain Henry. *A Sketch of the Kafir and Zulu Wars: Guadana to Isandhlwana*, London: C. Kegan Paul, 1880

Hamilton, Carolyn (ed.). *The Mfecane Aftermath: Reconstructive Debates in Southern African History*, Johannesburg: Witwatersrand University Press; Pietermaritzburg: University of Natal Press, 1995

Hamilton, Carolyn, Bernard K. Mbenga and Robert Ross (eds). *The Cambridge History of South Africa*, vol. 1, *From Early Times to 1885*, Cambridge: Cambridge University Press (2010), pb edn 2012

Hamilton-Browne, Colonel G. *A Lost Legionary in South Africa*, London: T. Werner Laurie, 1912

Hammond-Tooke, David. *The Roots of Black South Africa*, Johannesburg: Jonathan Ball, 1993

Harness, Arthur. 'The Zulu Campaign from a Military Point of View', *Fraser's Magazine*, new series 21, 101 (April 1880), pp. 539–50

Harrison, General Sir Richard. *Recollections of a Life in the British Army during the Latter Half of the Nineteenth Century*, London: John Murray, 1908

Hartley, Guy. 'The Battle of Dithakong and "Mfecane" Theory' in Carolyn Hamilton (ed.), *The Mfecane Aftermath: Reconstructive Debates in Southern African History*, Johannesburg: Witwatersrand University Press; Pietermaritzburg: University of Natal Press, 1995

Haythornthwaite, Philip J. *The Colonial Wars Source Book*, London: Caxton Editions, 2000

Headlam, Cecil. 'The Failure of Confederation, 1871–1881' in Eric A. Walker (ed.), *The Cambridge History of the British Empire*, vol. VIII, *South Africa, Rhodesia and the High Commission Territories*, Cambridge: Cambridge University Press, 1963

Heydenrych, D.H. 'The Boer Republics, 1852–1881' in T. Cameron and S.B. Spies (eds), *An Illustrated History of South Africa*, Johannesburg: Jonathan Ball, 1986

Houghton, H. 'Economic Development, 1865–1965' in Monica Wilson and Leonard Thompson (eds), *Oxford History of the British Empire*, vol. 2, *South Africa 1870–1966*, Oxford: Oxford University Press, 1971

Howard, Michael. *The Causes of Wars and Other Essays*, London: Temple Smith, 1983

H.S. 'The Kaffir War: By an English Officer in South Africa', *Fraser's Magazine*, February 1878

Hummel, Chris (ed.). *The Frontier War Journal of Major John Crealock 1878: A Narrative of the Ninth Frontier War by the Assistant Military Secretary to Lieutenant General Thesiger*, Cape Town: Van Riebeeck Society, 2nd series No. 19, 1989

Iliffe, John. *Honour in African History*, Cambridge: Cambridge University Press, 2005

Illustrated London News, 1878, 1882

Jones, Huw M. *The Boiling Cauldron: Utrecht District and the Anglo-Zulu War, 1879*, Bisley: Shermershill Press, 2006

Keegan, Tim. *Colonial South Africa and the Origins of the Racial Order*, Cape Town: David Philip, 1996

Kinsey, H.W. 'The Sekukuni Wars', *Military History Journal*, 2, 5 (June 1973), <http://samilitaryhistory.org/> (accessed 10 March 2013)

—— 'The Sekukuni Wars', Part II, *Military History Journal*, 2, 6 (December 1973), <http://samilitaryhistory.org/> (accessed 14 August 2013)

Kinsman, Margaret. ' "Hungry Wolves": The Impact of Violence on Rolong Life 1823–1836' in Carolyn Hamilton (ed.), *The Mfecane Aftermath: Reconstructive Debates in Southern African History*, Johannesburg: Witwatersrand University Press; Pietermaritzburg: University of Natal Press, 1995

Knight, Ian. *The Anatomy of the Zulu Army from Shaka to Cetshwayo 1818–1879*, London: Greenhill Books, 1995

—— *The Boer Wars (1) 1836–1898*, London: Osprey Military, 1996

—— *A Companion to the Anglo-Zulu War*, Barnsley: Pen & Sword Military, 2008

—— *Go to Your God like a Soldier: The British Soldier Fighting for Empire, 1837–1902*, London: Greenhill Books, 1996

—— (ed.). 'Kill Me in the Shadows', *Soldiers of the Queen*, 74 (September 1993)

—— *The National Army Museum Book of the Zulu War*, London: Sidgwick & Jackson in association with The National Army Museum, 2003

—— *Queen Victoria's Enemies (1): Southern Africa*, London: Osprey Military, 5th impression, 2005

—— *Warrior Chiefs of South Africa*, Poole: Firebird Books, 1994

—— *With His Face to the Foe. The Life and Death of Louis Napoleon, the Prince Imperial: Zululand 1879*, Staplehurst: Spellmount, 2001

—— *Zulu Rising: The Epic Story of Isandlwana and Rorke's Drift*, London: Macmillan, 2010

Kotze, J.S. 'Counter Insurgency in the Cape Colony, 1872–1881', *Scientia Militaria: South African Journal of Military Studies*, 31, 2 (2003), pp. 36–58

Kuper, Hilda. *An African Aristocracy: Rank among the Swazi*, London: Oxford University Press for the International African Institute, 1969

—— *The Swazi: A South African Kingdom*, New York: Holt, Rinehart and Winston, 2nd edn, 1986

Laband, John. *The Atlas of the Later Zulu Wars 1883–1888*, Pietermaritzburg: University of Natal Press, 2001

—— 'Bulwer, Chelmsford and the Border Levies: The Dispute over the Defence of Natal, 1879' in John Laband and Paul Thompson, *Kingdom and Colony at War: Sixteen Studies on the Anglo-Zulu War of 1879*, Pietermaritzburg: University of Natal Press; Cape Town: N & S Press, 1990

—— 'The Cohesion of the Zulu Polity and the Impact of the Anglo-Zulu War: A Reassessment' in John Laband and Paul Thompson, *Kingdom and Colony at War: Sixteen Studies on the Anglo-Zulu War of 1879*, Pietermaritzburg: University of Natal Press; Cape Town: N & S Press, 1990

—— (ed.). *Daily Lives of Civilians in Wartime Africa from Slavery Days to Rwandan Genocide*, Westport, CT: Greenwood Press, 2007

—— 'Durnford, Anthony William (1830–1879)', *Oxford Dictionary of National Biography*, Oxford: Oxford University Press, online edn, 2008 <http://www.oxforddnb.com/view/article/8325> (accessed 14 August 2013)

—— *Fight Us in the Open: The Anglo-Zulu War through Zulu Eyes*, Pietermaritzburg: Shuter & Shooter; Ulundi: KwaZulu Monuments Council, 1985

—— 'From Mercenaries to Military Settlers: The British German Legion, 1854–1861' in Stephen M. Miller (ed.), *Soldiers and Settlers in Africa, 1850–1918*, Leiden and Boston: Brill, 2009

—— *Historical Dictionary of the Zulu Wars*, Lanham, MD: The Scarecrow Press, 2009

—— 'Humbugging the General? King Cetshwayo's Peace Overtures during the Anglo-Zulu War' in John Laband and Paul Thompson, *Kingdom and Colony at War: Sixteen Studies on the Anglo-Zulu War of 1879*, Pietermaritzburg: University of Natal Press; Cape Town: N & S Press, 1990

—— *Kingdom in Crisis: The Zulu Response to the British Invasion of 1879*, Manchester: Manchester University Press, 1992; repr. Barnsley: Pen & Sword Military, 2007

—— 'Lord Chelmsford' in Steven J. Corvi and Ian F.W. Beckett (eds), *Victoria's Generals*, Barnsley: Pen & Sword Military, 2009

—— (ed.). *Lord Chelmsford's Zululand Campaign 1878–1879*, Stroud: Alan Sutton Publishing for the Army Records Society, 1994

—— 'Mbilini, Manyonyoba and the Phongolo River Frontier: A Neglected Sector of the Anglo-Zulu War of 1879' in John Laband and Paul Thompson, *Kingdom and Colony at War: Sixteen Studies on the Anglo-Zulu War of 1879*, Pietermaritzburg: University of Natal Press; Cape Town: N & S Press, 1990

—— 'Mfecane (1815–1840)' in Gordon Martel (ed.), *The Encyclopedia of War*, Oxford: Wiley-Blackwell, 2011

—— *The Rise and Fall of the Zulu Nation*, London: Arms and Armour Press, 1997

—— *The Transvaal Rebellion: The First Boer War 1880–1881*, London: Pearson Longman, 2005

—— 'The War-Readiness and Military Effectiveness of the Zulu Forces in the 1879 Anglo-Zulu War', *Natalia*, 39 (December 2009), pp. 37–46

—— ' "War Can't Be Made with Kid Gloves": The Impact of the Anglo-Zulu War of 1879 on the Fabric of Zulu Society', *South African Historical Journal*, 43 (November 2000), pp. 179–96

—— 'Zulu (amaZulu) War Rituals' in Bron R. Taylor and Jeffrey Kaplan (eds), *The Encyclopedia of Religion and Nature*, London and New York: Thoemmes Continuum, 2005, pp. 1824–5

—— 'Zulu Civilians during the Rise and Fall of the Zulu Kingdom, *c.*1817–1879' in John Laband (ed.), *Daily Lives of Civilians in Wartime Africa from Slavery days to Rwandan Genocide*, Westport, CT: Greenwood Press, 2007

—— 'Zulu Strategic and Tactical Options in the Face of the British Invasion of January 1879', *Scientia Militaria: South African Journal of Military Studies*, 28, 1 (1998), pp. 1–15

—— 'Zulu Wars' in Dennis Showalter (ed.), *Oxford Bibliographies Online: Military History*, New York: Oxford University Press, 2012

Laband, John and Ian Knight. *The War Correspondents: The Anglo-Zulu War*, Stroud: Sutton Publishing, 1996

Laband, John and Paul Thompson. 'African Levies in Natal and Zululand, 1838–1906' in Stephen M. Miller (ed.), *Soldiers and Settlers in Africa, 1850–1918*, Leiden and Boston: Brill, 2009

—— *The Illustrated Guide to the Anglo-Zulu War*, Pietermaritzburg: University of Natal Press, 2000

—— *Kingdom and Colony at War: Sixteen Studies on the Anglo-Zulu War of 1879*, Pietermaritzburg: University of Natal Press; Cape Town: N & S Press, 1990

—— 'The Reduction of Zululand, 1878–1904' in Andrew Duminy and Bill Guest (eds), *Natal and Zululand from Earliest Times to 1910: A New History*, Pietermaritzburg: University of Natal Press and Shuter & Shooter, 1989

Labuschange, Pieter. *Ghostriders of the Anglo-Boer War (1899–1902): The Role and Contribution of Agterryers*, Pretoria: University of South Africa Press, 1999

Landau, Paul S. *Popular Politics in the History of South Africa, 1400–1948*, Cambridge: Cambridge University Press, 2010

Le Cordeur, Basil and Christopher Saunders (eds). *The War of the Axe, 1847: Correspondence between the Governor of the Cape Colony, Sir Henry Pottinger, and the Commander of the British Forces at the Cape, Sir George Berkeley, and Others*, Johannesburg: Brenthurst Press, 1981

Legassik, Martin. 'The Great Treks: The Evidence', *South African Historical Journal*, 46 (May 2002), pp. 282–9

Legassick, Martin and Robert Ross, 'From Slave Economy to Settler Capitalism: The Cape Colony and Its Extensions, 1800–1854' in Carolyn Hamilton, Bernard K. Mbenga and Robert Ross (eds), *The Cambridge History of South Africa*, vol. 1, *From Early Times to 1885*, Cambridge: Cambridge University Press, 2010

Lewsen, Phyllis. The First Crisis in Responsible Government in the Cape Colony', *Archives Year Book for South African History, 1943 (2)*, Pretoria: Government Printer, 1943

—— '*John X. Merriman: Paradoxical South African Statesman*, New Haven, CT, and London: Yale University Press, 1982

—— (ed.). *Selections from the Correspondence of J. X. Merriman 1870–1890*, Cape Town: Van Riebeeck Society, 1960

Lieven, Michael. ' "Butchering the Brutes All Over the Place": Total War and Massacre in Zululand, 1879', *History*, 84, 276 (October 1999), pp. 614–32

Lock, Ron and Peter Quantrill (eds). *The Red Book. Natal Press Reports, Anglo-Zulu War 1879*, privately printed, n.d.

—— *Zulu Victory: The Epic of Isandlwana and the Cover-Up*, London: Greenhill Books, 2002

Lucas, Sir Charles. *The Empire at War*, vol. I, London: Humphrey Milford; Oxford: Oxford University Press, 1971

Lynn, John A. *Battle: A History of Combat and Culture from Ancient Greece to Modern America*, Boulder, CO, and Oxford: Westview Press, 2003

McClendon, Thomas V. *White Chief, Black Lords: Shepstone and the Colonial State in Natal, South Africa 1845–1878*, Rochester, NY: Rochester University Press, 2010

Machin, Ingrid. *Antbears and Targets for Zulu Assegais*, Howick, South Africa: Brevitas, 2002

MacKinnon, Aran S. *The Making of South Africa: Culture and Politics*, Upper Saddle River, NJ: Pearson Prentice Hall, 2004

Mahoney, Michael R. *The Other Zulus: The Spread of Zulu Ethnicity in Colonial South Africa*, Durham, NC, and London: Duke University Press, 2012

Manning, Stephen. 'Evelyn Wood' in Steven J. Corvi and Ian F.W. Beckett (eds), *Victoria's Generals*, Barnsley: Pen & Sword Military, 2009

Marks, Shula. 'Khoisan Resistance to the Dutch in the Seventeenth and Eighteenth Centuries', *Journal of African History*, 13, 1 (1972), pp. 55–80

Marks, Shula and Anthony Atmore. 'Firearms in Southern Africa: A Survey', *Journal of African History*, 12, 4 (1971), pp. 517–30

Martineau, J. *The Life and Correspondence of the Right Hon. Sir Bartle Frere, Bart., G.C.B., F.R.S., etc.*, vol. II, London: John Murray, 1895

Marwick, Brian Allan. *The Swazi: An Ethnographic Account of the Natives of the Swaziland Protectorate*, London: Frank Cass, 1966

Mathews, Jeffrey. 'Lord Chelmsford: British General in Southern Africa', unpublished D. Litt. et Phil. thesis, University of South Africa, 1986

Maylam, Paul. *A History of the African People of South Africa: From the Early Iron Age to the 1970s*, London: Croom Helm, 1986

Merensky, D.A. *Erinnerungen aus dem Missionsleben in Transvaal 1859–1882*, Berlin: Buchhandlung der Berliner evangel. Missionsgesellschaft, 2nd edn, 1882

Miers, Sue. 'Notes on the Arms Trade and Government Policy in Southern Africa between 1870 and 1890', *Journal of African History*, 12, 4 (1971), pp. 571–7

Miller, Stephen M. (ed.). *Soldiers and Settlers in Africa, 1850–1918*, Leiden and Boston: Brill 2009

Milton, John. *The Edges of War: A History of the Frontier Wars, 1702–1878*, Cape Town: Juta, 1983

Mitford, Bertram. *Through the Zulu Country: Its Battlefields and Its People*, London: Kegan Paul, Trench, 1883

Molyneux, Major-General W.C.F. *Campaigning in South Africa and Egypt*, London: Macmillan, 1896

Monteith, Mary. 'Cetshwayo and Sekhukhune 1875–1879', unpublished M.A. thesis, University of the Witwatersrand, 1978

Moodie, T. Dunbar. 'Black Migrant Mine Labourers and the Vicissitudes of Male Desire' in Robert Morrell (ed.), *Changing Men in Southern Africa*, Pietermaritzburg: University of Natal Press; London: Zed Books, 2001

Morrell, Robert (ed.). *Changing Men in Southern Africa*, Pietermaritzburg: University of Natal Press; London: Zed Books, 2001

—— 'The Times of Change: Men and Masculinity in South Africa' in Robert Morrell (ed.), *Changing Men in Southern Africa*, Pietermaritzburg: University of Natal PRess; London: Zed Books, 2001

Morton, F. 'Slavery' in Elizabeth A. Eldredge and Fred Morton (eds), *Slavery in South Africa: Captive Labour on the Dutch Frontier*, Boulder, CO: Westview Press; Pietermaritzburg: University of Natal Press, 1994

—— 'Slavery and South African Historiography' in Elizabeth A. Eldredge and Fred Morton (eds), *Slavery in South Africa: Captive Labour on the Dutch Frontier*, Boulder, CO: Westview Press; Pietermaritzburg: University of Natal Press, 1994

Mostert, Noël. *Frontiers: The Epic of South Africa's Creation and the Tragedy of the Xhosa People*, London: Pimlico, 1993

Moyer, Richard A. 'The Mfengu, Self-Defence and the Cape Frontier Wars' in Christopher Saunders and Robin Derrincourt (eds), *Beyond the Cape Frontier: Studies in the History of the Transkei and Ciskei*, London: Longman, 1974

Natal Mercury, Supplement, 22 January 1929

Ndlovu, Sifiso. 'A Reassessment of Women's Power in the Zulu Kingdom' in Benedict Carton, John Laband and Jabulani Sithole (eds), *Zulu Identities: Being Zulu, Past and Present*, New York: Columbia University Press, 2009

Norbury, Fleet Surgeon Henry F. *The Naval Brigade in South Africa during the Years 1877–78–79*, London: Sampson Low, Marston, Searle & Rivington, 1880

Norris-Newman, Charles. *In Zululand with the British*, London: W.H. Allen, 1880

—— *With the Boers in the Transvaal and Orange Free State in 1880–1*, London: W.H. Allen, 1882

Parsons, Norman. 'Reviving the Trek Debates', *South African Historical Journal*, 46 (May 2002), pp. 308–12

Peers, Chris. *The African Wars: Warriors and Soldiers of the Colonial Campaigns*, Barnsley: Pen & Sword Military, 2010

Peires, J.B. *The Dead Will Arise: Nongqawuse and the Great Xhosa Cattle-Killing Movement of 1856–7*, Johannesburg: Ravan Press, 1989

—— *The House of Phalo: A History of the Xhosa People in the Days of their Independence*, Johannesburg: Ravan Press, 1981

—— 'Ngqika c. 1779–1829' in Christopher Saunders (ed.), *Black Leaders in Southern African History*, London: Heinemann, 1979

Penn, Nigel. *The Forgotten Frontier: Colonists and Khoisan on the Cape's Northern Frontier in the 18th Century*, Athens: Ohio University Press, 2006

Philip, John Edward (ed.). *Writing African History*, Rochester, NY: Rochester University Press, 2006

Preston, Adrian (ed.). *The South African Journal of Sir Garnet Wolseley 1879–1880*, Cape Town: A.A. Balkema, 1973

Price, Richard. *Making Empire: Colonial Encounters and the Creation of Imperial Rule in Nineteenth-Century Africa*, Cambridge: Cambridge University Press, 2008

Prichard, Helen M. *Friends and Foes in the Transkei: An Englishwoman's Experiences during the Cape Frontier War of 1877–8*, London: Sampson Low, Marston, Searle & Rivington, 1880

Pridmore, Julie. 'Introduction' to John Laband (ed.), *The Journal of William Clayton Humphreys . . . Trader and Hunter in the Zulu Country during the Months July–October 1851*, No. 6, Colin Webb Natal and Zululand Series, Durban: Killie Campbell Africana Library; Pietermaritzburg: University of Natal Press, 1993

Pugh, Martin. 'Beach, Michael Edward Hicks, first Earl St Aldwyn (1837–1916)', *Oxford Dictionary of National Biography*, Oxford: Oxford University Press, online edn, 2008, <http://www.oxforddnb.com/view/article/33859> (accessed 14 August 2013)

Reid, Richard J. *Warfare in African History*, Cambridge: Cambridge University Press, 2012

Rider Haggard, Sir H. *The Last Boer War*, London: Kegan Paul, Trench and Trubner, 1899

Robson, Linda and Mark Oranje. 'Strategic Military Colonisation: The Cape Eastern Frontier 1806–1872', *Scientia Militaria, South African Journal of Military Studies*, 49, 2 (2012), pp. 46–71

Ross, Robert. 'Khoesan and Immigrants: The Emergence of Colonial Society in the Cape, 1500–1800' in Carolyn Hamilton, Bernard K. Mbenga and Robert Ross (eds), *The Cambridge History of South Africa*, vol. 1, *From Early Times to 1885*, Cambridge: Cambridge University Press, 2010

—— 'The !Kora Wars on the Orange River, 1830–1888', *Journal of African History*, 16, 4 (1975), pp. 556–576

Saunders, Christopher. 'Political Processes in the Southern African Frontier Zones' in Howard Lamar and Leonard Thompson (eds), *The Frontier in History: North America and Southern Africa Compared*, New Haven, CT, and London: Yale University Press, 1981

—— 'Great Treks?', *South African Historical Journal*, 46 (May 2002), pp. 300–7

Saunders, Christopher, Colin Bundy and Dougie Oakes. *Illustrated History of South Africa: The Real Story*, Pleasantville, NY: The Readers' Digest Association, 3rd edn, 1988

Saunders, Christopher and Iain R. Smith. 'Southern Africa, 1795–1910' in Andrew Porter (ed.), *The Oxford History of the British Empire*, vol. 2, *The Nineteenth Century*, Oxford: Oxford University Press, 2001

Schreuder, D.M. *Gladstone and Kruger: Liberal Government and Colonial 'Home Rule', 1880–5*, London: Routledge and Kegan Paul, 1969

—— *The Scramble for Southern Africa, 1877–1895*, Cambridge: Cambridge University Press, 1980

Shillington, Kevin. *Luka Jantjie: Resistance Hero of the South African Frontier*, London: Aldridge Press, 2011

Smith, Keith. *The Wedding Feast War: The Final Tragedy of the Xhosa People*, London: Frontline Books, 2012

Smith, K.W. 'The Fall of the Bapedi of the North-Eastern Transvaal', *Journal of African History*, 10, 2 (1969), pp. 237–52

Smithers, A.J. *The Kaffir Wars 1779–1877*, London: Leo Cooper, 1973

Soga, John Henderson. *The Ama-Xhosa: Life and Customs*, Alice, Eastern Cape: Lovedale Press; London: Kegan Paul, Trench, Trubner, *c.*1932

Special Reporter of the 'Cape Times' [R.W. Murray]. *Cetywayo, from the Battle of Ulundi to the Cape of Good Hope*, Cape Town: Murray & St Leger, 1879

Spiers, Edward M. *The Late Victorian Army 1868–1902*, Manchester: Manchester University Press, 1992

—— *The Victorian Soldier in Africa*, Manchester and New York: Manchester University Press, 2004

Stapleton, Timothy J. *Maqoma: Xhosa Resistance to Colonial Advance 1798–1873*, Johannesburg: Jonathan Ball, 1994

—— *A Military History of South Africa from the Dutch–Khoi Wars to the End of Apartheid*, Santa Barbara, CA: Praeger, 2010

—— 'South Africa' in Ian F.W. Beckett, (ed.), *Citizen Soldiers and the British Empire, 1837–1902*, London: Pickering & Chatto, 2012

—— ' "Valuable, Gallant and Faithful Assistants": The Fingo (or Mfengu) as Colonial Military Allies during the Cape-Xhosa Wars, 1835–1881' in Stephen M. Miller (ed.), *Soldiers and Settlers in Africa, 1850–1918*, Leiden and Boston: Brill, 2009

Stearn, Roger T. 'Lanyon, Sir (William) Owen (1842–1887)', *Oxford Dictionary of National Biography*, Oxford: Oxford University Press, online edn, 2006, <http://www.oxforddnb.com/view/article/16060> (accessed 14 August 2013)

Storey, William Kelleher. *Guns, Race, and Power in Colonial South Africa*, Cambridge: Cambridge University Press, 2008

Strachan, Hew. *European Armies and the Conduct of War*, London: G. Allen & Unwin, 1983

Sutton, J.B. 'The 1878 Rebellion in Griqualand West and Adjacent Territories', unpublished Ph.D thesis, School of Oriental and African Studies, University of London, 1975

Swinny, G.H. *A Zulu Boy's Recollections of the Zulu War* (1884), edited by C. de B. Webb, *Natalia* 8 (December 1978), pp. 8–21

Switzer, Leo. *Power and Resistance in an African Society: the Ciskei Xhosa and the Making of South Africa*, Madison, WI: University of Wisconsin Press, 1993

Theron, Bridget. 'King Cetshwayo and Victorian England: A Cameo of Imperial Interaction', *South African Historical Journal*, 56 (2006), pp. 60–87

Theron-Bushell, Bridget M. 'Puppet on an Imperial String: Owen Lanyon in South Africa, 1875–1881', unpublished D. Litt. et Phil. thesis, University of South Africa, 2002

Thompson, Leonard. 'Co-operation and Conflict: the High Veld' in Monica Wilson and Leonard Thompson (eds), *The Oxford History of South Africa*, vol. 1, *South Africa to 1870*, Oxford: Oxford University Press, 1969

—— *A History of South Africa*, New Haven, CT, and London: Yale University Press, 1990

—— 'Great Britain and the Afrikaner Republics, 1879–1899' in Monica Wilson and Leonard Thompson (eds), *The Oxford History of the British Empire*, vol. 2, *South Africa 1870–1966*, Oxford: Oxford University Press, 1971

Thompson, P.S. *Black Soldiers of the Queen: The Natal Native Contingent in the Anglo-Zulu War*, Tuscaloosa, AL: University of Alabama Press, revised edn, 2006

Trapido, Stanley. 'Reflections on Land, Office and Wealth in the South African Republic, 1850–1900' in Shula Marks and Anthony Atmore (eds), *Economy and Society in Pre-Industrial South Africa*, Harlow, Essex: Longman, 1980

Trollope, Anthony. *South Africa*, reprint of the 1878 edition with an introduction and notes by J.H. Davidson, Cape Town: A.A. Balkema, 1973

Tylden, George. 'The Development of the Commando System in South Africa, 1715 to 1922', *Africana Notes and News*, 13 (March 1958–December 1959), pp. 303–13

van der Waag, Ian. 'South Africa and the Boer Military System' in Peter Dennis and Jeffrey Grey (eds), *The Boer War: Army, Nation and Empire*, Canberra: Army History Unit, Department of Defence, 2000

Van Rooyen, T.S. 'Die Verhouding tussen die Boere, Engelse en Naturelle in die Geskiedenis van die Oos-Transvaal tot 1882', *Archives Year Book for South African History, 1951 (I)*, Cape Town: Government Printer, 1951

Vijn, Cornelius. *Cetshwayo's Dutchman: Being the Private Journal of a White Trader in Zululand during the British Invasion*, edited by Bishop J.W. Colenso, London: Longmans, Green and Co., 1880

Walker, Eric A. (ed.). *The Cambridge History of the British Empire*, vol. VIII, *South Africa, Rhodesia and the High Commission Territories*, Cambridge: Cambridge University Press, 1963

Warwick, Peter. *Black People and the South African War 1899–1902*, Johannesburg: Ravan Press, 1983

Webb, Colin de B. 'Lines of Power: The High Commissioner, the Telegraph and the War of 1879', *Natalia*, 8 (December 1978), pp. 31–7

Webb, Colin de B., and John B. Wright (eds). *The James Stuart Archive of Recorded Oral Evidence Relating to the History of the Zulu and Neighbouring Peoples*, 5 vols, Pietermaritzburg: University of Natal Press; Durban: Killie Campbell Africana Library, 1976, 1979, 1982, 1986, 2001

—— (eds). *A Zulu King Speaks: Statements Made by Cetshwayo kaMpande on the History and Customs of his People*, Pietermaritzburg: University of Natal Press; Durban: Killie Campbell Africana Library, 1978

White, Gavin. 'Firearms in Africa: An Introduction', *Journal of African History*, 12, 2 (1971), pp. 17–84

Wilson, Monica and Leonard Thompson (eds), *The Oxford History of South Africa*, vol. 1, *South Africa to 1870*, Oxford: Oxford University Press, 1969

—— (eds), *The Oxford History of the British Empire*, vol. 2, *South Africa 1870–1966*, Oxford: Oxford University Press, 1971

Winter, Jay and Antoine Prost. *The Great War in History: Debates and Controversies 1914 to the Present*, Cambridge: Cambridge University Press, 2005

Woodward, Sir Llewellyn. *The Age of Reform 1815–1870*, Oxford: Clarendon Press, 2nd edn, 1962

Worden, Nigel. *The Making of Modern South Africa: Conquest, Apartheid, Democracy*, Oxford: Wiley-Blackwell, 4th edn, 2007

Worger, William H. *South Africa's City of Diamonds: Mine Workers and Monopoly Capitalism in Kimberley, 1867–1895*, New Haven, CT: Yale University Press, 1987

Worsfold, Basil. *Sir Bartle Frere: A Footnote to the History of the British Empire*, London: Butterworth, 1923

Wright, John. 'Turbulent Times: Political Transformations in the North and East, 1760s–1830s' in Carolyn Hamilton, Bernard K. Mbenga and Robert Ross (eds), *The Cambridge History of South Africa*, vol. 1, *From Early Times to 1885*, Cambridge: Cambridge University Press, 2010

Yorke, Edmund. *Rorke's Drift 1879: Anatomy of an Epic Zulu War Siege*, Stroud, Glos: Tempus Publishing, 2001

Acknowledgements

The writing of any book is a long and arduous journey, and this has been no exception. I must thank my long-suffering commissioning editor at Yale University Press, Heather McCallum, for sticking with me while I squealed through several tricky bends. Ian Knight, my stalwart and long-time companion-in-arms in the historical arena of the Anglo-Zulu War, pushed me back onto the paved road when he saw me spinning my wheels in the mud. He also generously made many images from his collection available for inclusion in the book. I must also thank Graham Dominy, formerly the National Archivist of South Africa, for his assistance in tracking down suitable images, and Robert Hall of the McGregor Museum in Kimberley and Pieter Nel of the Pietermaritzburg Archives Repository for coming up with some essential ones. The Wilfrid Laurier University Library system was invaluable in obtaining all the printed materials I required for writing this book. Reading or re-reading the work of the scholars in my field, many of them my valued mentors, colleagues, co-authors and friends, I am conscious of the bottomless debt I owe their research. Any mistakes in this book are mine, not theirs.

Yale University Press's anonymous readers of my manuscript gave me good reason to reconsider and revise several aspects of my work. I have been very fortunate in the team of editors at the press—Candida Brazil, Rachael Lonsdale and Tami Halliday—as well as my copy editor, Tash Siddiqui, all of whom have worked hard to iron out the wrinkles in my work and ready it for publication. I am also grateful to my cartographer, Martin Brown, who transformed my clumsy sketches into elegant maps.

Nevertheless, I could never have pushed this book through to completion had it not been for the unfailing support and loving encouragement of my wife, Fenella, who also (and very practically) lent me invaluable help with proof-reading and indexing.

Index

Words from Nguni languages are entered under the root rather than under the prefix.